IMPROVING READING COMPREHENSION

IMPROVING READING COMPREHENSION

J. DAVID COOPER

Ball State University

HOUGHTON MIFFLIN COMPANY   BOSTON

Dallas   Geneva, Illinois   Lawrenceville, New Jersey   Palo Alto

To
Isabelle Cooper
Mother, Friend, Supporter

Photo credits for photographs reprinted from Teacher's Guide, pupil selection, and pupil workbook: page 69, Ed Dosien/The Stock Broker; page 70, Morton Beebe & Associates/The Image Bank; page 71, J. Claridge/Morton Beebe & Associates/The Image Bank; page 93, Taurus Photos; page 94, Archive Pictures, Inc.; page 183, Mimi Forsyth/Monkmeyer; page 184, Steve McCutcheon/Alaska Pictorial Service.

Printed in the U.S.A.

Library of Congress Catalog Card Number: 85-81501
ISBN: 0-395-39498-8
  BCDEFGHIJ-VH-89876

CONTENTS

TABLE OF CONTENTS

PREFACE

PURPOSE

Classroom teachers and reading specialists are doing a better job of teaching reading than they have ever done before. However, they want to be even better! To accomplish this goal, teachers want to know what new ideas have been discovered in the teaching of comprehension—and how they can incorporate them with the things that they are already doing well. This book was written to address this concern.

Teachers have always wanted to know—"How do I teach children to comprehend?" During the last decade, reading specialists, classroom teachers, and researchers have devoted much of their professional energy to discussing and exploring reading comprehension. Translating into classroom practices newly discovered insights, understandings, and ideas about teaching comprehension is the major purpose of *Improving Reading Comprehension*.

Throughout the text the emphasis is on *how to teach* comprehension. Its single greatest focus is its application of a direct instruction paradigm, with stress on the critical step of teachers' *modeling* new processes and skills *as* they teach, to the real-life teaching of reading comprehension. Every attempt has been made to summarize the supporting research and theory and translate it into practice. However, this book does not represent a compendium of all of the research in comprehension, for only those areas considered most likely to have direct impact on how teachers teach have been addressed. This is a practical book whose primary goal is to act as a helpful, guiding tool in the teaching of reading comprehension in today's classroom.

AUDIENCE

Improving Reading Comprehension focuses heavily on the elementary teacher because that is where much of reading instruction takes place. However, the book has been written so that it can be utilized by reading teachers and content teachers at all levels.

It is intended for undergraduate and graduate students in most reading courses, as well as for inservice teachers enrolled in workshops or classes run by their school systems. Additionally, it can be used on its own as an on-the-job resource by teachers and specialists. In short, this text can be used by anyone who is concerned with the effective teaching of reading comprehension.

COVERAGE AND FEATURES

In order to lay the groundwork for the rest of the book, Chapter One reports the latest findings in comprehension research, with special emphases on the reader's schema and background knowledge as well as on text structure. Chapter Two presents the author's Model of Direct Instruction and establishes the components of the total instructional program for reading comprehension. Both frameworks are pivotal for the remainder of the text. Chapters Three and Four discuss background and vocabulary development and offer myriads of practical ideas for better preparing a reader to approach a new selection. Chapter Five is central to the entire book. With simple clarity, it presents the concept of metacognition, a self-monitoring reading strategy, and then explains in step-by-step fashion how a teacher should model or demonstrate for students each new skill to be learned. The differences between narrative and expository text structure and the varying requirements they place upon a reader are discussed in Chapter Six. Finally, in Chapters Seven and Eight, the total reading comprehension program is fleshed out. How reading comprehension correlates with writing and how the teaching of comprehension skills applies to content teaching are fully treated.

In order to make this text easy to study and more appealing to use, the following features have been included:

Chapter Objectives list for students the major points to be learned in each chapter.

Introductions to chapters offer an overview of the chapter contents and give students a framework into which they can fit new ideas.

Summaries conclude chapters and highlight the major ideas presented in the chapter.

Fully-developed model lessons and teaching scripts demonstrate in an immediate fashion the text's concepts and translate these concepts into real-life instructional situations.

Basal reading selections and teacher's guide pages, many presented in original full color, act as real bases for the model lessons and activities. Together the selections and lessons illustrate how the teaching of reading comprehension can be accomplished in the classroom.

ACKNOWLEDGMENTS

There are many individuals to whom I owe a great debt of thanks for support and assistance throughout the development of the manuscript for this book. The editorial staff at Houghton Mifflin, both in the School Division and in the College Division, believed in my ideas, supported them in seeing this book to fruition, and offered skillful advice and direction in the shaping and creation of the manuscript. Dr. Susan Page, friend and colleague, critiqued the ideas, suggested changes and improvements, and offered encouragement when I became discouraged. Dr. Martha Zetzl of Butler University in Indianapolis, friend and colleague, helped to make the manuscript more readable for teachers by her endless hours of reading and critiquing. Michael D. Robinson, elementary teacher, assisted in developing sample passages and in evaluating the manuscript from a preservice teacher's point of view. Brenda Stone Anderson, secretary, typed and retyped the manuscript to meet many deadlines on short notice.

The following reviewers offered perceptive criticisms throughout the developmental stages of this text. Their comments helped immeasurably to focus and shape the book.

Dr. George F. Canney
University of Idaho

Dr. Adele Graef
Illinois State University

Dr. Joan Heimlich
University of Wisconsin at Whitewater

Dr. William McCarthy
Indiana State University

Dr. Nancy Marshall
Florida International University

Dr. Vincent Mikkelson
East Carolina University

Dr. Sidney Skolnick
Southern Connecticut State College

Dr. Charlene Swanson
Southern Utah State College

Of these reviewers I would like to especially thank Dr. Nancy Marshall, whose comments—both in breadth and in depth—went well beyond what was expected and helped particularly in the revision of the manuscript.

Finally, I would like to thank the teachers with whom I have worked for many years. Their questions—and their reactions to my answers to their questions—helped to show the need for this text and to give it a focus.

J. David Cooper

IMPROVING READING COMPREHENSION

CHAPTER

O   N   E

UNDERSTANDING READING

COMPREHENSION

Making sense of print is what reading is all about.
—Goodman, 1984, p. 112

In this chapter you will learn:

1. how the view of reading comprehension has changed since the turn of the century,
2. what reading comprehension is,
3. the role of schema in reading comprehension,
4. how text type influences reading comprehension,
5. the changed role of skills in reading comprehension,
6. what to teach in reading comprehension programs,
7. what factors other than text type influence reading comprehension,
8. five basic principles to guide the teaching and development of reading comprehension.

In a recent workshop, I asked fifty classroom teachers and reading specialists from a large metropolitan area to list the questions they had about reading comprehension. Their responses were very similar and are reflected in the questions of five participants:

Participant 1: What is reading comprehension?
Participant 2: I have heard a lot of talk about teaching reading comprehension, but I'm not sure I know how to teach it. What do I need to do to teach comprehension better?
Participant 3: Can I use the material in my basal reader to teach comprehension? Is the material in my basal up-to-date?

1

Participant 4: My principal said that she heard in a workshop that there are no skills of comprehension. Should I stop teaching the skill lessons in my manual?

Participant 5: I want to know what to do to help my kids better understand what they read, and I don't need a lot of stuff that can't help me tomorrow. They don't understand what they read. How can I help them?

The questions these five participants raised illustrate the breadth of the concern and frustration of the teachers in this workshop—and, I believe, the concern and frustration of teachers throughout the country—in knowing how to help students improve reading comprehension. The number of volumes written and discussions held about reading comprehension in the last decade is mind boggling; there is no question that educators have learned more about reading comprehension in the last ten years than was learned in the previous fifty. But the real question is, How can this information be used to improve the teaching of reading? How can classroom teachers who teach reading predominantly from a basal reader be guided to look critically at what they do in the name of reading comprehension and begin to alter some of their procedures?

It is the purpose of this text to help classroom teachers take a more critical look at reading comprehension, understand the processes of comprehension better, and see how to begin to incorporate some of the new information about teaching comprehension into the framework of their reading instruction. No attempt is made to present all the research and theoretical positions on reading comprehension; rather, the emphasis is on synthesizing this information into practical applications for the classroom. Although research offers some direction in the teaching of comprehension, it does not provide definitive answers to all the questions that teachers are posing (Tierney and Cunningham, 1984). Teachers can base many of their decisions about how to teach reading comprehension on research and then, on the basis of existing theories, speculate about those questions not answered by research. This chapter will present some of the background material needed by teachers to better understand and teach comprehension.

A CHANGED VIEW OF COMPREHENSION

Interest in reading comprehension is not new. Since before the turn of the century (Huey, [1908] 1968; Smith, 1965), educators and psychologists have noted the importance of comprehension as a part of reading and have been concerned with understanding what happens when a reader comprehends. Interest in comprehension has intensified in recent years, but the process of comprehension itself has not changed. As Roser points out, "Whatever children and adults did as they read in ancient Egypt, Greece, or Rome, and whatever they do today in order to derive or apply meaning to print is the same" (1984, p. 48). What has changed is our understanding of how comprehension takes place; it is hoped that this improved understanding of comprehension will enable reading specialists to devise improved teaching strategies.

During the 1960s and 1970s, a number of reading specialists believed that reading comprehension was an end product of decoding (Fries, 1962); if students could name the words, comprehension would occur automatically. This basic belief became the foundation for a series of reading texts that are still in use in many parts of the country (Fries et al., 1966). As teachers placed greater emphasis on decoding, however, they found that many students still were not able to understand; comprehension was *not* taking place automatically.

Educators then began to believe that the problem existed in the types of questions teachers were asking. Because teachers asked predominantly literal questions, students were not being challenged to use their inferential and critical reading and thinking abilities. The stress in reading instruction shifted, and teachers began asking students a greater variety of questions at differing levels according to some taxonomy such as the Barrett Taxonomy of Reading Comprehension (Clymer, 1968). However, it wasn't long before teachers began to realize that asking questions was primarily a means of checking comprehension and no teaching was being provided. This view was supported by research on the use of questions in classroom practices and in basal readers (Durkin, 1978; Durkin, 1981a).

In the 1970s and 1980s, researchers in education, psychology, and linguistics began to look in other directions to find answers to their concerns about comprehension. They began to theorize about how a reader comprehends and then attempted to verify certain aspects of their theories through research (Anderson and Pearson, 1984; Smith, 1978; Spiro et al., 1980). It is through the works of many of these individuals and others that reading specialists have come to a new understanding of comprehension.

Comprehension as it is currently viewed is a process by which the reader constructs meaning by interacting with the text (Anderson and Pearson, 1984). The understanding the reader achieves during reading comes from the accumulated experiences of the reader, experiences that are triggered as the reader decodes the author's words, sentences, paragraphs, and ideas. This does not mean that the reader must be able to orally decode every word on a page, but the reader must have some ability to decode in order to comprehend. The interaction between the reader and the text is the foundation of comprehension. In the process of comprehending, the reader relates the information presented by the author to information stored in his or her mind; this process of relating new information to old information is the process of comprehending.

Let's consider an example of this process. Read the following sentence:

The lazy, old cat spent his whole day curled up asleep by the fireplace.

You probably had no difficulty comprehending this sentence. You immediately pictured in your mind an old cat that you had seen, known, or heard about. You thought of all the qualities and characteristics of this cat and could picture it asleep by the warm fire. Although the writer of this sentence intended to convey a certain meaning to you, the reader, the exact meaning that you constructed related to the knowledge, information, feelings, and attitudes about cats that you have in your mind. You constructed your meaning from within your experiences (Pearson and Tierney, 1984). It is this interaction between the reader and the text that is the process of comprehending. As Anderson and Pearson note, "To say that one has comprehended a text is to say that she has found a mental 'home' for the information in the text, or else that she has modified an existing mental home in order to accommodate that new information" (1984, p. 255).

To comprehend the written word, the reader must be able to (1) understand how an author has structured or organized the ideas and information presented in text, and (2) relate the ideas and information from text to ideas or information stored in his or her mind. By doing these two things, the reader interacts with the text to construct meaning. This new understanding of comprehension clearly refutes the old belief that comprehension is getting meaning from the printed page. The meaning that the reader constructs does not come from the printed page alone; it comes from the reader's own experiences which are triggered or activated by the ideas the author presents. The reader constructs meaning by combining the new information provided by the author with the information stored in his or her mind. That is exactly what you did as you read the sentence about the cat.

The reader is usually presented with more material to read than a single sentence. As the reader proceeds through the text, additional information is gained; this information activates other ideas from the reader's memory and helps the reader construct further meaning.

An example will help to illustrate how this process works. Read the following two sentences:

I ran quickly through the tunnel trying to escape my captors. As I rounded a turn, the ground seemed to disappear beneath me.

From reading these two sentences, you probably gained some idea that the paragraph is about someone who is in trouble. You probably pictured a person running through a tunnel. At this point, you can't be sure what the writer means by the ground disappearing. You have constructed your meaning for the two sentences, but your understanding seems incomplete. Now read the complete paragraph to see what happens to your comprehension.

I ran quickly through the tunnel trying to escape my captors. As I rounded a turn, the ground seemed to disappear beneath me. I seemed to fall for hours. Just as I saw the ground approaching, a voice called, "Wake up! It's time for breakfast."

After reading the complete paragraph, your understanding of what is happening has changed because new information received from the author caused you to construct a different meaning. This is what happens as one reads and comprehends. As the reader gathers additional information from the text, he or she relates that information to the information stored in his or her memory and in this way constructs meaning. After reading the paragraph above, you picture someone who is having a dream. Your understanding of the meaning changed from the first two sentences to the last two. You were able to comprehend this paragraph by taking the author's ideas and relating them to the information you already had from your own experiences.

Comprehension is the process of constructing meaning by taking the relevant ideas from the text and relating them to ideas you already have; this is the process of the reader interacting with the text. No matter how long or short the text passage, the process occurs in the same manner. By identifying the relationships and ideas the author presents, you develop understanding of what you are reading. You relate the new ideas to ideas already stored in your memory.

SCHEMA, BACKGROUND, AND COMPREHENSION

One area of theory and study that has led to this new understanding of reading comprehension is schema and schema theory. Schema (singular) or schemata (plural) are structures that represent the generic concepts stored in an individual's memory (Rumelhart, 1980). Schema theory explains how these structures are formed and related to one another as an individual develops knowledge.

A reader develops schemata through experiences. If the reader has had no experience (or limited experience) with a given topic, he or she will have no schemata (or insufficient schemata) to recall, and comprehension will be difficult or impossible. Many studies on comprehension, schemata, and background have shown that the reader's background information greatly influences comprehension (Adams and Bertram, 1980; Durkin, 1981b; Pearson et al., 1979). The reader's background seems to have a greater influence on the comprehension of implied information than directly stated information, probably because readers understand implied information only when they can relate it to their existing knowledge and prior experiences.

Think back to the sentence about the old cat. As you read that sentence, you began to form a thought or picture in your mind about the cat, based on the information you had stored in your mind; you were using your schema about cats. If your schema about cats did not include anything about cats sleeping by a fire, you learned some new information about cats that you added to your cat schema. An individual's schemata are never really complete; the experiences of life constantly expand and change one's schemata.

The process of comprehension depends on the reader's schemata. The more nearly a reader's schemata match the schemata intended by the author, the easier it is for the reader to comprehend the text. Another example will help illustrate this point. Read the following paragraph:

Andrew was having a great time at his birthday party. He was playing games and opening presents. When it came time to blow out the candles on the cake, he blew and blew but they would not go out. As soon as he thought he had blown out the candles, they would light up again.

To comprehend this paragraph, you must have a schema about birthday parties. However, if your birthday party schema does not include anything about trick candles that you can't blow out, you will not be able to understand what has happened to Andrew. From the information in the paragraph, you could tell that Andrew was having a birthday party—the text stated this—and your schema for birthday parties helped you formulate and understand most of what was taking place at the party. The text helped you determine what Andrew was having, and your schema helped you understand it. However, to understand what type of candles were on Andrew's cake you must rely even more heavily on your schema. The text didn't tell you what kind of candles they were. Therefore, to fully comprehend this paragraph you have to use both your schema and clues from the text.

There is evidence to indicate that readers use their schemata and clues from the text in varying amounts as they comprehend (Spiro, 1979). It can be argued that if readers used only their schemata in comprehending, no two individuals would ever agree about the information in what they read. Alternatively, if readers used only clues from the text to comprehend, all readers would agree that a given selection had the same meaning (Strange, 1980). Clearly neither of these positions is completely correct. Effective comprehenders use an *interactive* process that both relies heavily on their schemata and requires them to obtain information from text. Even though these two processes occur simultaneously as readers comprehend, it is the reader's schemata that provide the structure needed to associate meaning with text (Anderson and Pearson, 1984).

In summary, schemata are the categories of knowledge (concepts, information, ideas) that are formed in the reader's mind through experiences. As reading comprehension occurs, the reader takes the ideas from text and relates them to his or her acquired knowledge—schemata. If the reader does not have schemata for a particular topic or concept, he or she may form a new schema for that topic if enough information is provided. As the reader constructs new knowledge, by relating new information to already stored information, his or her schemata continuously expand.

TEXT TYPE AND COMPREHENSION

The definition of comprehension presented in this book is based on the idea that the reader interacts with the text and relates the ideas from the text to prior experiences to construct meaning. A part of this process requires that the reader understand how the author has organized his or her ideas. The organization of ideas in a written selection is known as text structure.

There are two basic types of text: narrative and expository. Narrative text tells a story and is the type of text usually found in literature selections. Expository text provides information and facts and is the type of text usually found in science and social studies selections. Teachers have known for many years that students do not read science material in the same way they read literature. Narrative and expository writings are organized differently, and each has its own particular vocabulary and concepts. Readers must use their comprehension processes differently when reading these different types of text. There is evidence to show that teaching students strategies for focusing on text structure will enhance their comprehension (Taylor and Beach, 1984; Beach and Appleman, 1984). Thus a major element in understanding comprehension is awareness that readers need to be taught how to read different types of text. This means that readers must be shown how to comprehend narrative, or story, type material and expository, or informational, material. The topic of text structure is discussed in detail in Chapter 6.

COMPREHENSION SKILLS

Evidence presented thus far clearly supports the conclusion that comprehension is an interactive process between the reader and the text. However, there are skills that can be taught to help students learn to better use their interactive comprehension processes. Most individuals reading this text have either recommended to others that skills be taught or have themselves taught students comprehension skills with exercises in identifying the main idea of the text, the sequence of events, details, cause-and-effect statements, and the like. These and other skills have been listed as the skills of comprehension in basal readers and independent skills hierarchies such as the Wisconsin Design for Reading Skill Development (Otto et al., 1977). But are the skills listed in these sources really the skills of reading comprehension? Is there evidence that teaching any of these skills really improves a reader's comprehension? Have reading specialists placed comprehension skills in the wrong perspective?

A skill is an acquired ability to perform a task well (Harris and Hodges, 1981). The basic theory underlying the skills approach to comprehension is that there are specific parts of the comprehension process that can be taught. The assumption is that students can demonstrate increased success with a skill following instruction and practice in using that skill. Teaching a student these parts of comprehension supposedly improves the overall process.

Numerous studies have attempted to identify the skills of reading comprehension (Davis, 1968, 1972; Spearritt, 1972; Thorndike, 1973). Examination of the results of these studies reveals that they did not consistently identify the same skills. The only skill that appeared in three of the four studies was identification of word meanings; all other skills were found in no more than two of the four studies.

Rosenshine (1980), in a review of professional literature concerning the skill question in reading comprehension, drew the following conclusions:

1. It is difficult to confidently put forth any set of discrete comprehension skills.
2. Comprehension skills are simply not taught in a hierarchical fashion.
3. It is not clear whether all, or even any, of the skill exercises in reading comprehension are essential or necessary. (p. 552)

Research does not clearly support the identification of any set of comprehension skills; neither is there specific evidence to support the idea that teaching students main idea, sequence, cause-and-effect, or other skills as they have typically been taught will make them better comprehenders. This evidence, along with evidence already presented in this chapter, refutes the long-held belief that comprehension is a set of discrete skills. Comprehension is not a set of discrete skills. It is a *process* by which the reader constructs meaning by using clues in the text and relating them to his or her existing background.

Over the years, reading specialists and researchers have assumed that the sum of the parts of comprehension equals the whole; that is, learning each comprehension skill leads to the overall process, or learning all of the skills is the process of comprehension. The skills that have been taught have typically focused only on helping the reader learn the skill for the sake of learning the skill, not on helping the reader learn the process of using the skill. Many of the problems relative to skill instruction have been directly related to how the skill was taught and not to the fact that the skill was taught at all.

Because comprehension is a process of constructing meaning by relating information from the text to one's own experiences, the reader must be taught to identify the relevant information in the text and then to relate that information to his or her background. As has already been noted, there are different types of text. A major problem with traditional comprehension skill teaching is that skills have been taught without any regard for the type of text. For example, teachers have helped students note details of a story by asking them such questions as "Who did the trick?" or "What happened to Bob?" However, such questions do not help students really understand the story. Noting details is an inappropriate means of checking students' comprehension of narrative material. These teachers have not taught the skills of comprehension as processes, and they have taught them without any consideration for the type of text in which they were to be used.

Another problem with the traditional teaching of comprehension skills is that it has not included any processes to help the reader see how to relate the information obtained from the text to his or her past experiences. Obviously some changes must be made in comprehension instruction.

Where does this leave classroom teachers today? Should they abandon the comprehension skill lessons provided in their readers? No, but the teacher should teach the lessons differently from the way they have taught them in the past. Teachers should (1) focus on the skills and processes that will help the reader get clues from the text and relate those clues to prior experience, and (2) emphasize the process of using the skill rather than teaching the skill for the skill's sake.

The comprehension skills that are currently taught should be carefully evaluated in terms of whether they help the reader understand how a text selection is organized and whether they help the reader learn to use the process of comprehension. Most of the traditional comprehension skills are aimed at helping the reader focus on clues in the text and have not been appropriately taught. Only those skills that help readers get clues from the text and those that help the reader relate those clues to prior experience should be retained. In addition, new skills and processes should be added. These conclusions are based on the following considerations.

1. Although there is no consistent body of evidence to support the identification of a discrete set of skills that should be taught in reading comprehension programs, neither is there evidence of anything to replace the skills currently taught. Until researchers provide consistent evidence of what should be taught in place of the current comprehension skill lessons, we had better hold on to things that have produced some degree of success in improving comprehension. Data from the National Assessment of Educational Progress indicate that students are succeeding at improving more literal types of comprehension but are less successful at improving inferential and critical comprehension (National Assessment of Educational Progress, 1982). These latter types of comprehension are more dependent on teaching students the process aspects of comprehension, and these skills clearly need to be added to or strengthened in existing instructional programs.

2. The skills that typically have been called comprehension skills are nothing more than different tasks or types of comprehension that focus the reader's attention on the text. Although readers need to learn to perform some of these tasks in order to recognize how an author has organized his or her ideas, learning any one task alone is not essential to improving a reader's use of his or her overall comprehension processes.

3. In light of the nature of the comprehension process and its relationship to the reader's background, the teaching of comprehension must be viewed more broadly than the teaching of discrete skills or tasks. The program for developing comprehension is much more complex than teaching discrete skills; it also involves teaching readers the process of comprehension and how to use it.

4. Each reader's comprehension process is somewhat different because each individual has developed different schemata. Further, the ways in which a person makes use of the skills and processes taught as a part of reading comprehension also differ. Therefore, it is unlikely that any body of research will ever consistently support any given set of comprehension skills as being *the* skills to teach.

5. The manner in which comprehension skills are taught also needs to be examined. Most so-called skill teaching in comprehension has been isolated from the mainstream of reading. Some psychologists and educators have recommended that the teaching of any comprehension skill or process be closely connected to actual text reading (Palincsar and Brown, 1984; Cooper et al., 1979). The key issue in teaching comprehension may be not what is taught, but how it is taught. Sheridan (1978) pointed out that one result of the new research on comprehension may be that teachers will no longer teach skills in isolation. Research on direct instruction in comprehension supports the need to make certain that skills are taught and applied in natural text reading (Baumann, 1984).

In summary, teachers must critically review the comprehension skills they teach and select only the more essential ones to incorporate into their comprehension programs. At the same time, they must carefully restructure their teaching procedures to help students learn to *use* comprehension skills. That is, teaching must include showing students how to apply or use the comprehension skills in reading real text. In addition, teachers must teach these skills from a process point of view, and they must add to their teaching strategies the actual processes rather than merely the discrete skills of comprehension. Therefore, the question of what to teach in comprehension must be clearly addressed.

WHAT TO TEACH IN COMPREHENSION

The definition of comprehension being used in this chapter is that *comprehension is a process by which the reader constructs meaning by interacting with the text.* This process is dependent upon the reader being able to:

1. Understand how an author has structured his or her ideas and information in text. There are two basic types of text: narrative and expository.
2. Relate the ideas and information from text to ideas or information that the reader has stored in his or her mind. These are the schemata that the reader has developed through experiences.

The following outline summarizes the skills and processes that should be taught in comprehension programs. It is based on the research and ideas that have been discussed in this chapter. The categories of the outline are not presented in a hierarchy, and the order of the elements does not necessarily represent the order in which they should be taught. Neither does the order of the elements suggest that the reader uses these elements one at a time. When reading a passage of text, the reader uses many of these skills and processes simultaneously (Samuels & Kamil, 1984). The sole purpose of this outline is to suggest to teachers what should be taught in a reading comprehension program. The outline is divided into two main sections: the skills and processes that can provide clues to understanding text, and those skills and processes that are used for relating text to past experiences.

Skills and Processes to Teach in the Comprehension Program
I. Skills and processes that provide *clues to understanding text*
   A. *Vocabulary skills:* Teach students those skills that will make them independent in determining word meanings. The skills include:
   1. *Context clues:* The reader uses familiar words in a sentence or paragraph to determine the meaning of an unfamiliar word.
      Example

      Bob drove the *semi*, a very large truck, to haul the furniture.

   2. *Structural analysis:* The reader uses prefixes, suffixes, inflectional endings, base words, root words, compound words, and contractions to determine word meanings. (See Chapter 4 for detailed discussion.)

Example

The reader can determine the meaning of the word *reheat* by knowing the meaning of the base word *heat* and the prefix *re*, meaning "again." Thus, the word *reheat* means to heat again.

3. *Dictionary skills:* The reader uses the dictionary to determine the meanings of words. (See Chapter 4.)

Example

When a reader encounters an unknown word and has tried all other clues to meaning, he or she can refer to a dictionary to find the meaning.

B. *Identification of relevant information in text:* Teach students the skills they need to identify in text the information that is relevant or important to their purpose for reading. These skills include:

1. *Identifying relevant narrative details:* The reader uses knowledge of story structure to identify the information that he or she needs to understand a narrative. (See Chapter 6.)

Example

In the story of the "Three Little Pigs," the reader can identify the important elements of the narrative without labeling them.

Characters: three pigs and the wolf

Setting: the homes of the pigs

Problem: Wolf wants to get into the houses of the pigs and eat them up *or* the pigs are trying to save themselves from the wolf.

Action: The wolf goes to each pig's house and tries to blow it down. Each house is made of a different material. The wolf succeeds at the first two pigs' houses, forcing them to run to the third pig's house. The last pig's house is made of brick, and the wolf can't blow it down.

Resolution: Wolf meets his demise as he tries to enter the brick house through the chimney.

2. *Identifying how the events of a narrative are related:* After identifying the events of a narrative (not necessarily by name), the reader determines how they are related to develop an overall understanding of the story. To do this, he or she must understand the following processes:

a. *Cause and effect:* One event causes another to happen.

Example

The wolf blows on the first pig's house; it collapses.

b. *Sequence:* Events are sometimes related because they happen in a certain order.

Example

The wolf tries to get the pigs by going to the first house, then the second house, and so on.

3. Identifying relevant details in expository materials: The reader identifies details that are relevant or important to his or her purpose for reading expository material.
Example
A student is instructed to read the following passage to find out about some of the parts of a motorcycle that must be maintained. He or she must determine which details are important.

Motorcycles are popular as a means of transportation and as a hobby for people. They are much like cars; there are things that must be done to keep them running smoothly. The engine must be tuned and serviced regularly. It is also important that the brakes function properly. Many motorcycles have CB radios that must also be kept in the proper working order. The number of people who own motorcycles increases yearly.

4. *Identifying the main idea and supporting details in expository writing:* The reader determines the main idea in expository text and identifies those details that support it. Readers must be taught how to determine the author's main idea by using the supporting details.
Example
Determine the main idea in the following passage:

Trees are excellent resources. They provide a source for paper and wood. Trees also provide a source for business through farming. People use trees for shelter and for things of beauty.

The main idea is "Trees are excellent resources." All other points are supporting details.

5. *Identifying the relationships of ideas in expository writing:* The reader learns to recognize and interpret the following expository structures. Through these structures he or she can see the relationship of ideas in expository writing and thus gain comprehension. The structures are discussed in detail in Chapter 6.
   a. *Description:* The author presents information about a topic or gives characteristics of the topic.
   b. *Collection:* The author presents related ideas in a group; a sequence of ideas is apparent.
   c. *Cause-and-effect:* The author relates ideas in such a way that a cause-and-effect relationship is stated or implied.
   d. *Response:* The author presents a problem, question or remark that is followed by a solution, answer, or reply.
   e. *Comparison:* The author requires the reader to note likenesses or differences in two or more objects or ideas.

II. Processes and skills for relating text to past experiences
   A. *Inferencing:* The reader is taught to use information stated by the author to determine that which is not stated. The student will have to draw heavily from prior experiences.

Example

Tim was very upset. He cried as he saw the old man's coffin go by. Who could he talk to about his life now that dad was gone?

The reader must use inferencing to determine that Tim's father is dead. The reader is relating information from the text to prior experiences. The inference comes from the reader's experiences.

B. *Critical reading:* The reader is taught to evaluate and judge as he or she reads. This requires him or her to draw from prior experiences.

   1. *Facts and opinions:* The reader is taught to recognize that facts are true and can be proven and opinions are how a person feels or believes and are not necessarily true.
     Example

     Mr. Brown was thirty-five years old. Some people thought he looked like he was fifty.

     The first sentence is a fact; the second is an opinion.

   2. *Bias:* The reader is taught to recognize bias. An author is showing bias when he or she shows feelings either for or against something.
     Example

     Mr. Styles is the best candidate for mayor. He is sure to win.

   3. *Assumptions:* The reader is taught to recognize assumptions, statements that are taken for granted as being true.
     Example

     Since it has rained all week, tomorrow's picnic is sure to be postponed.

   4. *Propaganda:* The reader is taught to recognize propaganda, material that is written to persuade someone to be for or against something.
     Example

     Everybody in town is buying the new green lawn products; you should too.

Teach students processes that will help them pull together the elements of critical reading, such as:

   1. Reading to get a general idea of what the author is saying and trying to persuade them to think.
   2. Looking for techniques that might lead them to question what the author has said.
   3. Comparing the information they are reading with what they know, or looking for more information in another source.
   4. Evaluating what they read.

C. *Monitoring:* Students are taught processes to help them determine as they read whether their reading is making sense. Once students have assimilated these processes, they will be able to make clarifications, if needed, as they read.

1. Summarizing
2. Clarifying
3. Questioning
4. Predicting

(See Chapter 5 for a detailed discussion of this procedure.)

These are the elements that should be taught in reading comprehension programs. Current research indicates that comprehension can be taught (Baumann, 1984; Duffy et al., 1984). This means that the teacher must show readers how to think through the processes involved in performing each of these comprehension tasks and must also show students how to use or apply the processes when reading actual text. Improving comprehension instruction requires changing both what is taught and how it is taught.

FACTORS OTHER THAN TEXT TYPE THAT INFLUENCE COMPREHENSION

Each reader's comprehension is influenced by a number of factors that must be taken into account when teaching comprehension. These factors include the reader's oral language, attitudes, purpose for reading, and general physical and emotional condition.

Oral Language

An important factor that teachers must consider when teaching comprehension is the student's oral language abilities. Research has established that there is a significant relationship between a student's oral language ability and his or her reading ability (Loban, 1963; Ruddell, 1965; Menyuk, 1984). A student's oral language ability is very closely connected to his or her development of schemata and background experiences.

The student with limited oral language ability or an oral language base other than English will not have an understanding of the basic patterns and concepts of the language. Therefore, this student will not have the base on which to develop reading and comprehension.

Oral language and oral vocabulary form the foundation for building a reading vocabulary, which is an important part of comprehension. In the initial stages of learning to read, the reader's "meaning vocabulary" is developed almost exclusively from his or her "oral vocabulary." Therefore, the student who lacks a good oral vocabulary will be limited in developing an extensive meaning vocabulary, which in turn will make text comprehension more difficult. This situation is often seen in students who come from homes in which there are limited opportunities for the development of good oral language and in students who come from homes in which a language other than English is spoken. Before these students can learn to read and comprehend, they must develop some facility with oral language.

The development of oral language is not only important at the beginning stages of comprehension; it is important throughout the entire process of learning to comprehend, especially in the development of a meaning vocabulary. Thus, an on-going part of the reading program should be the development of oral language. One way for teachers to provide for this development is to continuously read aloud to students and present opportunities to discuss what was read. This topic is discussed in further detail in Chapter 2.

Attitudes

A student's attitudes toward reading can affect the way he or she comprehends. The student with a negative attitude toward reading will not be able to comprehend as effectively as the student with a positive attitude. A student who has developed a negative attitude about reading—for whatever reason—will not perform the tasks of reading as well as the student who has a positive attitude. The student with a negative attitude may have the skills needed to be a successful comprehender, but his or her attitude may interfere with the ability to use those skills.

The reader's attitudes influence comprehension in another way. The attitudes and beliefs that an individual develops about various topics can affect the way in which he or she comprehends. A student who has, for example, developed the attitude that all politicians are dishonest and crooked is likely to comprehend the following paragraph directly in relation to his or her attitude.

Mr. Barnes had decided to run for mayor again. He knew he had the people's support because he had been cleared of any wrongdoing in the last campaign.

The student with a negative attitude toward politicians is likely to still believe that Mr. Barnes had done something wrong. Attitudes and values directly influence critical reading because critical reading requires students to judge and evaluate. Many times these judgments and evaluations are based on the student's attitudes and values.

Purpose for Reading

The purpose an individual has for reading something directly influences how that person will comprehend the reading and to what that person will pay attention. If you are reading this chapter because you know you are going to have a multiple-choice test about it, you are probably focusing on every detail, no matter how small. If, on the other hand, you are reading this chapter to get a general idea of what you need to know to understand comprehension, you probably aren't paying attention to all the details; instead, you are focusing on the general ideas.

When you read a newspaper to get a general idea of the day's news, you might look at only the headlines. If you are reading to compare two articles in terms of reporting style, however, you will read much more carefully and pay attention to the details. This is called selective attention (LaBerge and Samuels, 1976). It is important for teachers to understand this concept because it influences how students will comprehend any text they read. If you ask students to focus on one purpose as they read a chapter, you should not expect them to know something unrelated to the purpose given for reading. Therefore, students should not be expected to read and know all the material in a text from a single reading.

General Physical and Emotional Condition

All learning is influenced by the learner's general physical and emotional condition; comprehension is no exception. Students who have good health, good vision, and enough to eat before they come to school, and who are not emotionally upset will best learn how to comprehend and will comprehend most effectively. The teacher must address all these factors to be certain that the needed conditions for effective learning are present before beginning instruction.

PRINCIPLES FOR GUIDING READING COMPREHENSION DEVELOPMENT

Helping readers learn to comprehend is the ultimate goal of reading instruction. In this chapter, some basic understandings relative to reading comprehension are presented. Within the framework developed, five basic principles for guiding the teaching and development of reading comprehension stand out:

1. *The reader's background is one of the major elements in his or her ability to comprehend text.* The theory and research about schemata and background knowledge clearly support the principle that background influences the ability to comprehend. The comprehension program must incorporate instructional procedures that help readers activate or develop the background relative to a particular topic to be read and relate that background to the text. This must be done in such a way that readers will learn how to draw from their backgrounds and relate old information to new information.
2. *Comprehension is a process of constructing meaning while interacting with the text.* Helping readers learn to comprehend involves teaching them to focus on the relevant features of a text and helping them relate those features to their prior experiences. This includes teaching students to read different types of text, focusing on how different authors structure their ideas.
3. *There are different types or tasks of comprehension, but they are not discrete skills of the overall process.* Students must be taught to use the skills of comprehension; they must learn to focus on the process behind the skill, not on the skill itself. The skills that are taught as a part of comprehension instruction should be seen as clues that enable the reader to interpret written language.
4. *The way in which each reader performs the tasks of comprehension depends on his or her background.* Because each reader's background is different, each reader may answer questions and perform comprehension tasks differently.

Teachers must be prepared to accept a variety of responses from students as long as those responses are reasonable and can be supported.

5. *Comprehension is a language process and should be developed as a part of the total language arts—listening, speaking, reading, and writing.* Oral language forms the foundation for reading comprehension, and instructional activities in reading comprehension programs should build on and expand the oral language base of readers. Every opportunity to relate reading to listening, speaking, and writing should be utilized.

These five guiding principles are the foundation on which the remainder of this text is written. It is believed that teachers who focus on these principles when developing their comprehension programs will be the most effective teachers of reading in schools of the future.

ORGANIZATION OF THIS TEXT

The remainder of this text is devoted to the presentation of specific teaching strategies that will fit into a reading program, based on the concept of reading comprehension developed in this chapter. Chapter 2 presents a design for an instructional program in reading comprehension. Chapters 3 through 7 describe ways in which teachers can develop instructional strategies to use in each aspect of the comprehension program. Chapter 8 focuses on how content teachers can help all students improve their understanding of text at any level.

SUMMARY

Reading specialists and researchers have changed their views of reading comprehension; it is no longer thought of as getting meaning from the page or as a set of discrete skills. Rather, reading comprehension is thought to be a process whereby the reader constructs meaning by interacting with text.

The reader's schemata are the basic categories of knowledge stored in the mind. By using clues from the text, the reader is able to activate his or her schemata to construct meaning. The meaning that the reader constructs is based on the reader's ability to select relevant clues from the text and relate them to his or her stored knowledge.

A reader's comprehension is influenced by the type of text that is read. Narrative text tells a story, and expository text presents information. The reader must learn to read each of these types of text.

Comprehension has been approached as a discrete set of skills. Research, however, does not support this point of view. It does appear that there are specific skills and processes that should be taught to improve students' comprehension. However, these skills must be taught from a process point of view, and more of the processes of comprehension must be added to the instructional program in reading. The specific items to be included in this program were identified in this chapter.

Comprehension is also influenced by the reader's oral language, attitudes, purpose for reading, and general physical and emotional condition. These factors must be considered by the teacher in developing the comprehension program.

The following basic principles should guide all comprehension development:

1. The reader's background is one of the major elements in his or her ability to comprehend.
2. Comprehension is a process of constructing meaning while interacting with the text.
3. There are different types or tasks of comprehension, but they are not discrete skills of the overall process.
4. The way in which each reader performs the tasks of comprehension depends on his or her background.
5. Comprehension is a language process and should be developed as a part of the total language arts—listening, speaking, reading, and writing.

REFERENCES

Adams, M., and B. Bertram. 1980. *Background knowledge and reading comprehension*. Reading Education Report No. 13. Urbana, IL: University of Illinois, Center for the Study of Reading (ERIC Document Reproduction Service No. ED 181 431).

Anderson, R. C., and P. D. Pearson. 1984. A schema-theoretic view of basic processes in reading comprehension. In P. D. Pearson (ed.), *Handbook of reading research*, pp. 255–291. New York: Longman.

Baumann, J. F. 1984. The effectiveness of a direct instruction paradigm for teaching main idea comprehension. *Reading Research Quarterly, 20*, 93–115.

Beach, R., and D. Appleman. 1984. Reading strategies for expository and literary text types. In A. C. Purves and O. S. Niles (eds.), *Becoming readers in a complex society*. Eighty-third yearbook of the National Society for the Study of Education. Chicago: University of Chicago Press.

Clymer, T. 1968. What is "reading"? Some current concepts. In H. M. Robinson (ed.), *Innovation and chance in reading instruction*. Sixty-seventh yearbook of the National Society for the Study of Education. Chicago: University of Chicago Press.

Cooper, J. D., et al. 1979. *The what and how of reading instruction*. Columbus, OH: Charles E. Merrill Publishing Company.

Davis, F. B. 1968. Research in comprehension in reading. *Reading Research Quarterly, 3*, 499–545.

Davis, F. B. 1972. Psychometric research on comprehension in reading. *Reading Research Quarterly, 7*, 628–678.

Duffy, G. G., L. R. Roehler, and J. Mason (eds.). 1984. *Comprehension instruction: Perspectives and suggestions*. New York: Longman.

Durkin, D. 1978. What classroom observations reveal about reading comprehension instruction. *Reading Research Quarterly, 14*, 481–533.

REFERENCES

Durkin, D. 1981a. Reading comprehension instruction in five basal reader series. *Reading Research Quarterly, 16*, 515–544.

Durkin, D. 1981b. What is the value of the new interest in reading comprehension? *Language Arts, 58*, 23–43.

Fries, C. 1962. *Linguistics and reading*. New York: Holt, Rinehart and Winston.

Fries, C., et al. 1966. *Merrill linguistic readers*. Columbus, OH: Charles E. Merrill Publishing Company.

Goodman, K. S. 1984. Unity in reading. In A. C. Purves and O. S. Niles (eds.), *Becoming readers in a complex society*. Eighty-Third Yearbook of the National Society for the Study of Education, pp. 79–114. Chicago: University of Chicago Press.

Harris, T. L., and R. E. Hodges (eds.). 1981. *A dictionary of reading and related terms*. Newark, DE: International Reading Association.

Huey, E. B. 1908. *The psychology and pedagogy of reading*. Cambridge, MA: M.I.T. Press. Reprinted 1968.

LaBerge, D., and S. J. Samuels. 1976. Toward a theory of automatic information processing in reading. In H. Singer and R. Ruddell (eds.), *Theoretical models and processes of reading*, pp. 548–579. Newark, DE: International Reading Association.

Loban, W. D. 1963. *The language of elementary school children*. Champaign, IL: National Council of Teachers of English.

Menyuk, P. 1984. Language development and reading. In J. Flood (ed.), *Understanding comprehension*, pp. 101–121. Newark, DE: International Reading Association.

National Assessment of Educational Progress. 1982. *The reading comprehension of American youth*. Denver, CO: Education Commission of the States.

Otto, W., et al. 1977. *The Wisconsin design for reading skill development: Comprehension*. Minneapolis, MN: NCS Educational Systems.

Palincsar, A. S., and A. L. Brown. 1984. Reciprocal teaching of comprehension-fostering and comprehension-monitoring activities. In *Cognition and instruction*, pp. 117–175. Hillsdale, NJ: Lawrence Erlbaum Associates, Inc.

Pearson, P. D., et al. 1979. *The effect of background knowledge on young children's comprehension of explicit and implicit information*. Urbana, IL: University of Illinois, Center for the Study of Reading.

Pearson, P. D., and R. J. Tierney. 1984. On becoming a thoughtful reader: Learning to read like a writer. In A. C. Purves and O. S. Niles (eds.), *Becoming readers in a complex society*. Eighty-third yearbook of the National Society for the Study of Education, pp. 144–174. Chicago: University of Chicago Press.

Rosenshine, B. V. 1980. Skill hierarchies in reading comprehension. In R. J. Spiro, B. C. Bruce, and W. F. Brewer (eds.), *Theoretical issues in reading comprehension*, pp. 535–554. Hillsdale, NJ: Lawrence Erlbaum Associates.

Roser, N. L. 1984. Teaching and testing reading comprehension: An historical perspective on instructional research and practices. In J. Flood (ed.), *Promoting reading comprehension*, pp. 48–60. Newark, DE: International Reading Association.

Ruddell, R. B. 1965. Effect of the similarity of oral and written patterns of language structure on reading comprehension. *Elementary English, 42*, 403–410.

Rumelhart, D. E. 1980. Schemata: The building blocks of cognition. In R. J. Spiro, B. C. Bruce, and W. F. Brewer (eds.), *Theoretical issues in reading comprehension*, pp. 33–58. Hillsdale, NJ: Lawrence Erlbaum Associates.

Samuels, S. J., and Kamil, M. 1984. Models of the reading process. In P. D. Pearson (ed.), *Handbook of reading research*, pp. 185–224. New York: Longman.

Sheridan, E. M. 1978. A review of research on schema theory and its implications for reading instruction in secondary reading. South Bend, IN: Indiana University. (ERIC Document Reproduction Service No. ED 167 947).

Smith, F. 1978. *Understanding reading*, 2nd ed. New York: Holt, Rinehart and Winston.

Smith, N. B. 1965. *American reading instruction*. Newark, DE: International Reading Association.

Spearritt, D. 1972. Identification of subskills of reading comprehension by maximum likelihood factor analysis. *Reading Research Quarterly, 8*, 92–111.

Spiro, R. J. 1979. Etiology of comprehension style. Urbana, IL: University of Illinois, Center for the Study of Reading.

Spiro, R. J., B. C. Bruce and W. F. Wheeler (eds.). 1980. *Theoretical issues in reading comprehension*. Hillsdale, NJ: Lawrence Erlbaum Associates.

Strange, M. 1980. Instructional implications of a conceptual theory of reading comprehension. *The Reading Teacher, 33*, 391–397.

Taylor, B. M., and R. W. Beach. 1984. The effects of text structure instruction on middle-grade students' comprehension and production of expository text. *Reading Research Quarterly, 19*, 134–146.

Thorndike, R. L. 1973. Reading as reasoning. *Reading Research Quarterly, 9*, 135–147. Reprint of 1917 article.

Tierney, R. J., and J. W. Cunningham. 1984. Research on teaching reading comprehension. In P. D. Pearson (ed.), *Handbook of reading research*, pp. 609–655. New York: Longman.

CHAPTER
T W O

THE INSTRUCTIONAL PROGRAM

IN READING COMPREHENSION

Reading comprehension is too complex to be classified
"school responsibility." Nonetheless, much can be done in
classrooms to help students develop into able processors of
print.—Durkin, 1983, p. 272

In this chapter you will

1. learn what the components of the instructional program in reading comprehension are and how they are related to one another,
2. develop an overall understanding of how to use direct instruction to teach comprehension.

Effective reading instruction requires the understanding of learning and the elements of instruction that lead to learning. Simply defined, learning is the acquisition of skill or knowledge. In reading instruction, learning takes place when a student acquires the skills and processes needed to read. The two main processes involved in reading are comprehension and decoding, and it is clear from research and professional opinions that both can and must be taught (Anderson et al., 1985; Reid, 1981; Duffy and Roehler, 1982; Hansen and Pearson, 1980; Hansen and Pearson, 1983; Baumann, 1984). The effective reader uses these processes simultaneously. Therefore, the processes must be taught and developed so that the reader learns to use them together when reading any text. Effective reading instruction includes separate lessons in decoding and comprehension, but these must be taught in such a way that the instruction concludes with an opportunity for the reader to use what was taught in the reading of natural text.

The nature of comprehension is such that the instructional program is the responsibility of all teachers, not only reading teachers. Reading teachers can teach students the basic processes of comprehension, but content teachers must account for those elements of the instructional program that help students comprehend when reading different types of content material.

MASTERY AND READING COMPREHENSION

Decoding and comprehension are different types of processes and must be treated accordingly in the instructional program. The elements (skills) of decoding can be taught and mastered. A student can be taught to identify and use a consonant blend to decode a word; the student learns the blend and can use it every time he or she encounters it in a new word.

The skills and processes of comprehension can also be taught at a given reading level and in a given type of text; a student can master the use of the process at that level. However, when the level of the material and type of text are changed, the process also changes. For example, although we may teach sequence to students reading at the fourth grade level in a narrative selection, we have to teach it again when those students encounter fifth grade level expository material in science. Because the level, presentation style, and topic of the material have changed from those in which the process of sequence was originally taught, the process has changed. Therefore, mastery of reading comprehension never occurs in the same sense that mastery of decoding does.

COMPONENTS OF THE INSTRUCTIONAL PROGRAM
IN READING COMPREHENSION

The instructional program in reading comprehension should include three components:

> developing background and vocabulary,
> building processes and skills,
> correlating writing with reading.

These three aspects of the instructional program are not discrete; as shown in Figure 2.1, these components are interrelated and blend together to make up comprehension instruction. In order for a reading comprehension program to be effective, it must be carried out during reading instruction as well as during all content teaching; some adaptations to the program are necessary for content teachers and will be discussed in Chapter 8.

Developing Background and Vocabulary

A person's background of experience has a direct influence on all aspects of his or her comprehension abilities (Adams and Bertram, 1980; Johnston and Pearson, 1982). Research and theory relative to schema development (see Chapter 1) are

COMPONENTS OF THE INSTRUCTIONAL PROGRAM

Figure 2.1   The Instructional Program in Reading Comprehension

supportive of the importance of the reader's background in comprehension. Learning vocabulary is a specialized form of background development. Therefore, the focus of this component of the instructional program is to help the reader develop the background, including vocabulary, needed to read selections; this development must take place so that background and vocabulary are viewed as related components and not separate entities.

A student who is reading a chapter on nuclear physics will comprehend it more effectively if he or she has the appropriate background concepts, including vocabulary, that form the foundation for the chapter. If the student lacks this background, comprehension of the ideas in the chapter can be exceedingly difficult or impossible. Therefore, a major component of the comprehension program is the development or retrieval from past experiences of needed background concepts and ideas before students read any selection in any class or content area. This component of the comprehension program is not a separate segment of instruction; it must be an integral part not only of all reading instruction, but also of all content teaching.

An important part of the teacher's responsibility in helping students improve their comprehension is developing the needed background before something is read. As students mature in their reading ability, they must begin to know how to draw independently on their own background and to recognize the need for more background before they read a given selection. Even adult readers often fail to comprehend text accurately because they lack the needed background.

A portion of background development relates to the general experience that an individual has with a given topic. For example, the student who has traveled to many places will be able to understand better a selection on problems of travel than will the student who has never traveled. However, if the selection focuses on the problems of travel seen through the eyes of airline personnel, the student may not have the needed experiences and background to comprehend fully. This example shows how important it is for a teacher to develop or help students recall background as related to the key ideas or concepts in a chapter or selection. If students have not experienced air travel as airline personnel or have not known anyone who has, it is necessary for the teacher to develop this background before students read the selection. Teachers can do this through teacher-directed discussion and through role playing. Such background development is clearly oriented toward helping the reader understand the selection as opposed to simply developing background on the related topic of air travel. Beck (1984) calls this type of instruction schema-directed development. All background development for a selection should have as its goal helping the reader relate his or her background directly to the ideas and concepts involved in a story line or main ideas.

Knowing the meanings of words accounts for a significant portion of a reader's ability to comprehend a given selection (Anderson and Freebody, 1979; Beck, Perfetti, and McKeown, 1982; Jenkins, Pany, and Schreck, 1978). Thus, a major component of the comprehension program must be the systematic teaching and development of vocabulary as a part of background development for specific selections and ongoing development for future reading. In the comprehension program, the teacher needs to

teach selected words prior to having students read selections,
enrich and expand students' vocabularies by providing them with many lessons with and about words,
teach vocabulary skills that will help students become independent in figuring out word meanings.

The words that are taught before students read selections must be only those that relate most directly to the key concepts of the selection. Key terms for a selection on airline personnel, for example, might be *personnel, flight attendant, ground crew*, and *pilot*. They would be the terms the teacher would thoroughly explain as a part of background development before the selection was read by students.

The vocabulary program must continue after students have completed their reading of a selection. Teachers should provide students with exercises that use the vocabulary in written context; the exercises should help students develop a deeper understanding of the words as they were used in the selection and they should expand and enrich the students' use of those words. For example, after reading the selection on airline personnel, students might be given sentences incorporating both key concept words taught prior to reading the selection and other words from the selection. Students would be instructed to read the sentences and think of or locate within each sentence synonyms for the underlined words.

Another aspect of vocabulary development is the systematic teaching of the vocabulary skills that will help students independently determine word meanings. These skills include

the use of affixes (prefixes, suffixes, inflectional endings), base words, and root words,
context clues,
dictionary skills.

The teaching of these skills in reading instruction helps students become independent in constructing the meanings of unfamiliar words when they are encountered in context. If students are taught to connect the meaning of such prefixes as *un* and *dis* with base words, they should be able to independently determine the meanings of words containing those elements. For example, if they encounter the words *unsafe* and *dissatisfied* in a selection, they should be able to determine the meanings without the teacher's help.

The background and vocabulary component should be viewed as the backbone or foundation of the reading comprehension program. By helping students learn the meanings of words and think about important concepts related to the key concepts in a selection prior to reading, the teacher is helping the reader activate and develop schemata, which is the basis for successful comprehension of a selection. By teaching specific lessons oriented toward expanding and enriching the reader's vocabulary and by teaching skills to help students independently determine word meanings, the teacher is helping the student establish background and vocabulary for future reading. Background and strategies for developing and activating it are discussed in greater detail in Chapter 3; Chapter 4 focuses on strategies for teaching vocabulary.

Building Processes and Skills

In order for students to learn the processes and skills of comprehension, they must be systematically taught those skills and processes. Think back to your experiences as a student: How many times were you asked by a teacher to pick out or state the main idea of a paragraph or selection? Then, try to recall the number of times the same teacher actually taught you how to do this. Chances are great that you won't be able to recall many, if any, instances of actual teaching. As teachers, we simply have not done much teaching of comprehension (Durkin, 1978). We have spent a lot of time asking questions but very little time showing students how to locate or figure out the answers. Questioning alone is not teaching comprehension. Instead of merely questioning, the teacher must model for students what is to be learned. Modeling is the part of teaching in which the teacher shows students how to use and think through various processes and skills. This concept will be developed more fully in a later section of this chapter and in Chapter 5.

Included in the building of processes and skills is showing students how to recognize and comprehend different structures of text. Evidence indicates that a part of comprehension is recognition of the way an author has organized or structured the ideas presented (Bartlett, 1978; Meyer, 1975; Taylor and Samuels, 1983). This concept is referred to as text structure. Once students have learned to use the basic skills and processes of comprehension, they must be taught how to apply those skills to understand the structure of different types of text.

The concept and terminology of text structure is new to many teachers. One way to think of text structure is along the lines of different content areas. Examine the story "Clyde Monster," reprinted in Example 2.1, and the science passage reprinted in Example 2.2. As you read the passages, you will notice that they are organized and written in different styles. "Clyde Monster" presents material in what is called a narrative structure whereas the science passage is presented in an expository structure.

Narrative structure is the form used in storytelling. It can have dialogue but does not always include it. Narrative writing can be easily distinguished from expository writing in that it has characters, a setting, a problem, action, and a resolution of the problem. In the story "Clyde Monster," the elements of the narrative can be clearly identified:

Characters: Clyde Monster, Mother Monster, and Father Monster

Setting: a forest

Problem: Clyde is afraid of the dark and afraid there are people in the cave.

Action: 1. Father lights the cave to show that there are no people inside.
2. Mother and Father ask Clyde if he would hide and scare people.
3. Father and Mother ask Clyde if he knew of a monster who had ever been scared by people.

Resolution: Clyde goes into the cave to go to bed, but he wants the rock open just a little.

Expository structure is the form used to present and explain ideas or facts. Different types of exposition are used by authors to accomplish different purposes. (For a discussion of different types of expository writing, see Chapter 6.) In the science passage in Example 2.2, the author explains how a living system converts energy and how this relates to cells. This is a descriptive expository passage.

No content area relies exclusively on one type of structure; however, certain areas utilize expository structure more than narrative, and vice versa. Science and social studies are areas that use more expository structure; literature uses more narrative. The instructional program in reading comprehension must teach readers to apply the basic processes of comprehension to different types of structures. Therefore, students must be taught how to determine the way in which authors have organized their ideas in different text structures, not just to identify different types of passages.

EXAMPLE 2.1   NARRATIVE SELECTION

Clyde Monster

by Robert L. Crowe

Clyde Monster is too scared to go into his cave.

Find out if Mother and Father can help Clyde.

188

Clyde wasn't very big,
but he was ugly.
And he was getting uglier every day.
He lived in the woods
with his mother and father.

Father Monster was a big monster.

He was very ugly, which was good.

Mother Monster was even uglier,
which was better.

Monsters laugh at pretty monsters.

All in all, Clyde and his mother and
his father were lovely monsters —
as monsters go.

190

All day Clyde played in the woods
doing lovely monster things.

He liked to make big holes and
he liked to walk into things.

At night Clyde lived in a cave.

But then one night he would not go
into his cave.

"Why?" asked his mother.

"Why won't you go into your cave?"

"I'm scared of the dark,"
said Clyde.

192

"Scared?" asked his father.
"What are you scared of?"

"People," said Clyde.
"I'm scared there are people
in the cave who will get me."

193

"That's silly," said his father.
"Come, I'll show you.
There.
Did you see any people?"

"No," said Clyde,
"but people can hide.
They may be hiding under a rock.
They will jump out and get me
after I go to sleep."

194

"That is silly," said his mother.
"There are no people here.
    Even if there were,
they wouldn't get you."

"They wouldn't?" asked Clyde.

"No," said his mother.
"Would you ever hide in the dark?
    Would you hide under a bed
to scare a boy or a girl?"

"No!" said Clyde.
"I would never do a thing like that!"

195

"Well, people won't hide
and scare you," said his father.
"It just so happens that
monsters and people have made a deal.
Monsters never scare people —
and people never scare monsters."

196

"Are you sure?" Clyde asked.

"Very sure," said his mother.
"Do you know of any monsters
that were ever scared by people?"

"No," said Clyde.

"Do you know of any people who
were ever scared by monsters?"
asked his mother.

"No," Clyde said.

"There!" said his mother.
"Now it's time for bed."

"And," said his father, "I don't want you to talk anymore about being scared by people."

"OK," said Clyde as he went into the cave.

"But could you leave the rock open just a little?"

198

Source: Adaptation of CLYDE MONSTER by Robert L. Crowe. Text copyright © by Robert L. Crowe. Reprinted by permission of the publisher, E. P. Dutton, a division of New American Library. In William K. Durr et al.: *Carousels*, pp. 188–198 (Houghton Mifflin Reading), 1986.

EXAMPLE 2.2   EXPOSITORY SELECTION: SCIENCE PASSAGE ——————

Living systems all convert energy in their own ways, and yet the basic chemical process is the same. When a burning piece of wood gives off heat, it is actually releasing energy that was contained within its chemical bonds. It would be simple if energy could be released from a cell by burning. But burning produces temperatures too high for a living cell to endure, and the burst of energy release is too short and too sudden. Organisms need a slow, steady energy source, and especially one that can be controlled and regulated, since the chemical reactions in organisms can use energy only in small packages. Cells have effective ways of regulating energy release.

Source: D. Ritchie and R. Carola, *Biology*, 2nd ed., p. 41. Reading, MA: Addison-Wesley Publishing Company, 1983.

——————————

In summary, the building processes and skills component of the comprehension program involves the teacher demonstrating the processes and thinking that the reader uses in performing different types of comprehension tasks; this includes teaching students how to understand different text structures. Chapter 5 presents strategies for modeling; Chapter 6 presents applications of these strategies to teaching text structure.

Correlating Writing with Reading

The third aspect of the instructional program in reading comprehension is that of correlating various types of writing activities with comprehension. Research has clearly shown the importance of the relationship between reading and writing and the benefits of correlating them (Tierney and Leys, 1984).

The writer strives, during writing, to organize his or her ideas so that they will be understood by the reader. The reader looks at what someone has written and attempts to determine how the author structured or organized the ideas presented. Because the processes of reading comprehension and writing are so similar, the correlation of activities in the two areas makes them mutually supportive. Correlating writing with comprehension does not mean having students write out answers to a long list of questions; it means giving students writing activities that relate to the material they have read. These ideas are developed further in Chapter 7.

Comprehension Instruction and the Total Curriculum

The three components of the instructional program in reading comprehension, although presented under separate headings, must be viewed as interrelated aspects in producing successful comprehenders. Just as the process of comprehension is complex, so is the process of producing a reader who is able to comprehend effectively. The components of comprehension instruction must be carefully woven together throughout the entire educational program to produce students who are excellent comprehenders.

All teachers must assume a certain responsibility for producing students who are able to comprehend what they read. Reading teachers, those teachers responsible for teaching reading as a separate subject, can and must incorporate these three components into their reading instruction. Content teachers, those teachers responsible for teaching students a body of content, must continuously help students comprehend text by guiding them to apply the comprehension skills and processes they have learned.

To ensure application of comprehension skills and processes to text, content teachers must account for certain elements of the comprehension program in their teaching. Content teachers are not being asked to formally teach reading, but rather to account for their students' reading needs in their content areas. Content teachers must guide their students through the special vocabulary, style of writing, and background needed for comprehension, in their particular content areas (Dupuis, 1984). This is not the same type of teaching that would be done by the reading teacher: The focus in the content class is on helping the student comprehend the material and learn the content, whereas the reading teacher's concern is helping the student learn the skills and processes of reading. Therefore, for a school's reading program to be complete, all teachers must assume responsibility for helping students learn to comprehend and to apply what they have learned to different texts.

A MODEL FOR DIRECT INSTRUCTION

Comprehension skills and processes can be taught through direct instruction (Duffy, Roehler, and Mason, 1984), the part of the reading program that teaches students the "how to" of reading. Direct instruction is a process by which the teacher

> clearly shows, demonstrates, or models for students what is to be learned,
> provides opportunities for students to use what was learned,
> provides corrective feedback and monitoring as students learn.

This process includes the following steps:

1. Teaching
   a. Let students know what is to be learned and help them relate it to prior experiences.
   b. Model the skill or process and verbalize the thinking that takes place.

   > Teacher models for students.
   > Students model for teacher.

   c. Provide guided practice in the use of the skill or process.
   d. Summarize what was learned and verbalize how and when to use it.

2. Practicing
Provide students with independent practice in the skill or process.
3. Applying
   a. Remind students of the skill, process, or strategy that is to be applied.
   b. Have students read the text selection to determine its intent.
   c. Discuss the text

        to check students' understanding of the selection,
        to check students' application of the skill or process taught.

   d. Summarize what was learned and how it was used in reading.

Figure 2.2 depicts the steps of direct instruction. These steps blend or flow together, but each of the three major steps has distinctly unique features. As can be seen in Figure 2.2, direct instruction is an ongoing process that may require reteaching at any point. Many times, when students have failed to apply what they have learned, teachers have thought they should provide more practice. In some instances more practice might be needed, but in all cases extra practice should be preceded by some teaching that includes, at least, modeling of what the students are going to practice. As students move through the steps of direct instruction, total responsibility for the learning activity gradually shifts from the teacher to the students.

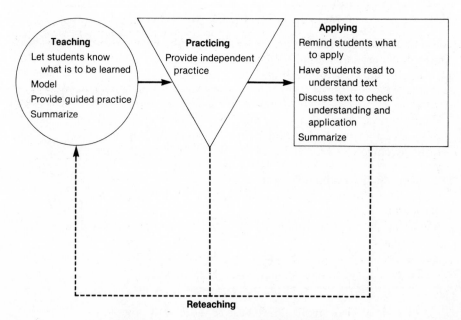

Figure 2.2   A Model for Direct Instruction

Numerous reading authorities have recommended models similar to that just described, both for direct instruction in reading in general and for comprehension specifically (see, for example, Cooper et al., 1979, and Mason, Roehler, and Duffy, 1984). Direct instruction can be used throughout the instructional program in reading comprehension. Therefore, a clear understanding of its component parts is necessary to understanding how to teach comprehension. The parts are discussed in detail in the following sections.

Teaching

Many educators use the terms teaching and modeling synonymously. Teaching is broader than modeling, however, and involves both the process of showing students how to use a skill, process, or strategy and that of guiding them to internalize it. The process of teaching includes four distinct parts.

Teachers should begin all teaching by letting students know exactly what they will learn in the lesson and why it is important, and by helping students draw on prior experiences and learnings to relate to the lesson. This part of teaching helps students begin to develop their thinking about what is to be learned (*metacognitive development*—see Chapter 5) and helps them relate the lesson to previous learnings. It thus develops a schema or frame of reference for the lesson.

The second part of teaching is modeling, the part of teaching in which the teacher shows the students how to use a skill, process, or strategy and verbalizes the thinking that takes place. After the teacher models for the students, they in turn model the same skill, process, or strategy for the teacher. This has been referred to as a "think aloud" technique because the teacher and students actually try to verbalize the thinking that they go through in performing the task (Clark, 1984). The importance of this step to direct instruction cannot be overemphasized. This is a difficult step to perform because the focus of teaching has traditionally been assigning students a comprehension task and expecting them to perform it or simply telling students to do something. For example, teachers have often thought they were teaching main idea by saying to students:

The main idea is the one sentence that all the others in a paragraph are about. Read the following paragraphs and pick out the one statement that best describes the main idea.

This is certainly not modeling and does not fit into the teaching step of direct instruction; it is part of the practice step.

In the modeling portion of teaching, the teacher uses samples of text, sentences, or paragraphs to illustrate the comprehension skill or process being taught. These samples should clearly show the skill or process in question and can be taken from any source.

After the modeling step is completed, students should be provided with guided practice, the part of teaching in which students complete a directed choice activity using the skill, process, or strategy under the teacher's direction. Throughout the activity, the teacher provides students with corrective feedback by letting them know whether they are right or wrong and why (Rosenshine and

Stevens, 1984). The activity should draw the students' attention to the skill or process that has been taught; devices such as multiple-choice activities, fill-in-the-blank exercises, matching, or completion exercises are most often used for practice activities. As students complete the guided-practice activity, reteaching is provided as needed. The general purpose for guided practice is for the teacher to ascertain that students have learned what they were supposed to learn in the modeling and to reteach to correct any problems that might occur.

The final part of teaching is the summary, the part of the lesson in which the teacher prompts students with questions to verbalize what was learned and how it can be used in reading. This step helps students further develop their ability to think about what they are learning and know how and when to use it; this part of metacognitive development is extremely important to effective comprehension (Baker and Brown, 1984). The students should summarize in their own words as much as possible. Often, this is difficult to achieve, but teachers should make every attempt to get students to express the learnings in their own words, prompting them with appropriate questions or guiding statements. It is the teacher's responsibility to provide those additional questions and guidance that will prompt students to express the points in their own words.

Summarization should occur twice during direct instruction—at this point in the lesson and after students have applied or used the skill, process, or strategy in reading natural text. Both summarizations are designed to foster the reader's metacognitive growth in comprehension.

Example 2.3 presents an outline script for the teaching step of direct instruction. In the script, a teacher uses direct instruction to teach students to make predictions from text. In the first step, you can clearly see how the teacher *informs students of what is to be learned* and why it is important. In the second step, *modeling*, notice how the teacher shows and verbalizes the process for making predictions and how the students then are required to model the same process the teacher used. Notice in the third step how the teacher uses samples of text with a directed-choice activity to provide *guided practice*. In the fourth step, the *summary*, the teacher uses prompting questions to get students to summarize what they've learned.

EXAMPLE 2.3   SAMPLE TEACHING SCRIPT FOR MAKING PREDICTIONS

Level: Second–third grade

Objective

Given a passage with explicitly stated information, students will be able to make justifiable predictions about what is likely to happen next.

Teaching

Let Students Know What Is to be Learned and Relate It to Prior Experiences
Say: You have learned how to note important details as you read, but does the author always tell you everything exactly as it happens or everything you need to know in a story? (Students respond.) No, the author doesn't. Sometimes you must use the author's information to guess or predict what will happen next. In this lesson, you will learn to use the information in a passage to make predictions about what is likely to happen next. This will help you improve your comprehension as you read.

Modeling: Teacher
Say: Listen to the following passage and tell me what you think is likely to happen next:

Mark and his dad sat in the car listening to the booming thunder and watching the pouring rain, wondering why they hadn't brought an umbrella. They couldn't figure out how they were going to get into the doctor's office without getting soaked or without Mark falling. The heavy cast on Mark's right leg made it impossible for him to run. The gushing water on the walks would make the bottom of the cast and the crutches slippery. As the time for Mark's appointment drew near, they knew they could wait no longer. Just as they were about to open the car door, one of Mark's teammates came out of the building.

(Have students make their predictions, and list them on the chalkboard. If students are unable to answer, give possible predictions of your own.)
Say: Now, let's look at each prediction and see if the clues in the story make it a good choice. (Go through each prediction pointing out the clue or clues in the story that justifies it. If there are no clues to support the prediction, point this out and note that this is not an appropriate prediction. Say something similar to the following to explain the thinking that would take place to reach *each* prediction:

Mark and his dad are going to get wet. I would predict this is going to happen because it is raining, they have no umbrella, and the story doesn't say anything about Mark's teammate having one.

Conclude the discussion by noting which predictions are appropriate.)
Say: Read the following paragraph silently and then tell me what is likely to happen next.

Larry and his family were excited about their vacation. Food was prepared, clothes were washed, and Mom and Dad helped get all the suitcases ready. The last minute packing and rushing were over. Everyone had settled into their place in the big van. They had been driving for a few hours. Mom said she was beginning to get hungry. "Let's stop for a hamburger for our first vacation lunch," Dad said. "Great!" was the cry from the rear of the van. They pulled into a small restaurant and tumbled out of the van. Just as they walked inside, Dad reached for his wallet and found that it was missing.

(After students have read the passage silently, read it aloud to them.)
Say: Here are some possible predictions that I would make about what is likely to happen next and why I think these might be true. (List each prediction on the

board and give your thinking, explaining how you reached your conclusion; underline supporting phrases in the passage:

The family ate and Mom paid for the meal. Mother is likely to have her purse because she always carries it with her. The story doesn't say that she left it at home.

The family ate and the kids paid for the meal. Since the family is going on vacation, the kids probably have their own spending money, and they might pay for the lunch. The story doesn't really say they have spending money, however.

The family searched the van to see if they could find the missing wallet. The first place to look for the wallet might be in and around the van. Maybe it dropped out of Dad's pocket, but there are no real clues to this.

The family went back home to see if they could find Dad's wallet. Since the family had not stopped anywhere before lunch, it is likely that the wallet could be at home. Therefore, it would be sensible for them to return home to find it.

Conclude the discussion by pointing out that more than one of these things could possibly happen. Tell which ones and why.
Say: We would not know which predictions were correct until we read the rest of the story. Now I want you to read the following part of the story to yourself to see which of my predictions were correct.

Dad was really upset about not having his wallet. He went to look for it in the van but couldn't find it. Everyone was very hungry.
"We will buy the lunch," said the kids. "And then we can go back home and find your wallet."
"Good deal," said Dad. "Let's enjoy our lunch."

(After students have read the paragraphs, point out the predictions that were correct, and why.)

Modeling: Students
Say: Now, I want you to read a paragraph silently and then tell me your predictions about what is likely to happen next. Tell me how you thought through your answers. (Have students read the following paragraph, make their predictions, and explain their thinking about how they reached their conclusions and the clues they used. Prompt students with questions if needed. Repeat this step with another paragraph if students are still having trouble making predictions.)

Nine-year-old Betty had a problem. Her mother's birthday was only three days away, and she didn't have any money. She was thinking about making her mother a pretty box in which to keep letters and cards. However, she really wanted to buy her something. Mrs. Brown came over while Betty was thinking about what to do. "Do you know of someone who could take care of my little girl for a few hours?" she asked Betty. "I will pay $1.25 an hour."

(After students have made their predictions and explained their thinking, have them finish reading the story to see if they were correct. Discuss their findings.)

A MODEL FOR DIRECT INSTRUCTION

Betty was really happy. Now she could make some money. "I'll stay with your little girl," she said. "I need some money to buy a birthday present." The next day Betty went shopping and bought her mother a gift.

Guided Practice

Say: Now I want you to read some paragraphs and make predictions about their outcomes. Read the first paragraph to yourself and select the statement that tells what you think will happen next. Be ready to explain the thinking you used to reach your answer. (Have students read each paragraph and explain their answers. If students are unable to make the predictions, do it for them and explain your thinking as you did in the modeling step, pointing out clues from the story that helped you. If students make errors, point them out and tell why their choices are incorrect.)

Jack had wanted to go swimming every day this week. The rain or his other activities had kept him from going. Today, it was warm and sunny. He didn't have other things to do.

_____ Jack stayed home and read a book.
_____ Jack went swimming.
_____ Jack went shopping with his mother.

It had snowed all night. When Terri and Ed got up in the morning, the ground was covered. They couldn't get their car out of the garage, but they just had to get to the store. There was no one else to open the store, and people would really need food today. "What will we do?" asked Terri. All at once Ed remembered his Christmas gift from Terri, the snowmobile.

_____ Terri and Ed went to work in a snowmobile.
_____ Terri and Ed stayed home from work.
_____ Terri and Ed drove their car to work.

Summary

Say: In this lesson you have learned to make predictions. Let's summarize what you have learned and let's think about when you might use what you've learned in your reading. Prompt students with the following questions to summarize the points they've learned in their own words:

1. *What does it mean to make predictions?*
   —Use the facts the author gives you as clues to tell what might happen.
2. *How do you make predictions when you read?*
   —Look at the author's clues and think about what they mean.
3. *How can you be sure that your predictions are correct?*
   —Read on in the text to check your prediction.
4. *When would you use the skill of predicting?*
   —When you are reading and trying to figure out who did something in a story.
   —In books that are mysteries.

Practicing

After the teaching step of direct instruction has been completed, practice is provided. Practice is the part of direct instruction in which the student uses the skill, process, or strategy in an independent, directed-choice activity. This activity should match what was taught and should resemble the type of activity the teacher used in guided practice. The teacher should check the activity after students have completed it and should provide corrective feedback when students are incorrect; this should consist not only of telling students that they are wrong but of showing them why. Example 2.4 presents a sample independent-practice activity that could be used following the *teaching* of making predictions.

EXAMPLE 2.4   SAMPLE INDEPENDENT-PRACTICE EXERCISE FOR MAKING PREDICTIONS ———————————

NAME _____ DATE _____

DIRECTIONS: You have learned to use the author's clues to help you make predictions. Read each of the following paragraphs and underline the sentence that tells what is most likely to happen next. The first exercise has been done for you.

1. Mr. Jones gave the class a test. He said they had to finish it in one hour. Everyone but Sue was done in half an hour. When time was up, Sue was still working.
   a. Sue had to turn in her test.
   b. Sue could take the test home.
   c. Sue finished her test the next day.
2. The directions for washing Lisa's new dress said drip dry; dryer will shrink garment. By mistake, Lisa's mother put the dress in the dryer with some other clothes. The next day Lisa went to her closet to get her dress. She was very sad.
   a. Lisa wore her new dress.
   b. Lisa's mother ironed her dress.
   c. Lisa's dress shrank, and she couldn't wear it.
3. Mrs. Lee was baking cookies. Ted could smell them out in the yard. He was really hungry. He kept going into the kitchen to see the cookies. Mrs. Lee left the cookies out to cool while she went to the store. When she came home, three cookies were missing.
   a. Mr. Lee took the cookies to work.
   b. Ted ate three cookies.
   c. Mrs. Lee took the cookies to her friend.
4. Mike had been having trouble with the tire on his bike. It wouldn't hold air. He stopped at the gas station to get it pumped up. On the way home, he thought

he heard air coming out of the tire, but he put his bike in the garage until morning.
a. Mike had a flat tire.
b. Mike rode his bike to school.
c. Mike got a new bike for his birthday.

Practice is the step in direct instruction that is typically overdone by teachers. Students do need practice, but they need only enough practice to fix in their minds the skill or process and make it possible for them to use it. Practice exercises are relatively easy to create and can be assigned to students for independent work. However, the amount of practice needs to be held to a minimum.

Applying

The final component of direct instruction is application of the skill or process to the reading of text. For reading instruction in general, the text may be words, sentences, or longer selections. For comprehension instruction, however, application must take place by having students read natural text. Application is the power of direct instruction because it prevents the teaching of skills and processes from being isolated teaching. The only reason to teach a particular comprehension skill or process is for students to use it in reading natural text. In instances in which students are having problems in reading comprehension, it is often because they are unable to apply what they have been taught to actual reading; such students can do well on practice activities, but they are unable to use the skill or process in reading selections. They need to be taught how to apply the skills or processes to the reading of text.

There are two types of application, guided and independent. Guided application takes place under the teacher's direction and provides the teacher with an opportunity to teach students how to apply their comprehension skills and processes to the reading of text and to determine if students are able to apply them. This is the same type of application that occurs in direct instruction. Independent application takes place when students are reading on their own in textbooks, trade books, newspapers, magazines, or other sources. The teacher has no control over independent application, but the effective comprehension program must provide sufficient time for students to read independently. It is through independent reading that students have repeated opportunities to use what they have learned about how to comprehend.

Within guided application, four steps occur. First, the teacher must remind the students about the comprehension skill, process, or strategy that is to be applied when reading the text. The teacher can do this orally, by simply calling to the students' attention the skill or process that they have learned and should apply in reading a given selection. A brief example can be included.

The second step of guided application is for students to silently read the text, using the comprehension skill or process they were to apply. Remember that in any reading situation, the reader is actually applying or using many skills at the same time, including both decoding and comprehension. However, the teacher should focus the students' attention on one particular skill by reminding them of the skill and by asking questions that require the use of the particular skill.

In having students read the text for application purposes, the first concern of the teacher should be that students understand the selection. Teachers can be assured of this by providing students with purpose-setting statements and questions to guide their reading. (For a detailed discussion of guided silent reading, see page 58.)

The third step of guided application, discussion, occurs after students have read the text. Teachers should use two different types of questions to direct the discussion. The focus of the first type should be on whether students have understood the selection. The focus of the second type should be on whether students have been able to apply the comprehension skill or process taught, practiced, and referred to in the skill reminder. This is done through teacher-posed questions that do not mention the skill but require the use of the skill for answering. The following examples illustrate the right and wrong ways to ask questions for application purposes for two comprehension skills, main idea and inference.

Main Idea
Right: 1. In this selection, what was the overall idea the author was trying to get across to the reader?
2. On page 234 of your selection, what point was being expressed about the use of rockets for peace purposes?
Wrong: 1. What is the main idea of this selection?
2. Find the sentence on page 234 that gives the main idea?

Inference
Right: 1. Why was Martha so unhappy in the story? (*Note:* All "why" questions are not necessarily inference; whether they are depends on the way the text is written.)
2. What kind of person was Andrew Williams? Be ready to read sentences that prove your answer.
Wrong: 1. What places in the story require you to infer about Martha's unhappiness?
2. To determine what kind of person Andrew Williams was, you must be able to infer. What places in the story require you to do this?

The examples that are labeled as wrong are more oriented toward practice than toward application because they direct students to the specific skill to use. The two types of questions suggested for discussion can be imbedded in the overall discussion; the teacher need not ask all questions oriented toward developing or checking understanding before asking application questions. However, the application questions should be asked so that they follow the story line and do not disrupt the flow of understanding of the selection. Keep in mind that while the teacher is focusing on the application of one skill or process, students are also using many other comprehension skills and processes.

The final step in guided application is the summary. Here the students again summarize what they have learned about using the comprehension skill or process being taught. The emphasis in this summary should be on how and when students used the skill in reading the text for application purposes and how and when the skill can be used in reading other texts. Again, the teacher will need to prompt students, with questions or statements, to verbalize their thinking. This step further develops and reinforces the student's ability to think about and know when to use the comprehension skill or process (metacognition).

The application activity should focus on one new comprehension skill or process at a time even though students use many skills and processes simultaneously. Students will need to complete more than one application activity for each skill. As students seem to develop the ability to use several skills and processes, it is appropriate for there to be an application activity that combines their use in reading text. In such an activity, the teacher would briefly remind students of the skills and processes they will be using before they begin to read. The discussion after reading would include teacher questions to check for the application of the skills referred to in the reminders. Such cumulative application checks more nearly approximate independent application.

In Example 2.5, the narrative "Birthdays" is presented, followed by an outline script in which a teacher helps students apply the skill of making predictions (taught earlier) to the narrative. Notice how the teacher first *reminds students of the skill to be applied*, then has students read the text *to determine the intent of the selection*. Notice that the teacher next discusses the text to ensure that students have understood the selection and were able to *make predictions* as they read. Finally, notice that the teacher guides students in *summarizing* what they have learned about making predictions to a reading selection. Marginal numbers show actual page division in original pupil text.

EXAMPLE 2.5   SELECTION AND SAMPLE APPLICATION LESSON
FOR MAKING PREDICTIONS

Selection: "Birthdays"

Little Owl rolled over in his bed and pulled the covers up around him. He liked   1
listening to the sound of the rain falling on the leaves outside. Suddenly, Little
Owl sat up.

"Tonight is my birthday!" he cried. He jumped out of bed and ran into the kitch-
en.

"Good evening, Little Owl," Mother said with a smile. "Are you ready for breakfast?"

"Yes, I'm hungry," said Little Owl, sitting down at the table. "Do you know what   2
tonight is?"

"Yes, I do," said Mrs. Owl. "Tonight is the night I must clean the cupboards."

"No, no!" said Little Owl. "I mean, do you know what *tonight* is? It's a special
night."

Mother laughed. "Special? There's nothing special about cleaning cup-boards."

"She forgot," Little Owl said to himself.

After breakfast, Little Owl went down the steps of the Old Tree. "She forgot that tonight is my birthday," Little Owl sighed. "This never happened before."

3   Little Owl walked slowly to the tall trees. He saw Raccoon sitting under a tree. "Hi, Raccoon," said Little Owl. "Do you know what tonight is?"

"Sure I do," said Raccoon.

"You do?" cried Little Owl.

"Tonight is the night my cousin promised to show me her secret fishing place," said Raccoon.

"Oh," said Little Owl, "I thought you *knew* what's special about tonight."

"I've been waiting here since sunset," Raccoon went on, "but she hasn't come yet. Well, I can't wait any longer. Listen, Little Owl. When my cousin comes by, tell her I'm down at the river. Will you do that, Little Owl?"

Then Raccoon hurried off without waiting for an answer.

4   Little Owl stood for a while looking down the path, but no one came.

"I'm not going to stand here all night," he thought, "not on my birthday."

Little Owl wrote a note for Raccoon's cousin and stuck it on the tree. Then he stepped back and looked at the note.

5   "Suppose that note were a sign," he thought. "Suppose it said, 'Tonight is Little Owl's Birthday.' And suppose there were signs just like it all over the forest. Then everyone would know about my birthday!"

"That's it!" he cried. "I'll make some signs."

Little Owl ran back to his house, laughing all the way. First he found some boards, then he opened a can of paint. He stuck one wing into the paint and wrote on the first board:

"TONIGHT IS LITTLE OWL'S BIRTHDAY."

"I'll put this sign down by the river," Little Owl thought.

He painted a picture of some water at the bottom of the sign to help him remember that this sign should go near the water. He decorated each sign to help him remember where to place it.

6   After he had finished the signs, Little Owl carried them down the path. When he got to the big tree in the woods, he remembered that he needed a hammer and some nails. He left the pile of signs near the bottom of the big tree and ran home.

When he came back, all the signs were gone. Little Owl could hear someone hammering down in the woods, so he went down into the woods.

7   Suddenly, the hammering stopped. Mole poked his head around the stump of a tree. "Is that you, Little Owl?" he said in a slow, sad voice.

"Hello, Mole," said Little Owl. "I haven't seen you in a long time."

"No one does," said Mole. "But I saw *you,* Little Owl," he said shyly. "And you have made me very happy."

"I have?" asked Little Owl. "You don't look happy."

"Oh, I always look like this," sighed Mole. "But tonight I *am* happy. Do you know what tonight is, Little Owl?"

8   "I know what tonight is," cried Little Owl." "Do you know what it is?"

"Tonight is my birthday," said Mole.

"*Your* birthday?" shouted Little Owl.

"Every year it's my birthday," Mole went on proudly, "but no one ever knows. Now *you* remembered, Little Owl."

"I did?" asked Little Owl.

"Yes, you did," Mole went on. "You said to yourself that tonight must be Mole's birthday. So you made that present, Little Owl. You brought it here and set it down near my hole, then you hurried off so that I would be surprised. Oh, Little Owl," said Mole getting up slowly. "I'm so happy! Come and see."

Mole took Little Owl farther down into the woods. "Look!" he said. "My new house. Isn't it beautiful?"

Little Owl could hardly believe his eyes. Mole was building a house out of Little Owl's signs.   9

"I've always wanted a real house," said Mole. "And now, because of your wonderful present, I shall have one. I'll sit in it all day and look at the lovely decorations you painted for me."

Mole could not read. In fact, he could not even see very well.

"Oh, it will be a happy home for me," said Mole.

Little Owl looked at his signs. Some of them were already nailed together.   10 "Now no one will ever know about my birthday," he sighed to himself.

Then Little Owl looked at Mole's happy face. He picked up his hammer and helped Mole build his house.

When Mole and Little Owl finished building the house, they sat together on the stump and admired the house.

"Do you know what tonight is, Mole?" said Little Owl. "It's *my* birthday, too."   11

"*Your* birthday and *my* birthday are on the same night?" cried Mole.

"That's right," said Little Owl.

"Let's go to my house and celebrate our birthdays together," said Little Owl.

Mole was delighted. He had never celebrated anything with anyone before.

Little Owl and Mole walked together along the path to Little Owl's house. Little Owl opened the door.

"Surprise!" everyone shouted. "Happy birthday, Little Owl!"   12

Little Owl couldn't believe his eyes.

The kitchen was all decorated with lights and colored paper. The table was set for a party, and around it stood all of Little's Owl's friends.

"What's going on, Little Owl?" Mole whispered.

"A birthday party!" cried Little Owl.

He ran over to his mother and gave her a big hug. "You did remember my birthday! It's Mole's birthday, too," said Little Owl.

"Happy birthday, Mole!" said Mrs. Owl.

"Happy birthday, Mole and Little Owl!" everyone cried.

Mole and Little Owl looked at each other. Each was thinking the same thing. "A birthday is more fun when it's shared."

Source: Adaptation of "Birthdays" from LITTLE OWL, KEEPER OF THE TREES by Ronald and Ann Himler, illustrated by Ronald Himler. Copyright © 1974 by Ronald and Ann Himler. Reprinted by permission of Harper & Row, Publishers, Inc. In William K. Durr et al.: *Discoveries,* pp. 77–91 (Houghton Mifflin Reading). Boston: Houghton Mifflin Company, 1986.

Sample Lesson

Application

Remind Students of Skill to Apply
Say: You have learned how to make predictions as you read. You use the author's clues to determine what is likely to happen next or later. As you read our story today, try to use what you have learned about making predictions.

Have Students Read Text to Determine Intent of the Selection
Say: Today, we are going to read the story "Birthdays." (Background and vocabulary would already have been developed. See page 56.) Remember to use what you have learned about making predictions. (Students should be able to read the first half of the story by themselves for a single purpose. *Note:* Purpose for reading is broadly based and requires students to focus on the entire first half of the selection. Purpose leads to an understanding of the selection and checks the application of making predictions.)
Say: Read pages 1–6 to see what is happening in Little Owl's life and to tell what you think is going to happen to Little Owl.

Discuss the Text to Check Understanding of the Selection
(After students read this part of the selection, lead a discussion using the following questions. Note that these questions are designed to help the reader develop an overall understanding of "Birthdays." *Note:* The questions are designed to ensure that the reader has an overall understanding of the story and how the ideas are related. The questions follow the order of the story and lead students to form a map or overall mental picture of the story. None of these questions check application. Page numbers refer to marginal numbers in story.)

1. *Who are the characters (animals) in our story?*
   —Little Owl, Mrs. Owl, Raccoon, and Raccoon's cousin.
2. *Where did our story take place?*
   —In the woods around Little Owl's home.
3. *What was the problem Little Owl was having?*
   —It was his birthday and no one seemed to know it.
4. *What did Little Owl do to try to remind his mother that it was his birthday?*
   —He asked her if she knew what night it was. (page 2)
5. *Did Little Owl's mother remember that it was his birthday?*
   —No. (page 2)
6. *What did Little Owl ask Raccoon?*
   —Do you know what tonight is? (page 3)
7. *What did Raccoon tell Little Owl?*
   —It was the night he and his cousin were going to the secret fishing place. (page 3)
8. *Did Raccoon remember that it was Little Owl's birthday?*
   —No. (page 3)

9. *What did Little Owl do that helped him decide how to tell everyone it was his birthday?*
   —He left a note for Raccoon's cousin telling her to meet Raccoon at the river. (pages 4–5)
10. *What did Little Owl do to let everyone know it was his birthday?*
    —He made signs to put up. (page 5)
11. *What did Little Owl forget to take with him when he went to put up the signs?*
    —Hammer and nails. (page 6)
12. *When little Owl returned, what had happened to his signs?*
    —They were gone. (page 6)
13. *What was the big problem that Little Owl was having?*
    —No one seemed to remember his birthday and someone had taken his signs.

Discuss Text to Check Application of Skill and Extend Students' Thinking about the Selection

1. How do you think Little Owl felt? Why?
2. How would you have felt if you had been Little Owl?
3. What do you think is going to happen in the next part of our story? As students make predictions, list them on the board and save them for the next reading period. In the next reading period:

Say: Now we are going to read the next part of the selection. You made these predictions about what is going to happen in this part of the story (refer to students' list). Now read pages 7–12 to see if your predictions were correct. (After students have read the second part of the selection, discuss the accuracy of their predictions. Lead students through a discussion similar to the one in the last class period to ensure that they understand the second part of the story and the overall story. Conclude the discussion of the story by asking the following two questions.)

Questions to Bring out the Lesson of Selection and to Check Application of Making Predictions

1. What did Little Owl and Mole learn about birthdays?
2. How do you think Little Owl and Mole will spend their birthdays and the birthdays of other friends in the future?

Summarize
Say: In this selection, you used what you had learned about making predictions to help you understand the story. How did you use making predictions? (Have students tell in their own words how they used the skill of making predictions in this selection. Prompt with questions if necessary.)
Say: When do you think this skill will help you in your reading? (Have students answer in their own words.)

The concept of direct instruction provides a systematic framework for teachers to follow when teaching students how to comprehend. (The same framework can be applied to teaching decoding.) To ensure that students learn to comprehend more effectively when reading natural text, all parts of direct instruction must be used systematically. Table 2.1 summarizes the steps of direct instruction and provides a brief description of each.

Table 2.1   Steps of Direct Instruction in Comprehension

Steps of Direct Instruction	Description
1. Teaching	
Let students know what is to be learned and relate it to prior experience.	Teacher helps students begin to think about what is to be learned and develop a frame of reference or schema for it. This helps students develop metacognitive processes.
Model skill or process and verbalize thinking.	
Teacher modeling	Teacher shows students how to use the comprehension skill or process and explains the thinking that takes place in doing so. Sentences or paragraphs are used as examples.
Student modeling	Students show teacher the same process and explain their thinking.
Provide guided practice.	Students try out the comprehension skill or process under the teacher's direction. Corrective feedback is provided. Teacher reteaches as needed. Directed-choice activities are used.
Summarize.	Students explain in their own words how to use the comprehension skill or process; teacher prompts with questions. This helps students develop metacognitive abilities.
2. Practicing	Students use the comprehension skill or process in an independent, directed choice activity. Teacher provides corrective feedback as needed after completion of the activity.
3. Applying	
Remind students of the skill they are going to apply.	Teacher tells students what comprehension skill they should apply in reading natural text; an example of the skill can be given. This step further develops students' metacognitive processes.
Students read text.	Teacher provides purpose or guide questions to help students gain an understanding of the overall text.
Discuss text read.	
Check understanding.	The discussion following reading is first focused on being certain that students understand the intent of the selection.
Check application.	Teacher asks questions to determine whether students applied the comprehension skill or process in question.
Summarize	Students tell in their own words how and when to use the comprehension skill or process; teacher prompts with questions. Relates to metacognitive development.

USING DIRECT INSTRUCTION WITH A DIRECTED READING LESSON

The use of a Directed Reading Lesson (DRL), Directed Reading Activity (DRA), or Directed Reading Thinking Activity (DRTA) is not new to the teaching of reading (Harris and Sipay, 1980; Stauffer, 1969). Authorities in reading instruction have long recognized the merits of some instructional plan and have recommended the DRL as a sound way to carry out reading instruction. A DRL is not an approach to or method of teaching reading; it is a way of thinking about and organizing reading instruction that ties together the components of good teaching.

The basal readers, which are the most widely used approach to teaching reading in the United States, follow a directed reading model; the names each author uses for the parts of the lesson vary, but the basic organizational structure is the same. Therefore, inservice teachers are very familiar with some form of the DRL.

Although the DRL has been most commonly used with basal reading materials, it can be used in any class with any type of material to help foster improved comprehension. The DRL can be used as a means to integrate the elements of direct instruction and at the same time to account for the components of the instructional program in reading comprehension. The idea of the DRL being an appropriate way to tie together the components of direct instruction is not new (Cooper et al., 1979).

Traditionally, the parts of the DRL recommended by many reading authorities have included (1) getting ready to read, (2) guided silent reading, (3) skill building, and (4) follow-up, using various labels for each part. The problem with this traditional order is that it leads teachers to believe that skills are taught after reading has been completed. Furthermore, this order does not clearly indicate to teachers the ways in which the parts of the DRL relate to one another. Therefore, a new order has been suggested (Cooper et al., 1979):

1. skill building
2. background and readiness
3. guided silent reading and discussion
4. extension

This sequence helps teachers clarify how the parts of direct instruction fit together with an overall concept of a good reading lesson and good reading instruction. Although the parts of the DRL are presented in a sequential order, they can be used flexibly to meet the instructional needs of students. The parts are discussed in the following sections.

Skill Building

The skill building portion of a DRL is the part of the lesson in which new skills and processes of reading are taught. This is the phase of the lesson that utilizes the teach and practice steps of direct instruction; it is at this point in the lesson that the teacher teaches the skills and processes of reading comprehension and provides practice for students. Thus, it accounts for the building processes and skills component of the instructional program in reading comprehension. During skill building, instruction should alternate between decoding, comprehension, and study skills, depending on what skills or processes need to be taught. Refer back to the sample lessons for teaching students to make predictions (Examples 2.3 and 2.4). Two parts of direct instruction—teaching and practice—occur in the skill building portion of the DRL. Only one new comprehension skill or process should be taught at a time.

Background and Readiness

The background and readiness portion of the DRL develops the background concepts and vocabulary that students will need in order to read a particular selection. The activities carried out in this part of the lesson help to build students' motivation to read the selection and help develop the students' frame of reference or schema, which will lead to better comprehension. The background developed for the selection should be more than just the general topics to be covered in the reading. It should be a schema-directed plan that will help the reader develop an understanding of the selection (Beck, 1984).

Teachers often skip or rush through this part of the lesson. However, background and vocabulary are so significant to comprehension that this segment of the lesson must be given a fair portion of time (Pearson, 1982).

In addition to the less formal instruction teachers use to provide background and motivation, the background and readiness portion of the lesson also makes use of direct instruction in teaching and practicing vocabulary. This phase of the lesson accounts for the developing background and vocabulary component of the instructional program in reading comprehension. Example 2.6 illustrates a sample background and readiness lesson that could be used with the narrative "Birthdays" (see page 49). You will recall that this narrative was used earlier with a lesson on applying the skill of making predictions, which was taught and practiced using direct instruction in skill building. As you study this example, notice how the background development is leading to a frame of reference for the students' overall understanding of the selection and is not focusing only on background of the topic itself.

EXAMPLE 2.6   SAMPLE BACKGROUND AND READINESS
LESSON* ——————————————————————

Purpose

To develop background relative to understanding

1. how one would feel when it is a special day in his or her life and no one seems to remember or care.
2. that owls sleep in the day and stay awake at night.

*Note that this lesson is based on "Birthdays," the selection on pages 49–51.

Vocabulary

special and *birthday*
Say: We are going to read a story about owls. Has anyone ever seen an owl? (Students respond; briefly discuss.) Do you know when owls like to sleep? (Students respond. If they do not know that owls sleep in the daytime and stay awake at night, explain this.)
Say: Owls do sleep all day and stay awake all night. Have you ever heard anyone say that somebody is a "night owl"? People are called "night owls" if they stay up all night. Our story today is a make-believe story about Little Owl, who is having a special day but no one seems to know it. Have you ever had a special day in your life that no one seemed to know? (Students respond. Encourage them to tell their experiences, bringing out that even though others did not seem to notice, they probably did care.)

Teaching Vocabulary Prior to Reading and Relating It to Background
Write the following sentence on the board: It was a <u>special</u> day in Little Owl's life.
Say: Use what you have learned about letter sounds and the sense of the sentence to figure out the underlined word in this sentence. Who can read this sentence for me? (Students respond. If no one can read it, the teacher reads it aloud, calling attention to the underlined word.) What does "special" mean? (Students respond. Encourage students to give examples of special days.)
Say: For Little Owl, the special day was his birthday. (Write the following sentence on the chalkboard: It was Little Owl's <u>birthday</u>.)
Say: Who can read this sentence for me? (If students are unable to read the sentence, read it aloud for them.)

Guided Practice With Vocabulary After It Has Been Taught*
Say: What is a birthday? (Discuss birthdays. Have students give another sentence with the words *special* and *birthday*. Write the sentences on the board and have other students read them aloud and tell what the words mean in each sentence.)
Say: It is Little Owl's birthday and no one seems to notice. How would you feel? (Students respond.) Maybe the animals around Little Owl are just pretending not to notice. Why might they do that? (Students respond. Discuss, bringing out that they might have a surprise for him.)

Summary
(Here, you summarize background for students, orienting your summary toward an overall understanding of the story.)
Say: In our story called "Birthdays," it is Little Owl's birthday, which is a special day for him. No one seems to notice, but maybe that's not totally true. As you read this story, think about this situation.

---

*No additional practice should be needed for this selection.

Guided Silent Reading and Discussion

The guided silent reading and discussion portion of the DRL is its keystone. This is the segment of the lesson that draws together everything the teacher has been aiming toward. The primary purpose for guided reading is to provide students with opportunities to apply the comprehension skill or process that was taught and practiced in the skill building portion of the lesson. The vocabulary and background for the selection will have already been developed (in the background and readiness portion of the lesson).

In terms of direct instruction, guided silent reading and discussion is the portion of the lesson in which application takes place; students use the comprehension skills and processes they have been taught while reading natural text. Thus, the activities included in the application portion of direct instruction take place during the guided silent reading segment of the DRL. These include

1. reminding students of the comprehension skill to apply.
2. having students read silently under teacher guidance to gain a general understanding of the selection.
3. discussing the text with students to be sure they understand the selection and to ensure that they were able to apply the comprehension skill taught.
4. summarizing what students learned about using the comprehension skill or process taught and applied in the reading.

The sample application lesson presented in Example 2.5 illustrates what should be taking place in guided silent reading.

In addition to applying the comprehension skill taught, students are applying the vocabulary that was taught in the background and readiness portion of the DRL and drawing on the experiences that were developed or activated to construct their own understanding of the selection. Teachers can check students' application of the vocabulary during the general discussion of the students' overall understanding of the text.

Using Questions in Guided Reading

Questions are an important part of guided reading and discussion activities, but questions do not teach comprehension (Durkin, 1981a, 1981b; Herber and Nelson, 1975). They do, however, help students develop an understanding of specific selections and let the teacher know whether students are able to apply the comprehension skills and processes taught. Many sound recommendations concerning questions during guided reading can be made based on current research and professional opinions (Beck, Omanson, and McKeown, 1982; Pearson, 1982, Beck, 1984); some of these recommendations follow.

There are two basic formats that can be used for guided reading. The first is page-by-page or section-by-section guided reading, in which the teacher asks specific questions, students read to find the answers, and then there is a discussion; this is continued until the entire selection is read. This format is typically used in the primary grades and for students who are having difficulty learning to read.

In the second format, students are given a single purpose to guide their reading of an entire selection, and their reading is followed by discussion. This procedure is typically used in the intermediate grades and for students who are capable readers.

With either format, the first set of questions teachers ask should lead their students to an overall understanding of the text by proceeding in an order that matches the order of events in the selection. Further, this set of questions should lead students to see how the events of the selection are interrelated. With page-by-page guided reading and discussion, questions asked before students read the selection should lead students to an overall understanding of the selection; the discussion following guided reading should include questions that help students pull together the ideas of the entire selection. These questions should also proceed in the order of events in the selection and should help students see how those events are related. In other words, guided reading and initial discussion questions should lead students to formulate what Beck calls a story map or overall mental picture of the selection (Beck, 1984).

After the guided reading and the initial discussion have been completed and students have an overall understanding of the selection, questions can be asked that extend the selection and check application of specific skills. The application questions can also be asked as a part of the questions that are meant to develop an overall understanding of the story, provided that they fit into the flow of ideas. Example 2.7 illustrates the type of lesson that can be used in page-by-page or section-by-section guided reading and discussion. The lesson uses the first part of the selection "Birthdays," reprinted on page 49. Remember that this selection was used to teach students to apply the skill of making predictions to the reading of natural text. The following example has the same focus.

EXAMPLE 2.7   SAMPLE SECTION-BY-SECTION GUIDED READING
LESSON* ─────────────────────────────

Remind students of skill to apply.

Say: You have learned how to make predictions as you read. You use the author's clues to determine what is likely to happen next or later. As you read our story today, try to use what you have learned about making predictions.

*Note to teacher: The outline script in Example 2.7, which illustrates section-by-section guided reading, assumes that the background and readiness portion of the DRL has already been completed. The focus of this guided reading and discussion is the application of making predictions.

Have students read text section-by-section to determine the overall intent of the selection.

(Page numbers refer to marginal numbers in story on page 49.)

Set purpose for reading.

Say: Read page 1 to find out what Little Owl did when he got out of bed.

Discussion

Check purpose for reading.
Develop intent of the selection.
Check application of making predictions.

1. What did Little Owl do when he got out of bed?
2. What special day was it for Little Owl?
3. What do you think he is going to do on his birthday?

Set purpose for reading.

Say: Read page 2 to see what Mrs. Owl said about the special day.

Discussion

Check purpose for reading.

1. What did Mrs. Owl say about the special day?

Develop intent of the selection.

2. Did Mrs. Owl seem to know it was Little Owl's birthday?

Set purpose for reading.

Say: Read page 3 to see what Little Owl did after breakfast.

Discussion

Check purpose for reading.
Bring out the problem of the selection.

1. What did Little Owl do after breakfast?
2. How did Raccoon answer Little Owl's questions about it being a special day?
3. What did Raccoon ask Little Owl to do?

Set purpose for reading.

Say: Read pages 4 and 5 to find out what Little Owl decided to do.

Discussion

Check purpose for reading.
Bring out intent of selection.

1. What did Little Owl decide to do?
2. Why didn't Little Owl want to stand and wait for Raccoon's cousin?

USING DIRECT INSTRUCTION

Set purpose for reading.	*Say:* Read page 6 to find out what Little Owl did about his signs.

Discussion

Check purpose for reading.
Bring out intent of selection and set scene for next section.

1. What did Little Owl do about his signs?
2. What happened when he was ready to put up the signs?
3. What did Little Owl discover when he returned?

Discussion Following Reading

Questions to help students pull together the story and develop an overall understanding.

1. Who are the characters in our story?
2. Where does our story take place?
3. What problem does Little Owl have?
4. How does he try to solve it?
5. How would you feel if you were in Little Owl's place?

Question to extend thinking about the selection and relate it to student's experiences.

Check application of predictions.

Say: What do you think is going to happen in the next part of our story?

In the second format of guided reading, students are given a single purpose to guide their reading of the entire selection, and discussion follows their reading. The purpose given for reading should be broadly based and require students to focus on the entire selection as much as possible (Pearson, 1982). In the discussion immediately following reading, the first questions the teacher should ask should check the purpose and help students develop an overall understanding of the ideas in the selection and the ways the ideas are related. Thus, the questions should proceed in the order of the ideas presented in the selection and should lead students to formulate their "map" of the selection. The teacher can then ask questions that extend the selection and check application. Again, the application questions can be asked as part of the initial discussion, provided they fit into the flow of ideas. This type of guided reading was used in Example 2.5 (p. 49), the application activity using "Birthdays." Notice that the teacher in Example 2.5 first gives students an overall purpose to guide their reading, then, in the initial follow-up discussion, brings out an overall flow or map of the story, and concludes with questions extending the selection by requiring students to relate their feelings to the story and asking them to make their predictions about what is likely to happen in the second part of the selection.

Guided reading is a tool to be used for instructional purposes. The goal should always be for students to read full selections as soon as possible. Therefore, page-by-page or section-by-section guided reading should be discontinued as soon as students are able to read and comprehend entire selections. The reading of entire selections gives students a better feel for "real reading" and helps them see that they are learning how to read in order *to be able to read.*

Extension

The final part of the directed reading lesson is extension. It is during this part of the lesson that students

use what they have learned in their reading in some type of creative activity,

extend their vocabulary by learning words related to the vocabulary they were taught for the selection, thus developing background for future reading,

carry out a writing activity that correlates with the type or content of the selection read,

read other related selections to expand the concepts they've just learned,

complete an activity that requires further application of the reading skills used in the selection.

In terms of direct instruction, the extension portion of the DRL accounts for further application and provides additional teaching and learning experiences related to the content or type of selection. Extension also helps to build more positive attitudes toward reading. This is the major place in the lesson where the correlating writing component of the instructional program in reading comprehension is accounted for. The extension portion of the DRL must not be viewed as the "fringe benefits" or the "only if time allows" portion of the lesson. Extension activities should be given to all students. Example 2.8 illustrates various types of extension activities that could be used for the selection "Birthdays," presented in Example 2.5. Students' needs should dictate the types of activities a teacher uses.

EXAMPLE 2.8   SAMPLE EXTENSION ACTIVITIES ———————

Writing
(Directions to students) Write a paragraph about your favorite character in "Birthdays." In your paragraph, describe the character and tell why you like him or her.

Vocabulary
(Directions to students) The selection "Birthdays" has some words that you think of when you think about a birthday. For example, the word *present* on page 51 would be a birthday word. Look through the story to find other birthday words, and think of words on your own. Make a list of them. Write a sentence using each word. Be ready to share your list and sentences with others.

Creative Activity
Have students take parts from the story and act the story out. Have one student be a narrator, one Little Owl, and so on. Encourage students to say their parts in their own words.

Making Predictions
Have students select a favorite comic strip from the newspaper and bring it to class. Have them read it to see if there are clues that would help them predict what will be in the next day's strip. Follow up by having them check the newspaper the next day. This can be done over several days.

In summary, the DRL is an already-familiar format to many teachers that can be used to account for the elements of direct instruction and the components of the instructional program in reading comprehension. Table 2.2 summarizes the parts of the DRL and shows how they can account for these elements. Authors of basal readers are beginning to incorporate the direct instruction concept into their suggested teaching plans. Example 2.9, a sample lesson from the 1986 Houghton Mifflin Reading *Triumphs*, illustrates how this is being done. Note how the steps of direct instruction are employed in the skill preparation for reading "The Slim Butte Ghost" to teach making inferences from narrative. Also note how students are reminded to apply this skill under Reading (page 389) and how this application is checked during the discussion under Thinking It Over (page 392).

INDEPENDENT READING AND COMPREHENSION DEVELOPMENT

The instructional program in reading comprehension is designed to teach students *how to comprehend*, and direct instruction places focus on the "how to" of comprehension. However, a student's growth in reading comprehension comes through repeated *use* of what he or she has been taught to do. In essence, the reader must have many opportunities to independently apply the comprehension skills and processes he or she has been taught.

In every reading program at every level, there must be a segment of time allowed for students to independently read materials they have selected themselves. Each student should read something that relates to his or her own interests. Students should be encouraged to share and talk about their reading with others, including the teacher, but they should not be asked to write traditional book reports.

As students are given time to read independently, they should be told to try to make use of all the things they have learned about reading. Beyond this, there should be no direct teaching of reading during the independent-reading period—no worksheets, no workbook pages, no detailed questioning, no testing —just reading for fun and enjoyment.

**Table 2.2   The Directed Reading Lesson, Direct Instruction,
and the Instructional Program in Comprehension**

Lesson Component	Description	Comprehension Program Element
SKILL BUILDING		
Teaching	In this segment of the DRL, skills and processes are taught and practiced.	Accounts for the building processes and skills component of comprehension and for developing vocabulary.
Let students know what is to be learned and relate it to prior experiences.		
Model skill or processes.		
Provide guided practice.		
Summarize.		
Practicing (Independent)		
BACKGROUND AND READINESS		
Develop background for selection.	Helps reader develop or activate background that leads to a better understanding of the selection, not just of the topic.	Accounts for the developing background and vocabulary component of comprehension.
Teach and practice new vocabulary using direct instruction.	Direct instruction is used to teach and practice key vocabulary for the selection; vocabulary is a part of background development.	
Build motivation for reading selection.		
GUIDED SILENT READING AND DISCUSSION		
Applying	Students are applying the skills and processes learned to the reading of "natural text." The application step of direct instruction is accounted for.	Accounts for the building processes and skills component of comprehension and for developing vocabulary.
Remind students of skill to apply.		
Students read text.		
Discuss text.		
Summarize.		
EXTENSION		
Focus on extending and enriching reading and on further applying what has been learned.	Activities are directed toward further application and expansion of learnings from reading.	Accounts for the correlating writing component of comprehension. Also builds background and vocabulary for future reading.
	Writing activities are correlated to reading.	

EXAMPLE 2.9 SAMPLE BASAL READING LESSON USING DIRECT INSTRUCTION ———

3 Skill Preparation for Unit 23

The Slim Butte Ghost

Comprehension

Making Inferences from Narrative (C2 · G1a–e,2a,b) Lesson 24

Note

This lesson brings together skills taught in earlier levels. If some students need a brief review, you may use the following Optional Review lessons:

Unit 22: Drawing Conclusions
Unit 23: Inferring Cause-Effect Relationships
Unit 25: Predicting Outcomes

Introduction

Remind students that they have found it is often necessary to make inferences as they read; that is, they have to use what they already know to figure something out because the author did not tell them everything. Explain that authors assume that their readers will be able to do such things as draw conclusions, predict outcomes, and so on, without lengthy explanations. Tell students that good inferencing skills make good readers and that in today's lesson they will learn more about how to develop their inferencing skills.

Instruction

Duplicate [Teacher's Notebook: Instruction Master page 34]

In discussing inferencing, be sure to make the following points:

- Inferencing is based in part on information and clues provided by the author.

- In addition, readers bring with them their own knowledge and experience.

- Readers make inferences by putting together their own background of information and what the author tells them.

Point out to students that they have already had a lot of experience with inferencing because it is involved in a variety of skills that they have practiced.

These include drawing conclusions, predicting outcomes, and recognizing cause-effect relationships. Remind students that in the last unit, they learned that sometimes cause-effect relationships are very straightforward but that other times they may have to infer either the cause or the effect. For an example of this, have them turn in their books to "Raymond's Run" (pages 306–318).

Ask students to recall why Squeaky was so happy at the end of the race that she was willing to smile at Gretchen. Students may give the most obvious explanation, that it was because Gretchen had run a good race and didn't seem like such a bad sort after all. Tell students that as good readers, they could figure out that the real source of Squeaky's elation is that she felt very good about herself just then, having just decided to do something unselfish for her less-fortunate brother, and she realized that there were many things she could accomplish even if she had lost the race (page 316). Point out that in order to figure out these cause-effect relationships, they had certain information the author provided, in this case, Squeaky's own words about what happened and how she felt. In addition, readers could recognize, from their own experience, the feeling of elation that Squeaky had that comes from feeling good about oneself. By putting these two understandings together, they could infer that Squeaky was ready to allow that Gretchen had indeed done a good job and that maybe girls could be friends. To emphasize this, ask students how they think Squeaky might have acted toward Gretchen if she had done badly in the race and if she had not thought of something that would help Raymond. Suggest that they put themselves in Squeaky's place.

Distribute the following material:

Martin leaned against a palm tree and took a final look at the little house where he had spent so many happy days. Soon he would be leaving it behind for a far different climate. He wondered if he was too old to learn how to ski and to ice skate. He hoped that he would not be so busy with his studies and other campus activities that he never had a chance to try.

After students have read the paragraph, explain to them that though the author doesn't say these things specifically, they, as readers, can make the following inferences:

Martin is presently in the South.

He is moving north to a colder climate.

Martin has mixed feelings about leaving.

He will be going to school or college.

Point out that many of the clues on which they based their inferences were supplied by the author, such as Martin leaning against a palm tree; mention of the change of climate, skiing and ice skating, and studies and campus activities. Point out that it is the students' own experience that would allow them to interpret these clues. For example, they would have to know that palm trees grow in the South; realize that skiing and skating are common in the colder North; understand that campus activities suggest school or college; know that it is easier to learn such sports as skiing and ice skating when young.

Refer students to the following:

Suddenly the heavy air exploded in the flash and crash of a sudden storm. Rover whipped around and raced under the porch. Jo tried to coax him out before the rains came. "Come out, you silly canine," she said. "It's only thunder."

After students have read the paragraph, tell them that though the author doesn't specifically explain why the dog is frightened, the reader is able to infer it. There is the clue of Jo's trying to "coax him out" and saying "It's only thunder." The reader may also, from his or her own experience, know that dogs are often frightened by thunder and will try to hide from it. The reader, therefore, infers the cause-effect relationship, or what is actually a series of causes and effects: The thunder is the cause of Rover's fear, which in turn causes the dog to hide under the porch, which then causes Jo to try and get him out. Point out that as good readers, they would not pause in a story to figure out such cause-effect relationships. But because they are able to make such inferences, they are able to understand the whole story better.

Refer students to the following:

The service manager at the garage looked annoyed. He had promised Mr. Haversham's car at four o'clock, that was true, and he admitted as much to the red-faced man on the other side of the counter. But, as he explained, the mechanics had found that there was a part that had to be replaced, and though they had ordered a new one immediately, it wouldn't arrive for two days.

"I really think you should leave the car here, Mr. Haversham. I really can't be responsible if . . ."

Mr. Haversham interrupted him. "I'm a busy man, Mr. Collins. I need my car."

"Well, I can't force you to leave it. But try not to drive it over forty miles an hour."

Mr. Haversham raised an eyebrow at that. "On the turnpike? That would be an accomplishment."

A moment later, he roared out of the garage. Andy Collins shook his head.

After students have read the excerpt, tell them that the author has left many clues in both the dialogue and the narrative that would allow them to predict what may happen to Mr. Haversham. They have learned, for example, that there is part that needs to be replaced; that the service manager doesn't want Mr. Haversham to drive the car at all; that he feels it would certainly be dangerous over forty miles an hour. Readers can also infer that Mr. Haversham drives on the turnpike and that he is a hasty and impatient man. From their own experience, readers know that maximum speed on a turnpike is, under normal conditions, over forty miles an hour. Putting all these clues together, the reader can infer that Mr. Haversham will probably drive his car too fast and that he will have some kind of trouble with it, which may be serious. As they continued in the story, students would experience a sense of anticipation that something was going to happen, thus adding to their involvement in the story and making it hard to put down.

Guided Practice

Workbook page 95, or **Teacher's Notebook Guided Practice** page 19

Tell students that now they will have a chance to practice what they have learned about making inferences. Have students read the first paragraph. Then have them read and answer question one, which asks them to make an inference based on what they read and what knowledge they bring to their reading. Then ask for volunteers to read aloud their answers. Discuss any disagreements about the answers, which may be based on the varied experience readers bring to their reading.

    Continue in the same manner with the next two paragraphs and their follow-up questions.

Summary

Go over the following summary points with students. Then encourage them to summarize in their own words what they have learned about making inferences in narrative selections and to tell how this skill will help them in their studies. Tell them that they will have a chance to apply this skill in the next selection.

● A reader makes inferences by using information supplied by the author in the selection combined with what background the reader brings to the selection.

● Inferencing is involved in a variety of reading skills used by good readers; these include drawing conclusions, recognizing cause-effect relationships, and predicting outcomes.

Independent Practice

Ask students to turn to **Workbook** page 96 and complete the page independently.

Reteaching Lesson:
    Making Inferences from Narrative
    See page 727 in this Guide.

Optional Resources

Instruction Transparencies:
    Unit 22

Teacher's Notebook:
    Assessment Forms A and B pages 53–54

Workbook page 95
or Teacher's Notebook Guided Practice page 19

Making Inferences
Guided Practice

  Michael's first sight of the campus left him breathless. There were so many buildings and so many people that he did not know how he would ever make any sense out of it.

1. Where is Michael, and why is he there? Explain your answers.
Michael is on the campus of a school, probably a large college or university. A large college or university would be likely to have many buildings, as well as many people. Michael is probably about to begin life as a student at the school. This is suggested by : "he did not know how he would ever make any sense of it." Apparently, Michael plans to spend some time here — or this phrase would make no sense.

  Michael finally located his dorm and lugged his baggage up the stairs to Room 302. He took one look at the tiny room with its bare walls and drab furniture and wondered if he'd made the right decision.

2. Is Michael planning to be a day student or a boarder? How do you know?
Michael is planning to be a boarder. He has located his dorm. (A dormitory is a building in which students who live at a school sleep.) Michael also has luggage with him, suggesting that he will live at the school.

3. Michael wonders if he has made the right decision. To what do the words "right decision" refer? Explain your answer.
The words may refer to Michael's decision to board at the school rather than live at home. He is obviously not too pleased with the appearance of his room. Or, the words may refer to Michael's choice of schools, or to his decision to continue his education.

  Suddenly a cheerful voice said, "You must be Michael. I'm Paul. Welcome to our room."

4. How do you think Michael will respond? Explain your answer.
Michael will probably feel much relieved. Although the school itself seems overwhelming, at least he has a friendly roommate.

Name _____ Date _____

Comprehension: Making Inferences from Narrative   Unit 22 • TRIUMPHS   95

Workbook page 96
Independent Practice

Making Inferences

● Read the paragraph and the statements that follow. Each statement is an inference that could be made, based on the paragraph. Explain why, using your own background knowledge and what you know about cause-effect relationships, drawing conclusions, and predicting outcomes.

  Bill pedaled faster and faster, weaving his way through the piles of dead leaves that lined the side of the road. The air was crisp but not yet cold, and the exercise felt good. After a while, Bill's leg muscles began to ache, so he switched gears. He was climbing steadily and was about to pass Miss Morgan's house. When he noticed that Miss Morgan was in her yard, raking leaves, he slowed down. Bill waved and the young woman waved back. Then, with a burst of renewed energy, he pedaled to the top of the hill. At the crest, he smiled, sat back, and relaxed his legs. It was an easy coast down the other side Bill knew. He had covered this route many times. He wanted to be sure he was familiar with every mile of it on the day of the triathlon.

1. Bill is riding a bicycle.
Bill is pedaling; his leg muscles begin to ache; he switches gears.

2. Bill is in a suburban or rural area.
There are piles of leaves by the side of the road; Miss Morgan has a yard.

3. The time of the year is autumn.
There are piles of dead leaves in the road; the air is crisp but not yet cold; Miss Morgan is raking her yard.

4. Miss Morgan and Bill know each other.
Bill notices Miss Morgan in her yard; he slows down and waves; she waves back.

★ Decide which of the following statements is an inference that can be made, based on the paragraph. Mark the space for the answer.

○ Miss Morgan is Bill's coach.   ○ Bill has a three-speed bike.
● Bill is in training for a race.   ○ Bill lives near Miss Morgan.

Name _____ Date _____

96   Comprehension: Making Inferences from Narrative   Unit 22 • TRIUMPHS

3

1 Reading the Selection

The Slim Butte Ghost
by Virginia Driving Hawk Sneve
pages 320–331

Summary

City-bred Hank is visiting his grandfather, who lives in Lokota Indian country. When he hears Mr. High Bear tell his grandfather that the Slim Butte ghost has been seen again, he is curious and excited, especially as he has been invited along to try to catch it. He learns that the ''ghost'' is a wild white stallion — actually, several different ones that have been seen from time to time over the years. Each time, a group of riders goes out to try to catch it, but never does. Hank's grandfather has gone every time, ever since he was a young cowboy, but now he is too old. Sending Hank is the next best thing, though. As he helps Hank prepare for his adventure, Hank imagines himself a tough hero in a Western movie. He tries to maintain this feeling on the chase, in spite of intruding disappointments. Then, when the mare responds to the call of the stallion, Hank suddenly finds himself on a runaway horse, and he must fight to regain control of it. Finally the trail ends as the stallion's sharp hoofprints disappear at a steep incline. The men seem content to give up the search and return home, but Hank is angry at the abrupt ending. Then he realizes that they never expected to catch the stallion, that it is all a ritual they repeat each time the ghost appears. After all, as Grandpa says with satisfaction upon their return, ''You can't catch a ghost.''

Preparation
Vocabulary/Concept Development

Ask students to share what they know about wild horses, based on what they have learned from their own experience, from books, and from movies. Then have them try to describe the type of country where wild horses could live. Tell them that in the story they are about to read, the people of such an area have a very special feeling toward one particular wild horse.

Display *stirrup, hobble, bridle*

Ask students what the words have in common. *(equipment used with horses)* If there are students in the group who are familiar with horses and their gear, ask them to describe each item and explain how it is used. Otherwise you can use the following information and discussion questions:

- **A stirrup is a loop or ring hung by a strap from either side of a horse's saddle. The loop or ring has a flat base on which the rider's foot rests. What is the purpose of a stirrup?** *(to support the rider's foot; to allow the rider to mount)*

- **A hobble is a rope or strap put around the legs of a horse to limit, but not prevent entirely, its movement. Why and when might you need to hobble a horse?** *(to prevent it from roaming when there is no other means of doing so, such as a corral or barn)*

- **A bridle is a device made up of straps, including a bit (the part that goes into the horse's mouth), and reins, which fits on a horse's head. What is the purpose of a bridle?** *(to allow the rider to control the horse; for example, to slow or stop it, to turn it, to give it freedom to move at a faster pace)*

Explain that they will find these and other terms about horses in the story they are about to read, ''The Slim Butte Ghost.''

Display *Lakota*

Tell students that this story takes place somewhere in the Dakotas, specifically in Lakota Indian country, and that all the characters are Lakotas. The word *Lakota* also refers to the language of the Lakota people.

Comprehension: Making Inferences from Narrative (C2 · G1a–e,2a,b)

Tell students that as they read the story, they will be making inferences based on direct and indirect clues supplied by the author. When they combine these clues with the knowledge they themselves bring to the story, they will understand and enjoy it more fully.

Reading

Purpose Setting/Silent Reading

Have students turn to page 320 in their books. Read aloud the title, the author's name, and the opening question. Explain that Hank, the main character, has, like them, just heard of the Slim Butte ghost, and, like them, he is wondering: How do you catch a ghost?

1

The Slim Butte Ghost

by Virginia Driving Hawk Sneve

"The shrill call sounded again and again, fading into the night with the pounding hoof beats." The Slim Butte Ghost was back. Maybe this time they would catch it!

320

"We've seen the ghost again," Mr. High Bear calmly announced. "Up on the Slim." He nodded his head north toward the butte[1] jutting out of the prairie.

Hank looked up, wondering if Mr. High Bear was serious. A real ghost? Hank wanted to ask, but one thing he had learned from Grandpa was that a person didn't rush conversation or anything else in Indian country. So he kept his mouth shut and tried to sit quietly while the neighbor and Grandpa visited.

"How long has it been?" Grandpa asked.

"Must be — ten, twelve years." Mr. High Bear sipped his coffee, eyes squinted in thought. "Can't be the same one."

"No," agreed Grandpa.

Hank blew into his steaming mug to keep from blurting the questions racing in his head. He sipped and gasped back a yelp as the scalding brew burned his tongue.

"Going after him?" Grandpa asked, still gazing out of the window.

Mr. High Bear nodded.

"Guess I won't be going this time." Grandpa smiled, but Hank, blowing air over his smarting tongue, heard the yearning in the old man's voice.

"Where'd you hunt before?" Mr. High Bear asked, eyes on the butte.

"All over the hill," Grandpa chuckled.

Mr. High Bear smiled and Hank almost dropped his mug as the neighbor asked, "The boy want to come?"

Instantly, as the men turned to him, Hank closed his mouth over his painful tongue. "He ain't been on a horse this visit," Grandpa said, giving Hank a quizzical glance.

"I can ride," Hank blurted.

Mr. High Bear nodded and stood. "We'll start about four this afternoon," he told Hank. "Better take a bedroll."

---

[1]**butte** (byo͞ot): a hill rising abruptly from an otherwise flat area, with sloping sides and a flat top.

321

1

Hank managed a cool nod, still stifling his curiosity. But after the neighbor had left, the questions tumbled out. "What ghost? Where are we going?"

"You're going after the Slim Butte ghost." Grandpa grinned and rose from his chair. "Let's see if we can fix up a bedroll for you."

"A real ghost?" Hank persisted. "What'll I ride?"

"High Bear'll bring you a mount," Grandpa said, rummaging through an old trunk. He pulled out two worn, faded army blankets, reeking of moth balls. "Whew," Grandpa wrinkled his nose. "Better hang these out to air before we roll 'em."

"There isn't a real ghost on the butte, is there?" Hank asked after he had draped the blankets over the clothesline.

Grandpa stared out at the butte. "I was a young man first time I saw it," he mused. "Old folks used to tell about a ghost that appeared every so often on or around Slim Butte. They said it was big and white; would jump up in front of a horse and rider out of nowhere, scare 'em silly, and take off like lightning.

"I was riding Nelly over to a branding job one day before sunrise. As it started to get light, we rode into fog in the lowlands along the creek below the butte. It was so thick that I could barely see Nelly's ears. I slowed her to a walk and started whistling to keep myself company, but stopped when I remembered the old folks saying that whistling called ghosts."

Hank vividly pictured the scene in his mind, but it was himself he saw — not Grandpa — on the horse cautiously riding through damp mist.

"The sun lightened up the fog," Grandpa went on. "I could see better, so I kicked Nelly into a trot. Just as we topped a rise, I saw the ghost.

"Nelly saw it too. She reared up, bucked, and kept me busy trying to stay mounted; but all the while I watched the ghost. It was pale, whiter than the fog, and the breeze that came about then made it sort of come and go in the mist. It lit out, and Nelly took after it. I hung on, trying to rein her in — didn't have time to be afraid.

"Nelly was sure-footed, but she was running low to the ground at top speed when we couldn't see much ahead. I worried she'd step in a prairie-dog hole and break a leg — besides what I might break if

322

she went down. But I couldn't stop her. I began to wonder if the ghost had put a spell on Nelly to run her to death. Then the fog cleared.

"It was no ghost Nelly was chasing; it was the biggest white stallion I'd ever seen. I didn't blame Nelly for going after him." Grandpa paused and nodded as if agreeing with himself.

"What happened?" Hank demanded.

"Well, I wanted to go after the stallion and see if I could catch him, but I had to get to my job and we'd gone miles in the wrong direction. Even though Nelly was fast, she was only good for top speed for about a quarter mile. She'd never catch up with that stallion, who looked like he could run forever."

"Did you ever try to find him again?"

"Sure did. When I got to my job I told the boys, and we all had a good laugh over a horse being mistaken for a ghost. A few days later when the branding was done, we went looking for the stallion. We never saw him again — not then. About every ten years or so, someone sights the stallion — 'course it ain't the same one, probably a descendant of the one I saw. But every time, a bunch rides out and tries to catch him." Grandpa sighed and gazed at the butte. "I've been on every hunt 'cept now. Don't think my rusty old bones can handle another one."

Grandpa put his hand on Hank's shoulder. "Guess you going is about as good as me being along." He gave Hank a pat.

"Wish I had one of those sleeping bags for you to use." Grandpa changed the subject and showed Hank how to make a blanket bedroll. "Understand they're more comfortable than a blanket on the ground."

"It'll be okay, Grandpa. If you could sleep on the ground, I can too," Hank reassured the old man and himself too.

"S'pose so. But the ride's going to be rough — longer and harder than any riding you've ever done. Think you can handle it?"

"Sure," Hank said as calmly as he could despite the anxious excitement drying his mouth.

Mr. High Bear and two other men rode up with sleeping bags tightly rolled and tied to their saddles along with other nylon bags bulging with provisions and gear for a night's camp.

323

Mr. High Bear's son Joe followed, leading a horse all saddled and bridled for Hank. The horse, an old mare called Babe, stood munching grass while Hank tied his blanket roll and a plastic water bottle to the saddle. He was disappointed in the mare, but didn't complain. He knew Mr. High Bear had picked Babe because she was calm and an easy ride for an inexperienced, city-raised kid.

Hank mounted and the mare moved after the others. He turned to wave at Grandpa standing forlornly in the yard, and despite Hank's excitement, he felt sorry for the old man who understood that stallion-chasing was for the young and strong.

Hank tried to get Babe into line with the men and Joe, who rode abreast; but the mare set her own pace in the rear.

After an hour's ride the party reached the creek below Slim Butte, and Hank was glad to get there. Babe had a gentle gait, but Hank's tailbone was sore and his inner thigh muscles ached. He dismounted, following the lead of the others, who watered and unsaddled their horses before they took care of themselves.

324

Hank imagined himself the tough hero in a Western movie whose life might depend on the care he gave his mount; but his daydreaming ended when Joe had to help halter and hobble Babe. "I'd be the greenhorn," Hank thought in disgust. "Just like I really am!"

Still, the fantasy of being a different person in another time stuck with Hank as he and Joe were sent to gather dry wood for a cook-fire.

Hank didn't try to talk to Joe who, in Hank's imaginary movie, typified the silent, stoic Indian. He was surprised and disillusioned when Joe spoke.

"Ever camped out before?"

"Sure," Hank replied.

"Where?"

"At home." Hank tried to keep his comments terse, as a tough movie cowboy might.

"In the city?" Joe said in disbelief.

"No," Hank explained. "In the country along the river," but didn't add that his camping had been at a boys' camp.

The boys carried the wood to Mr. High Bear, who had a pit dug and ringed with rocks, just the way Grandpa told about doing when he was a young cowboy. Hank expected Mr. High Bear to use flint or twirl fire sticks to start the fire, but he didn't even use matches. Hank felt cheated as the man flicked a butane lighter and the dry twigs flared.

One of the other men set a wire grate over the rocks, and soon the aroma of boiling coffee and sizzling wieners and beans set Hank's mouth to watering.

Hank's imaginary movie scene dissolved as he ate from paper plates and drank from a foam cup — not tin, like Grandpa would have used. But, Hank mused, he didn't have to wash dishes in the creek either, just throw them in the fire. On the other hand, he thought of another change since the old man's cowboy days: The water in the creek was no longer safe to drink.

Hank spread his blankets on the ground as the others unrolled their sleeping bags. "People have gotten soft," he sneered to himself as he watched Mr. High Bear place a foam pad under his bag. Hank

325

was proud to sleep the way Grandpa had — the ground for his mattress. He didn't use his saddle for a pillow since no one else did, but lay back, arms under his head, and watched the stars begin to twinkle in the vast sky. How he loved this prairie sky, so clear, with stars undimmed by city smog and lights. He sighed contentedly and relaxed.

The men spoke to each other in Lakota and laughed. Hank wished he could understand. He had the uneasy feeling that the Lakota speakers were talking about him. Maybe by the end of the summer, he'd be able to speak — if Grandpa kept up the lessons. Hank closed his eyes, giving in to his weariness.

"You in high school?" Joe asked from his sleeping bag near Hank's blankets.

"Yeah," Hank said shortly, not really wanting to talk now. He was so tired and sore from the ride.

"What grade?"

"Going to be a junior."

"Me too."

Hank, arms numb under his head, rolled to his side and felt a rock pressing into his hip.

"You sore from riding?" Joe asked.

"Some," Hank admitted.

"Gonna be worse tomorrow," Joe flatly stated.

"Probably," Hank agreed and shifted his hips away from the rock.

"Should be fun," Joe said, his sleeping bag rustling as the boy settled into it. "This is my first stallion hunt. I was too little the last time," Joe yawned.

"Do you think we'll catch him?" Hank asked and heard more yawning from Joe, but no answer. Hank rolled to his other side and found the rock again; he wiggled around it and closed his eyes.

The hobbled horses sent slight tremors through the ground as they stamped over the grass they chomped. One of the men coughed as Hank drifted into sleep.

A slight, cool breeze sent smoke from the dying fire into Hank's face and he coughed and choked. He curled himself into a ball, tucking the blanket under his boots and over his head, and slept.

326

Hard thumps and tremors in the earth jolted the boy into alarmed awakening. "Wha——!" he cried at the shrill trumpeting that rang over the horses' frantic neighing.

Confused, Hank tried to rise, but the blanket tangled about his feet and he fell. He heard Mr. High Bear and the other men shouting and running to the horses. He stumbled to his feet; the trumpet-like call rang again, raising the hair on his neck, and pounding hooves seemed to be heading right at him.

He ran to the men, who were struggling to hold the hobbled horses. He grabbed at Babe's halter, but the mare tossed her head away. Again he reached for the halter, clutched it, and was almost yanked off his feet as Babe reared.

The shrill call sounded again and again, fading into the night with the pounding hoof beats. "Okay, girl, okay," Hank whispered, stroking Babe's neck, stilling the shivers rippling her hide.

"She'll stay now." Mr. High Bear's voice startled Hank. "The stallion's gone."

"Was it the stallion that made that — sound?" Hank wasn't sure what to call the wild trumpeting he had heard.

"Yes, he was calling the mares," Mr. High Bear said. "Sure is a nervy one," he chuckled. "Almost into camp before we woke up."

"Did you see him?"

"No. Just heard him and smelled him." Mr. High Bear gave Babe a pat. "We'd better get back to sleep. It'll be morning soon and we'll go after the stallion."

Hank smoothed the blankets he had tossed when he had gotten up and saw that Joe was still snoring in the comfort of his warm sleeping bag; he'd slept through the whole commotion.

Hank shivered himself into a ball, tucking the blanket about his body, thinking that the stallion's visit seemed a dream — a nightmare — a ghost horse appearing out of nowhere, its shrill summons trumpeting through the fog. Hank was not surprised to awaken to a morning mist rolling damp and cold along the creek. "Just like Grandpa said," he thought, stretching to unkink stiff, aching muscles.

Hank rolled his blankets and enviously watched Joe crawl, warm and dry, from his sleeping bag. He gave Hank a sheepish grin

327

1

as the men teased, "We could have had that horse, but your snores scared him off." He handed Hank a granola bar. Hank nodded his thanks, eagerly biting into it, washing its dry nourishment down with water. There was no hot coffee to ease the damp chill; Mr. High Bear couldn't get the wet wood to fire.

The men and boys moved quickly to saddle and bridle the horses, mounted, and followed the stallion's trail up the butte. Babe stayed in her end place as the single file traversed the slope, but Hank was content to let her follow. He felt as though he were in a dreamworld as the other riders blended into the fog blanketing the butte. At times his head broke through the cloud into blinding sunlight, and he could see only the tips of Babe's ears; the rest of her was in the fog.

Babe stumbled up the steep trail and then walked above the fog onto the sunlit summit. Hank gasped at the vista about him; the flat summit was an enchanted island in a fluffy sea of cloud. He sat, reins slack, open-mouthed, enthralled, until, abruptly, it all changed and the fog dispersed into tattered ribbons and the rough slope of the butte emerged.

"Hey!" Hank was jolted out of his dreamworld by Joe's call. Babe followed the others across the butte and down the far trail.

Babe lurched stiff-legged down the slope, every jolting step jarring Hank's spine. He leaned back in the saddle, feet braced in the stirrups and reins loose, when Babe suddenly snorted and her head snapped up. All around the butte the wild call of the stallion reverberated, and the mare responded to the command, swerving and shoving to pass Joe's pinto. "Whoa!" Hank shouted, gathering the slack reins, but Babe ignored the tight pull and the pinto's lashing hooves. A sharp jab sent waves of pain flashing up Hank's leg as a hoof caught his calf.

The ringing summons sounded again, sending all of the horses into turmoil, while the riders yelled and tried to keep their mounts to the trail. Hank struggled with Babe, ignoring his throbbing leg, trying to avoid the pinto until they were on the plain; and Babe broke, racing past the others. Hank clung to the saddle horn, reins flopping uselessly on the mare's neck as she pounded flat out over the prairie.

328

"Hold her!" Mr. High Bear yelled.

Thought she'd step in a prairie-dog hole. Grandpa's voice echoed in Hank's mind, reminding the boy of the danger of a runaway. Hank forced his hands from the horn, leaned back in the saddle, braced and pulled as hard as he could on the reins.

Babe's neck arched as she fought the bit, but her run gradually slowed to a jouncing trot, making Hank grab for the saddle horn again. "Whoa, whoa," he called, steadily tightening the reins until Babe slowed to a walk; then, flanks heaving, she stopped.

Hank, as sweaty as the horse, felt his heart throb in his ears. The horizon shimmered dizzily before him as his breathing became short, quick gasps. Deliberately he took a deep breath and exhaled slowly again and again until the roaring in his ears stopped.

"Old Babe thought she was a filly again," Mr. High Bear laughed as he and the others caught up to Hank. "Ain't seen her run like that

329

1

for years." His eyes betrayed his concern. "You did okay," he praised, and Hank managed a weak smile, not trusting his voice to speak.

Grateful that none of the men or Joe spoke of the mare running away or acknowledged his losing control of the horse, Hank turned Babe to follow the others.

The party rode slowly on, circling the butte, but the stallion's sharp hoofprints ended at a steep incline, almost as if he had run into the butte. Silently the men looked up at the butte, then turned away. The hunt was over.

"Is that all?" Hank cried to himself, and he winced at the pain in his leg as he heeled Babe about. All of the discomfort of the night — the rough ride, the pain of his swelling calf and, he admitted to himself, his fear — all of that, to have it end with such abruptness did not make any sense. Why, he wondered almost angrily, and then he understood.

No one — Mr. High Bear, Joe, the others, or Grandpa — had expected to catch the stallion. "They didn't want to," Hank's thoughts whirled. It was all a game — no, not a game, but a ritual that was repeated every time the stallion appeared. "Like my pretend-movie," Hank wonderingly concluded.

Grandpa watched the riders trail into the yard. "Didn't get him?" he asked, but Hank heard the satisfaction and relief in the old man's voice.

"No," Mr. High Bear answered.

Grandpa nodded. "You can't catch a ghost," he said.

Author

Virginia Driving Hawk Sneve, Native American author of stories and books for young people, was born and grew up on the Rosebud Sioux Reservation in South Dakota. She is a graduate of the South Dakota State University and has been a teacher, guidance counselor, and editor. Mrs. Sneve's first book was given an award by the Council on Interracial Books for Children.

330

Thinking It Over

Comprehension Questions

1. If the Slim Butte ghost was a real horse, why wasn't it ever caught?

2. Why didn't Hank ask more questions about the Slim Butte ghost when the adults were discussing it?

3. Hank asked his grandfather a direct question: "There isn't a real ghost on the butte, is there?" Why didn't Grandpa answer yes or no directly?

4. How would you describe the mood of the story? How does the author use setting to help establish the mood?

5. What clues does the author offer to prepare you for the fact that the Slim Butte ghost is not going to be caught?

6. Why did Hank feel "cheated" when things were not done the way he imagined his grandfather had done them?

Vocabulary

How well do you know your cowboy jargon? Match the numbered words with their definitions below.

1. filly
2. paint
3. chuck
4. mustang
5. tenderfoot

a. a spotted horse
b. a wild horse
c. a young female horse
d. a newcomer
e. food

Writing a Description

Imagine that Hank has asked an artist to make a painting of his or his grandfather's encounter with the Slim Butte ghost. Write a description that the artist could follow. Before you begin to write, list some of the details, such as setting, that you want to have included.

331

Thinking It Over

Comprehension
Page 331

Comprehension Questions: Text

1. Purpose/Skill Application
If the Slim Butte ghost was a real horse, why wasn't it ever caught? (The chase was a ritual, and no one really wanted it to end. That way they could look ahead to something out of the ordinary, something mysterious.)

Interpretive: making inferences

2. Why didn't Hank ask more questions about the Slim Butte ghost when the adults were discussing it? (He knew that it would be considered impolite to rush the answer; the answer would come when the person was ready to give it.) **Page 321**

Literal: cause-effect

3. Hank asked his grandfather a direct question: "There isn't a real ghost on the butte, is there?" Why didn't Grandpa answer yes or no directly? (Grandpa obviously wanted to get the best effect for his story, building up to the answer only after first setting the mood.) **Page 322**

Interpretive: character's motivation

4. How would you describe the mood of the story? (Answers may vary. Examples: mysterious, spooky, ghostly.) How does the author use setting to help establish the mood? (The lonely campfire in the dark night, the fog, and the butte rising out of the prairie emphasize the story of the "ghost.") **Pages 324–327**

Literary: mood and setting

5. What clues does the author offer to prepare you for the fact that the Slim Butte ghost is not going to be caught? (The fact

Literary: foreshadowing

that it has been around a long time without being caught is emphasized. Also, Hank keeps finding parallels between his adventure and his grandfather's. Even though everyone knows that a real horse is involved, it is constantly referred to as a ghost, and, as Grandpa says, "You can't catch a ghost.")

6. **Why did Hank feel "cheated" when things were not done the way he imagined his grandfather had done them?** *(He wanted to think of himself as capable of being everything his grandfather was; also, if things were too easy, they would not fit in with his fantasy of being a tough cowboy movie hero.)* **Page 325**

Interpretive: characters' feelings

Additional Questions

1. **How does Hank's background differ from his grandfather's?** *(Hank was city-bred; his grandfather lived in ranching country and was an experienced cowhand.)* **Pages 321, 322, 323, 325**

Literal: noting details

2. **How does Hank's chase experience compare with his grandfather's?** *(They were similar, since in both there was a fog and each was riding a mare that took off suddenly. In neither case was the stallion in any danger of being caught. They were different in that Hank was a tenderfoot with little riding experience, while his grandfather was a real cowboy. Also, Grandpa was alone, while Hank was with a group of friends.)* **Pages 322–323, 328, 329**

Interpretive: making comparisons

Vocabulary
Page 331

Ask students to read the Vocabulary section and to follow the directions. You may wish to ask students to list other cowboy terms they know, either from the story or from other sources, and then discuss their meanings. *(Answers: 1. c; 2. a; 3. e; 4. b; 5. d)*

Writing a Description
Page 331

Have students read the section Writing a Description and follow the directions. Encourage students to share their descriptions with a peer and then make revisions based on their discussion. Students who are interested in art may be able to evaluate the specifications from the point of view of the artist.

Workbook
 page 97 Vocabulary and Comprehension

Workbook page 97
Vocabulary/Comprehension

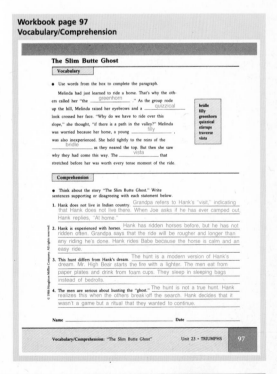

The Slim Butte Ghost

Vocabulary

● Use words from the box to complete the paragraph.

Melinda had just learned to ride a horse. That's why the others called her the "___greenhorn___." As the group rode up the hill, Melinda raised her eyebrows and a ___quizzical___ look crossed her face. "Why do we have to ride over this slope," she thought, "if there is a path in the valley?" Melinda was worried because her horse, a young ___filly___, was also inexperienced. She held tightly to the reins of the ___bridle___ as they neared the top. But then she saw why they had come this way. The ___vista___ that stretched before her was worth every tense moment of the ride.

bridle
filly
greenhorn
quizzical
stirrups
traverse
vista

Comprehension

● Think about the story "The Slim Butte Ghost." Write sentences supporting or disagreeing with each statement below.

1. Hank does not live in Indian country. Grandpa refers to Hank's "visit," indicating that Hank does not live there. When Joe asks if he has ever camped out, Hank replies, "At home."

2. Hank is experienced with horses. Hank has ridden horses before, but he has not ridden often. Grandpa says that the ride will be rougher and longer than any riding he's done. Hank rides Babe because the horse is calm and an easy ride.

3. This hunt differs from Hank's dream. The hunt is a modern version of Hank's dream. Mr. High Bear starts the fire with a lighter. The men eat from paper plates and drink from foam cups. They sleep in sleeping bags instead of bedrolls.

4. The men are serious about hunting the "ghost." The hunt is not a true hunt. Hank realizes this when the others break off the search. Hank decides that it wasn't a game but a ritual that they wanted to continue.

Name _____ Date _____

Vocabulary/Comprehension: "The Slim Butte Ghost"   Unit 23 • TRIUMPHS   97

Source: William K. Durr et al.: *Triumphs, Teacher's Guide*, pp. 383-385, 388-393 (Houghton Mifflin Reading). Boston: Houghton Mifflin Company, 1986. Used by permission.

The exact amount of time that should be devoted to independent reading will vary from class to class and level to level. The Commission on Reading recommended at least two hours a week for independent reading beginning at the third grade level but made no recommendations for the primary levels (Anderson et al., 1985). As soon as students develop some skill in reading in kindergarten and first grade and are able to read independently, some time each week should be devoted to this activity. The amount of time should gradually increase to one or one and one-half hours by the end of second grade.

Directly related to independent reading is reading aloud to students. There are so many values in developing all aspects of comprehension and the other language arts that reading aloud should assume a primary position in all areas of the curriculum as well as being a part of the at-home activities of parents. Reading aloud can be tied to an area of study, but sometimes it should be just for fun; this helps to develop the base for long-term vocabulary development. Jim Trelease, in *The Read-Aloud Handbook* (Trelease, 1982), presents a wonderful bibliography of his favorite read-aloud books for all age levels along with many important DOs and DON'Ts of reading aloud:

Do
Begin reading aloud to children as early as possible.
Read as often as you can.
Vary the length and subject matter of your reading.
Allow time for discussion after reading.
Read with expression and feeling.
Read slowly enough for the listener to follow along and form mental pictures.
Add a real-life dimension to a book or story. For example, have a bowl of blueberries to be eaten after reading Robert McCloskey's *Blueberries for Sal*.
Allow students to draw or write while listening if it helps them pay attention. (This is not the completion of an assignment.)

Don't
Don't continue reading a book once you discover that you have made a poor choice.
Don't read above a child's emotional level.
Don't be unnerved by questions during reading; answer them patiently.
Don't use reading as a punishment for misbehaving.

MISCONCEPTIONS ABOUT DIRECT INSTRUCTION

There are many misconceptions that arise about the use of direct instruction in teaching reading in general and comprehension specifically. Some of these misconceptions stem from the misunderstanding of direct instruction, and others come from its misuse. In either case, being aware of the misconceptions should help combat them.

Misconception 1. Direct instruction is isolated skill teaching. Direct instruction is not isolated skill teaching. Each of the component parts of direct instruction systematically leads the learner from being shown by the teacher how to perform and think about a particular comprehension skill or process to being able to apply that skill or process in reading natural text. The only way that direct instruction can become isolated skill teaching is if the application step is left out. It is through the application step that the reader sees both how and why to use a comprehension skill or process in reading text.

Misconception 2. Teaching is telling learners about a skill or process. Teaching is not telling; it involves showing students how to use a comprehension skill or process and letting them know the thinking processes that one goes through to use it. In the modeling part of teaching, the teacher models a process, and the students are expected to repeat the process for the teacher using a different example. During guided practice, the student tries out the comprehension skill or process, and the teacher provides corrective feedback and reteaching as needed. Throughout this process, the emphasis is on the teacher showing and sharing the thinking about how to use a skill; students then follow this step by demonstrating their ability to perform the same process. Teaching is not telling.

Misconception 3. Direct instruction constitutes the whole instructional program in reading. Wrong! Direct instruction is only that part of the reading program that is concerned about teaching students the "how to" of reading. Direct instruction must be balanced with sufficient opportunities for students to read independently and use, in that reading, what they have been taught.

Misconception 4. Teachers know how to use direct instruction and have been using it for years to teach comprehension. This may be true for some "good" teachers, but for the most part, teachers have not been taught how to teach comprehension. The primary reason is that educators have not known how to teach comprehension, as is clearly revealed by examination of some of the leading professional texts in reading from the past ten years (Burns, Roe, and Ross, 1984; Durkin, 1983; Harris and Sipay, 1980; Heilman, Blair, and Rupley, 1981). These texts concentrate on providing teachers with strategies for questioning or making assignments in comprehension. Most do not even discuss what it means to teach; they assume that the teacher automatically understands this.

SUMMARY

Comprehension can be directly taught with an instructional program that includes three components:

> Developing Background and Vocabulary
> Building Processes and Skills
> Correlating Writing with Reading

Direct instruction built into a directed reading lesson model can account for each of these program components and can be used to systematically help students learn how to comprehend.

The instructional program in comprehension must be balanced by sufficient time for students to read independently, using what they have learned in their reading. This time should be devoted to the students reading, enjoying what is read, and sharing what is read with others; it should not include any of the aspects of direct instruction or more formal teaching.

REFERENCES

Adams, M., and B. Bertram. 1980. *Background knowledge and reading comprehension.* Reading Education Report No. 13. Urbana, IL: University of Illinois, Center for the Study of Reading. (ERIC Document Reproduction Service No. ED 181 431)

Anderson, R. C., and P. Freebody. 1979. *Vocabulary knowledge and reading.* Reading Education Report No. 11. Urbana, IL: University of Illinois, Center for the Study of Reading. (ERIC Document Reproduction Service No. ED 177 470)

Anderson, R. C. et al. 1985. *Becoming a nation of readers: The report of the Commission on Reading.* Washington, DC: The National Institute of Education.

Baker, L., and A. L. Brown. 1984. Metacognitive skills and reading. In P. D. Pearson (ed.), *Handbook of reading research*, pp. 353–394. New York: Longman.

Bartlett, B. J. 1978. Top level structure as an organizational strategy for recall of classroom text. Ph.D. dissertation, Arizona State University, Tempe.

Baumann, J. F. 1984. The effectiveness of a direct instruction paradigm for teaching main idea comprehension *Reading Research Quarterly*, *20*, 93–115.

Beck, I. L. 1984. Developing comprehension: The impact of the directed reading lesson. In R. C. Anderson, J. Osborn, and R. J. Tierney (eds.), *Learning to read in American schools: Basal readers and content texts.* Hillsdale, NJ: Lawrence Erlbaum Associates.

Beck, I. L., R. C. Omanson, and M. G. McKeown. 1982. An instructional redesign of reading lessons: Effects on comprehension. *Reading Research Quarterly*, *17*, 462–481.

Beck, I. L., C. A. Perfetti, and M. G. McKeown. 1982. Effects of long-term vocabulary instruction on lexical access and reading comprehension. *Journal of Educational Psychology*, *74*, 506–521.

Burns, P. C., B. D. Roe, and E. P. Ross. 1984. *Teaching reading in today's elementary schools.* Boston: Houghton Mifflin Company.

Clark, C. M. 1984. Teacher planning and reading comprehension. In G. G. Duffy, L. K. Roehler, and J. Mason (eds.), *Comprehension instruction: Perspectives and suggestions*, pp. 58–70. New York: Longman.

Cooper, J. D., et al. 1979. *The what and how of reading instruction.* Columbus, OH: Charles E. Merrill Publishing Company.

REFERENCES

Duffy, G. G., and L. R. Roehler. 1982. Direct instruction in reading comprehension: What does it really mean? *Reading Horizons, 23*(1), 35–40.

Duffy, G. G., L. R. Roehler, and J. Mason (eds). 1984. *Comprehension instruction: Perspectives and suggestions.* New York: Longman.

Dupuis, M. M. (ed.). 1984. *Reading in the content areas: Research for teachers.* Newark, DE: International Reading Association.

Durkin, Dolores. 1978. What classroom observations reveal about reading comprehension instruction. *Reading Research Quarterly, 14,* 481–533.

Durkin, D. 1981a. Reading comprehension instruction in five basal reader series. *Reading Research Quarterly, 16,* 515–544.

Durkin, D. 1981b. What is the value of the new interest in reading comprehension? *Language Arts, 58*(1), 23–43.

Durkin, D. 1983. *Teaching them to read,* 4th ed. Boston: Allyn and Bacon.

Hansen, J., and P. D. Pearson, 1980. *The effects of inference training and practice on young children's comprehension.* Arlington, VA. (ERIC Document Reproduction Service No. ED 186 839)

Hansen, J., and P. David Pearson. 1983. An instructional study: Improving the inferential comprehension of fourth grade good and poor readers. *Journal of Educational Psychology, 75,* 821–829.

Harris, A. J., and E. R. Sipay. 1980. *How to increase reading ability,* 7th ed. New York: Longman.

Heilman, A. W., T. R. Blair, and W. H. Rupley. 1981. *Principles and practices of teaching reading.* Columbus, OH: Charles E. Merrill Publishing Company.

Herber, H. L., and J. Nelson. 1975. Questioning is not the answer. *Journal of Reading, 18,* 512–517.

Jenkins, J. R., D. Pany, and J. Schreck. 1978. *Vocabulary and reading comprehension: Instructional effects.* Technical Report No. 100. Urbana, IL: University of Illinois, Center for the Study of Reading. (ERIC Document Reproduction Service No. ED 160 999)

Johnston, P., and P. D. Pearson. 1982. *Prior knowledge, connectivity, and the assessment of reading comprehension.* Technical Report No. 245. (ERIC Document Reproduction Service No. ED 217 402)

Mason, J., L. E. Roehler, and G. Duffy. 1984. A practitioner's model of comprehension instruction. In G. G. Duffy, L. R. Roehler, and Jana Mason (eds.), *Comprehension instruction,* pp. 299–314. New York: Longman.

Meyer, B. J. F. 1975. *The organization of prose and its effects on memory.* Amsterdam: The Hague North-Holland Press.

Pearson, P. D. 1982. Asking questions about reading. Ginn Occasional Paper No. 15. Columbus, OH: Ginn and Company.

Reid, E. R. 1981. Comprehension skills can be taught. *Educational Leadership, 38,* 455–457

Rosenshine, B., and R. Stevens. 1984. Classroom instruction in reading. In P. D. Pearson (ed.), *Handbook of reading research,* pp. 745–798. New York: Longman.

Stauffer, R. G. 1969. *Teaching reading as a thinking process*. New York: Harper & Row, Publishers.

Taylor, B. M., and S. J. Samuels. 1983. Children's use of text structure in the recall of expository material. *American Educational Research Journal, 20,* 517–528.

Tierney, R. J., and M. Leys. 1984. What is the value of connecting reading and writing? Reading Education Report No. 55. Urbana, IL: University of Illinois, Center for the Study of Reading.

Trelease, J. 1982. *The read-aloud handbook*. New York: Penguin Books.

CHAPTER

T H R E E

DEVELOPING BACKGROUND

Understanding is based on some type of previous experience. —Lamoreaux and Lee, 1943, p. 40

In this chapter you will learn

1. more about how the reader's background and schemata influence reading comprehension,
2. how to decide what background should be developed before students read a selection,
3. strategies that you use to help students develop background.

As was discussed in previous chapters, the background of the reader is closely related to his or her ability to comprehend text (Adams and Bertram, 1980). Research indicates a causal relationship between the development of background and the ability of the reader to comprehend (Tierney and Cunningham, 1984). If the reader has specific background understandings about a selection before reading it, he or she will comprehend it better. While this causal relationship does exist, there is no conclusive evidence in current research that one approach to developing the reader's background is better than another (Tierney and Cunningham, 1984). The teacher must decide what provisions are necessary to ensure that the reader has the background needed to read and comprehend a selection. Therefore, one of the major components of the instructional program in reading comprehension is developing background and vocabulary. This chapter focuses on background development in general by clarifying what is included in background development, presenting guidelines for deciding what background should be developed and suggesting a number of strategies for background development. This is done within the context of the directed reading lesson using direct instruction. Chapter 4 expands the concept of background development by focusing solely on vocabulary development.

BACKGROUND DEFINED

The term *background development* is not new to teachers or reading specialists. For many years, educators have maintained that learning is enhanced if the learner has background related to the topic under study (Smith, 1965). Reading authorities have, for many years, recommended that teachers make provisions within the directed reading lesson to ensure that the reader has the background he or she will need to comprehend the selection to be read. The importance of background development has been given even greater emphasis with the recent increase in theory development and research on schema. Future research and further work in classrooms may well support the hypothesis that in any reading situation, background development is the most important aspect that the teacher must consider in helping readers comprehend more effectively.

Background as it relates to learning and reading comprehension has been defined as "the sum of a person's previous learning and development; experience; . . . experiences which precede a learning situation, story, etc." (Harris and Hodges, 1981). The specific background that a reader needs to comprehend a selection varies from selection to selection. Each reader will either have the background, have part of the background, or have none of the background for the selection. As has been noted in previous chapters, the schemata the reader develops through experiences form the basis for his or her background on a particular topic. The reader stores these concepts, ideas, and relationships in memory and uses them when they are needed. For example, the first thing you do as you begin to read a magazine article about the pleasures of automobile racing as a hobby is think about automobile racing and what you know about it. You are activating your schemata for automobile racing, which may have been formed many years ago. If your schemata for automobile racing include positive, pleasant ideas, you will read the article differently than if they include negative, unpleasant ideas. If you have no schema or very limited schemata for automobile racing, you will begin to form a schema as you read the article, and you will relate the information you gain to any other schemata you have about cars. Throughout the process of reading, you constantly take the information gained from the text and relate it to an existing schema, expanding that schema, or form a new schema. This process occurs continuously as the reader interacts with the text. As more information is gained, other schemata are activated, new ideas are formed, more information is gained, and so on. Figure 3.1 illustrates this process.

Therefore, the role of the teacher in comprehension instruction is to help the reader activate, or call up from his or her past experiences, the background needed for comprehending a particular selection and to help the reader develop that background if it is lacking. The procedures and activities the teacher uses are called background-development activities. Such procedures and activities help readers learn that during reading they must constantly draw on background to build meanings.

In Chapter 2, the concept of the directed reading lesson (DRL) was presented. The four parts of that lesson are skill building, background and readiness, guided silent reading and discussion, and extension. It is during the background and

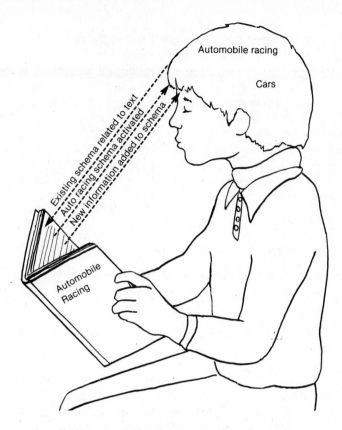

Figure 3.1   Reader Interacting with the Text

readiness portion of the lesson that the teacher provides for background development for a specific selection. All of the activities that take place in this part of the lesson are a part of background development, including the preteaching of vocabulary that is used in the selection. In the extension portion of the lesson, background for future reading is also developed.

The specific background needed by a reader to comprehend a selection includes

1. knowledge of the topic,
2. understanding of specific concepts in the selection,
3. understanding of terminology.

Assume that your students are going to read a selection entitled "Birds in Winter." From the title, you learn that students will need to know something about the topic of birds and winter. You could speculate that they might need to know about the habits of birds in winter or the specific birds that can be seen in winter. Without reading the selection, you are unable to tell in any more detail what background would be needed. Too often teachers and authors of instructional materials develop the topic of the selection but overlook the important concepts that students must also understand to comprehend the selection. If the article "Birds in Winter" is about the survival of birds during a blizzard, students must understand the concepts of survival and of a blizzard as well as know the terminology related to these concepts. Simply developing background related to birds and winter would not be sufficient to help students comprehend the selection effectively. Background development must be related to the specific topic and concepts of the selection. The overall purpose is to help the reader relate his or her existing schemata to the selection or develop a schema that will ultimately help him or her comprehend the selection more effectively. This type of background development is known as schema-directed background development (Beck, 1984).

DECIDING WHAT BACKGROUND TO DEVELOP

When deciding what background needs to be developed for a selection the teacher must take into consideration the following factors:

1. the text,
2. the teacher,
3. the students.

First, the teacher must examine the text to determine the author's main points or general story line. Thus, the teacher must read the text that students are expected to read. Even if the teacher's edition of the text provides a summary or listing of the main points of the selection, it is best for the teacher to read the entire selection and make his or her own assessment of the main points.

You will recall that there are two basic types of text, narrative and expository. (See Chapters 2 and 6 for more discussion on types of text.) For a narrative selection, the teacher should develop a story map that includes the setting, characters, problem, action, and resolution of the problem. This map should be written out. From the map, the teacher can identify the key concepts of the selection, which he or she should use to identify the background and vocabulary that need to be developed before students read the selection.

For expository text, the teacher should identify the main ideas the author develops in the selection. These ideas comprise the key concepts of the selection and should be written out; they are the basis for determining the background and vocabulary the teacher needs to develop before students read the selection.

Next, the teacher must determine exactly what he or she wants students to learn from the reading. The teacher's purpose may differ from the author's main points. For example, assume that the author's main point in the article "Birds in Winter" is that birds must be helped by persons in order to survive severe winter weather. However, the article also discusses the types of birds that usually suffer the most in blizzard conditions. The teacher may be more concerned that students learn these types of birds than focus on the author's main point. If so, the teacher should develop background directed more toward different types of birds than toward the author's main point.

Finally, the teacher must consider the students' backgrounds. If the students already have the background they will need for the reading, the background-development activity should be one that activates or brings to a level of consciousness the background the students already possess. If the students have no background for the selection, the background development activity should be one that develops as much of the needed background as possible before students read the selection. This assessment of students' existing background is made through observations and getting to know students. Sometimes it is not possible to anticipate a student's background until teaching has begun. In such instances, it may become necessary for the teacher to alter teaching plans for on-the-spot background development.

Typically, basal readers and content texts have not included the type or amount of background development that readers need to help them relate their schemata to the selection in a way that will lead to improved comprehension (Beck, Omanson, and McKeown, 1982). Further, the teacher's guides have usually included very general or topical development and not development that relates directly to the story line or main ideas in the selection. Authors of more recent basal readers are making great efforts to correct these inadequacies.

Think back to the article about birds in winter. Example 3.1 illustrates the wrong way and the correct way for teachers to develop background for this article.

EXAMPLE 3.1   INCORRECT AND CORRECT METHODS FOR DEVELOPING BACKGROUND ───────

Sample 1: Incorrect Method
(typical of what has been found in basal readers)

Today, we are going to read the article "Birds in Winter." Have you ever seen birds during the winter? What kinds of birds do you usually see in winter? How do birds get food in winter? (The discussion continues in this manner.)

Sample 2: Correct Method
(schema-directed to help reader relate background to the selection)

Today, we are going to read the article "Birds in Winter." Before we read it, I want you to think about some important ideas that will help you understand what you read. From the title, what would you say this article is going to be about? (Record student responses; discuss them.) This article is about how birds survive during a blizzard. (Relate the students' predictions to surviving in a blizzard.) What is a blizzard? (Students respond. Write a sentence on the chalkboard that contains the word *blizzard,* and discuss its meaning.) What does it mean to survive in a blizzard? What kind of problems might birds have surviving during a blizzard?

Discuss these questions; list students' responses on the board and discuss them. Add your own points to the discussion. Conclude the discussion by developing a list of points about how birds survive in a blizzard. The list should include such points as

1. A blizzard is a bad snowstorm with high winds.
2. Birds could have many problems surviving in a blizzard. These could include

> getting food,
> not freezing to death,
> having water to drink,
> having a place to sleep that is protected from the wind.

Notice that the discussion in the first part of Example 3.1 is topical and general. It does not include background development related to the main point or key concepts of the article. The discussion in the second part of the example clearly requires students to use whatever past experiences or schemata they have developed about birds and winter to make predictions. The teacher develops what students already know by relating that information to the concepts of survival and blizzard. He or she also teaches key-concept vocabulary within the context of the background development. Finally, the teacher guides the students in summarizing the key points from the background-development activity to make sure that students have a schema for reading the article "Birds in Winter" that relates directly to the main point or key concept of the article. The discussion in the second part of Example 3.1 is more thorough than that in the first part and, unlike the discussion in the first part, develops background directly related to the article.

The strategy used in the second part of Example 3.1 is not the only one that could have been incorporated in the background development. There are many alternative strategies for developing background; each has advantages and disadvantages that should be considered before and during its use.

STRATEGIES FOR DEVELOPING BACKGROUND

In background development, the teacher should do more than simply tell students information or give a lecture. The process of background development should be an interactive one, including teacher-student and student-student interactions. At the same time, teachers should not feel that the process of developing background requires them to do things they will find difficult or impossible. To be effective in developing background for students, teachers must systematically work at the process and utilize strategies that work best for them and their students. Many of the strategies discussed in the following sections of this chapter have overlapping characteristics. Teachers should become familiar with each of the strategies and try it several times so that they can make it a part of their teaching repertoire.

Discussion

Discussion is probably the most widely used of all strategies for helping students activate their existing background or develop background that they are lacking. Discussion is something that all teachers think they are able to conduct in their classrooms, and they generally perceive it as being easy to prepare for and carry out. Nothing could be further from the truth. Good discussions require careful preparation and considerable development skill. But, they are a good way to provide background development for students. Research is being conducted that should eventually lead to new directions in classroom discussions (Alvermann, 1984). For now, the guidelines presented in this section should be followed; they have proven effective in background development.

A discussion is an interactive procedure whereby the teacher and students talk about a given topic; a discussion is not simply the teacher telling students a body of information. Teachers should consider each of the following guidelines when preparing a background-development discussion:

1. Know exactly what points need to be made in the discussion. These points should relate to the story line or main ideas of the text.
2. Ask questions that require students to respond with more than *yes* or *no*. Students should be required by the question to elaborate and explain their answers. A teacher who is just learning to lead a discussion should write out the questions in advance to be sure that he or she has created questions that require more than *yes* or *no* responses. The suggested questions in the teacher's guides to basal readers or content texts can be used as long as they fulfill this requirement.
3. Call on individual students to answer questions; don't always wait for volunteers to answer.
4. When calling on individual students to answer questions, ask the question before calling on the student. This practice encourages everyone to listen and encourages all members of the group to participate.
5. After asking a question, allow students sufficient time to answer. Teachers frequently do not give students enough time to think about the answers they want to give to a question.
6. Encourage students to raise their own questions about the topic or to raise questions about the answers of other students. It is a good idea for the teacher to model such behavior for the students and tell them that they can ask similar questions of the teacher or other students.
7. Participate in the discussion and model good questioning and question-responding behavior for students; tell students that they should try to ask questions in a discussion in the same manner you do.
8. Don't allow the discussion to drag on for an unnecessarily long time, losing students' attention. A short, lively discussion is better and more motivating than one that is too lengthy.

9. Conclude the discussion by having students summarize the points that were made. Provide guidance as needed, but don't simply tell students what was covered in the discussion. For the discussion to be of value to the students, they must be able to internalize and verbalize the ideas that were presented.

Although the teacher's guides to basal readers and other textbooks usually present information to help teachers build background through discussion, it is the teacher's responsibility to actually turn that information into a discussion. Teachers should not simply relay the information in the teacher's guides to the students. In addition, as discussed earlier, the background provided in teacher's guides may not meet the needs of a given class or may not be the points that need to be developed to help the reader relate his or her background directly to the main point of the selection in a way that will improve comprehension. Therefore, it is necessary for the teacher to evaluate the information given in teacher's guides and develop a discussion that will meet the needs of the students.

The following dialogue illustrates an effective discussion between a teacher and students for developing background for the narrative selection "Clyde Monster," which was presented on page 27. (You may wish to reread that selection and its accompanying story map at this time.) You will recall that Clyde was a monster who was afraid of the dark in his cave because he thought there might be people in the cave who would attack him.

EXAMPLE 3.2 DISCUSSION DIALOGUE ⸺⸺⸺⸺⸺⸺⸺

Teacher: Today, we are going to read a story about a monster who was afraid of the dark. What is a monster, Mark?

Mark: A big, ugly, grizzly thing.

Teacher: It sounds scary to me. What else would you say about monsters? (Lisa volunteers.)

Lisa: All monsters aren't scary; some of them could be nice. Monsters aren't real.

Teacher: Can you think of any questions you could ask me or someone else in our group about monsters? (Fred volunteers.)

Fred: Miss Greenwood, have you ever seen a monster?

Teacher: No, but around Halloween I've seen some people dressed like monsters.

Mark: I saw a monster once.

Lisa: But it wasn't real. It was somebody dressed up like a monster.

Mark: He looked real to me.

Teacher: What kinds of things do you think monsters might be afraid of, Sara?

Sara: I don't know.

Teacher: What things have you ever been afraid of, Sara?

Sara: The man next door and his dog.

Teacher: Well, what kinds of things do you think monsters can be afraid of, Bob?

Bob: Maybe they're afraid of other monsters,—BIG UGLY GREEN ONES!

Teacher: Maybe they are. What else could they be afraid of? (Lisa volunteers.)

Lisa: Maybe they're afraid of people. Some people are like monsters.

Teacher: In our story today, we are going to read about a monster who is afraid of something. His name is Clyde. (Write *Clyde* on the chalkboard.) When do you think Clyde might be afraid, Alan?

Alan: Maybe at night or when he is not with a friend.

Bob: Maybe he is afraid in the woods.

Teacher: We have talked about things that you could be afraid of. What were some of them, Alan?

Alan: Other people, dogs, monsters.

Mark: The dark, too.

Teacher: As you read the story about Clyde Monster, I want you to think about the things you're afraid of and see what Clyde is afraid of. Read the story to find out what Clyde is afraid of and what he finally does.

Discussion is one of the background-developing strategies that is frequently combined with other techniques. It is good to use discussion in situations in which students already have some background related to the selection they are going to read or have a schema for the selection to be read. However, if students have very limited or no background, discussion should not be used alone because it is often too abstract to help the reader develop the background he or she really needs. Many times, teachers depend on discussion alone when more concrete background-developing activities should be used.

Background-Generating Activity

A background-generating activity provides an opportunity for students to think of all the information they know about a given topic. The students can work individually or in pairs. They first are asked to generate all of the ideas they have for a particular topic and then to share their ideas with the group. The teacher lists the ideas on the chalkboard, and then the teacher and students discuss them. The background-generating activity is an excellent way to get students to activate the background and information they have on a particular topic; by hearing the ideas of others, students activate additional information they have stored in their memories or learn new information. Use the following steps to carry out a background-generating activity:

1. Provide students, individually or in pairs, with cards they can record information on.
2. Tell students that they are to write on the cards any words, ideas, or phrases that they know about the given topic. Provide a time limit for the activity, and tell students not to be concerned about spelling.
3. After students have completed the activity, have them read their lists aloud to the group, and record their ideas on the chalkboard or overhead projector.

4. Discuss the information recorded, pointing out ideas that are directly related to the selection students are going to read. If incorrect information is on the list, note the errors and remove the items from the list. Don't just refuse a student's ideas and not include them on the list.
5. Direct the discussion of the ideas generated by the students to the story line or main ideas of the selection. Conclude the discussion by helping the students set a purpose for reading or give them a purpose for reading.

The background-generating activity can be used with all students. At the primary levels or with less able readers, the activity may have to become a group activity in which the teacher records on the chalkboard or overhead projector the ideas provided by the students instead of having the students write their own lists. The following example illustrates how a fourth-grade teacher used this activity to induce students to generate the background they had on the topic of whales; the students were about to read an expository article about why whales are an endangered species.

EXAMPLE 3.3   BACKGROUND-GENERATING DIALOGUE

Teacher: Today, we are going to read an article about whales and why they are in trouble. I want you to write on this card all the things you can think of about whales. Don't worry about spelling. (The ideas of two students are pictured on the accompanying cards. After a few minutes, the teacher asked the students to stop writing.)
Teacher: I want each of you to read what you have written on your card, and I will write your ideas on the board. (The teacher listed all the students' ideas on the board, accepting all responses from each student. When students had the same responses, the teacher recorded the idea only once.)
Teacher: Let's look at our list of ideas to see if there is anything that is incorrect.

> Whales are mammals
> Whales live in the ocean
> There are killer whales
> Whales can talk
> Fish
> Big
> Eat people
> Can be made into oil
> Can be eaten
> Are hunted by fishermen

(Students examined the list. When no one identified any incorrect information, the teacher proceeded.)

TED

Whales are mammals.

Whales live in the ocean.

There are killer whales.

Whales can talk.

ELSIE

fish

big

eat people

Teacher: Whales are sort of like fish because they live in the ocean; they look like fish, but they are much bigger than most fish. Therefore, we don't want to say that whales are fish. (The teacher removed *fish* from the list.)

Teacher: You know that dinosaurs once lived on the earth, but they are no longer around. For many reasons, we don't have dinosaurs. The same thing is happening to whales. Look at this list of characteristics of whales to see if you can identify any reasons for why whales might be in trouble or in danger of disappearing. (The students responded. The teacher then discussed their answers. The teacher identified those items the students missed.)

Teacher: We are going to read the article entitled "Disappearing Whales," which is on page 46 of your book. Based on the information that we have just

discussed about whales and why they might be in danger of disappearing, what do you think would be a good thing for us to think about or look for as we read?
Student: Maybe we could look to see if our reasons about why whales disappear are right and find some others.
Teacher: That's a good idea. (The teacher wrote the student's response on the board and had students read the article silently, telling them that they would later discuss the article based on that purpose.)

The background-generating activity, like discussion, is best used when students have some background to draw from. However, if students have no background on a topic, this strategy should either not be used or it should be used in combination with one of the other strategies that develops background more concretely.

Prequestions, Purpose-Setting Activities, and Objectives

As a part of background development, teachers must help students focus their attention on the topic that is covered in the selection before they begin to read. There are three similar techniques that teachers can use: prequestions, purpose-setting activities, and objectives. These strategies are usually preceded by a discussion or background-generating activity. There is evidence that all three of these activities have advantages for helping readers improve comprehension in different reading situations (Tierney and Cunningham, 1984). Their primary objective is to help readers attain a purpose for reading. When students are directed to read any text in any class, they should always have a clear purpose in mind to guide their reading.

Prequestions

Prequestions are those questions posed by the teacher for students to answer as they read. In order to formulate questions, the teacher must know the story line or main ideas of the selection and what he or she wants students to learn as a result of reading the selection. One of the disadvantages of many prequestions is that they often focus the reader's attention on such small segments of information that the reader overlooks the main points or ideas in the selection. For example, one of a teacher's prequestions for a selection might be: How many men flew in the plane? If the answer to this question comes early in the text, students would quickly accomplish their purpose for reading and might lose interest in the rest of the text. They would have no purpose for the remainder of their reading. The question would miss the main point of the text. Better background-developing prequestions are those that require the reader to make inferences and judge or evaluate as they read. Such questions require readers to relate prior knowledge and background experience to their reading.

The questions that teachers pose in guided silent reading (see Chapter 2 for a discussion of guided silent reading) are prequestions. They focus the reader's attention on a specific purpose for reading and help him or her relate existing knowledge to reading.

All prequestions should require the reader to use as much of the text as possible; the questions should not focus on one specific point. Many times teachers become discouraged with prequestions because they find that students are only reading to locate the specific answers. If this becomes the case, the questions the teachers are asking are too literal or too precise and need to be more interpretive. The role of the prequestion is to help readers activate their backgrounds and focus attention as they read.

Let's look again at the article "Birds in Winter," which was discussed earlier in this chapter, and examine some examples of good and bad prequestions. You will recall that the article was about survival of birds during a blizzard. The article identified many birds that have difficulty surviving during a blizzard and listed many of the specific problems that birds encounter during blizzard conditions. The main point developed in the article was that birds have to depend on humans in many instances to survive under these extreme winter conditions.

The following prequestions would not be good ones to use for "Birds in Winter" because they focus on specific points and do not direct the reader's attention to the overall text. Furthermore, these questions do not require the reader to draw extensively from his or her prior knowledge:

1. What two birds have the greatest difficulty surviving during blizzard conditions?
2. What three reasons are stated by the author to justify why people should help birds during blizzards?

The second question is better than the first but still fails to direct the reader to relate prior knowledge to the text.

Better prequestions to use include

1. How do the problems faced by the birds in this article compare to the problems you have seen birds experience during bad winter storms?
2. Based on the article "Birds in Winter" and on your own experience, why do you think it is important for people to help birds during winter storms?

These questions require readers to focus their attention on the entire text and require the reader to draw on prior experience. For these and any other purpose questions to be of value to the reader in helping him or her improve comprehension, they must be discussed after the reading has been completed. Too often, teachers ask the purpose questions and then never discuss them (White, 1981).

Purpose-Setting Activities

Purpose setting is a variation of prequestioning. Its purpose is also to help the reader activate background and relate it to the selection that is to be read. Purpose-setting activities usually take the form of a discussion and conclude by giving the student a purpose for reading the selection. The purpose for reading might be formulated in a question, as mentioned above. This strategy incorporates elements of discussion and prequestioning.

Purpose setting can also be done by readers without the teacher's involvement. In fact, as readers mature in their ability to read, they should be encouraged to set their own purpose for reading because that is what the effective comprehender must ultimately do. For this reason, students must be taught techniques such as SQ3R, which can help them set their own purposes as they read material. (See Chapter 8 for a discussion of this technique.)

An appropriate purpose-setting discussion for the article "Birds in Winter" might begin

You have discussed some of the problems that birds can have surviving in winter. Read this article to find out if there are other reasons for why birds have difficulty surviving in blizzards.

You will notice that the only real difference between this purpose and the questions given earlier is the form in which the purpose is stated.

Objectives

Objectives are statements that let readers know what they can expect to accomplish from reading a chapter or text. These statements focus the reader's attention and also help to activate prior knowledge and background. Objective statements are most useful for readers at the intermediate, middle school, junior high, and high school levels in reading expository texts. The objectives are stated at the beginning of a chapter and are stated in a form similar to the following:

In this chapter you will learn
1. the most important uses of wood,
2. the ways people can protect forests,
3. the ways in which people have come to depend on wood products.

For the objectives to be of value, teachers must call them to the readers' attention prior to reading and must show the readers how to make use of the objectives as they read.

As you can see, prequestioning, purpose-setting activities, and objectives are very similar; their intent is to help the reader focus attention during reading and relate prior knowledge to reading. Prequestions and purpose-setting activities have the greatest similarity and are usually better strategies than objectives for directly requiring the reader to relate prior knowledge to the reading. Objectives, on the other hand, clearly let the reader know what to expect in the reading and create a mind-set that will help the reader think about and activate prior knowledge relative to the topic. There is certainly nothing wrong with the teacher using all three of these procedures in combination. If the text to be read does not list objectives, the teacher could easily provide them. For prequestions, purpose-setting activities, and objectives to be useful in helping the reader activate background and improve comprehension, they must be followed up in the discussion that follows the reading.

Advance Organizers and Story Previews

The teacher can present some of the key ideas, concepts, or vocabulary related to a topic to be read in the form of an advance organizer. For example, if students are to read a selection about how to build a doghouse, the advance organizer might include statements about how to use a hammer, how to saw wood, and how to read a blueprint. The teacher should provide the advance organizer in written form and should read and discuss it with the students. The advance organizer is similar to the objective statements that appear at the beginning of a chapter.

There is research to support the advantages of advance organizers for improving a reader's comprehension as well as research to the contrary (Ausubel, 1960; Barnes and Clawson, 1975; Feller, 1973; Tierney and Cunningham, 1984). The best that can be concluded about advance organizers is that they may be helpful in developing background for some readers in some situations. Example 3.4 includes an advance organizer that was used in a lesson designed to teach students how to read social studies text. The purpose of this advance organizer was to help students think about the functions of an archaeologist before they read an article on that topic.

A variation of the advance organizer is the story preview, which is a statement that summarizes some of the key ideas that will appear in a selection. Many times the story preview ends with a question that students should use to direct their reading. Story previews are usually written out, as in Example 3.5, and distributed to students to read; they can, however, be presented orally by teachers as a part of background discussion before the selection is read.

Advance organizers are usually more useful with expository material, and story previews are more useful with narrative material. Many of the strategies presented in this chapter incorporate elements of the advance organizer. For advance organizers or story previews to be of value in helping the reader activate prior knowledge, they must be discussed with students, and students must be told their purpose.

Webbing and Semantic Mapping

Two very similar strategies that teachers can use to help readers activate prior knowledge and further develop an understanding of relationships and ideas before they read a selection are webbing and semantic mapping. Both techniques help the reader activate existing schemata related to a particular topic and develop a specific schema for a selection that is to be read. One of the most important advantages of these strategies is that they help the reader develop relationships

EXAMPLE 3.4   ADVANCE ORGANIZER FOR SOCIAL STUDIES

Digging for Clues to the Past

by Bruce Porell

There are lots of clues to the mystery of how people lived long ago — but it takes careful work to find them.

Archaeologists study how people lived in the past. They learn from objects that people used in their daily lives. Their work is important because there are few written records of long-ago life. They help to fill holes in the puzzle of history.

Revealing Artifacts

The objects that archaeologists study are called artifacts. They are the pots we cook in and the dishes we eat from. Artifacts are the chairs and tables in your living room, the rubber ball in your bedroom, the toothbrush in the rack over your bathroom sink, and the chicken bones you threw away after supper last night. They are everywhere. They are our tools, toys, decorations, furniture, clothes, and weapons, and even the buildings we live and work in. Look around you. You are wearing artifacts, and you are surrounded by them.

Very old artifacts have often been changed by nature's forces. Some materials stand up better than others. Cloth, paper, and wood can be destroyed by water, fire, and insects. They can be impossible to recognize after only a few years. Metals such as iron, bronze, and copper can rust or corrode, if they are in damp places. Pots and stone tools are the artifacts most often found, because they last the longest. Modern plastics may last as long as pottery and stone. Some of these new materials will be around for ten thousand years before breaking down and returning to the soil.

Archaeologists at work
Opposite: Israel
Above: Mexico

97

EXAMPLE 3.5 STORY PREVIEW

Ed and Art are two very competitive basketball players. They both like to be the top scoring player on the team. In the regional tournament, they are both determined to score the most points. What do you think the outcome will be?

---

among ideas, which is crucial to their developing the appropriate schema or frame of reference for comprehending text. Both techniques are more concrete than discussions or background-generating activities because they present for the reader a picture of how ideas are related. Webbing and semantic mapping are types of advance organizers; they are often called graphic organizers because they graphically show students how ideas are related.

Webbing

Webbing, a technique that is also discussed in Chapter 4 in the context of vocabulary development, is a procedure designed to help students visualize the relationships between ideas. In this technique, the teacher leads a discussion in which he or she has students tell how various ideas might be related. The teacher writes the ideas on the board and then draws lines to show the relationships. The ideas used in the web can come from the teacher, from the students, or from both. Example 3.6 shows the steps the teacher can use in carrying out a webbing strategy to activate and build students' background prior to their reading a selection. The selection is about the problems of being an oldest child in a family with three children, in which the parents always select the oldest child to do everything.

EXAMPLE 3.6 CREATING A BACKGROUND DEVELOPMENT WEB

Step 1: Tell students that you are going to discuss with them some ideas related to the topic of the problems of being an oldest child, which will be covered in their next reading selection. Or, have students generate the ideas using the background-generating activity mentioned earlier. With both approaches, ask students to list some of the things that may happen to an oldest child simply because he or she is the oldest child in a family. Add ideas from the reading selection to the students' list.

Step 2: List the ideas on the chalkboard. Have a student read them aloud. The list may look like the following:

> *Ideas*
> You are expected to do everything right.
> You get to have special privileges like staying up later.
> You have to take care of younger brothers and sisters.

Younger brothers and sisters get more attention.
You get to do some things alone.

Step 3: Record the topic under discussion on the chalkboard and put a box around it. Select one of the ideas from the list to begin the discussion and write it somewhere on the chalkboard near the topic. Discuss whether the idea is really related to the topic. If it is related, have a student draw a line from the idea to the topic to show that they are related.

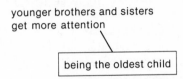

Step 4: Next, have students read the remaining ideas and select another one for discussion. Record it on the chalkboard and discuss if and how it is related to the topic and the other idea or ideas on the board. Have a student draw lines to show any relationships.

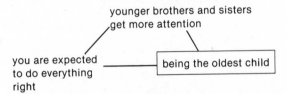

Step 5: Continue the discussion in the same manner until all ideas have been discussed. Students should be actively involved in the discussion and drawing the lines. The completed web is shown below.

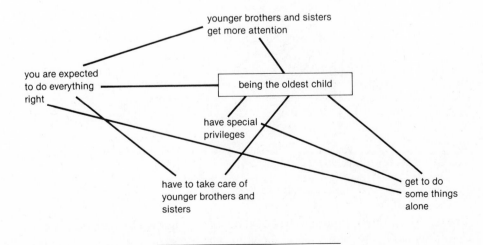

Webbing can also be used after a story has been read to help students organize the ideas presented in the story and see how they are related. A variation of webbing is the story map, which is discussed in detail in Chapter 6.

Semantic Maps

Pearson and Johnson described a strategy called semantic mapping, which can be used to help students build background and see relationships between ideas and concepts in a given topic (Pearson and Johnson, 1978). This strategy is similar to webbing.

A semantic map is a visual representation of a particular concept or concepts and their various relationships. Ovals are used to represent the concepts and lines with arrows and words written above them represent the relationships. The relationships depicted on the map can be class, example, or property. Example 3.7 shows a partial semantic map for pine trees that was created with a group of third graders preparing to read a science article about the uses of pine trees.

EXAMPLE 3.7   SEMANTIC MAP FOR PINE TREES ———————————

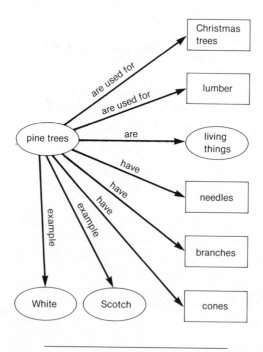

The teacher of the third-grade class used the following steps to direct the discussion for creating the map about the uses of pine trees.

1. The teacher wrote the major concept or topic for the discussion on the chalk-board and drew an oval around it. In this example the major concept was *pine trees*.
2. The teacher asked students to think of words to describe the topic, pine trees. Those words were written in boxes and linked with arrows to the main-concept oval. The teacher wrote words above the arrows, such as "have," to indicate the relationship between the main concept and the boxed words.
3. Next, the teacher asked students to give some examples of the topic, pine trees. The examples were written in ovals with arrows indicating *example*.
4. Finally, the teacher asked students to tell some uses of pine trees. Those were listed in boxes with arrows indicating *are used for*.

There is no one right way to develop a semantic map. The words written on the arrows to show relationships will vary according to the topic being discussed. Semantic mapping is a good procedure to follow when students are going to read several selections or chapters related to a given topic. The teacher and students can start the map before students begin the reading and can add to it as students gain new background information from their reading. In this way, students will clearly see that reading helps build background for further reading. After students have completed their reading, they can return to the map to make additions or changes that resulted from their reading.

When teachers use either webbing or semantic mapping, they are actually conducting a discussion that is visually represented for students. Therefore, they should apply the guidelines for good discussion to their lessons on webbing and semantic mapping.

Pictures

The value of pictures in improving comprehension is a topic that has received much attention by numerous researchers. Some researchers indicate that pictures are of little or no value to students as they comprehend; others report conflicting evidence (Samuels, 1970; Schallert, 1980; Thomas, 1978). It appears that the best conclusion that can be drawn from the research on pictures and comprehension is that for a picture to be helpful to readers, the teacher must provide the student with instruction and direction to help him or her understand the picture and relate it to the text being read. Instruction and direction are especially needed when the picture interprets the text rather than presents something that is literally or explicitly stated in the text.

Pictures can, however, be very useful in both activating and developing background for the reader. The pictures in a text can be used as a basis for discussion about the topic of the selection. The teacher can use additional pictures in the background-building portion of the lesson to illustrate concepts or simply to provide readers with vicarious experiences with the topic to be read. The following points should help guide teachers in their use of pictures to develop or activate a reader's background on a given topic:

1. Before beginning the background building for the lesson, read the selection and examine the pictures and illustrations to determine whether any can be used to help readers develop background. Determine whether the pictures and illustrations are literal representations of the text, whether they interpret the text, or whether they were simply added to make the text attractive.
2. Decide whether topical background or concepts in the selection can be easily developed using pictures other than those in the text.
3. As you use pictures in background building, be certain that students understand how they relate to the topic that is to be covered in the reading. Clearly explain the relationship of the pictures being used to the topic of the selection.
4. As you use pictures as a basis for discussion, encourage students to share any of their own experiences that relate to the pictures.

Pictures are concrete ways to develop background even when students have very limited background or no background on the topic to be covered in the reading. Pictures, diagrams, and illustrations are often more useful in developing background for expository text than for narrative text; however, even with narrative text, pictures can be used to develop selected background concepts. Usually, teachers must combine the use of pictures with discussion to ensure that students are developing the background that relates to understanding the overall selection rather than simply focusing on the topic of the selection. Recall the background-generating dialogue about whales becoming an endangered species (Example 3.3). Showing pictures of whales would have been an appropriate strategy for helping the student who had never seen a whale or a picture of a whale. However, just showing the pictures would not have been sufficient to develop the needed understandings about why whales and other animals are in danger of becoming extinct.

Another precaution that teachers must exercise when using pictures to develop background is to be sure that the pictures actually illustrate the correct relationship for students. If the two pictures in Example 3.8 had been used to discuss the differences between whales and fish, students might come away with the conclusion that whales and fish are about the same size. Many times published materials provide pictures that lead students, especially those at beginning reading levels, to form incorrect concepts and relationships.

Concrete Materials, Role Playing, and Field Trips

Background can also be activated or developed through the use of concrete materials, role playing, and field trips. Concrete materials and field trips help to develop real experiences for students; role playing helps to create vicarious experiences for students.

Assume that students are going to read a story or an article about computers but have never had any experiences with computers. The best way to build background for the reading would be to bring a computer into the classroom or take

EXAMPLE 3.8   PICTURES SHOWING A MISLEADING SIZE
                RELATIONSHIP ───────────────

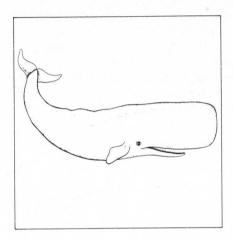 

students to a computer lab for demonstration and discussion. Through direct observation, students would be able to see for themselves what a computer does and begin to learn some of the related terminology. Simply seeing a computer, however, is not enough; the students must have the opportunity to talk about and ask questions about computers and to participate in their use. The teacher plays a vital role in directing the discussion using the guidelines presented earlier in this chapter.

Teachers can also use role playing to create an experience that will help students develop background for a selection. Assume that students are going to read a selection about newspaper reporters' experiences. Students could assume the role of the newspaper reporter and interview the teacher. As the one being interviewed, the teacher could respond in ways that would allow students to experience the role of a reporter conducting an interview. Role playing immerses the students in a situation with very realistic experiences. The teacher should follow role playing with a discussion that brings out points that relate to the background the teacher wants to build. Role playing is especially useful in helping students develop such background concepts as understanding prejudice or unfairness.

Field trips are another alternative for building background for students. It is not realistic, however, to plan a field trip for each selection or chapter that students are going to read. Field trips should be planned around a given theme or topic when there are several selections to be read on that topic. For example, if students are going to read several chapters with topics related to water pollution, a trip to the local water company might be appropriate. The objective would be to learn how water is purified and to learn some of the problems that are related to water pollution, thereby helping students build background for the reading that is to come. The teacher should prepare students for the field trip by giving them direction in what to look for when they are at the water company. Following the trip, there must be a discussion that helps students pull together the information they learned on the trip. A semantic map about the water company might be developed to help students relate the ideas that they learned.

Prior Reading

The prior reading that students have done also helps to develop background for future reading. Therefore, when possible, it is important for teachers to relate a selection that students have already read to one that they are going to read. For example, if students have recently read an article on snakes and they are about to read an article on other reptiles, the teacher should help them relate what they learned about snakes to other reptiles. Many times simply bringing the information from previous reading to students' attention is sufficient for helping them activate their own background on the topic. Reading is a powerful background builder.

Reading aloud to students affords the teacher many opportunities to help them develop background for a particular selection or a group of selections. This activity should be continued in all grades, not just in the elementary grades. For example, if students are preparing for a unit on astronomy, the teacher could read aloud Judith Herbst's *The Sky Above And Worlds Beyond*, an amusing book about astronomy and outer space; such an activity would help to build background for the upcoming reading in astronomy. Again, reading aloud must be accompanied by discussion that helps students relate the points they learn to their prior experiences.

SELECTING STRATEGIES TO USE FOR DEVELOPING BACKGROUND

Fourteen strategies for helping readers activate or develop prior knowledge before reading a selection have been described. All of the strategies will not be used at one time; certain strategies lend themselves to developing background in some situations more than others. Most of the time teachers will find it most helpful to use several strategies in combination rather than one strategy alone. Teachers should base their decisions about which strategies to use in developing and activating the reader's background on (1) what they know to be the existing background of their students in relation to the topic and (2) the type of text that they are having students read.

When students have some background relative to a particular topic, strategies that activate and expand existing background can be used. These include

> discussion,
> background generating activity,
> prequestions,
> purpose setting activities,
> objectives,
> advance organizers,
> story previews,
> webbing and semantic mapping, and
> prior reading.

However, when students have very limited background or no background on a topic, the teacher needs to use activities that more concretely develop background. These include

> pictures,
> concrete materials,
> role playing,
> field trips, and
> prior reading.

In such instances, the teacher should combine the use of one or more of these five strategies with some of the strategies listed in the first group. For example, the combination of a field trip, semantic mapping, and discussion would thoroughly develop the background needed by students for a particular selection or group of selections.

In addition to considering the background students already possess, the teacher must also consider the type of text to be read when selecting strategies to use in background development. If students are going to read narrative text, the teacher should provide them with a means of developing background that is directly related to the story line and not just related to the topic of the story. Thus, the teacher might combine

> discussion,
> background generating activity,
> prequestions,
> purpose setting,
> story previews,
> webbing,
> role playing, and
> prior reading.

If students are going to read expository text, the teacher should provide them with a means of developing topical background related to the main ideas of the selection. The teacher might use

> discussion,
> background generating activity,
> prequestions,
> purpose setting,
> objectives,
> semantic mapping,
> pictures,
> concrete materials,
> role playing,
> field trips, and
> prior reading.

You will notice that the two lists overlap. Certainly, these lists are not absolute. The teacher must simply think about what his or her students need to know in order to comprehend the text they are going to read and must select the procedures that will help the students develop or activate this background most effectively.

PRETEACHING VOCABULARY AND BACKGROUND DEVELOPMENT

Activating the readers' schemata and developing a specific schema for a selection must involve not only developing specific background concepts but also helping readers learn the key-concept words for the selection. Therefore, background and vocabulary for a specific selection should be developed in relation to one another. The more closely connected these two elements are, the more helpful they will be in improving students' comprehension of selections. Chapter 4 presents strategies for preteaching vocabulary and illustrates how vocabulary teaching and background development can be woven together in a lesson.

SAMPLE LESSONS ILLUSTRATING BACKGROUND DEVELOPMENT

As was noted in Chapter 2 and earlier in this chapter, the directed reading lesson (DRL) incorporating direct instruction can be used to help the reader learn how to comprehend. The background and schema that are needed for reading a selection are developed in the background and readiness portion of the DRL. The following two examples (3.9 and 3.10) illustrate the development of background for a narrative selection and for an expository selection, respectively. Vocabulary preteaching is woven into each example.

The Third Avenue Elevated

by Carla Stevens

A ride on the elevated train in the Great Blizzard of 1888 turned into an exciting adventure for Anna and her grandfather. How did Anna help the other people on the train?

12

Anna's grandfather Jensen was visiting her in New York City in 1888. He was bored with city life and said he didn't like the city too much. For something to do, he offered to take Anna to school as it had started to snow very hard. Anna was eager to get to school because she was doing well in spelling and hoped to win that day's spelling bee. So they set out.

Anna followed Grandpa up the long flight of steps to the Fourteenth Street El station. No one was at the ticket booth, so they ducked under the turnstile to the platform. They stood out of the wind at the head of the stairs. Anna could see only one other person waiting for a train on the uptown side.

Anna looked at her rosy-cheeked grandfather. Snow clung to his mustache and eyebrows and froze. They looked like tiny icebergs.

"Here comes the train!" Grandpa shouted. A steam engine, pulling two green cars, puffed toward them. When the train stopped, Anna and Grandpa hurried across the platform and stepped inside. There were lots of empty seats. They sat down behind a large woman. She took up most of the seat in front of them.

Anna pulled off her hat. Her pom-pom looked like a big white snowball. She shook it, spraying the floor with wet snow. The conductor came up the aisle and stopped at their seat.

Grandpa said, "No one was at the station to sell us a ticket."

"That will be five cents," the conductor said. "Each."

"You mean I have to pay for her too?" Grandpa's eyes twinkled.

Grandpa and the conductor laughed. Anna didn't like to be teased. She turned away and tried to look out, but snow covered the windows.

Grandpa leaned forward. "Quite a storm," he said to the woman in the seat in front of them. "Nothing like the Blizzard of '72, though. Why it was so cold, the smoke froze as it came out of the chimney!"

A woman holding a basket sat across from them. She leaned over. "In Poland, when I was a little girl, it snowed like this all winter long."

The woman in the seat ahead turned around. "This storm can't last. First day of spring is less than two weeks away."

"That's just what I was telling my daughter this morning!" Grandpa said.

Anna could see that Grandpa was growing more cheerful by the minute.

Suddenly the train stopped.

"What's the trouble?" the woman from Poland asked. "Conductor, why has the train stopped?"

The conductor didn't reply. He opened the car door and stepped out onto the platform. No one inside said a word.

Then Grandpa stood up. "I'll find out what's the matter."

Anna tugged at his coat sleeve. "Oh, please sit down, Grandpa." He didn't seem to understand how scared she felt. How she wished she had stayed home!

The door opened again, and the conductor entered the car. He was covered with snow. "We're stuck," he said. "The engine can't move. Too much snow has drifted onto the tracks ahead. We'll have to stay here until help comes."

"Did you hear that, Anna?" Grandpa almost bounced up and down in his seat. "We're stuck! Stuck and stranded on the Third Avenue El! What do you think about that!"

When Anna heard the news, she grew even more frightened. "Mama will be so worried. She doesn't know where we are."

"She knows you are with me," Grandpa said cheerfully. "That's all she needs to know." He leaned forward again. "We might as well get acquainted," he said. "My name is Erik Jensen, and this is my granddaughter, Anna."

The woman in the seat ahead turned around. "Josie Sweeney," she said. "Pleased to meet you."

"How-dee-do," said the woman across the aisle. "I'm Mrs. Esther Polanski. And this is my friend, Miss Ruth Cohen."

Someone tapped Anna on her shoulder. She turned around. Two young men smiled. One man said, "John King and my brother, Bruce."

A young woman with a high fur collar and a big hat sat by herself at the rear of the car. Anna looked in her direction. "My name is Anna Romano," she said shyly.

"I'm Addie Weaver," said the young woman. She smiled and wrapped her coat more tightly around her.

It was growing colder and colder inside the car. When the conductor shook the snow off his clothes, it no longer melted into puddles on the floor.

'We'll all freeze to death if we stay here," moaned Mrs. Sweeney.

"Oooooo, my feet are so cold," Addie Weaver said.

Anna looked at her high-button shoes and felt sorry for Addie Weaver. Even though Anna had on her warm boots, her toes began to grow cold too. She stood in the aisle and stamped her feet up and down.

Suddenly Anna had an idea. "Grandpa!" she said. "I know a game we can play that might help keep us warm."

"Why Anna, what a good idea," Grandpa replied.

"It's called 'Simon Says.' "

"Listen, everybody!" Grandpa shouted. "My granddaughter, Anna, knows a game that will help us stay warm."

"How do we play, Anna?" asked Mrs. Polanski. "Tell us."

"Everybody has to stand up," said Anna.

"Come on, everybody," Grandpa said. "We must keep moving if we don't want to freeze to death."

Miss Weaver was the first to stand. Then John and Bruce King stood up. Grandpa bowed first to Mrs. Sweeney, then to Mrs. Polanski and Miss Cohen. "May I help you, ladies?" he asked. They giggled and stood up. Now everybody was looking at Anna.

"All right," she said. "You must do only what Simon tells you to do. If *I* tell you to do something, you mustn't do it."

"I don't understand," Mrs. Sweeney said.

"Maybe we'll catch on if we start playing," Grandpa said.

"All right," Anna said. "I'll begin. Simon says, 'Clap your hands.' "

Everybody began to clap hands.

"Simon says, 'Stop!' "

Everybody stopped.

"Good!" Anna said. "Simon says, 'Follow me!' " Anna marched down the aisle of the car, then around one of the poles, then back again. Everybody followed her.

"Simon says, 'Stop!' "

Everyone stopped.

Anna patted her head and rubbed her stomach at the same time.

"Simon says, 'Pat your head and rub your stomach.' Like this."

Everyone began to laugh at one another.

"Simon says, 'Swing your arms around and around.' "

"Ooof! This is hard work!" puffed Mrs. Sweeney.

"Now. Touch your toes!"

Mrs. Sweeney bent down and tried to touch her toes.

"Oh! oh! You're out, Mrs. Sweeney!" Anna said.

"Why am I out?" she asked indignantly.

Anna giggled. "Because Simon didn't say to touch your toes. *I* did!"

Mrs. Sweeney sat down. "It's just as well," she panted. "I was getting all tired out."

"Is everyone warming up?" Grandpa asked.

"Yes! yes!" they all shouted.

Snow was sifting like flour through the cracks around the windows. Just then, the door opened. A blast of icy cold air blew into the car. Everyone shivered. It was the conductor coming back in again.

"Get ready to leave," he said. "The firefighters are coming!"

Everyone rushed to the door and tried to look out. The snow stung Anna's eyes. The wind almost took her breath away.

The conductor closed the door again quickly. "The wind is so fierce, it's going to be hard to get a ladder up this high. We're at least thirty feet above Third Avenue."

"Ladder! Thirty feet!" Anna shivered.

"Oh, help me," groaned Mrs. Sweeney. "I'll never be able to climb down a ladder." She gave Grandpa a pleading look.

"Oh, yes, you will, Mrs. Sweeney," he said.

"Once you get the hang of it, it's easy."

"In all that wind?" Mrs. Sweeney said. "Never!"

"Don't worry, Mrs. Sweeney. You won't blow away," said Grandpa.

Anna looked at Grandpa. "I'm scared too," she said.

"And what about me?" asked Mrs. Polanski. "I can't stand heights."

The door opened and a firefighter appeared. He shook the snow off his clothes. "We'll take you down one at a time. Who wants to go first?"

No one spoke.

"Anna," said Grandpa. "You're a brave girl. You go first."

"I'm afraid to climb down the ladder, Grandpa."

"Why, Anna, I'm surprised at you. Don't you remember how you climbed down from the hayloft last summer? It was easy."

"You can do it, Anna," said Miss Cohen.

"Pretend we're still playing that game. Simon says, 'Go down the ladder,'" said Mrs. Sweeney.

"So go now," Miss Cohen said. "We'll see you below."

"I'll be right below you to shield you from the wind. You won't fall," said the firefighter.

Anna shook with fear. She didn't want to be first to go down the ladder. But how could she disappoint the others?

Grandpa opened the door. The conductor held her hand. Anna put first one foot, then the other, on the ladder. The fierce wind pulled her and pushed her. Icy snow stuck to her clothes, weighing her down.

The firefighter was below her on the ladder. His strong arms were around her, holding her steady. With her left foot, Anna felt for the rung below.

Step by step by step, she cautiously went down the ladder—thirty steps. Would she never reach bottom? One foot plunged into snow and then the other. Oh, so much snow! It covered her legs and reached almost to her waist.

"Stay close to the engine until the rest are down," the firefighter said.

Anna struggled through the deep snow to the fire engine. The horses, whipped by the icy wind and snow, stood still, their heads low. Anna huddled against the side of the engine. The roar of the storm was growing louder.

First came Mrs. Polanski, then Ruth Cohen—then Bruce and John King—then Addie Weaver. One at a time, the firefighter helped each person down the ladder. Now only Grandpa and Mrs. Sweeney remained to be rescued.

Anna could see two shapes on the ladder, one behind the other. The firefighter was bringing down someone else.

"Oh, I hope it's Grandpa," Anna said to Addie Weaver.

Suddenly she gasped. She could hardly believe her eyes. One minute the two shapes were there. The next minute they weren't!

Everyone struggled through the deep snow to find out who had fallen off the ladder.

Anna was the first to reach the firefighter who was brushing snow off his clothes. "What happened?" she asked.

"Mrs. Sweeney missed a step on the ladder. Down she went, taking me with her," the firefighter replied.

Mrs. Sweeney lay sprawled in the snow nearby. Her arms and legs were spread out, as if she were going to make a snow angel.

"Are you all right, Mrs. Sweeney?" Grandpa asked. Anna had not seen Grandpa come down the ladder by himself. Now he stood beside her.

"I'm just fine, Mr. Jensen. I think I'm going to lie right here until the storm is over."

"Oh, no, you're not!" Grandpa said. He and a firefighter each took one of Mrs. Sweeney's arms and pulled her to her feet.

Anna couldn't help giggling. Now Mrs. Sweeney looked like a giant snow lady!

"Climb onto the engine," said a firefighter. "We must get the horses back to the firehouse. The temperature is dropping fast."

"We live only two blocks from here," Mrs. Polanski and Miss Cohen said. "We're going to try to get home."

"We'll see that you get there," John King said. "We live on Lafayette Street." The young men and the two ladies linked arms and trudged off through the snow.

"What about you, Miss Weaver?" Grandpa asked. She looked confused.

"Hey, everybody, this is no tea party! Let's go!" said the firefighter.

"You come with us then, Miss Weaver," Grandpa said. "You too, Mrs. Sweeney."

Anna's fingers were numb with cold. She could hardly hold onto the railing of the engine. Often she had seen the horses racing down the street to a fire. Now they plodded along very, very slowly through the deep snow.

No one spoke. The wind roared and shrieked. The snow blinded them. One firefighter jumped off the engine and tried to lead the horses forward.

Anna huddled against the side of the engine, hiding her face in her arms. It was taking them forever to reach the firehouse.

Just then, the horses turned abruptly to the left. The next moment they were inside the stable, snorting and stamping their hooves.

Several men ran forward to unhitch the engine. Everyone began brushing the icy snow off their clothes.

Suddenly Grandpa became very serious. "The thermometer says five degrees above zero, and the temperature is still dropping. We must get home as fast as possible. Mrs. Sweeney, you and Miss Weaver had better come with us."

"Here, Miss," a firefighter said. "Put these boots on. You can return them when the storm is over."

"Oh, thank you," Addie Weaver said.

Anna had forgotten about Addie's high-button shoes.

"Whatever you do, Anna, you are not to let go of my hand," Grandpa said firmly.

"Mr. Jensen, would you mind if I held your other hand?" asked Mrs. Sweeney.

"Not a bit," said Grandpa. "Anna, you take hold of Miss Weaver's hand. No one is to let go under any circumstances. Do you all understand?"

Anna had never heard Grandpa talk like that before. Was he frightened too?

They plunged into the deep snow, moving slowly along the south side of Fifteenth Street. The wind had piled the snow into huge drifts on the north side of the street.

When they reached Broadway, the wind was blowing up the avenue with the force of a hurricane. Telephone and telegraph wires were down. Thousands of them cut through the air like whips. If only they could reach the other side, Anna thought. Then they would be on their very own block.

No one spoke. They clung to one another as they blindly made their way across the avenue. Mrs. Sweeney lost her balance and fell forward in the snow. For a moment Anna thought she was there to stay, but Grandpa tugged at her arm and helped her get to her feet.

They continued on until they reached the other side. Now to find their house. How lucky they were to live on the south side of the block. The snow had reached as high as the first-floor windows of the houses on the north side. At last they came to number 44. Up the seven steps they climbed. Then through the front door and up more stairs. A moment later, Mr. Romano opened their apartment door. "Papa, you're home," Anna cried, and fell into her father's arms.

Several hours later, Anna sat in the kitchen watching a checkers game. Mrs. Sweeney, wearing Grandpa's bathrobe, was playing checkers with Grandpa, while Miss Weaver, in Mama's clothes, chatted with Mama. Outside, the storm whistled and roared. Tomorrow would be time enough to study her spelling, Anna decided. Now she just wanted to enjoy the company.

Suddenly Grandpa pushed his chair back. "You win, Mrs. Sweeney. Where did you learn to play checkers?"

"I belong to a club," Mrs. Sweeney replied. "I'm the champ. We meet every Tuesday. Maybe you will come with me next Tuesday, Mr. Jensen?"

"Why, I'd like that," answered Grandpa.

Anna said, "I think Grandpa likes the city better now."

Mrs. Romano smiled. "It took a snowstorm to change his mind."

"You call this a snowstorm?" said Grandpa. He winked at Anna. "When you are an old lady, Anna, as old as I am now, you will be telling your grandchildren all about our adventure in the great blizzard of 1888!"

The Great Blizzard of 1888
There really was a great blizzard in 1888. It began to snow early Monday morning, March 12th. Before the snow stopped on Tuesday, four to five feet had fallen in New York City. Seventy inches fell in Boston and in other parts of the East.

The winds blew at 75 miles an hour and piled the snow in huge drifts. Everywhere, people were stranded. In New York City, about 15,000 people were trapped in elevated trains. Like Anna and Grandpa, they had to be rescued by firefighters with ladders.

By Thursday of that same week, the sun was out again. The snow began to melt. Anna went to school and won the spelling bee. And Grandpa walked down to Sullivan Street to play checkers again with Josie Sweeney.

Author
Carla Stevens grew up in New York City, where she rode the Third Avenue Elevated as a child. Riding on the El was always a great adventure for her. Mrs. Stevens has been a teacher as well as a writer. Another of her books that is set in the past is *Trouble for Lucy*.

Source: Adapted from ANNA, GRANDPA, AND THE BIG STORM by Carla Stevens. Copyright © 1982 by Carla Stevens. Reprinted by permission of Ticknor & Fields/Clarion Books, a Houghton Mifflin Company. Approximately 2679 words from ANNA, GRANDPA AND THE BIG STORM by Carla Stevens (Viking Kestrel Books, 1984), copyright (c) Carla Stevens, 1982. In William K. Durr et al.: *Flights*, pp. 12–30 (Houghton Mifflin Reading). Boston: Houghton Mifflin Company, 1986.

Sample Lesson

Note: The Third Avenue Elevated will be used to illustrate background development for a narrative selection. Read the story before proceeding with the lesson to determine the background that an average fourth-grade reader would need in order to understand this selection. Assume that the students do not live in a large city with an elevated train. As you identify the background, note the key terms that students will need to learn.

Background Needed

The major story line is that Anna and her grandfather get trapped on an elevated train during a blizzard, and the story develops around how they are rescued and get home. Students need to understand what an elevated train is and the problems that can develop by being trapped in a train and stranded during a snowstorm.

Key terms:
Elevated
El
stranded
conductor

Techniques to Be Used in Developing Background

picture
background-generating activity
discussion
story preview
purpose setting

The Lesson

Say: Today, we are going to read the selection, "The Third Avenue Elevated." Look at the picture on page 105 of your book. It is a picture of a train that is called an elevated train or an El. Describe the train for me. (Students respond. Make certain that students realize that the train is about thirty feet above the ground. *Note: This is using a picture to develop background.* Have a *brief* discussion about student responses. Note that *discussion* is used here and throughout the lesson to develop background.) Usually elevated trains are in cities like Chicago and New York. (Put the following sentence and words on the board.

Anna and her grandfather rode on the Third Avenue El.

elevated train

Read the sentence aloud. *Note: This is the preteaching of a related key term.*)

Say: El is the abbreviation for elevated train. In today's story, Anna and her grandfather get stranded on the train during a blizzard. (Pass out 3 x 5 cards or have students use their own paper.) I want you to write down anything you can think of that might happen while being trapped on this train during a snowstorm. Don't worry about spelling. (Give students time to write their responses. *Note: This is a background-generating activity.*)

Say: Now, I want you, one at a time, to read what you have written. (Have students read their answers, and record their responses on the chalkboard or overhead projector. Discuss the responses, eliminating any that are in error. Be certain that students realize that being trapped on the El could pose problems getting down to the ground and getting home in a blizzard.)

Say: In today's story, Anna and the other people on the train get stranded in a blizzard. (Write the following sentence on the board:

The people on the train get <u>stranded</u> and don't think they can get home.

Have a student read the sentence and discuss the meaning of stranded.)

Say: There is a man who works on the train. (Write the following sentence on the chalkboard:

The <u>conductor</u> takes tickets on the train.

Ask a student to read this sentence aloud and tell you what the underlined word means.)

Say: There are some names of people in our story that you might not know. (List names on the chalkboard and pronounce them or have students pronounce them.

> Erik Jensen, grandfather
> Anna Romano
> Mrs. Esther Polanski
> Miss Ruth Cohen
> John and Bruce King
> Mrs. Sweeney
> Addie Weaver)

Say: We have talked about some words and ideas that are important in our story. Give me a sentence using these words:

> stranded
> conductor
> El or Elevated

(Students respond. *Note: This is guided practice with words.*)

Say: We have discussed some of the problems that could happen by being stranded on an El in a snowstorm. What were some of those? (Students respond. *Note: This is summarizing background.*)

Say: Now open your books to page 106 and read the story preview to find out why Anna and her grandfather were on the train. (Students read and respond. *Note: This is using a story preview provided in text.*)
Say: I want you to read this story to find out how Anna and the people on the train solved their problem of being stranded. *(Note: This is setting a purpose that focuses on the entire selection.)*

Comments About the Lesson

This lesson used five different techniques to help students develop the background needed for this selection; three key-concept terms were also pretaught. For students who have no background about blizzards, the short article about the blizzard of 1888 could be used as prior reading. This part of the directed reading lesson (the preteaching of background and vocabulary) should move along quickly, but teachers should allow sufficient time to ensure that the background is developed for the selection. After students have completed the story, there must be a discussion of the purpose for reading as well as other points.

EXAMPLE 3.10 EXPOSITORY SELECTION AND SAMPLE BACKGROUND DEVELOPMENT LESSON FOR STUDENTS IN THE SECOND HALF OF THIRD GRADE

What Makes a Bird a Bird?

by May Garelick

There's something special about birds that makes them different from any other kind of animal. What is that something special?

In trees and in bushes, on the ground, and in the air, birds are flying, singing, calling, and nesting.

How do we know that a bird is a bird? What makes it different from any other type of animal? What makes a bird unique?

Is a bird unique because it flies? A fly flies, and so do butterflies, ladybugs, dragonflies, and bees. But these animals are not birds. They are insects.

Many insects fly. They do not fly as fast as birds, but many insects do fly.

And what is this furry-looking creature, flying around in the middle of the night? It's not an insect, and it's not a bird. It's a bat.

Bats sleep during the day, hanging upside-down in hollow trees or in caves. At night they fly around, trying to catch insects for food.

Bats, insects, and birds are not the only animals that fly.

What do you think this creature is, flying above the water? Is it a bat? An insect? A bird? No, it's a flying fish that has been frightened by an enemy under water. Like all fish, flying fish live most of the time in water. If an enemy comes near, however, a flying fish can jump out of the water, glide through the air, and escape.

If there are flying insects, flying bats, and even flying fish, then it is not flying that makes a bird unique. As a matter of fact, you know a bird that doesn't really fly.

Have you ever seen a chicken fly? Sometimes a chicken attempts to fly, but it doesn't get far. To get anywhere, a chicken walks. Is a chicken a bird? Yes.

Can you think of another bird that can't fly? Penguins cannot fly; they walk. Down to the water they waddle and into the sea for a swim. Penguins are excellent swimmers. They use their flipper-like wings to paddle through the water.

Another bird that cannot fly is the ostrich, the biggest bird in the world. Although it can't fly, the ostrich's long legs make it a very swift runner. An ostrich can run as fast as forty miles an hour.

If ostriches, penguins, and chickens cannot fly, what makes them birds? Are they birds because they have wings?

Birds definitely have wings, but look at a fly flying around. You can see its wings. Dragonflies, butterflies, and bees have wings too. If some insects have wings, then it is not wings that makes a bird unique.

Is a bird a bird because it sings? Birds sing and call messages to each other, especially in the spring. That's how birds communicate with one another.

One bird's song may be a warning to other birds to keep away. Usually the other birds will keep away. If they don't, there may be a fight.

A mother hen clucks to her chicks to tell them that there is food. The chicks recognize her call and come running for the food.

A duck quacks to signal her ducklings to follow her. Baby robins make peeping sounds to let their parents know they are hungry.

Birds sing and call messages to each other, but many insects communicate by singing and calling. Crickets chirp, and grasshoppers hum. Katydids repeat their rhythmic song all night long.

If there are insects that can sing and call, then it is not singing and calling that makes a bird unique. What *is* the special thing that makes a bird a bird?

Is a bird unique because it builds a nest? Birds build nests in trees, in bushes, under caves, and in barns. They build nests wherever their eggs and their babies will be safe.

Some birds, however, build no nests at all. A whippoorwill lays her eggs among the leaves on the ground.

Birds are not the only animals that build nests. Ants, bees, snakes, fish, rabbits, mice, and other animals make nests too.

If other animals build nests, then it is not nest building that makes a bird a bird.

Egg laying is not what makes a bird unique, either. It's true that all birds lay eggs, but so do frogs, snakes, fish, bees, mosquitoes, and many other animals.

So—it isn't flying that makes a bird different from anything else alive.

And it's not having wings.

And it's not singing or calling.

And it's not building nests or laying eggs.

What is it, then, that makes a bird a bird?

Birds have something that no other living thing has. What is it?

FEATHERS! Only birds have feathers. That's the special thing that makes a bird unique. A bird has to have feathers to be a bird. Whether it flies or not, any animal with feathers is a bird.

Feathers are strong. Try to break or tear one, and you'll see how strong a feather is. Bend a feather so the tip touches the bottom. Watch it spring back. It won't break.

Feathers are light. Hold a feather, and you'll see how light it is. You've probably heard people say that something is "light as a feather."

Feathers are beautiful, and they come in many colors. There are feathers from red cardinals, blue jays, blackbirds, white doves, green parrots, brown sparrows, and many other colored birds.

Feathers are useful too. They do many things for birds. Feathers make birds the best flyers. Even though some other animals fly, no living creature can fly as long or as far as a bird.

Feathers also help keep birds warm in winter. Watch a bird on a cold day. It looks like a fat puffball because it has fluffed out all its feathers to keep out the cold.

Feathers help keep birds dry in the rain. Put a drop of water on a feather, and watch the water slide off.

Birds take good care of their feathers by cleaning and smoothing them with their beaks. This is called *preening*. Most birds also oil their feathers while they preen. They get the oil from their tails. When they apply it to their feathers, it waterproofs and softens the feathers.

Most birds also bathe to keep their feathers clean. Some birds bathe in water, and others bathe in fine dust. However, no matter how well birds clean their feathers, they get brittle and wear out. At least once a year, birds *molt*—their worn-out feathers fall out. Birds don't shed all their feathers at once, just one or two at a time. As the old feathers fall out, new ones grow in.

You may find some of these old feathers on the ground. Pick them up and look at them.

Feathers are the special things that make a bird a bird.

Source: May Garelick, "What Makes a Bird a Bird?" In William K. Durr et al.: *Journeys*, pp. 200–207 (Houghton Mifflin Reading). Boston: Houghton Mifflin Company, 1986. Used by permission.

Sample Lesson

Note: What Makes a Bird a Bird will be used to illustrate background development for an expository selection. Read the selection before proceeding with the lesson to determine the background that would be needed by an average reader in the second half of third grade. As you identify background, note the key terms that students will need to learn.

Background Needed

The main idea developed in this selection is that the only thing that distinguishes birds from other animals is their feathers. The author develops this idea by illustrating that many other creatures have characteristics that birds have but only birds have feathers.

Key terms:
feathers
Katydids
ostriches
penguins

Techniques to Be Used in Developing Background

semantic mapping
discussion
purpose setting

The Lesson

Say: Today, we are going to read an article about birds. Before we read it, I want us to think about what we know about birds. (Write the word *birds* on the chalkboard and circle it.)

(birds)

Say: Tell me some things that describe what birds look like. (Students respond. If they need help getting started, give an example. Record responses and draw boxes around them. Draw an arrow between the word *birds* and the words given by students. Write the word *have* above the arrow. A sample is given below. *Note: Here and in the sections that follow the teacher is using semantic mapping.*)

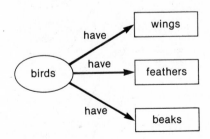

Say: Now, I want you to tell me some things that birds do. (Students respond. Use the same procedure as above to record the responses. Draw ovals around these words.)

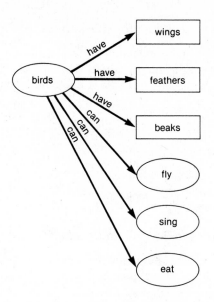

Say: Tell me the names of some birds that you know. (Students respond. Follow the same procedure as above. Put boxes around these words.)

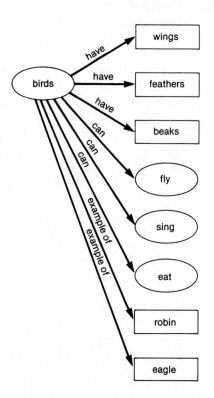

SUMMARY

Say: We have drawn a map of some of the things that we know about birds. In today's article, we are going to learn some more information about birds that we can add to our map. There are some words in the article that we need to know before we read. I want each of you to read the following sentences to yourself to see if you can figure out what the underlined words mean. (Print the following sentences on the board and have students read them silently and then aloud. Discuss the meanings of the underlined words. If students are unable to determine the pronunciations of the words, pronounce the words for them.

1. Birds have <u>feathers</u> on their bodies.
2. A <u>penguin</u> is a black and white bird that lives where it is cool.
3. <u>Katydids</u> are little insects that are like grasshoppers.
4. An <u>ostrich</u> is a bird with very long legs and a long neck.)

Say: Now I want you to give me a sentence with each of these words. (Students respond. If they have problems with any words, discuss the meaning of the words with them. *Note: This is guided practice with vocabulary.*)

Say: We have talked a lot about birds, but did you ever think about the thing that really makes a bird a bird? (Point to the semantic map.) Look at all the things we have said about birds. Can things other than birds fly? (Student respond. Discuss their answers briefly. *Note: This is discussion orienting the background students have developed thus far to the main idea of the selection.*)

Say: Today's article will help you learn what makes a bird a bird. Open your book to page 114 and read the first two sentences to yourself. (Then have a student read these aloud.) I want you to read this article to find out what the something special is that makes a bird a bird. (*Note: This is setting the purpose for the article.*)

Comments About the Lesson

After students have read the selection, discuss their responses to the purpose question. Have students look back at the semantic map about birds and add any information they learned from their reading. Make sure that students understand that even though having feathers is the one thing that really makes a bird a bird, the other ideas listed about birds are still true.

This lesson used three different techniques to help students develop the background needed to read this expository article. Four key terms were also pretaught as a part of background development. As with the narrative selection in Example 3.9, the teacher must follow the reading of this expository selection with a discussion of the purpose for reading as well as other points.

SUMMARY

The reader's background directly influences his or her ability to comprehend text. Background involves all of an individual's prior learning and experience that form the basis for the reader's schemata for various ideas, concepts, and relationships. The reader stores this information in his or her memory.

The role of the teacher in teaching comprehension is to help the reader activate prior experiences in order to develop the background or schema for comprehending a particular selection. The background that a reader needs for a selection includes knowledge of the topic, understanding of specific concepts in the selection, and understanding of key terminology. Therefore, a major part of the instructional program in reading comprehension is developing background and vocabulary.

What background should be developed for a particular selection depends on the type of text, the teacher and what he or she wants students to learn, and the existing background of the students. There are numerous strategies that teachers can use to help students develop background. These include

> discussion,
> background generating activity,
> prequestions, purpose setting activities, and objectives,
> advance organizers and story previews,
> webbing and semantic maps,
> pictures,
> concrete materials, role playing, and field trips,
> prior reading.

Within any given lesson, the teacher is likely to use several of these strategies in combination with one another.

REFERENCES

Adams, M., and B. Bertram. 1980. *Background knowledge and reading comprehension.* Reading Education Report No. 13. Urbana, IL: University of Illinois, Center for the Study of Reading. (ERIC Document Reproduction Service No. ED 181 431)

Alvermann, D. E. 1984. Using textbook reading assignments to promote classroom discussion. *Clearing House, 58,* 70–73.

Ausubel, D. P. 1960. The use of advance organizers in the learning and retention of meaningful verbal material. *Journal of Educational Psychology, 51,* 267–272.

Barnes, B. R., and E. U. Clawson. 1975. Do advance organizers facilitate learning? Recommendations for further research based on an analysis of 32 studies. *Review of Educational Research, 45,* 637–659.

Beck, I. L. 1984. Developing comprehension: The impact of the directed reading lesson. In R. C. Anderson, J. Osborn, and R. J. Tierney (eds.), *Learning to read in American schools: Basal readers and content texts.* Hillsdale, NJ: Lawrence Erlbaum Associates.

Beck, I. L., R. C. Omanson, and M. G. McKeown. 1982. An instructional redesign of reading lessons: Effects on comprehension. *Reading Research Quarterly, 17,* 462–481.

REFERENCES

Feller, W. A. 1973. The effects of two types of advance organizers and two types of spaced questions on the ability of a selected group of tenth grade biology students to recall, comprehend and apply facts from written science. Ph.D. dissertation, Temple University, Philadelphia.

Harris, T. L., and R. E. Hodges. 1981. *A dictionary of reading and related terms.* Newark, DE: International Reading Association.

Lamoreaux, L. A., and D. M. Lee. 1943. *Learning to read through experience.* New York: Appleton-Century-Crofts.

Pearson, P. D., and D. D. Johnson. 1978. *Teaching reading comprehension.* New York: Holt, Rinehart and Winston.

Samuels, S. J. 1970. Effects of pictures on learning to read, comprehension and attitudes. *Review of Educational Research, 40,* 397–407.

Schallert, D. L. 1980. The role of illustrations in reading comprehension. In R. J. Spiro, B. C. Bruce, and W. F. Brewer (eds.), *Theoretical issues in reading comprehension,* pp. 503–524. Hillsdale, NJ: Lawrence Erlbaum Associates.

Smith, N. B. 1965. *American reading instruction.* Newark, DE: International Reading Association.

Thomas, J. L. 1978. The influence of pictorial illustrations with written text and previous achievement on the reading comprehension of fourth grade science students. *Journal of Research in Science Teaching, 15,* 401–405.

Tierney, R. J., and J. W. Cunningham. 1984. Research on teaching reading comprehension. In P. D. Pearson (ed.), *Handbook of reading research,* pp. 609–655. New York: Longman.

White, R. E. 1981. The effects of organizational themes and adjunct placements on children's prose learning: A developmental perspective. *Dissertation Abstracts International, 42,* 2042A–2043A. (University Microfilms No. 81-25, 038)

CHAPTER
F O U R

VOCABULARY DEVELOPMENT

What is needed for all learning is interest. A sense of excitement about words, a sense of wonder, and a feeling of pleasure—these are the essential ingredients in vocabulary development.—Deighton, 1959, p. 59

In this chapter, you will learn

1. the goals of vocabulary instruction,
2. a model for vocabulary development,
3. ways to create a vocabulary atmosphere in the classroom,
4. strategies for preteaching vocabulary,
5. strategies for teaching students the skills needed to be independent in determining word meanings,
6. techniques for teaching specific vocabulary lessons.

An essential part of comprehension is knowing the meanings of words (Davis, 1944; Davis, 1972; Johnston, 1981). Therefore, an important component of the instructional program in reading comprehension must be vocabulary development, which is a specialized form of background building. Within this part of the instructional program, there are two primary goals:

1. To help students develop a stock of words they can instantly recognize, understand, and relate to their overall background.
2. To teach students how to independently determine the meanings of words they have not been taught.

IMPORTANCE OF INSTANT-RECOGNITION VOCABULARY

As a mature reader, you know the meanings of and can recognize thousands of words; these words constitute your instant-recognition vocabulary. The term instant-recognition vocabulary is used instead of sight vocabulary in this text because the term sight words or sight vocabulary has, for many individuals, taken on the meaning of only those words we have memorized. Instant-recognition vocabulary is more than that—it is those words you recognize immediately in your reading and understand. For example, all of the words in the following sentence are part of your instant-recognition vocabulary; you will be able to recognize and know the meaning of each word without hesitation.

The children cooked hot dogs and marshmallows and had a wonderful time.

Sometimes, as you read, you encounter a word that you do not instantly recognize or understand. Such words are not a part of your instant-recognition vocabulary. Read the following sentence, paying special attention to the underlined word:

The old man carried his parlimp very carefully.

When you encountered *parlimp*, you had to draw your attention away from comprehension of the sentence and focus instead on determining the meaning of the unknown word. An extensive instant-recognition vocabulary enables the reader to focus attention on the comprehension of natural text rather than dividing attention between total comprehension and comprehension of vocabulary.

Traditionally, a sight word has been defined as "a word which is immediately recognized as a whole and does not require word analysis for identification" (Harris and Hodges, 1981, p. 245). Sight or recognition vocabulary has been defined as "the number of different words known without the necessity of word analysis; words understood quickly and easily" (p. 272). These definitions reflect a focus on decoding with little or no attention to word meaning. Many teachers, when asked how they evaluate sight vocabulary, reply, "I have my students read the Dolch word list." However, an evaluation of students' abilities to read word lists reflects only their abilities to pronounce words correctly and is an extremely narrow way to define sight vocabulary. Educators often make the mistaken assumption that if a student pronounces a word correctly, he or she already has the word in his or her oral language background.

Thus, a broader definition than that of sight vocabulary and a different term are needed to reflect the reader's ability to immediately pronounce words and associate meaning with them—that term is instant-recognition vocabulary. It is used in this text to mean words the reader can recognize, pronounce, and understand instantly.

Any word can become an instant-recognition word for a reader. The reader's goal should be to develop an extensive instant-recognition vocabulary so that he or she does not have to analyze each word encountered in terms of pronunciation and meaning. Further, the teacher's goal of increasing the student's recognition vocabulary should focus on the student's ability to instantly recognize words during the reading of natural text instead of on the student's ability to pronounce and define words in isolation. When direct instruction is used properly, students apply their instant-recognition vocabulary in the reading of text.

An important distinction exists between words in a reader's instant-recognition vocabulary and words that must initially be taught as whole words. Words that must be taught as whole words are those that are phonetically irregular in the English language or those for which students do not yet have the ability to apply phonetic analysis. These words must be introduced in written context. Many of the words in this category are referred to as high-frequency words, indicating that they have a high degree of use in the language. Two lists of such words are the Dolch List (Dolch, 1936) and the Johnson Basic Vocabulary for Beginning Reading (Johnson, 1971a; Johnson and Pearson, 1984). The Johnson list is the more current of the two (Johnson, 1971b). This text does not focus specifically on the teaching of high-frequency words; it focuses instead on the teaching of instant-recognition vocabulary from a key-concept-word point of view.

As stated in the beginning of this chapter, the first goal of an instructional program in vocabulary development is to help students develop a stock of words that they can instantly recognize and relate to their overall background. For this goal to be accomplished, direct instruction involving word meaning must be followed by consistent and frequent opportunities for students to read the words they have learned in natural text. The second goal of vocabulary instruction is to teach students how to determine word meanings independently, that is, without the teacher's help.

DEVELOPING INDEPENDENCE IN DETERMINING WORD MEANING

Some of the skills that are taught as a part of word recognition also help the reader determine word meaning. These include use of context clues, structural analysis, and dictionary skills. Table 4.1 summarizes the various skills taught as a part of word recognition and vocabulary development and indicates whether they are important to pronunciation or meaning. Notice that only phonics is exclusively an aid to pronunciation. As teachers help students develop their vocabularies, they must be aware that the students are applying their word-recognition skills not only to determining word meaning but also to determining word pronunciation. Further, teachers must be conscious of whether they are teaching a particular structural analysis skill or dictionary skill to enable students to pronounce a word or to determine the meaning of a word. There is a definite link between word recognition and comprehension, and students should be helped to see this link. If students are able to determine the pronunciations of words that are already in their oral language, they are likely to know the meanings of the words. Effective vocabulary instruction will enable the students to make a smooth transition from decoding to vocabulary meaning.

Remember the sentence presented earlier:

The old man carried his <u>parlimp</u> very carefully.

You tried to read the underlined word by

Table 4.1 Word Recognition and Vocabulary Skills and Their Purposes for Teaching

	Purposes for Teaching	
Skills	Pronunciation	Meaning
phonics	×	
structural analysis	×	×
context clues	×	×
dictionary	×	×

using the context of the sentence,

looking for structural elements that you recognized, such as prefixes or base words,

using your phonic skills to decode the word.

At the conclusion of these attempts, you might have had some idea how to pronounce the word, but you did not know its exact meaning, and upon decoding the word, you realized it was not in your oral language experience. Therefore, you might have used three alternative strategies to help you determine the meaning of the word: you could have looked it up in the dictionary, asked someone about the word, or, had you been given more text, read further in an attempt to determine the meaning from context. You have developed these strategies for independently determining both pronunciations and meanings for words. In this case, none of your strategies would have worked because parlimp, which in the story means a glass container for carrying water, was coined by the author to illustrate the importance of a reader's oral language experience to vocabulary development. If the word had been in your oral language background, you probably would have been able to verify the pronunciation and determine the meaning using your existing skills and knowledge without going to another source.

A critical point about vocabulary development is that students can learn to pronounce and associate meaning with words more readily when they have had oral language experiences with them. However, all words that students come across in their reading are not in their oral vocabularies. Therefore, a major consideration in selecting a strategy to help students develop reading vocabulary must be whether the words in the lesson are in the students' oral language background. Because parlimp was not in your oral language background, you immediately tried to use one of the strategies you have developed to independently determine word pronunciation and meaning. The context probably would have given you the strongest clue to the word's meaning; the phrase "carried very carefully" could indicate that a parlimp is fragile. If parlimp had been a real word, you could have used the dictionary to determine its meaning.

When a word is a part of a reader's oral language, the reader basically knows the meaning of the word. Therefore, once the reader is able to pronounce the word, he or she should automatically be able to associate the meaning with it. This, however, is not always true. In some instances, beginning readers and less mature readers still need direct instruction in words that are in their oral language backgrounds because they do not have the meanings clearly associated with the symbols for the words. In other instances, the reader may have only one meaning for a word in his or her oral vocabulary and the text in which the word is used requires another. Such multiple-meaning words must be taught because the reader has had no background experience with them.

In teaching reading vocabulary and vocabulary skills, the teacher must always consider the reader's background and oral language. If there is a word in the reader's oral language background that needs to be taught, the teacher may only need to teach it from a pronunciation point of view with minimal attention given to meaning. Because the word is already in the reader's oral vocabulary, the reader probably knows the meaning and only needs to learn the pronunciation. However, the teacher should not automatically assume that words that are a part of a reader's oral language need to be taught only from a pronunciation point of view; many times students also need some instructional attention focused on the meanings of these words.

DEVELOPING WORD OWNERSHIP

When a student sees how a word relates to his or her overall background, the student develops "ownership" of the word (Beck, 1984) and has really learned the word. Students develop networks of words and their relationships through repeated experiences using the words in their reading and writing and through activities specifically designed to help them build relationships among words. The teacher's initial introduction of a word will help the student learn its meaning, but it is through the repeated experiences of using the word that the student develops ownership of the word.

As readers develop ownership of words, they are able to relate them to their existing schema and develop new schema. It is the process of relating new words to words already known that makes a word belong to an individual.

MODEL FOR VOCABULARY DEVELOPMENT

Vocabulary development, as used in this text, is the process of helping students develop ownership of words by teaching them the meanings of words and those skills that will help them independently determine word meanings. Within this framework, vocabulary development consists of three parts, as shown in Figure 4.1:

> preteaching vocabulary,
> teaching skills to determine word meanings,
> teaching specific vocabulary lessons.

Preteaching Vocabulary

Prior to having students read selections in their basal readers or other textbooks, the teacher should teach, in written context, the new vocabulary the students will encounter in their reading. Preteaching of vocabulary helps students learn

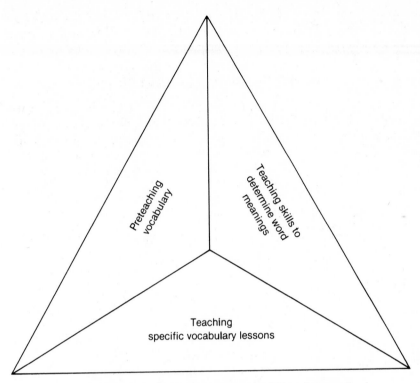

Figure 4.1   Model for Vocabulary Development

the words needed for the selection and at the same time helps them develop some of the background needed to comprehend the text. At the primary levels, the preteaching of vocabulary must include the basic or high-frequency words as well as the key-concept words for the selection. By the time students reach the intermediate levels, the preteaching will focus primarily on the key-concept words. The key-concept words selected for teaching should be those that relate most directly to the overall idea or concept developed in the text. By teaching words prior to having students read texts, the teacher helps students build the instant-recognition vocabularies that will enable them to become mature comprehenders. The words taught prior to reading will include words that may or may not be in the students' oral vocabularies.

Teaching Skills to Determine Word Meanings

Students cannot be taught every word they will encounter in reading. Therefore, they must be taught skills that will make them independent in determining word meanings. These skills include use of context clues, structural analysis (prefixes, suffixes, base words, root words, inflectional endings, compound words, and contractions), and the use of the dictionary. By learning these skills, students will be able to more readily determine the meanings of words that are not already in their oral vocabularies as well as the meanings of words that are.

Teaching Specific Vocabulary Lessons

In this part of the vocabulary program, students are taught the specific vocabulary lessons that will make them more aware of words and their relationships and will expand their instant-recognition vocabulary. The lessons should help students improve their overall vocabulary knowledge as well as make them more aware of word meanings. The lessons should be developed around

> synonyms/antonyms/homonyms/homographs,
> denotation/connotation,
> semantic maps,
> vocabulary webs,
> semantic feature analysis,
> analogies,
> etymologies,
> the thesaurus,
> multiple-meaning words.

These lessons will not only expand the reader's vocabulary but will also help the reader develop ownership of words.

VOCABULARY DEVELOPMENT AND THE DIRECTED READING LESSON

The format of the directed reading lesson (DRL) with an emphasis on direct instruction affords numerous opportunities to systematically account for the elements of vocabulary development. In the skill building portion of the DRL, lessons devoted to teaching skills to determine word meanings and specific vocabulary lessons can and should be taught. During the background and readiness portion, key concept words and basic vocabulary should be taught and practiced. During the guided silent reading portion of the lesson, students will apply what they have learned about vocabulary as well as learn new words and new meanings from their reading experience. In the extension portion of the DRL, specific vocabulary lessons oriented toward expanding the student's vocabulary as well as lessons that provide opportunities for students to apply what they have learned should be taught. Therefore, an important characteristic of the DRL is that it offers a framework that encourages the integration of vocabulary development with the other components of the instructional program in reading comprehension. Teaching vocabulary alone will not produce the most effective comprehender possible. The elements of the instructional program in reading comprehension must be woven together. The remainder of this chapter presents specific strategies and lessons for developing vocabulary within the context of the directed reading lesson described in Chapter 2.

CREATING A VOCABULARY ATMOSPHERE

Vocabulary development must begin with the creation of a vocabulary atmosphere in the classroom, an atmosphere in which students are constantly made aware of words and in which there are many activities focusing on words. To develop a vocabulary atmosphere, the teacher must first convey an attitude that lets students know that words are important. They can do this by having students be on the lookout for new words in their reading and listening and by constantly providing activities in the classroom that focus on words.

One way to help focus students' attention on words is to have them look for interesting words or words they don't know in their reading or when they are listening to others talk, watching television, seeing movies, and so forth, both in and out of class. Students should be instructed to bring those words into class, writing as best they can the words they can't spell (inventive spelling). The teacher and students should look up each of the words in the dictionary, discuss its meaning, and use it in several oral and written sentences. The words can then be put on a vocabulary bulletin board, in a student's word bank, or in a word book, all of which will be described later in this chapter.

The teacher should constantly call students' attention to interesting and unusual words, and, occasionally, the teacher should bring words to class to add to those brought in by students. By doing so, the teacher lets students know that he or she values words, too.

The vocabulary atmosphere of a classroom (and the general learning atmosphere) is enhanced by stimulating learning devices placed around the room for students to use and discuss. Books, displays, recordings, tapes, filmstrips, computer games or activities, and art that relates to a topic of study all make a classroom rich with learning tools that foster discussion and lead to new vocabulary and many other new language learnings. At the beginning of every school year, all teachers (elementary, reading, science, history, English, and so on) should plan what they are going to do to make the classroom atmosphere one that is conducive to better vocabulary learning. Such an atmosphere will help to improve all language learning.

Word Banks and Word Books

Word banks and word books are two devices that can add to the vocabulary atmosphere of the classroom. They are the students' personal files of words they have learned or want to learn. The words can be taken from those taught prior to selections, from areas of study such as science, from interest areas, and from other sources. Each word is either put on a card with a sentence the student has written using the word and placed in a word bank or written in a word book, again with a sentence. At the primary levels, the bank idea is motivational because words can be written on cards shaped like coins and dropped into the banks. Banks can be made of plastic bottles, boxes, or other containers. Words can be taken from the bank and reviewed periodically or used to create games the students can play.

For higher-level students, the word book is more appropriate. Students can use loose-leaf notebooks for their word books, or they can make them from pages held

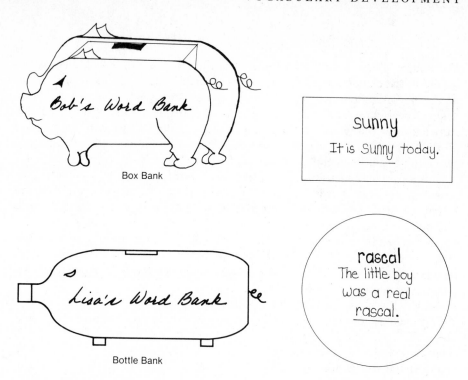

Box Bank

sunny
It is sunny today.

Bottle Bank

rascal
The little boy was a real rascal.

together with fasteners that will allow other pages to be added. Sections can be organized alphabetically. The words in the book can be used for periodic review and practice, can be read and discussed with other students, can be used in oral and written stories, and can be incorporated into activities such as learning to alphabetize.

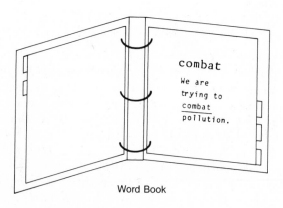

Word Book

Bulletin-Board Activities

Bulletin board displays can also stimulate the vocabulary atmosphere of the classroom. They can be used for both vocabulary practice and motivation. Manipulative activities, such as that shown in Example 4.1, can be used for vocabulary practice and reinforcement; other displays can feature words brought in by students or words being studied. The displays should be changed frequently. In this
way, bulletin boards become useful teaching tools instead of burdensome decorations that require teacher preparation time. Titles of popular songs, television shows, or movies can be used as motivational themes for the displays.

Vocabulary Games

Students enjoy playing games. Teachers can capitalize on this by making many vocabulary practice games available in the classroom. Manila folders can be used to make very simple game boards that can be easily stored in file cabinets. Word cards should be used with the game boards, with numbers on the cards indicating

the spaces to move. The teacher can have students draw cards from the central pile, complete the activity written on the card, and move the indicated number of spaces, if correct. The activities on the cards can be varied for different games. For example:

Write a sentence on each card using a new vocabulary word. Underline the word. Have students read the sentence and tell what the underlined word means. Write the correct meaning on the back of the card.

EXAMPLE 4.1   SAMPLE BULLETIN BOARD ACTIVITY ━━━━━━

BE A GREMLIN: GET INTO WORD TROUBLE

<u>Directions:</u> Read each sentence and place
the correct word in the
blank. Check with the key.

1. Mark and Bob _____ football after school.

2. The _____ team scored ten points.

3. The three _____ gave the team yell.

4. The team listened to the _____ each time
he talked to them.

Write a sentence on each card using a blank in place of a new vocabulary word,
and include on the card three choices to complete the sentence. Write the correct answer on the back of the card.

The space shuttle was carried _____ by the rocket.

abroad   aloft   apart

Provide categorizing activities such as "Pick the word that does not belong with the others":

airplane
horse
truck
window

Instruct students to select the correct word and justify their answer.
Write analogies on each card. Have students fill in the blanks.

Teacher is to students as
doctor is to _____ .

As students are taught words for a selection or chapter, the teacher should write each word and a sentence using the word on 3 × 5 cards. On the back of each card, the teacher should write the source from which the word was taken.

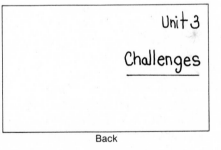

Front   Back

All cards with words from a common source should be held together with a rubber band and filed so that they can be located easily. The cards can be used for many simple games such as:

Draw
Place the cards in a box or paper bag. Have students take turns drawing cards, saying the word, reading the sentence, and telling what the word means.

Build-a-Stack
Deal five cards to each player. Place the remaining cards in the middle. Have students take turns laying down a card, reading the word and the sentence, and telling what the word means. If the student is correct, he or she draws another card from the pile. The student with the largest stack of cards wins.

Round-the-Table
Deal five cards to each player. Place the remaining cards in the middle. Have students take turns drawing a card from the person on their right. If the player can read the sentence on the card and explain the meaning of the underlined word, he or she lays the card down, and the student from whom the card was drawn takes a card from the stack in the middle. Once the middle stack is depleted, students continue around the table until one person runs out of cards. The person with the most cards read is the winner.

Using these sets of word cards, the teacher can create many meaningful practice activities with little preparation. In addition, students can use the cards to practice vocabulary with a partner during free time or when other work is finished.

The vocabulary atmosphere of the classroom stimulates students to learn words and leads students to develop word ownership. Constant awareness of words helps students see the importance of learning words.

PRETEACHING VOCABULARY

Preteaching vocabulary can accomplish three goals. It can

1. help students learn the meanings of important words in the selection,
2. help students learn to pronounce any key-concept words that might cause them difficulty in reading the selection,
3. ultimately help students develop a large stock of meaning vocabulary that eventually becomes instant-recognition vocabulary.

Research indicates a strong relationship between meaning vocabulary and comprehension (Johnston, 1981). However, the evidence does not show a causal relationship. Some researchers who have examined the effects of the preteaching of vocabulary on comprehension have reached positive conclusions; others have reached negative conclusions (Tierney and Cunningham, 1984). Still, it is defensible for teachers to devote *some* instructional time to the teaching of vocabulary before selections are read. The strength of the relationship between vocabulary and comprehension and the fact that some studies on the preteaching of vocabulary have produced positive results are sufficient justification for teachers to include this component in the comprehension program. However, the teacher should follow several guidelines that are supported by the research when preteaching vocabulary:

1. Preteach only the significant, key-concept words for a selection (Beck, Perfetti, and McKeown, 1982). If it seems necessary to teach a large number of words, the material assigned is too difficult for the students or is too far removed from their backgrounds.
2. Develop the words to be pretaught in written context reflecting the context in which they will be used in the selection (Gipe, 1978-79). If possible, words should be grouped into topical or semantic categories (Stevens, 1982).

3. Thoroughly teach the words (Jenkins, Pany, and Schreck, 1978). Teachers should not gloss over the words, but should instead take time to discuss word meanings in depth and have students give sufficient examples to make certain they understand the words.
4. Integrate the preteaching of vocabulary into the background development for the selection. Teachers should discuss with students the relationship between the words they are being taught and the concepts they will need to understand the selection.

These four principles should guide the preteaching of key-concept vocabulary. Teachers should always remember that the teaching of large numbers of unrelated words is not likely to lead to improved vocabulary learning or improved comprehension.

Selecting Words to Preteach

Each teacher must decide which words to teach students before they read a selection. The teacher should use as a guide the words suggested for preteaching in the teacher's guides of basal readers and content textbooks. However, teachers may find that as students gain more experience in reading, the words listed in the guide may not seem like the right words for their students. Therefore, it is ultimately the teacher's responsibility to select the words that should be pretaught, and that decision must be based on the students' abilities. Although there is no absolute, definitive answer to which words should be pretaught before material is read, there are four questions the teacher can ask that may facilitate this decision-making process. Before applying the questions, however, the teacher must read the selection under consideration to determine its general story line or key ideas. This procedure is the same as that suggested in Chapter 3 for determining which background to develop. If the text is a narrative, the teacher should develop a map of the story; if it is expository, the teacher should make a list of the main ideas (see Chapter 3). Each of the following questions should then be addressed:

1. *Which words in the selection are likely to cause the students difficulty?*
   Each group of students will have different backgrounds and different reading skills, which the teacher must take into account when determining the words that should be pretaught for a selection. Students with limited backgrounds will have greater needs in learning the words from a selection than will those with more experiences. Students with greater abilities to decode words and independently determine meanings will encounter fewer words that will cause them difficulty in a selection than will those with lesser skills in these areas. For example, if students have the skills to independently determine the pronunciations and meanings of words and the words are already in their oral language backgrounds, the teacher will probably not have to conduct vocabulary preteaching or will be able to conduct less preteaching than for other words. Students can deal with these words as they encounter them in

their reading. Therefore, in answering this question, the teacher must think about the students' overall backgrounds of experience, their abilities to decode words, and their abilities to independently determine word meanings. It should be with these points in mind that the teacher determines the words that are likely to cause students difficulty as they read the selection. The decision will still be somewhat arbitrary, but it will be much less so when guided by the points suggested here.

2. *Which of the words identified are key-concept words from the selection?*

Key-concept words are the words that relate most directly to the overall intent or main ideas developed in the selection. The teacher's choice of key-concept words is influenced by what the teacher wants the students to learn as a result of reading the text. The key-concept words are the major meaning carriers in a selection and are much like the words in a telegram:

Mom-Dad

Send $200.00 for school.

Love,
Bill

The words in the telegram convey the intended meaning without explanation. Key-concept words from a selection do the same thing—they carry much of the meaning intended. The teacher must look over the words selected in answer to Question 1 and identify the key-concept words. They are the words that should be pretaught; the other words should be dropped from the list. If there are a large number of words on the list that are not key-concept words and are likely to cause students difficulty, the text is probably too difficult for students and its use should be reevaluated.

3. *Which of the key-concept words identified are adequately defined and/or have pronunciation clues in the text?*

Some of the key-concept words will be defined in the text through context clues or by direct definitions. Further, pronunciation guides may be given for words that are not likely to be in the students' oral vocabularies and backgrounds of experience. A word does not have to be pretaught if the text contains adequate clues to the word's meaning and pronunciation. Students will be able to determine such words on their own. These words can be deleted from the list.

4. *Will students be able to define and/or pronounce any of the words remaining on the list by using structural analysis (prefixes, suffixes, root words, or base words)?*

Some of the key-concept words remaining on the list will include structural elements that students can use to determine pronunciation and/or meaning. If students know how to use these elements, the words containing them will not need to be taught.

The words remaining on the list are the ones that the teacher should teach before students read the selection. These are the words that relate most directly to the key concepts and do not have sufficient clues in the text for students to determine meaning on their own. By the time the teacher answers all four questions, the number of words on the list should have been reduced considerably. If the number exceeds five or six, the vocabulary should be developed over several days before the selection is read. If the teacher consistently finds that a large number of words must be pretaught for the chapters in a text or for selections in a basal reader, the difficulty level of the text probably exceeds the students' abilities.

Remember that there is no absolute or right way to select the words to teach before students read a selection. At the primary levels, teachers should seriously consider the words suggested in the teacher's guides because they include many of the basic or high-frequency words that students must learn. At the intermediate levels, teachers will need to make more decisions about which words to preteach. In making these decisions, teachers must always consider the students' backgrounds of experience and decoding abilities in relation to the key concepts of the selection. The words selected for preteaching should be the words that are most likely to assist the student in building background for the selection and comprehending it. Figure 4.2 summarizes the decision-making steps suggested in this section for identifying words that should be pretaught. The example that follows (Example 4.2) can be used to illustrate how a teacher would think through this process when selecting the words to preteach for the narrative, "The White Stallion." Read the narrative before studying the analysis; the story is approximately third-grade level of difficulty.

Which Words Should Be Pretaught?

First, read "The White Stallion," a narrative selection, to determine the general story line. This is a story about how a little girl, Gretchen, was saved by a wild, white stallion; the story takes place during pioneer times. The story shows how wild things can be helpful. One of the points that should be discussed after students have read the selection is whether this really could have happened.

Next, think about the backgrounds and reading abilities of the students in relation to the selection. Assume that the students who are going to read this selection are able to read third-grade level material, have fairly well-developed backgrounds of experience, and have fairly adequate skills for determining pronunciation and meaning of words. With these points in mind, identify the words that might cause students difficulty. The words might include

> Conestoga wagons,
> household goods,
> mustangs,
> mare,
> Guadaloupe River,
> stallion,
> cornmeal,
> faithful,
> coyote.

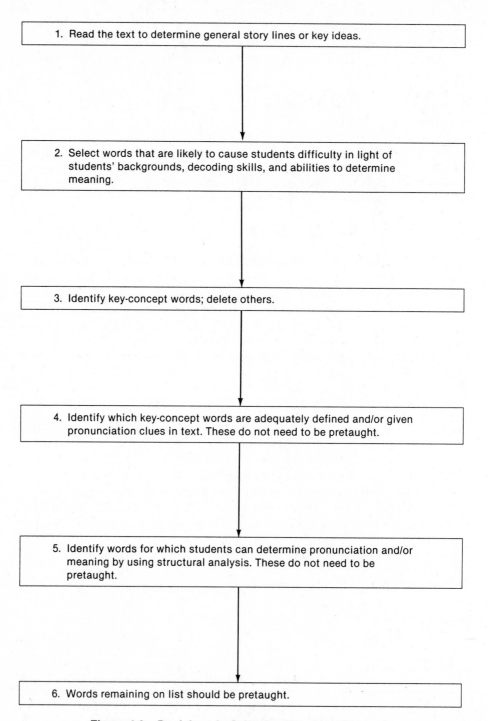

1. Read the text to determine general story lines or key ideas.

2. Select words that are likely to cause students difficulty in light of students' backgrounds, decoding skills, and abilities to determine meaning.

3. Identify key-concept words; delete others.

4. Identify which key-concept words are adequately defined and/or given pronunciation clues in text. These do not need to be pretaught.

5. Identify words for which students can determine pronunciation and/or meaning by using structural analysis. These do not need to be pretaught.

6. Words remaining on list should be pretaught.

Figure 4.2   Decisions in Selecting Words to Preteach

The White Stallion

by Elizabeth Shub

Long ago, a girl named Gretchen was on a
horse that strayed from the wagon train.
When Gretchen became surrounded by a herd
of wild horses, would the white stallion
be able to rescue her?

26

This is a story that has been told in Gretchen's family for many, many years. It is about an adventure Gretchen's great-great-grandmother was believed to have had when she was a girl about Gretchen's age. Gretchen's mother is telling the story to Gretchen.

It was 1845. Three families were on their way West. They planned to settle there. They traveled in covered wagons. Each wagon was drawn by four horses. These wagons were called Conestoga wagons.

Gretchen and her family were in the last wagon. Mother and Father sat on the driver's seat. The children were inside with the household goods. Bedding, blankets, pots and pans, a table, chairs, and a dresser took up most of the space.

There was not much room left for Trudy, John, Billy, and Gretchen. Gretchen was the youngest.

Behind the wagon walked Anna, the family's old mare. She was not tied to the wagon but followed faithfully. She carried two sacks of cornmeal on her back.

It was hot in the afternoon sun, and the children were too warm. The wagon cover shaded them, but little air came in through the openings at the front and back.

27

John kicked Billy. Billy pushed him, and he bumped Gretchen. Trudy, the oldest, who was trying to read, asked them to be good. Their quarrel was stopped by Father's voice.

"Quick, everybody! Look at the mustangs."

The children rushed to the back of the wagon. In the distance, they could see the wild horses. The horses galloped away and, in minutes, were out of sight.

"Look at Anna," John said.

The old mare stood still. She had turned her head toward the mustangs. Her usually floppy ears were lifted high. The wagon had moved some distance before Anna trotted after it.

It was hotter than ever inside.

"Father," Gretchen called, "may I ride on Anna for a while?"

Father stopped the wagon and came to the back. He lifted Gretchen onto the mare. The cornmeal sacks made a nice seat. He tied her onto the mare carefully so that she would not fall off.

As the wagon train moved on, Gretchen fell asleep in the warmth of the sun. The wagon train was following a trail in Texas along the Guadaloupe River. The back wheel of the first wagon hit a big rock, and a wheel broke off. The whole train stopped. Anna trotted away, with Gretchen sleeping on her back, and no one noticed.

28

The travelers decided to stay there for the night. Children gathered firewood and got water from the river. The grownups prepared food. It was not until the wheel had been fixed, and they were ready to eat, that Gretchen and Anna were missed.

The men tried to follow the mare's tracks but soon lost them. It was getting dark, and there was nothing to do but stay where they were. They would search again at the first sign of light. Faithful Anna, they thought, would return. She probably had found some grass to eat. She would come back when she had eaten all she wanted.

29

Gretchen awoke to the sound of lapping. Anna was drinking noisily from a stream. A short distance away stood about ten wild horses. They were light brown with dark brown stripes down their backs or on their legs.

After Anna had finished drinking, she moved toward the mares. They trotted up to her as if to say hello. Then they crossed necks with Anna. They were so friendly that Gretchen was not afraid. She did not even know that Anna had trotted away from the wagon train.

Suddenly the horses began to nibble at the sacks on Anna's back. They had smelled the cornmeal. In their eagerness, they nipped Gretchen's legs. Frightened, Gretchen screamed and tried to get out of the way. She tried to loosen the ropes that held her, but she could not free herself.

Out of nowhere, there came a great white stallion. He pranced and whinnied. He swished his long white tail. He stood on his hind legs, his white mane flying.

The mares moved out of his way. The white stallion came up to Anna. He carefully bit through the ropes that tied Gretchen. Gently, he took hold of the back of her dress with his teeth and lifted her to the ground. He seemed to motion to the mares with his head, and then he galloped away.

30

31

The mares followed at once, and Anna followed them.

Gretchen was left alone. She did not know what to do. "Father will find me soon," she said out loud to make herself feel better. She was hungry, but there was nothing to eat. She walked to the stream to get a drink of water. Then she sat down on a rock to wait.

Gretchen waited and waited, but there was no sign of Father, and no sign of Anna. The sun went down. It began to get dark. "Anna!" Gretchen called. "Anna! Anna! Anna!" There was no answering sound.

Gretchen sat up frightened. She heard the sound of a coyote, but it sounded as if it were far away.

She heard the sound of leaves and the call of redbirds. Gretchen began to cry. She made a place for herself on some dry leaves next to a tree. She curled up against the tree and cried until she fell asleep.

Morning light woke Gretchen. The stream sparkled in the sunlight. Gretchen washed her face and took a drink of water from the clear stream. She looked for Anna. She called her name, but Anna did not come. Gretchen was so hungry that she tried to eat some grass, but it had a nasty taste. She sat on her rock near the stream.

She looked at the red spots on her legs where she had been nipped by the horses. Then she began to cry again. A rabbit came by. It looked at her in such a funny way that she stopped crying. She walked along the stream. She knew she must not go far. "If you are lost," Mother had warned, "stay where you are. That will make it easier to find you." Gretchen walked back to her rock.

It was afternoon when she heard the sound of a galloping horse. A moment later, Anna trotted up to the stream. The sacks of meal were gone. As the old mare took a drink of water, Gretchen hugged her and she patted her back. Anna would find her way back to the wagon train.

33

Gretchen tried to climb on Anna's back, but even without the sacks, the mare was too high. There was a fallen tree not far away. Gretchen thought she might be able to stand on it to climb onto the mare. She tugged at Anna, but Anna would not move. Gretchen pulled and pushed, but Anna wouldn't move.

Then she heard hoofbeats coming up behind her. Before she could turn around, she felt something pulling at the collar of her dress. It was the white stallion. Again he lifted Gretchen by the back of her dress and sat her on Anna's back. He nuzzled and pushed the old mare. Anna began to walk.

The white stallion walked close behind Anna for a moment. Then, as if to say good-by, he stood on his hind legs, whinnied, and galloped away.

Gretchen always believed that the white stallion had told Anna to take her back to the wagon train. For that is what Anna did.

Long ago, a proud white stallion roamed the plains of Texas. Cowboys said he was the greatest horse that ever lived. And Gretchen must have felt that the cowboys were right.

Source: Entire text of THE WHITE STALLION by Elizabeth Shub. Copyright © 1982 by Elizabeth Shub. Adapted by permission of Greenwillow Books (A Division of William Morrow & Company). In William K. Durr et al.: *Caravans*, pp. 26–35 (Houghton Mifflin Reading), 1986.

The next point to consider is whether these words are key-concept words for this selection. Think about each word in relation to what you learned from reading the selection; you will see that all the words except Guadaloupe River and coyote relate directly to the general story line and setting. However, Guadaloupe River and coyote might cause students some difficulty—one is a foreign name for which the text offers no pronunciation clues, and the other, coyote, is a difficult word for many students to pronounce and some may not know its meaning. For these reasons, both words should remain on the list of words to preteach. All other words should remain on the list because they are key-concept words.

Next, consider which words are defined adequately in the text. Household goods, a term that might be new to some students, is defined through the context, and students should be able to use what they know about compound words to determine its pronunciation. Conestoga wagon is also defined in the text, but some students may have trouble with its pronunciation. Therefore, there is no reason to preteach household goods, but there is reason to teach Conestoga wagon. Eliminate household goods from the list of words to preteach.

Examine the remaining words on the list to determine whether students can figure out any of their pronunciations and/or meanings by structural analysis. Two of the words, cornmeal and faithful, seem to fit into this category. Students should have no trouble figuring out the pronunciation and meaning of cornmeal using their knowledge of compound words and their prior experience. Faithful, a word formed by a base word (faith) and suffix (ful), should also be an easy word for students to analyze; they have learned the suffix *ful* and they know the meaning of *faith*. Therefore, cornmeal and faithful do not need to be pretaught.

The list of words that have to be pretaught has been reduced to six:

> Conestoga wagon
> mustangs
> mare
> Guadaloupe River
> stallion
> coyote

These are the words that are likely to cause students difficulty in reading the selection, "The White Stallion," and should be pretaught. All except Guadaloupe River and coyote are key-concept words; however, these exceptions also need to be pretaught because of the problems they might cause some students. All six words should be pretaught.

Preteaching Strategies

The ultimate focus of preteaching vocabulary is on helping students learn the meanings of key-concept words for a selection. However, in the process of learning vocabulary, students are required to make use of their decoding skills, such as phonics, to determine the pronunciations of words. Students (and teachers) should see that the decoding skills help students figure out the pronunciations of words and at the same time assist them in determining word meanings.

Seven strategies for preteaching vocabulary will be presented. The teacher should select the strategies that will work best, depending on

1. the backgrounds of the students,
2. the word attack abilities of the students,
3. the type of words to be taught.

As was already noted, words that are in the students' oral vocabularies will be easier to teach because students already know their meanings. Students must only learn to associate the meanings with the graphic symbols for the words. At the primary levels, the words that are pretaught will already be a part of most students' oral vocabularies. At the intermediate levels and beyond, the situation changes; some words that must be pretaught will not be in the students' oral vocabularies. These words will require more oral development and meaning development as a part of vocabulary preteaching. Therefore, the teacher must consider the students' vocabulary backgrounds when selecting preteaching strategies.

The teacher must also consider the students' word attack abilities. Strategies that incorporate skills the students do not know how to use should not be chosen.

Finally, the teacher must consider the characteristics of the words to be pretaught. All strategies are not equally good for teaching all words. For example, words with structural elements such as prefixes are best taught with a strategy that focuses the students' attention on these elements.

The concept of direct instruction should be an integral part of whatever strategy is chosen for preteaching vocabulary. The following examples (Examples 4.3 to 4.9) illustrate seven strategies that can be used to teach many different words. Each strategy is presented in the same format with examples to illustrate how it can be used. The teacher may often incorporate several strategies into the same lesson to accommodate the different types of words that must be taught.

EXAMPLE 4.3 STRATEGY FOR CONTEXT PLUS PHONICS ————

Purpose

To direct students in applying phonic skills and context clues to determine the pronunciations and meanings of words.

When To Use

This strategy should be used after students have learned to use phonics and context clues. It is mainly used for words that are a part of the students' background experiences and oral language; determining pronunciation of such words should lead to meaning. In the primary grades, these words need to be pretaught. In the intermediate levels and beyond, most students will be able to use this strategy independently. If students do not have the words as part of their oral language vocabularies, more extensive meaning development will be necessary in Step 8.

Materials

Chalkboard, overhead projector, chart, or prepared sentence strips.

Procedures

Step 1: Remind students that they are going to use skills they have already learned to figure out some new words. Give a brief example to help them review and recall the skills they are going to use. For context clues, write a sentence like the following on the chalkboard:

Bob was a _____ boy. He always had fun.

Ask students what word would fit in the sentence. Accept all reasonable answers and discuss with students how they knew what word to put in the slot. For decoding skills, write two or three words on the chalkboard that students know and that illustrate a particular decoding skill. For example, to review digraphs, write the following words on the board:

ship
shoe
show

Have students read the words and note the *sh*. (This should be done very quickly.)

After you review context clues and decoding skills with your students, stress that they will now be using these skills to help them pronounce some new words.

Step 2: Write a sentence or sentences on the chalkboard, and underline the word to be pretaught.

Help me stop that cat. It wants to get the <u>fish</u>.

Step 3: Have students read the sentence(s) to themselves, trying to determine the underlined word.

Step 4: Have a student read the sentence(s) aloud.

Step 5: If students are unable to pronounce the underlined word, tell them to read the sentence(s) again, trying to use the sense of the other words and the letter sounds to figure out what the word is. If students are still unable to determine the word, read the sentence(s) aloud leaving a blank for the underlined word. Have students try to supply the word that would fit in the blank. If students are still unable to come up with the word, read it for them.

Step 6: Ask students how they knew this word was not *bird*. (It doesn't begin with the correct sounds; this helps students see that they are using phonics.)

Step 7: Ask students how they knew this word was not *finish*. (*Finish* doesn't make sense in the sentence; this helps students see that they are using context.)

Step 8: Discuss the meaning of the word *fish*.

Step 9: Have students use the new word in another sentence.

Comments

Context in combination with phonics is one of the most significant identifiers of words for readers. Therefore, the strategy for using these skills should be reinforced many times when preteaching vocabulary.

The teacher must be certain that students have learned the decoding skills required to analyze the words and that they know how to use context clues. More than one decoding skill can be used at a time in conjunction with context clues, provided the students know how to use each of the decoding skills. Teachers must remember that students need to read new words in written context, and they need to be given the opportunity to figure out the meanings of words for themselves. When teaching vocabulary, teachers are often too quick to tell students what a new word is, instead of following the necessary procedures to help students figure it out for themselves. *This situation should be avoided.*

EXAMPLE 4.4 STRATEGY FOR CONTEXT CLUES

Purpose

To direct students in using context clues to determine the meanings of words.

When To Use

This strategy can be used to preteach any word after students have learned to use context clues. It is a sound strategy to use when students have not been taught the phonic or structural skills needed to analyze a word or when the word is not a part of the students' oral language vocabularies. Students will perform better with this strategy if the word being taught is in their background experience; however, the strategy can also be used when the word is not a part of the students' backgrounds, provided that sufficient time is allotted to developing the needed background.

Materials

Chalkboard, overhead projector, chart, or prepared sentence strips.

Procedures

Step 1: Tell students that they are going to use the words in a sentence or paragraph that are familiar to them to figure out some new words. Briefly review the use of context clues by reading a sentence such as the following to students and having them fill in the blank:

The children laughed and played in the _____ as they built the snowman.

Ask students how they arrived at their answers. Point out that they used the other words in the sentence to help them determine a word that would fit in the blank.

Tell them that they should try to use context clues to figure out the underlined words in the sentences you are now going to give them.

Step 2: Write a sentence on the board, such as the following. The sentence should include a context clue that will help students determine the meaning of the underlined word. (For a discussion of types of context clues, see page 166.)

The leaves on the trees were green.

or

An interstate is a highway where many cars travel rapidly without having to stop for stop signs or stoplights.

Step 3: Direct students to read the sentence to themselves, trying to figure out the underlined word.

Step 4: Have a student read the sentence aloud. If the student pronounces the new word incorrectly, tell the students the correct pronunciation.

Step 5: Ask students what they think the new word means, and have them note clues in the sentence that helped them determine the meaning. Use pictures, objects, or other concrete examples to develop additional background if students need it to understand the meaning of the word.

Step 6: Have students think of other sentences using the word. Print at least one sentence on the chalkboard, and underline the new word. Then have a student other than the one who gave you the sentence read the sentence aloud. Conclude by restating the meaning of the word.

Comments

This strategy focuses on the application of context clues to determine word meaning. Even as students are using this strategy, they are probably using phonics to help them verify the words; there can never be a pure context strategy. The sentences the teacher writes on the board should provide strong enough context clues to assist the students in determining the meanings of the new words. If students are unable to figure out the meaning of a word after using the steps suggested, the teacher should tell them the meaning, but the teacher shouldn't be too quick to do this.

EXAMPLE 4.5   STRATEGY FOR STRUCTURAL ANALYSIS ————

Purpose

To direct students in applying structural analysis skills to determine the pronunciations and meanings of words.

When To Use

This strategy should be used after students have learned the particular structural analysis skills they will need to analyze the word under consideration. If the students' backgrounds and experiences do not include the words being taught, more time will have to be devoted to developing meaning after the initial meaning analysis.

Materials

Chalkboard, overhead projector, chart, or prepared sentence strips.

Procedures

Step 1: Tell students that they are going to use skills they have already learned to determine the pronunciation and meaning of some new words. Give a brief example to help them recall the type of skill they are going to use. For practice in the skill of using prefixes plus base words to determine meaning, write a word such as *unhappy* on the board. Point out that both the pronunciation and meaning of this word can be determined by looking at the prefix *un* and the base word *happy*. *Un* means not, and *happy* means glad, excited, or pleased. Therefore, the meaning of *unhappy* is "not glad, not excited, or not pleased."

Step 2: Write another sentence on the board that includes a new word made up of a prefix and base word. Underline the new word.

It is <u>unwise</u> to eat too much food.

Direct students to read the sentence to themselves, using the context plus word structure to figure out the pronunciation of the underlined word. Do not tell them the word.

Step 3: If students are unable to pronounce the word, break the word into parts and review the structural elements:

un wise

This step helps students relate directly the structural analysis skills being applied. If students are still unable to pronounce the word, read the sentence aloud leaving a blank for the underlined word, and asking them to look at the word on the board and try to supply the word that would fill in the blank.

It is _____ to eat too much food.

If students still fail to figure out the word, tell them what it is.

Step 4: Have students explain the meaning of the word by pointing out the meaning of each of the structural parts:

```
     un = not
+   wise = intelligent
   unwise = not intelligent
```

Step 5: Have students give several sentences using the word. Print at least one of the sentences on the board and ask a student other than the one who gave you the sentence to read it aloud.

Comments

This strategy focuses on the use of structural analysis skills to determine word pronunciation and meaning. If several words using the same structural elements are being taught at once, the teacher can skip Step 1 after the initial word is introduced.

EXAMPLE 4.6 STRATEGY FOR WEBBING ───────

Purpose

To teach students new vocabulary by helping them build relationships among words from a selection.

When To Use

This strategy should be used for words that students already have in their background experiences. To use this strategy effectively, students should have well-developed phonic and structural analysis skills.

Materials

Chalkboard, overhead projector, or large sheets of paper.

Procedures

Step 1: Select a group of key-concept words from a selection to be read.

Step 2: Tell students that they are going to learn some words that relate to the selection they are going to read. Print the words in a list on the chalkboard:

> covered wagon
> dangerous
> yoke
> oxen
> fever
> mules
> journey

Have students read the words aloud or read the words to them. (Alternatively, you can present the words in sentences and encourage students to use their decoding skills plus context to figure out the pronunciations of the words.)

Step 3: Select one word from the list and print it in a separate area of the chalkboard. Ask a student to read the word.

> dangerous

Discuss the meaning of *dangerous*. If the meaning given by the student differs from that used in the story, elicit or give the meaning appropriate to the story.

Step 4: Select another word. Write it somewhere near the first word.

dangerous

fever

Have a student read the new word, or read the word to the class. Discuss the meaning of the new word, *fever*. Then ask students if this word can be related to the first word. If students see a relationship between the two words, ask them to explain how the words are related, and draw a line between the words (or have a student draw the line). If students do not see a relationship, give them some possibilities; in most instances students will see a variety of relationships.

dangerous
fever

Step 5: Continue adding words to the web until all words from the list have been used. As each new word is added, discuss how it might be related to others already presented, and draw lines to show the relationships. A completed web might look like this:

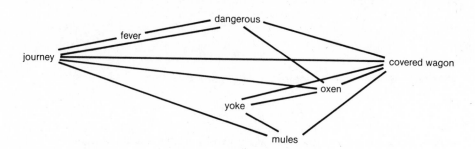

Step 6: Have students give sentences using each word. Print the sentences on the chalkboard and ask students to read them aloud. Underline the new word in each sentence.

The fire was <u>dangerous</u>.

Comments

This strategy builds on the students' backgrounds and also helps the students develop a framework or schema for reading the material. It is an excellent means of weaving together background and vocabulary development. Webbing can aid students in making predictions about the upcoming selection. It can also be used as a specific vocabulary lesson following the reading of a selection to expand and enrich vocabulary. (See page 187.)

EXAMPLE 4.7   STRATEGY FOR LISTENING-DISCUSSING-READING —

Purpose

To help students develop the oral language concept of a word and learn the word's meaning.

When To Use

This strategy should be used when the reader has limited or no oral language experience with the words being taught.

Materials

Chalkboard, overhead projector, large sheets of paper, prepared sentences or paragraphs using the words.

Procedures

Step 1:   Tell students that you want them to listen as you read a paragraph (or sentences) aloud and tell you what the passage is about:

The troops from the king's army <u>liberated</u> the prisoners, who were all glad to be free. The real <u>predicament</u> now faced by the freed captives was finding enough food to eat.

Step 2:   Discuss the passage with students, asking such questions as

What did the troops do?
What problem did the freed prisoners face?
What does *liberated* mean?
What does *predicament* mean?

Tell students the meanings of the two words if they are unable to determine the meanings from their listening.

Step 3:   Read the paragraph (or sentences) aloud again, asking students to pay particular attention to the words *liberated* and *predicament*.

Step 4:   Print the words *liberated* and *predicament* on the chalkboard.

Step 5:   Have students listen to another paragraph and select one of the two words to fill in each blank:

The baby bear was in a _____ ; it was caught in the hunter's trap. It knew it could not be _____ until someone came to help it.

Step 6:   Ask students to give other oral sentences using the words being taught. Further discuss the meanings as needed.

Step 7:   Write one of the students' sentences using each word on the chalkboard and have students other than the ones who gave you the sentences read them aloud.

Comments

The listening development portion of this strategy may need to be conducted over several days or weeks to ensure that students have sufficient oral language experiences with the new words. This type of development can be planned in advance of particular readings and can be used to build the needed background and vocabulary for selections or chapters.

EXAMPLE 4.8 STRATEGY FOR SELF-EVALUATION

Purpose

To teach students to be responsible for determining on their own the meaning and pronunciation of words they do not know in a selection.

When To Use

This strategy should be used after students have developed sufficient independence in reading to begin to become responsible for their own learning.

Materials

Chalkboard, overhead projector, or student notebooks in which students compile their own lists of words, using each word in a sentence.

Procedure

Step 1: Provide students with a list of key words from a selection (or have students skim a selection to locate the words they don't know).

> rocket
> blast-off
> atmosphere
> space shuttle
> tracking station

Step 2: Ask students to tell you if there are any words on the list that they cannot pronounce or understand. Circle the words they identify.

> rocket
> blast-off
> (atmosphere)
> space shuttle
> (tracking station)

Step 3:   Have students give a sentence for each word that you have not circled. Discuss the words and clarify their meanings, if necessary. Make certain that the sentences reflect the meaning of the words as they are used in the selection.

Step 4:   If a student in the group thinks he or she knows the meaning of one of the circled words, have the student give a sentence using the word. With the students, look the word up in the dictionary to verify the student's use of the word, and thoroughly discuss its meaning. Have the student who asked that the word be circled give another sentence using the word.

Step 5:   If any of the circled words cannot be defined in this way, have students locate them in the dictionary and use them in a sentence. (Do not ask students to write the definitions.) Be certain the meaning discussed relates to the meaning used in the selection. (Students can put the new words and sentences in their vocabulary notebooks.)

Comments

This strategy can be used as soon as students begin to develop some independence in reading. It is a good strategy to use at the intermediate and junior high levels because it is different from what students have become accustomed to in being taught new words. It also begins to put the responsibility for determining the meanings and pronunciations of the words in a selection on the students.

EXAMPLE 4.9   STRATEGY FOR DICTIONARY SKILLS

Purpose

To direct students in using a dictionary to determine word meanings and pronunciations.

When To Use

This strategy can be used to teach words for which students lack background. Students must, however, already know how to use the dictionary to determine word meanings. (See page 176 for a discussion on teaching dictionary skills.)

Materials

Chalkboard or overhead projector and dictionaries appropriate to the students' reading level.

Procedure

Step 1:   Briefly remind students that the dictionary can be used to determine both the pronunciation and meanings of words.

Step 2:   Print the word to be taught on the chalkboard. For example:

march

Direct students to locate the word in the dictionary.

Step 3:   Once students have found the word, have a student give the pronunciation. Discuss any variations in correct pronunciation.

Step 4:   Have another student read the meanings given.

Step 5:   If more than one meaning is given, print a sentence on the board using the word as it is used in the selection. Underline the new word.

The children had to <u>march</u> to bed.

Have students select the meaning from the dictionary that matches the sentence. Then have students give another sentence using the same meaning of the word. (If only one meaning is given in the dictionary, do not devise a sentence yourself, but instead have students give a sentence using the word and print that sentence on the board. Have students read the sentence aloud.)

Step 6:   Continue in this pattern until all words to be pretaught have been discussed.

Comments

Students can learn to use the dictionary effectively if directed in this manner. Teachers should be cautious to not teach dictionary skills by having students look up many words and write their definitions. The dictionary has often become distasteful to students because of this practice. The emphasis in teaching reading vocabulary using the dictionary should be on encouraging students to use the dictionary as a valuable tool for determining word pronunciations and meanings.

This strategy can be varied by having individual students or pairs of students locate different words in the dictionary and share their pronunciations and meanings with the group. Have students give a sentence using the word, and have other students try to figure out the meaning. Remember: Students should *not* be required to look up lists of words and write definitions.

The strategies for preteaching vocabulary, presented in Examples 4.3 to 4.9, can be varied to keep interest high, but the basic steps in the strategies should be retained. In some lessons, the teacher will find it necessary to use only one strategy, while in other lessons, several strategies will have to be used in order to introduce several different types of words.

The lesson shown in Example 4.10 illustrates the background and readiness portion of the directed reading lesson using direct instruction for the selection "The White Stallion," which is reprinted on page 139. Note how background development and vocabulary teaching are closely related.

EXAMPLE 4.10 SAMPLE LESSON FOR DEVELOPING BACKGROUND AND VOCABULARY ━━━━━━━━━━━

Purposes

1. To help students develop the following background:

    knowing about travel in pioneer days,
    understanding how wild things might sometimes be helpful to people.

2. To teach the words Conestoga wagon, mustangs, Guadaloupe River, mare, stallion, coyote.

Materials

Overhead projector or chalkboard.

Teaching

Letting Students Know What They Are Going to Learn
Say: You didn't live in pioneer days, but you have read about or seen on TV or in the movies how pioneers lived. Today, you are going to think about some ideas and learn some words that will help you understand our next story, which is about a pioneer family. How did pioneers travel? (Students respond. Discuss their suggestions and then write the following sentence on the chalkboard:

Pioneers traveled in <u>Conestoga wagons</u>, or covered wagons with cloth tops.

Have a student read the sentence aloud.)

Modeling
Say: What is a Conestoga wagon? (Students respond. Have students use *Conestoga wagon* in another sentence and discuss its meaning.)
Say: As pioneers traveled, there were many wild animals that they had to face. Can you think of any? (Students respond. Write the following sentences on the chalkboard:

There were many <u>mustangs</u> or wild horses in pioneer times. The <u>coyote</u>, an animal that is like a wolf, was often seen and heard by pioneers.

Ask students to read each sentence aloud. If no student is able to do so, read the sentences to them. Discuss the underlined words, and have students give another sentence using each word.)
Say: The pioneers depended on horses they had tamed for work and travel. However, there were also wild horses that roamed the countryside. (Write the following sentences on the board:

A <u>mare</u> is a female horse. A <u>stallion</u> is an adult male horse.

Have students read the sentences, or read them to the students. Have students give other sentences using the underlined words.)

Say: The story we are going to read today takes place in Texas as a pioneer family is traveling near the Guadaloupe River. (Write the following sentence on the board:

The Guadaloupe River is in Texas.

Have a student read this sentence aloud.)

Providing Guided Practice with New Vocabulary

Say: We have talked about six new words today. (List the words on the board —Conestoga wagon, mustangs, mare, Guadaloupe River, stallion, coyote.)

Say: I want you to think of sentences using each of these words. (Write at least one of the sentences for each word on the chalkboard, and have students read the sentences aloud. Ask a student to underline the new word in each sentence.)

Say: As pioneers traveled, they had to live with the wild creatures like the horses and the coyotes. Are wild things usually helpful? (Students respond.) How do you think wild things can help you? (Students respond. Help them bring out the idea that sometimes wild things can be helpful.)

Summarizing Vocabulary and Background

Say: Today, we have talked about pioneers and some words that are in our next story. What were the words? (Students respond. List the words again for students.) What ideas have we discussed about pioneers as they traveled? (Students respond. Help them bring out the following points:

Pioneers traveled in Conestoga wagons.
They used horses for travel, but there were also wild animals including
    horses that roamed the countryside.
Wild things can sometimes be helpful to people.)

Practicing

Some students will need independent practice with the new words before they read the selection. For others, it will be enough to review the words after the reading has been completed. The following exercise can be used for independent practice with the vocabulary taught for "The White Stallion." The independent practice would occur before students read the selection.

Name _____ Date _____

Directions: Following are six definitions and a list of words. Read the definitions and determine which word goes with each. Write that word in the spaces next to the number of the definition. If your answers are correct, the letters that fall in the boxes will spell one of the new words. Write that word on the line at the end.

PRETEACHING VOCABULARY

mare	Guadaloupe
coyote	mustangs
stallion	Conestoga

1. A type of covered wagon
2. An adult male horse
3. A wild wolf-like animal
4. A river in Texas
5. Wild horses
6. A female horse

1. ☐ _ _ _ _ _ _ _ _

2. _ _ _ _ _ _☐_

3. _ _☐_ _ _

4. _ _ _ _ _☐_ _ _

5. _ _ _☐_ _ _ _

6. _ _ _☐

New word: _____

Applying

Students will apply the vocabulary that was pretaught when they read the selection, "The White Stallion." They will also be applying other comprehension skills as they read. If no additional skills are being applied, the application proceeds as follows.

Reminding Students of What to Apply
Say: We talked about some new words related to pioneers and how they travel. (Repeat the words; list them on the chalkboard if a day has lapsed between this part of the lesson and the first part.) We also discussed how wild things can sometimes be helpful. Now, we are going to read "The White Stallion."

Have Students Read Text
Say: I want you to read this story about Gretchen and her family to find out what happened to Gretchen. Pay close attention to the new words and the ideas we have discussed. *(Note: This is setting the purpose for reading, which will lead to a better overall understanding of the selection.)*

Discussion Questions to Check Overall Understanding of the Story
Ask students the initial purpose-setting question (the first question listed) and discuss their responses. Then ask the remaining questions to further check students' understanding. The questions follow the order of the story.

1. What happened to Gretchen in this story?
2. Who were the other characters in "The White Stallion"?
3. Where did the story take place?
4. What problem did Gretchen have while riding on Anna?
5. What did the men try to do when they realized Anna and Gretchen were gone?
6. What did the wild horses try to do while Anna was on Gretchen's back?
7. Who took Gretchen off of Anna's back?
8. Who led the mares away from Anna?
9. How did Anna feel when she was all alone?
10. Who came back in the afternoon?
11. How did Gretchen get back on Anna?
12. Who directed Anna to take Gretchen back to the wagon train?

Discussion Questions to Check Application of Vocabulary
1. What caused the old mare, Anna, to lift up her ears and pay attention?
   —The mustangs.
2. Who untied the ropes so Gretchen could get off Anna?
   —The white stallion.
3. What kind of horse was Anna?
   —A mare.

Discussion Questions to Extend Comprehension
1. Why do you think Anna wandered off?
2. How do you think Gretchen felt during this experience? Why?
3. Do you think this story really happened? Why or why not?

Planning Vocabulary Preteaching and Reinforcement

In planning vocabulary preteaching, the teacher must consider not only the points made in this chapter, but also the suggestions given in the teacher's guides for the materials being used. Most basal readers include lists of suggested vocabulary for preteaching. These words are more than likely the key-concept words for the selection, identified by the authors and editors. Each teacher must consider these words in relation to his or her students' backgrounds and reading abilities and must decide whether the identified words are the ones that are important to his or her students. Then, the teacher must consider the strategies suggested for the preteaching of those words and decide whether the strategies meet the needs of his or her students. Example 4.11 is a reprint of a vocabulary preteaching lesson suggested in the Riverside Reading Program.

EXAMPLE 4.11 SAMPLE VOCABULARY PRETEACHING LESSON ——

 1 Preparing to Read

Learn New Words

Instructional Words *Look at page 14. We will use the sentences on this page to learn new words for the next selection. Let's review the steps.*

How to Learn New Words
1. *Look at the letters in the word.*
2. *Think of the sound clues.*
3. *Use the sentence clues.*
4. *Read the word.*

1. astronomers
Use the steps to figure out any unfamiliar words. Look at the letters in the word and think of the sound clues. Use the sentence clues. Then read the word. Read the first sentence. Who can name the word in darker type in the first sentence and tell what the word astronomers means? (**Astronomers:** People who study stars and planets.) *Ask students to explain how sentence clues helped them to know what the word means.*

Have students read the other sentences aloud and explain the meaning of each word in darker type. Students may use the glossary to check word meanings. Brief definitions are provided here for your convenience.

2. **axis** an imaginary line through the North and South Poles
3. **cosmic** dealing with the universe as a whole
4. **craters** bowl-shaped dents in the surface of a moon or planet
5. **diameter** a straight line passing through the center of a circle
6. **equator** an imaginary line around the earth midway between the poles
7. **evaporate** to change to a vapor
8. **intense** very strong
9. **molten** melted
10. **probes** devices sent to gather information

 LEARN NEW WORDS

1. Scientists who study the stars and the planets are called **astronomers.**
2. The earth spins on its **axis**, an imaginary line running through the North and South poles.
3. The science fiction story described **cosmic** explosions taking place far beyond our solar system.
4. In the past, meteors have hit the surface of the moon, leaving deep, hollow **craters** behind.
5. We found the **diameter** of the circle by placing a ruler across the center of the circle and measuring from one side to the other.
6. The imaginary line that goes around the middle of the earth is called the **equator.**
7. My cousin says last summer was hot enough to make all the water in the pond **evaporate.**
8. The heat from the fire was so **intense** that the iron railings on the steps melted.
9. Rock or metal in a hot, liquid state is said to be **molten.**
10. Scientists have sent space **probes** to most of the planets to take photographs and gather information.

GET SET TO READ

What would a voyage to the planets be like? What would you see and learn on such a trip?

Listen as your guide takes you on a grand tour of the planets. Find out why there's no place quite like home.

14

Special Words Before students read the selection, write these names and pronounce them: **Antarctica, Apollo 17, Caribou, Maine, Hawaiian Islands, Jupiter, Martian, Mercury, Olympus Mons, Saturn, Uranus, Venus.**

Finally, write the words **carbon dioxide, eddies, hydrogen, meteor,** and **sulfuric acid** on the chalkboard. To introduce each word: point to it; read the context sentence aloud, omitting the new word; and help students use phonics and context clues.

People breathe in oxygen and breathe out carbon dioxide.

The paper swirled around in eddies of wind above our heads.

Water is made up of two parts hydrogen and one part oxygen.

A bright trail behind the meteor crossed the night sky.

Sulfuric acid is a strong chemical and must be used with care.

Get Set to Read

Before we read, let's review the steps we use to read for meaning.

How to Read for Meaning
1. *Set a purpose for reading.*
2. *Think about what you already know.*
3. *Read the selection.*
4. *Answer the purpose question.*
5. *Apply the information.*

Have students read the Get Set to Read section. *In reading this selection, our purpose will be to answer the question: Why is there nö place in the entire solar system quite like home?*

Discuss the questions in the first paragraph of Get Set to Read. Then ask *Why would you like to make such a voyage across the solar system? After reading the selection, we will answer the purpose question. Then we will see how this information applies to other things we know.*

Source: Leo Fay et al., *Previews,* Teacher's Edition, p. 7. The Riverside Reading Program, Copyright 1986 by The Riverside Publishing Company, Chicago, IL.

Throughout the reading program, the teacher should reinforce the vocabulary that was pretaught. Such reinforcement can come through practice following the initial teaching, through application in other selections beyond the initial selection, as well as through practice during the extension portion of the DRL. It is through repeated application that students develop word ownership.

TEACHING SKILLS TO DETERMINE WORD MEANINGS

For readers to develop their vocabularies and become independent in figuring out word pronunciations and meanings, they must be able to use certain vocabulary skills. Although the teaching of selected key-concept words before students read stories or chapters will help them develop large sight and meaning vocabularies, students must also develop the vocabulary skills that will make it possible for them to figure out the meanings of words independent of the teacher. These vocabulary skills include the use of context clues, structural analysis, and the dictionary. Lessons in each of these skill areas should be taught as part of the skill-building portion of the DRL. The sections that follow present strategies for teaching each of these skills.

Teaching Context Clues

When readers use the familiar words around an unknown word in a sentence, paragraph, or longer text to figure out either the pronunciation or meaning of the unknown word, they are using context clues. Rarely, if ever, does a reader depend on the use of context alone to determine the pronunciation or meaning of an unknown word. In most instances, the reader uses context in combination with phonics, structural analysis, or both to determine the unknown word (Cunningham, 1979).

Mature readers probably use context clues more frequently than any other skill to determine unknown words during reading. As the reader comes to an unknown word in a selection, he or she is likely to skip it and go on to see if the other words in the sentence or paragraph help determine the meaning of the word. Think back to the example of *parlimp* presented earlier in this chapter. The strongest clue to the meaning of *parlimp* was the context even though it did not lead to an exact meaning.

Context clues are most valuable to the reader when the word in question is in his or her oral vocabulary. However, context clues can be helpful even when a word is not in the reader's oral vocabulary. Read the following sentence, paying special attention to the underlined word:

The boots were made of <u>poromeric</u>, a leather substitute, instead of the real thing.

Even if the underlined word is not in your oral vocabulary, the context clue gives you a clear definition of the word. In many instances the context will not give as precise a definition as this example did, but any context clue is valuable in helping the reader reach an approximate meaning for words even when the words are not in the reader's oral vocabulary.

Types of Context Clues

There are many ways in which authors provide context clues, but four methods are most common. Readers must be taught to use these different types of context clues to determine the meaning of unknown words as they read.

Direct Definition—The author directly states the definition of a word in the sentence.

The **submarine** is a ship that can travel completely below the water's surface.

Appositive—The author gives clues to the definition of a word by including in the text a word or statement in apposition to the word.

Sara wore a bright red **fedora**, a hat, to her sister's wedding.

Synonym/Antonym—The author uses a synonym or antonym for a word instead of repeating that word in the passage. Most often this context clue is done with synonyms.

Mark's mother **pampered** him all the time. She *spoiled* him by giving him everything he wanted.

Surrounding Sentences—The author provides clues to a word's meaning in sentences surrounding the word.

The *wickedness of the old man* was known throughout the town. He pulled *many evil tricks*, too numerous to mention. His **vices** were a cause of concern for everyone. Even his own family knew *he was a bad person.*

Strategy for Teaching Context Clues

The strategy outlined here employs direct instruction in teaching context clues. (For a discussion of direct instruction, see Chapter 2.) With this strategy, the teacher develops a sequence of lessons that will lead students to see how to make use of the different types of context clues in their reading.

First, the teacher must help develop the concept of using context to determine word meanings. Instruction can begin in kindergarten with simple oral activities in which students are given sentences with blanks and asked to supply an appropriate word. The type of word that is left out of the sentence should proceed from concrete to abstract. For example:

> *Example A:* On the way to school I saw a _____.
> *Example B:* I like to play _____ with my friends.
> *Example C:* The _____ boy in class makes me laugh.
> *Example D:* I live _____ my mom and dad.

Each answer should be discussed with students, and they should be guided to see that only those words that make sense can be used. The teacher should point out to students that they are using the context, or other words in the sentence, to figure out the possible words to use in completing the sentences.

Teachers can carry out concept-development activities while reading to students or during any instructional period. When older students are being taught context for the first time, concept-development activities should be provided to ensure that the students understand the concept of using context. As soon as students are able to perform these types of tasks, they have developed the concept of using context clues and are ready to be taught how to use specific context clues in their reading.

In the teaching step of direct instruction, the first portion of the lesson is to let the students know exactly what they are going to learn in the lesson and why it is important. The second portion of the lesson is modeling. There are several steps in modeling that can be used to teach each of the specific types of context clues (Cooper et al., 1979). These steps are illustrated in the following sections for the appositive context clue.

Step 1: Develop the Context Clue at the Listening Level: The first part of the modeling process should be checking to see that students can use the context clue while listening. This step in the modeling ensures that students are able to make use of the skill in their oral language.

When modeling the use of the appositive type of context clue, the teacher should read a sentence that includes an appositive context clue to the class.

Say: Listen to the following sentence and tell me the meaning of the word *just.*

It was not just, right or fair, for the little boy to be punished.

The teacher should ask students to tell the meaning of the word *just* in the sentence and how they were able to determine that meaning. If the students are unable to answer, the teacher should tell them the meaning and point out that the words immediately following *just* tell the meaning. It is sometimes useful to reread the example for the students. The teacher should indicate to the students that this is one type of context clue. The age and maturity of the students will determine whether the teacher would tell them this type of context clue is called an appositive.

If students have difficulty with the listening step, the teacher should repeat it with several more examples. For students who have limited oral language abilities, it might be necessary to stop at this point in the modeling and provide several exercises practicing this type of context clue in listening. When students are able to use the context clue in listening activities, they are ready to proceed to the next step of modeling.

Step 2: Model the Context Clue in Reading: In this step of modeling, the teacher shows the students how to use the context clue in their reading and how to verbalize their thinking (thinking aloud) processes. After the teacher models the context clue, the students repeat the same process with another example.

Say: Read this sentence to yourself as I read it aloud and determine the meaning of the word *tender.* (Print the sentence on the chalkboard.)

The president of the club did not <u>tender</u>, or offer, his resignation even though everyone was angry with him.

Say: As I read this sentence, I can figure out the meaning of the word *tender* by using the context clue that follows it. The words set off by commas (point to the commas)—"or offer"—tell me what *tender* means; this type of context clue is called an appositive. Now, I want you to read another sentence and explain how you can determine the meaning of the word *haggard*.

The haggard, tired looking, old man was helped by the people.

After students have read the sentence to themselves, the teacher would instruct one student to repeat the modeling as done by the teacher in the example before. If students need more practice, the teacher should provide additional examples.

The modeling of the use of appositive context clues would be followed by the appropriate guided practice and summary to complete the teaching portion of the DRL. Independent practice and application would follow. Example 4.12 shows a sample practice exercise that can be used for either guided or independent practice for the appositive context clue.

EXAMPLE 4.12   SAMPLE PRACTICE ACTIVITY FOR THE APPOSITIVE CONTEXT CLUE

Directions: Read each sentence and determine the meaning of the underlined word. Circle the words in the sentence that gave you clues to the meaning of the word. Write the meaning of the word on the line below.

1. The urn, a large pot for flowers, was filled with roses.

   _____

2. Everybody carried large flasks, bottles, to use for fresh water.

   _____

3. The old man wore a wescot, a vest, under his coat.

   _____

4. Peonies, large puffy flowers, are beautiful in the spring.

   _____

   _____

To give students practice in applying this skill, the teacher should provide students with a selection to read that contains several examples of the appositive context clue. The teacher should not preteach the words defined by the appositives, but should instead remind students to use what they have learned about context clues when reading the selection. After students have completed the reading, the teacher should ask the students questions where answers would indicate whether the students were able to determine the meanings of the words defined by the context clues; the questions should not require the students to identify the clues.

There are many commercial materials on the market that provide practice with context clues. It should be remembered, however, that these materials are for practice, not teaching. An example of a context clue practice activity is shown in Example 4.13.

Teaching Structural Analysis

Structural analysis is the study of word parts. Students can use the structural elements in words to determine their meanings and pronunciations. The components of structural analysis include:

base words—meaningful linguistic units that can stand alone and contain no smaller meaningful parts; these are also called free morphemes. (re*sell*: sell is the base word)

root words—words from which other words are derived; usually the derivational word is from another language and is a bound morpheme—it cannot stand alone. (Scribble comes from the Latin root scribere meaning to write). Teachers frequently use the terms *base word* and *root word* synonymously, but they are not the same.

prefixes—units of meaning that can be added to the beginnings of base words or root words to change their meanings; these are bound morphemes and cannot stand alone. (*un*happy: "un" is the prefix meaning "not")

suffixes—units of meaning that can be added to the ends of base or root words to change their meanings; these are bound morphemes. (tear*ful*: "ful" is the suffix meaning "full of")

inflectional endings—word parts that can be added to the ends of root or base words to change their case, gender, number, tense, or form; these are bound morphemes. (boy*'s*: possessive case; steward*ess*: gender; tree*s*: number; walk*ed*: tense; funni*est*: form)

compound words—two or more base words that have been combined to form a new word with a meaning that is related to each base word. (run + way = runway)

contractions—shortened forms of two words in which a letter or letters have been replaced by an apostrophe. (do + not = don't; girl + is = girl's)

Readers can use structural analysis to determine the meanings of words that are not in their oral language vocabularies. By knowing the meanings of various parts of words, readers can determine the approximate meaning of the unknown word. For example, if students encounter the word *fearless* in their reading and they know the meanings of the base word *fear* and the suffix *less*, they can determine the meaning of *fearless*. The actual meaning of a word depends on the context in which the word is used. However, structural analysis skills will help the reader begin to determine the meanings of unknown words.

Direct instruction can be used to teach students structural analysis skills. Lessons on structural analysis should be included in the skill-building portion of the

EXAMPLE 4.13   SAMPLE CONTEXT CLUE PRACTICE ACTIVITY ——————

Unit 21

In ten days a tiny baby eats enough food to equal its own weight. An adult takes about five times as long to (1) .... as much food as he (2) ....

1. (A) sold   (B) eat   (C) hide   (D) frozen

2. (A) pays   (B) paints   (C) weighs   (D) looks

The custom of giving Easter eggs is old. People in Egypt painted eggs thousands of years ago. They exchanged them during the new moon in April. The custom meant that life had (3) .... to the (4) ....

3. (A) left   (B) upset   (C) failed   (D) returned

4. (A) earth   (B) dust   (C) paper   (D) cupboard

The Taj Mahal in India is one of the most beautiful buildings in the world. Built by an Indian ruler in memory of his wife, the building is over three hundred years old. It (5) .... many (6) ....

5. (A) hides   (B) lost   (C) scares   (D) attracts

6. (A) babies   (B) insects   (C) visitors   (D) fish

Bees air-condition their hives. They fan their wings to push out the hot air. After they spread water on the combs, they (7) .... again to make the (8) .... cool.

7. (A) sleep   (B) fan   (C) cut   (D) sing

8. (A) brushes   (B) lost   (C) air   (D) time

Single steers that run away from a herd are often called "windies." Cowboys who try to overtake the "windies" are likely to be (9) .... of (10) .... before the job is done.

9. (A) silent   (B) time   (C) eat   (D) out

10. (A) dipper   (B) message   (C) wind   (D) rainbow

Source: Robert A. Boning, *Using the Context*, Unit 21. Baldwin, NY: Barnell Loft, Ltd., 1976. Used by permission.

DRL. However, they are also an appropriate part of the extension portion of the lesson. There, teachers can expand on the structural elements that students encountered in the reading.

Strategy for Teaching Prefixes, Suffixes, Inflectional Endings, Base Words, and Root Words

Students can begin to learn prefixes, suffixes, inflectional endings, base words, and root words as soon as they have developed a basic reading vocabulary. The following general steps for modeling can be utilized in direct instruction for teaching all these elements. The steps illustrate the teaching of base words and the prefix *un*.

Step 1: Begin with a base word that students know. Print it on the board:

happy

Ask students what the word is and what it means.

Step 2: Add a prefix to the word. Tell students that you are going to add a part to the beginning of the word *happy* that will change its meaning.

unhappy

Pronounce the new word for them and explain that *un* is a prefix meaning "not." When it is added to the base word *happy*, it changes the meaning to "not happy."

Step 3: Have the students add the prefix *un* to another base word and tell you how the prefix changes the word's meaning. For example, write the word *safe* on the board. Ask students to add the prefix *un* and tell you the meaning of the new word. Students should respond by adding *un* to *safe* and verbalizing the meaning change.

Step 4: Show students how this knowledge will help them in reading. Write a sentence such as the following on the board and ask students to read it to themselves:

It was <u>unfair</u> for the teacher to give a test right after Christmas.

Discuss with students how even if they don't know the word *unfair*, they know that *fair* means right or just and *un* means not, and with that information they can figure out that *unfair* means not right or not just.

Step 5: Write a sentence on the board that includes a word using the prefix *un* and a base word the students already know.

Bob was <u>unable</u> to finish his work.

Ask students to read the sentence and explain how they can use the prefix *un* to help them determine the meaning of the underlined word.

The modeling portion of the lesson should be followed by guided practice and a summary. Independent practice and application should also be provided.

This basic strategy can be adapted for modeling suffixes, inflectional endings, base words, and root words. Identification of root words can also be taught in conjunction with etymologies (see page 190). Following is a list of common prefixes, suffixes, and inflectional endings with examples of words that include these structural elements. The list is reprinted from Johnson and Pearson (1984, pp. 129–131).

Prefixes

Invariant Prefixes

apo-	apoplexy, apogee
circum-	circumnavigate, circumvent
equi-	equidistant, equilibrium
extra-	extracurricular, extrasensory
intra-	intravenous, intramural
intro-	introspection, introvert
mal-	maladjusted, malapropism
mis-	misapply, misunderstand
non-	nonentity, nonprofit
syn-	synagogue, synapse, synonym

Variant (more than one meaning) but Common Prefixes

bi-	a. bicycle
	b. biannual
de-	a. dethrone, deactivate
	b. demerit, devalue
fore-	a. forewarn, forecast
	b. foreword, foreleg
in-	a. inept (also *ir*responsible, *il*legal, *im*material)
	b. indoors
pre-	a. preschool, preadolescent
	b. precaution, prearrange
pro-	a. pro-war, pro-life
	b. proceed, project
semi-	a. semicircle, semiannual
	b. semiabstract, semiautomatic
re-	a. redraw, rearrest
	b. recall, reaction
un-	a. unable, unbecoming
	b. unlock, untie

Suffixes

Noun Suffixes
Fourteen noun suffixes that indicate part of speech:

-ance, tolerance	-ness, wholesomeness
-ence, violence	-dom, freedom
-ation (-tion, -ion), starvation	-ery, drudgery

-ism, relativism

-ment, judgment

-acity, tenacity

-hood, manhood

-mony, harmony

-ty, loyalty

-tude, solitude

-ship, friendship

Eight noun suffixes that indicate agent:

-eer, auctioneer

-ess, governess

-grapher, photographer

-ier, financier

-ster, mobster

-ist, cellist

-stress, seamstress

-trix, aviatrix

Twenty-four noun suffixes with specific meanings:

-ana, Americana

-archy, monarchy

-ard (-art), drunkard

-aster, poetaster

-bility, susceptibility

-chrome, ferrochrome

-cide, suicide

-ee, payee

-fer, conifer

-fication, glorification

-gram, telegram

-graph, photograph

-graphy, photography

-ics, gymnastics

-itis, gastritis

-latry, idolatry

-meter, speedometer

-metry, geometry

-ology, biology

-phor, metaphor

-phobic, claustrophobic

-ric, meteoric

-scope, telescope

-scopy, bioscopy

Adjective Suffixes

Seventeen adjective suffixes:

-est, brightest

-ferous, odoriferous

-fic, scientific

-fold, tenfold

-form, uniform

-genous, autogenous

-scopic, telescopic

-wards, backwards

-wise, clockwise

-less, careless

-able, laughable

-ible (-ble), edible

-most, foremost

-like, humanlike

-ous, humorous

-ose, cellulose

-acious, tenacious

-ful, beautiful

Inflectional Endings

Plural

-s,   girls

-es,   watches

Comparison

-er,   taller

-est,   tallest

Tense

-ed,   jumped

-ing, jumping

-s,   jumps

Possessive

-'s,   Ann's

-s',   boys'

Strategy for Teaching Compound Words and Contractions

Two other components of structural analysis must be taught to students to help them become independent in determining word meanings. These are compound words and contractions.

Johnson and Pearson (1984) present a detailed analysis of different types of compound words but suggest that the types not be overemphasized in instruction. According to these researchers, the important point is that students learn what compound words are and how they can be used in determining word meanings as one reads. The following steps should be helpful to the teacher in developing direct instruction lessons on how to read and interpret compound words:

Step 1: Begin by explaining the concept and definition of compound words and showing students how compound words are formed:

school + house = schoolhouse
foot + ball = football
day + break = daybreak

Step 2: Present sentences containing compound words. Have students read the sentences. Then ask them questions about the meanings of the compound words. Use sentences and questions appropriate for the type of compound word. Point out how the two words that make up the compound word are related to the overall meaning of the word. For example, write the following sentence on the board:

We lived all summer on a houseboat.

Ask students what a houseboat is. (It's a boat that is *like* a house.) Some other examples of types of compound words follow:

We went to the ballpark.

Ask students what a ballpark is. (It's a park *for* playing ball.)

Mark got a bad sunburn.

Ask students what a sunburn is. (It's a burn *from* the sun.)

I saw a bluebird in the tree.

Ask students what a bluebird is. (It's a bird that *is* blue.)

By exercises such as these, students will begin to see that compound words have two parts that are related but that the parts do not always have the same relationship to one another.

Students also need to learn what contractions are and how to interpret them. The same type of direct-instruction procedure that was used with compound words can be used for contractions:

Step 1: Show students what a contraction is and discuss the meaning of contractions.

is + not = isn't
do + not = don't

Step 2:   Present contractions in sentences and discuss the meanings of the contractions. For example, write the following sentence on the board:

These old houses <u>aren't</u> very nice.

Then ask students what *aren't* means. Write another sentence on the board:

<u>Larry's</u> going to school on the bus.

Then ask students what *Larry's* means.
   The following is a list of common contractions.

Contraction	Meaning	Contraction	Meaning
shouldn't	= should not	I'm	= I am
don't	= do not		
couldn't	= could not	won't	= will not
wouldn't	= would not		
weren't	= were not	I've	= I have
hadn't	= had not	you've	= you have
wasn't	= was not	we've	= we have
didn't	= did not		
haven't	= have not	I'd	= I had, would
isn't	= is not	you'd	= you had, would
		he'd	= he had, would
we're	= we are	she'd	= she had, would
you're	= you are	they'd	= they had, would
they're	= they are		
I'll	= I will	where's	= where is
you'll	= you will	she's	= she is
he'll	= he will	he's	= he is
we'll	= we will	there's	= there is
they'll	= they will	what's	= what is
		that's	= that is

After teaching compound words and contractions, teachers should provide students with many opportunities to practice and apply the skills they learned in the reading of selections. Teachers should also encourage students to make use of compounds and contractions in their writing.

Teaching Use of the Dictionary

The dictionary is an invaluable tool for determining both the pronunciations and meanings of words. It is especially useful when students have tried all other skills and have still not determined the meaning or pronunciation of an unknown word. Unfortunately, the way students are often exposed to the dictionary is a turn-off to them. Therefore, there are some Don'ts about the dictionary that every teacher should keep in mind:

Don't give students long lists of isolated words to look up and define. Words out of context have no meaning. Therefore, students do not know which definition to select. Furthermore, this type of activity becomes dull and boring to students. It is not teaching.

Don't use the dictionary as a means of punishment. Too many teachers turn to the dictionary to punish students by having them copy pages. Who would ever want to see a dictionary again?

Don't require that every word on each week's spelling list be looked up in the dictionary and defined. This becomes a deadly, useless activity.

Don't teach phonetic respelling unless it is taught in relation to determining the pronunciation of words in the dictionary.

The *don't*s for teaching dictionary skills can be balanced with some positive *do*s:

Do teach students how to use a dictionary.

Do show students how to make use of a dictionary in their reading and writing.

Do show students how to use a dictionary in all content areas.

Do let students know that you, the teacher, often turn to the dictionary to check the spelling, pronunciation, and meanings of words.

The use of the dictionary must be taught in a manner that will leave students with positive attitudes. The teaching should begin in kindergarten and proceed through the primary grades until students know and understand the components of the dictionary and can use them effectively. The following sequence should guide the development of direct instruction in the use of the dictionary:

1. Use picture dictionaries to introduce the concept of the dictionary in kindergarten and first grade. Have students learn to locate words in the dictionaries, and teach them to make picture dictionaries of their own.
2. As soon as students have some knowledge of the alphabet, teach them how words are arranged in the dictionary. Give them practice in locating words.
3. Show students how words in the first half of the alphabet fall in the first half of the dictionary, and words in the second half fall in the second. Point out how, with this knowledge, students can save time by not having to turn through lots of extra pages.
4. Introduce the concept of phonetic respelling in relation to the pronunciation key, and show students how the pronunciation key can help them figure out the pronunciations of words in the dictionary.
5. Teach students to locate the meanings of words; point out that the dictionary lists more than one meaning for some words.
6. Complete the teaching of locating words alphabetically, showing students how words are alphabetized not just through the first letter but through the second, third, fourth, and subsequent letters.

7. Have students learn to select the correct dictionary definition for multiple-meaning words that are presented in written context.
8. Teach the special symbols used in dictionaries, such as *n* for noun, *v* for verb, and *sing.* for singular.
9. Show students all the other types of information that can be found in the dictionary, including lists of synonyms, an atlas, and geographic listings.
10. Provide students with experiences using many different dictionaries and glossaries.

Each of the items in this list will need to be translated into many direct instruction lessons involving several school years. Once students have learned the basics of using the dictionary, activities involving the dictionary can be used to introduce words in vocabulary preteaching lessons (see page 159). These activities should, however, be group activities under teacher direction; they should not be written activities independent of the teacher.

TEACHING SPECIFIC VOCABULARY LESSONS

The purpose of the third component of the vocabulary program, teaching specific vocabulary lessons, is to make students more aware of word meanings and to expand their vocabularies. Some of these lessons are taught during the skill-building portion of the DRL; others take place during extension portion or in lessons in other subject areas. Vocabulary should always be developed in relation to a particular theme, content area, or selection so that students will have a frame of reference for learning and retaining words.

Throughout the reading program and during all content classes, lessons should be planned with the focus of expanding and enriching students' vocabularies. These lessons should be based on the following principles:

1. *Build on vocabulary and vocabulary skills that have been taught.* Use the vocabulary and vocabulary skills that were taught before students read the selections to further develop vocabulary. Create activities that will challenge students to use the previously learned information in many different contexts.
2. *Relate specific vocabulary lessons to a topic of study.* For vocabulary learning to be valuable and lasting for students, it must be related to an existing schema or set of background experiences that students have. Therefore, expansion and enrichment activities should be tied to an area of study the students have completed or are working on, such as a story that was read or a unit of study in science.
3. *Develop vocabulary activities that correlate listening, speaking, reading, and writing.* Listening and speaking vocabularies form the foundation for reading and writing vocabularies. The development of vocabulary in these four areas is closely related, and their relationship should be accounted for in instructional activities.

4. *Make vocabulary learning fun.* A part of creating a vocabulary atmosphere is making learning fun. Students learn better if they enjoy what they are learning. The specific vocabulary lessons should be the lessons that help students develop a love of words.

Teachers often get so caught up in developing the basics of reading that they forget to provide lessons in vocabulary expansion and enrichment, especially for the less able students. All students should be given specific vocabulary lessons with emphasis on expansion and enrichment; such lessons not only broaden reading vocabularies, but they also develop the base for future vocabulary growth through listening and speaking. It is through this part of the vocabulary program that students get some of that extra spark that helps them maintain high motivation for learning. The life of any part of the reading program comes as much from the way the teacher presents material as from the lessons the teacher presents.

Teaching Synonyms, Antonyms, Homonyms, and Homographs

By teaching synonyms, antonyms, homonyms, and homographs, teachers help students expand their vocabularies. Synonyms are words that mean nearly the same thing—little and small, for example. Antonyms are words that are opposite in meaning, such as happy and sad. Homonyms, or homophones, are words that are spelled differently but pronounced the same and have different meanings—deer and dear. Homographs are words that are spelled the same but have different pronunciations and meanings—for example, we listen to a *record* player, but we *record* a song.

The teacher can use the following steps to teach synonyms, antonyms, homonyms, and homographs:

Step 1: Present a sentence or pair of sentences containing underlined synonyms, antonyms, homonyms, or homographs.

Step 2: Read the sentence or sentences to the students, or have the students read the sentences. Discuss the meanings of the underlined words.

Step 3: Present the term for the underlined words (synonym, antonym, homonym, homograph), and guide students to define the term from the way the words were used in the sentences.

The following sentences could be used in the above steps:

Synonyms
Mark said I made one <u>mistake</u>, but I said I made one <u>error</u>.
The automobile <u>accident</u> was reported in the newspaper as a <u>mishap</u>.
We picked up the <u>little</u> box. Sara said she would be glad to carry the <u>small</u> box.

Antonyms
The tribal chief was <u>old</u>, but the braves were <u>young</u>.
First the car would <u>stop</u>, and then it would <u>go</u>.
The cold syrup poured <u>slowly</u> from the can, but when it was heated it poured <u>quickly</u>.

Homonyms
Martha said she would <u>meet</u> her mother at the <u>meat</u> counter.
I <u>blew</u> out the <u>blue</u> candles on my cake.
The <u>fare</u> to ride the shuttle bus at the <u>fair</u> was fifteen cents.

Homographs
The singer was going to <u>record</u> his new <u>record</u> at the studio.
As I began to <u>wind</u> the rope around the pole the <u>wind</u> started to blow.
The stranger tried to <u>console</u> the old man at the scene of the accident. The movers carried the <u>console</u> into the dining room.

Once students have been taught synonyms, antonyms, homonyms, and homographs, they should be given many opportunities to practice recognizing and using these types of words in a variety of situations. Games like the following and exercises similar to those in Examples 4.14 and 4.15 can be used.

Match

Write synonyms, antonyms, or homonyms on cards. Deal five cards to each player, and place remaining cards in the middle. Students draw a card from the pile, lay down any pairs they have (made up of synonyms, antonyms, or homonyms, depending on the game they are playing), and then discard one card. The person who gets rid of all cards first is the winner. Many variations of this game can be created.

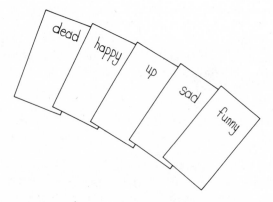

Homonym or Homograph Draw

Write sentences containing pairs of homonyms or homographs on cards. Underline the homonyms or homographs. Students take turns drawing cards, reading them aloud, and explaining the underlined words. Give students a point for each correct answer. The student with the most points when all cards are drawn wins.

The man with <u>bare</u> feet

ran after the <u>bear.</u>

King of the Mountain

Make a simple game board like the one pictured. Have a single die, and have a marker for each player. Use cards similar to those suggested in the first two games. Place a stack of cards by the board. The players take turns rolling the die

and drawing a card from the stack. If the player can read the card, give a synonym, antonym, or homonym for the word on the card or read the sentences and explain the meanings of the underlined words, he or she can move the number of spaces rolled on the die. Penalties can be added to make the game more exciting.

After students have learned to recognize synonyms and antonyms, they should be taught to use a thesaurus. The ability to use a thesaurus will help them expand and enrich their vocabularies as they write (see page 191).

Denotation-Connotation

Denotation and connotation are terms that describe the different meanings that words have. *Denotation* refers to a word's literal meaning. As shown in the following sentences, some words have more than one denotation; these are called multiple-meaning words.

Mark was the next player up at <u>bat</u>.
The <u>bat</u> came out from under the house at night.

Connotation refers to the feelings, emotions, or shades of meaning suggested or implied by a word. In the following sentences, note the differences in meaning implied by the underlined words:

Ted and Mark tied the <u>boat</u> to the dock.
Ted and Mark tied the <u>yacht</u> to the dock.

The first sentence doesn't make you think that Ted and Mark have anything special, whereas in the second sentence the connotations of the word *yacht* lead you to think that Ted and Mark might be wealthy. Teachers should provide systematic instruction to help students become aware of the denotations and connotations of words. The following modeling strategy can be used:

Step 1:   Present students with pairs of sentences containing words with similar denotations but different connotations. For example:

1. The old man <u>walked</u> down the street.
2. The old man <u>trudged</u> down the street.

Have students read the sentences aloud. Discuss with them how the words *walked* and *trudged* have very similar meanings. In both sentences, they should be able to tell that the old man is moving down the street on his own legs. Explain that the exact meanings of *walked* and *trudged* are called their denotations.

Step 2:   Ask students to think about and tell you what pictures *walked* and *trudged* form in their minds. Emphasize that *walked* brings to mind normal physical movement and that *trudged* brings to mind a person barely moving or having great difficulty moving. Explain that the pictures words make you think of or the feelings they make you have are their connotations. Discuss how trudged and walked make you have very different feelings and form different pictures of the old men in the two sentences. Remind students that when they read, they should be aware of the different denotations and connotations of words.

EXAMPLE 4.14   HOMONYM (HOMOPHONE) PRACTICE EXERCISE

6 Building Vocabulary with Homophones

Homophones are words that sound alike but have different meanings. Usually homophones are spelled differently.

PRACTICE EXERCISE   **A.** Underline the homophones in each pair of sentences. Use the Answer Key to check your answers.

1. The <u>site</u> for the start of the parade is Elm Street and First Avenue.
   Yesterday's sunset was a beautiful <u>sight</u>.
2. Moles are able to dig <u>burrows</u> with astonishing speed.
   Some states are divided into <u>boroughs</u> as well as counties.
3. The baseball hit the <u>pane</u> and the glass shattered.
   The doctor told Ms. Herrera to soak her leg in warm water to ease the <u>pain</u>.
4. The forecast was for <u>fair</u> weather so Ramón left his umbrella home.
   The <u>fare</u> for the trip from South Orange to Bedford is $3.50.

B. Match the words in column I with their definitions in column II. Write the letter of the correct definition in the space provided. Use the Answer Key to check your answers.

	I		II
c	1. site	a.	money charged to ride on a bus or train
e	2. sight	b.	an ache or soreness
g	3. fair	c.	a place
a	4. fare	d.	political divisions of a city or state
f	5. pane	e.	that which is seen
b	6. pain	f.	a sheet of glass set in the frame of a window
h	7. burrows	g.	clear and bright; sunny
d	8. boroughs	h.	holes or tunnels dug in the ground by animals

18

Source: Margaret Early et al., *Golden Voyages*, p. 18 (Reading Skills Workbook). HBJ BOOKMARK READING PROGRAM, Eagle Edition. Orlando, FLA: Harcourt, Brace, Jovanovich, Publishers, 1983. Used by permission.

EXAMPLE 4.15   SAMPLE ANTONYM PRACTICE EXERCISE ——————

17 Building Vocabulary with Antonyms

Antonyms are words that have opposite, or nearly opposite, meanings.

PRACTICE EXERCISE   The boldfaced and the italicized words in the sentences below are antonyms. Use the italicized word to help you figure out the meaning of the boldfaced word. Then underline the word or phrase that best defines the boldfaced word. Use the Answer Key to check your answers.

1. Usually **punctual**, Julio apologized for being *late*.
   punctual: a. on time
            b. quiet and shy
            c. talkative

2. It is important to be **precise** about measuring windows for curtain rods. If you are *careless*, they won't fit.
   precise: a. neat
          b. exact
          c. relaxed

3. Although Lena is only a **remote** cousin of mine, we feel like *close* relatives.
   remote: a. first
           b. younger
           c. distant

4. The building was **demolished** in the earthquake, but the owners were determined to *rebuild* it.
   demolished: a. completed
              b. moved from side to side
              c. destroyed

5. Although at first I thought it would be *dull*, the book turned out to be quite **engrossing**.
   engrossing: a. interesting
              b. a best seller
              c. sparkling

6. The day seemed so **overcast**, we put off our picnic for a *sunny* day.
   overcast: a. beautiful
            b. cloudy and gray
            c. hot and dry

55

Source: Margaret Early et al., *Golden Voyages*, p. 55 (Reading Skills Workbook). HBJ BOOKMARK READING PROGRAM, Eagle Edition. Orlando, FLA: Harcourt, Brace, Jovanovich, Publishers, 1983. Used by permission.

Step 3: Ask students to read sentences you write on the board and explain differences in the underlined words' denotations and connotations. For the following sentences, guide them to see the different denotations and connotations for car and limousine:

Harry drove up in his father's car, but Jeff arrived in his father's limousine.

The modeling should be followed by the appropriate guided practice and summary. Students should then be given independent practice and opportunities to use denotations and connotations in their reading. To provide practice, the teacher could give students, among other things, a selection to read in which there were words with different connotations but similar denotations.

Many fun activities can be built around denotation and connotation:

1. Have students pantomime or role play to show the different denotations or connotations for words.
2. Have students select a newspaper article, greeting cards, or other material and change the intended meanings by changing words with similar denotations to words with very different connotations.
3. Encourage students to use the denotative and connotative properties of words as they write.

Semantic Maps

For many years, teachers have instructed students to put words into categories to show relationships. More recently, this exercise has been adapted to one of building word maps, which not only show that words relate to one another, but show *how* words relate to a given word or concept. The term used to describe this activity is semantic mapping.

Semantic maps display concepts in categories and indicate how words are related to one another or how they "go together." Children learn new words, view "old" words in a new light, and see the relationships among words on the map. (Johnson and Pearson, 1984, p. 37)

Words can be related by class, example, or property. *Horses* and *pigs* are words related by class: They belong to the same class, called animals. Words are example relations if they name things that belong to the same class: a quarter horse is an *example* of a particular type of horse, but it also belongs to the *class* of animals. The name for a particular horse, such as Dapple, is also an *example* of horses. Property relations describe specific features of a class or an example of a class. Four-legged describes horse and is a particular feature of horses.

By developing semantic maps, students can think about these relationships and expand their vocabularies. The following steps should be useful in carrying out direct instruction in vocabulary, using semantic maps.

Step 1: Select a word or category from the material students have read. As students progress in this activity, they can select their words and categories.

Step 2: Ask students to think about the word selected and tell you as many words as they can that are related to the word. List all the words on the board.

Step 3: Write the category word in the center of the chalkboard, a large sheet of paper, or a bulletin board display. Then ask students to look at the words they listed and group the ones that are alike. In some instances, it might be necessary to give the students labels for the various categories of words.

Step 4: Proceed by discussing the words and having students explain how each is related to the main word. As each word is added to the map, cross it off the main list.

A partially completed map could look like the one in Example 4.16. As the teacher works with students in developing the map, he or she can give other words and categories of words to help expand the students' thinking. As students progress in this activity, they can begin to work on their own, in pairs, or small groups.

EXAMPLE 4.16 PARTIALLY COMPLETED WORD MAP ─────────

Topic: buildings

List of Words Generated by Students:

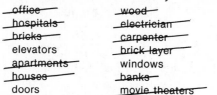

~~office~~   ~~wood~~
~~hospitals~~   ~~electrician~~
~~bricks~~   ~~carpenter~~
elevators   ~~brick layer~~
~~apartments~~   windows
~~houses~~   ~~banks~~
doors   ~~movie theaters~~
stairway   wire
carpet   pipes
~~cement~~   ~~plumber~~

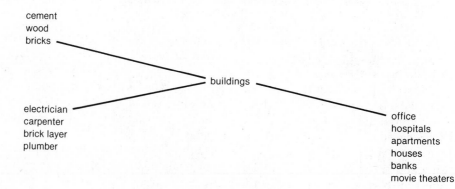

cement
wood
bricks

buildings

electrician
carpenter
brick layer
plumber

office
hospitals
apartments
houses
banks
movie theaters

The most important aspect of this activity is the discussion that takes place between the teacher and students and among the students. As words for the map are discussed, students see new relationships among words and learn new words. This type of activity leads students to word ownership. The teacher should freely prompt students to focus on particular words or ask questions that will lead students to identify new words for the map. For example, in discussing the map in Example 4.16, the teacher might ask students what they would call the category including electrician, carpenter, brick layer, and plumber. Students might come up with such labels as workers or construction crew. The teacher could then ask what other types of workers could be included in this category. If students cannot answer, the teacher could suggest architect, interior designer, landscape architect, and so forth, and then discuss what each of these persons might do in relation to buildings. Students expand their vocabularies through this type of discussion.

Semantic maps are really never completed. However, when the class reaches a point at which work on a map is to be discontinued, the map can be used for other purposes:

1. Students can select a particular map as a focus for a piece of writing. They can incorporate words and category ideas into their writing.
2. Students can put maps into their vocabulary notebooks and add to the maps as they encounter new words. Students can also make their own maps for their notebooks.
3. Semantic maps can be placed on bulletin boards, and students can add to them throughout the school year.
4. Students and teachers can use maps made from science, social studies, or other content chapters to review the content of chapters before a test.

Vocabulary Webs

Webbing was suggested earlier in this chapter as a technique for preteaching vocabulary by which students think about how words can be related; it can also be used as a means of expanding and enriching vocabulary. After students have read a selection or chapter, they can be instructed to select a list of words from their reading that are of interest to them and to work individually or in pairs to create a web showing how the words can be related. After the webs are completed, the students can discuss them with the group, and other students can suggest words to add to the web. At the conclusion of the activity, the students should be instructed to use the words from the web in oral and written sentences. Webs can be directed toward different categories of words, such as places, feelings, or methods of travel, or can be developed around the specific characters or events of a story. A completed web might look like the one in Example 4.17. Webbing leads students to see word relationships and develop word ownership.

EXAMPLE 4.17   COMPLETED VOCABULARY WEB

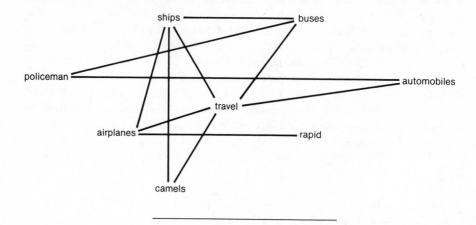

Semantic Feature Analysis

Another activity for expanding and enriching vocabulary is semantic feature analysis. With this procedure, students develop vocabulary and learn important concepts by looking at how a group of related words differ and how they are alike (Johnson and Pearson, 1984). The activity should be conducted after students have read a selection or group of selections on a given topic. In this activity, the students and teacher set up a grid like that in Example 4.18, following the steps outlined below:

1. Select a category (e.g., vegetables).
2. List items that fall into this category down the left side of the grid.
3. List features that some of the items have in common across the top of the grid.
4. Put pluses (+) and minuses (−) in the squares of the grid to indicate whether the items in the category have the feature under consideration. Each item is discussed, and the teacher should make sure students understand that some items are sometimes characterized by a feature, sometimes not. For example, for the grid in Example 4.18, the teacher should be sure students understand that the tomato can be both green and red but is usually cooked when green.
5. Add additional words and features to the grid.
6. Complete the grid and discuss each word.

The process should be repeated many times using different categories, moving from the concrete to the abstract. The teacher should encourage students to continuously look for new words to add to the grids. Students can keep grid sheets in folders or notebooks and can add to them throughout the year. For young students, semantic feature grids using very simple categories and features can be developed as oral language activities.

EXAMPLE 4.18   SEMANTIC FEATURE ANALYSIS GRID ——————

VEGETABLES	green	have peelings	eat raw	seeds
potatoes	−	+	+	−
carrots	−	+	+	−
tomatoes	− +	+	− +	+
broccoli	+	−	+	−
squash	+ −	+	+	+
cabbage	+	−	+	−

After completing a semantic feature grid, students should examine the pattern of pluses and minuses to determine how the words are alike and how they are different. This exercise will lead students to expand their vocabularies as well as refine the meanings of words they already know.

Analogies

Analogies are comparisons that suggest that two things are alike in some way: for example, fire is to hot as ice is to cold. When students make analogies, they are expressing their thinking patterns. Johnson and Pearson (1984, pp. 46–47) suggest thirteen analogy categories that teachers can use in vocabulary-development lessons.

1. Opposites in sensation: *Ice cream* is to *pickle* as *sweet* is to *sour*.
2. Object/Function: *Wine* is to *bottle* as *crackers* are to *box*.
3. Characteristics: *Rain* is to *wet* as *sun* is to *dry*.
4. Part/Whole: *Leaf* is to *tree* as *feather* is to *bird*.
5. Whole/Part: *Cup* is to *handle* as *clock* is to *hands*.
6. Location: *Teacher* is to *classroom* as *sailor* is to *ship*.
7. Action/Object: *Run* is to *track* as *swim* is to *pool*.
8. Agent/Action or Object: *Teacher* is to *students* as *doctor* is to *patients*.
9. Class or Synonym: *Smell* is to *sniff* as *see* is to *look*.
10. Familial: *Uncle* is to *nephew* as *aunt* is to *niece*.
11. Grammatical: *Hear* is to *heard* as *look* is to *looked*.
12. Temporal or Sequential: *Fifth* is to *first* as *twenty-fifth* is to *fifth*.
13. Antonyms: *Smile* is to *happy* as *frown* is to *sad*.

Teachers should incorporate analogies into their vocabulary-development programs because analogies help students expand their meaning vocabularies. The following steps can be used to develop analogy lessons using direct instruction:

Step 1: Present a simple, concrete analogy and explain the relationships to students. For example:

Car is to drive as airplane is to fly.

Explain to students that this statement is an analogy because it tells how two things are related. A car you can drive; an airplane you fly. In this statement, a car and an airplane are being compared.

Step 2: Present another analogy following the same pattern and have students explain it the way that you explained the first analogy. For example, you could write:

Bike is to pedal as boat is to row.

If students are unable to explain the relationships, repeat the process used in Step 1.

Step 3: Present incomplete analogies with choices of words to fill in the blanks. Ask students to use these words to complete the analogies.

Bed is to sleep as chair is to _____ .
  stand   sit   eat

Discuss the students' answers.

In the beginning stages of teaching analogies, the teacher should work with one pattern at a time. Once students seem comfortable using analogies, the patterns can be mixed. Analogies not only help students expand their vocabularies, they also help students improve their thinking processes.

Etymologies

The study of the origin and development of words is called etymology. Many words originate in other languages and become a part of the English language over years of use. Some words change in meaning through the years.

Students should be taught that words have different origins and histories and that they can get clues to a word's meaning and expand their vocabularies by learning the origin and history of the word. It is a good procedure to teach etymology gradually. As students learn new words and learn to recognize root words, the teacher should note that some words originated in other languages. When dictionary skills are taught, students should be shown how the dictionary indicates the language from which a word originated.

Assume that one of the words being introduced before a selection is to be read is *decade.* The teacher could present the word in a sentence and point out that the origin of the word is the Greek word *deka* meaning ten. The teacher could then ask students to try to determine the meaning of decade from the sentence.

Lisa had not visited her friend in years; it had been nearly a *decade* since she had seen her.

By using etymology in this way the teacher is showing students how word origin can help them determine word meanings as well as expand their vocabularies.

After introducing students to the concept of etymology, the teacher can put a large outline map of the world, such as that shown in Example 4.19, on a bulletin board. As students study vocabulary throughout the year, they can look up the origin of the words they are learning in the dictionary and put the words from each country in envelopes surrounding the map, color-coded for each country. Each new word would be put on a card with its origin, any comments that seem appropriate, and a sentence using the word. The teacher can periodically take the words from a pocket and have students read and discuss them. The teacher should encourage students to use the words in their speaking and writing.

EXAMPLE 4.19   WORD ORIGINS MAP ————————————

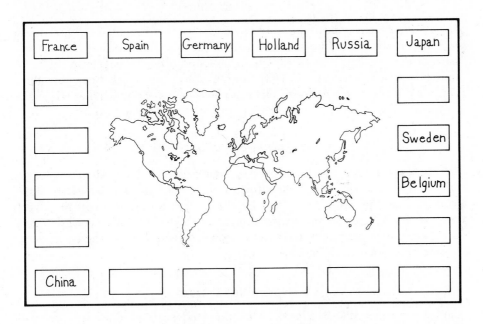

Using a Thesaurus

A thesaurus is a dictionary of synonyms and antonyms. The most famous thesaurus, *Roget's Thesaurus* (1965), is very useful in helping more mature readers and writers locate synonyms and antonyms for words. The thesaurus, however, is also a valuable resource to be used in teaching vocabulary and helping students expand their vocabularies. Teachers can introduce elementary-grade students to the use of the thesaurus with *Words to Use: A Junior Thesaurus* (Drysdale, 1971).

It is much easier to learn to use a thesaurus than a dictionary. Once students know how to alphabetize and have learned the concepts of synonyms and antonyms, they can be taught to use the thesaurus. Students must be taught how the thesaurus is organized, how to locate a word, and how to read the synonym or antonym entries. Students should be shown how writers use the thesaurus to locate words that they want to change in their writing to avoid repetition.

After students have learned to use the thesaurus, teachers should show them how it can be a valuable resource for expanding their vocabularies. To do this, the teacher can develop many interesting activities that require students to locate words in the thesaurus and select an appropriate synonym or antonym. A few such activities are described in the following sections.

Cartoon Capers

Have students select one of their favorite cartoons from the comics section of the newspaper. Have them use the thesaurus to select words to substitute for selected parts of the dialogue to make the dialogue sound different but mean the same (practice with synonyms). Students can share their writing and compare their versions to the original cartoon. Then, students can select words that will make the dialogue have an opposite meaning (practice with antonyms).

Editors at Work

Select an article from the newspaper or another source and underline selected words. Have students use the thesaurus to locate synonyms for the words. Have students read their edited versions aloud and discuss the synonyms they have used. A similar activity can be done using antonyms—the students would discuss the changes in meaning they have introduced. The same activity can be conducted using headlines from the newspaper.

Overworked Words

On a bulletin board keep a list of words that students tend to use repeatedly in their writing. Have students locate the words in a thesaurus and list synonyms for the words on the bulletin board, as shown in Example 4.20. Encourage students to use these synonyms in their writing. The words should be changed periodically. Students can also make a list of these or other overworked words in their vocabulary notebooks.

Multiple-Meaning Words

One problem readers encounter in comprehending is the extensive number of words in the English language that have more than one meaning; these are called multiple-meaning words. At the same time, the large number of multiple-meaning words shows the beauty and history of the language. Teachers must

EXAMPLE 4.20   BULLETIN BOARD DISPLAY ━━━━━━

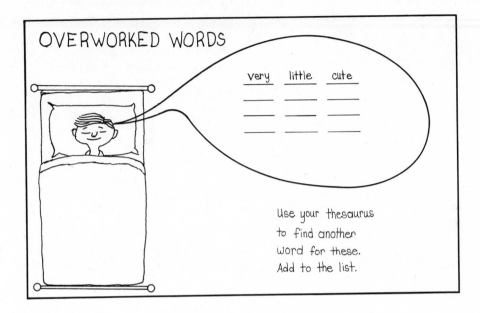

focus on multiple-meaning words to help their students expand and enrich their vocabularies.

Without vocabulary preteaching, students who know only one meaning for the word *list*, would have real difficulty constructing meaning from the following sentence:

The ship began to *list* to the right.

Students who think that *list* means only to write out a group of things would become very confused trying to understand how a ship could make a *list*.

An important part of vocabulary development and comprehension is teaching students that

1. nearly all words in the English language have more than one meaning, and
2. the specific meanings for words in reading selections will vary according to the context in which the words are used.

Oral language is the foundation for a reader's vocabulary. Many times an individual will have one meaning for a word well developed in his or her oral language and will not be aware of other possible meanings. Therefore, the new meanings must be taught. One of the best ways to deal with such words is to treat them as new words and teach their new meanings. For strategies for preteaching vocabulary, see page 149.

After students read a selection or several related selections that have a number of interesting multiple-meaning words, the teacher should review the meanings as they were used in the selections and teach other meanings. For example, if students have learned one set of meanings for *bank*, *ring*, *light*, and *saw*, they can be introduced to new meanings for the words using the following steps:

Step 1: List the words on the board and have students read them aloud.

> bank   light
> ring   saw

Step 2: Have students give a sentence using each word.

> I took my money to the <u>bank</u>.
> Mary wore a ruby <u>ring</u>.
> The box was so <u>light</u> that I could lift it.
> Barry <u>saw</u> the car turn the corner.

Step 3: Give students another sentence using each word in which the word has a new meaning. Have students discuss the meaning of the word. Tell students the new meaning if they do not know it and illustrate with other examples:

> Tom stood on the <u>bank</u> of the river to fish.
> We heard the bell <u>ring</u> from inside the room.
> The <u>light</u> from the candle made the room bright.
> We used a <u>saw</u> to cut down the tree.

Step 4: Have students give new sentences using the new meanings of the words. Have other students check to see that the students giving the sentences have used the words correctly.

After these steps have been completed, the teacher should provide exercises so that students can practice using the words.

Computer Activities for Vocabulary Development

The computer is a viable part of an increasingly large number of classrooms. Although much of the available software is oriented to drill and practice as opposed to direct instruction, these materials can be used effectively after the teacher's initial teaching. The following are some of the available software packages for vocabulary development:

Title   Game Show
Source   Advanced Ideas
Grade   All grades

This program is an educational tool for vocabulary development in a practice game format. It is designed like a quiz show and includes an easy-to-use authoring system so that teachers can adapt the program for their specifications. Additional subject diskettes are available.

Title Analogies Tutorial
Source Hartley Courseware, Inc.
Grade 5–10

This tutorial program helps students identify different types of analogies. It uses branching to provide assistance when the student needs it and is adaptable in that the teacher may add his or her own word lists.

Title Antonyms/Synonyms
Source Hartley Courseware, Inc.
Grade 5–8

This program assists students in learning to recognize and use synonyms and antonyms. It is adaptable, and the teacher may modify it or create lessons. Similar programs are available on the topic of homonyms from the same company.

SUMMARY

Vocabulary development is a specialized form of background development and is an important part of the instructional program in reading comprehension. Students develop reading vocabulary from their oral vocabulary, but not all words encountered in reading are in the students' oral vocabularies. Therefore, the vocabulary program must help students recognize words in their oral vocabularies and learn those words not in their oral vocabularies.

The program for vocabulary development must be carried out in a vocabulary atmosphere that helps make students conscious of words. The program should include three components that operate simultaneously:

> Preteaching Vocabulary
> Teaching Skills to Determine Word Meanings
> Teaching Specific Vocabulary Lessons

The purpose of preteaching vocabulary is to help students develop an extensive instant-recognition vocabulary. This comes about by preteaching the key-concept words from a selection before it is read. Seven strategies for preteaching words were suggested. Once words have been taught, they become instant-recognition words for students, and students develop ownership of words through repeated practice and application in the reading of real text.

Students must be taught skills for independently determining word meanings. These skills include structural analysis, context clues, and use of the dictionary.

The vocabulary program must also include specific vocabulary lessons designed to expand and enrich a reader's vocabulary. Specific lessons should focus on synonyms, antonyms, homonyms, homographs; denotation/connotation; semantic maps; vocabulary webs; semantic feature analysis; analogies; etymologies; use of a thesaurus; and multiple-meaning words.

REFERENCES

Beck, I. L. 1984. Developing comprehension: The impact of the directed reading lesson. In R. C. Anderson, J. Osborn, and R. J. Tierney (eds.), *Learning to read in American schools: Basal readers and content texts.* Hillsdale, NJ: Lawrence Erlbaum Associates.

Beck, I. L., C. A. Perfetti, and M. G. McKeown. 1982. Effects of long-term vocabulary instruction on lexical access and reading comprehension. *Journal of Educational Psychology, 74,* 506–521.

Cooper, J. D., et al. 1979. *The what and how of reading instruction.* Columbus, OH: Charles E. Merrill Publishing Company.

Cunningham, J. W. 1979. An automatic pilot for decoding. *The Reading Teacher, 32,* 420–424.

Davis, F. B. 1944. Fundamental factors of comprehension in reading. *Psychometrika, 9,* 185–197.

Davis, F. B. 1972. Psychometric research on comprehension in reading. *Reading Research Quarterly, 7,* 628–678.

Deighton, L. C. 1959. *Vocabulary development in the classroom.* New York: Bureau of Publications, Teachers College, Columbia University.

Dolch, E. W. 1936. A basic sight vocabulary. *Elementary School Journal, 36,* 456–460.

Drysdale, P. 1971. *Words to use: A junior thesaurus.* New York: William H. Sadlier.

Gipe, J. P. 1978–1979. Investigating techniques for teaching word meanings. *Reading Research Quarterly, 14,* 624–644.

Harris, T. L., and R. E. Hodges (eds.). 1981. *A dictionary of reading and related terms.* Newark, DE: International Reading Association.

Jenkins, J. R., D. Pany, and J. Schreck. 1978. *Vocabulary and reading comprehension: Instructional effects.* Technical Report No. 100. Urbana, IL: University of Illinois, Center for the Study of Reading. (ERIC Document Reproduction Service No. ED 160 999)

Johnson, D. D. 1971a. The Dolch list reexamined. *The Reading Teacher, 24,* 449–457.

Johnson, D. D. 1971b. A basic vocabulary for beginning readers. *Elementary School Journal, 72,* 29–34.

Johnson, D. D., and P. D. Pearson. 1984. *Teaching reading vocabulary,* 2nd ed. New York: Holt, Rinehart and Winston.

Johnston, P. 1981. Prior knowledge and reading comprehension test bias. Ph.D. dissertation, University of Illinois, Champaign.

Roget, P. 1965. *St. Martin's edition of the original Roget's thesaurus of English words and phrases.* New York: St. Martin's Press.

Stevens, K. C. 1982. Can we improve reading by teaching background information? *Journal of Reading, 25,* 326–329.

Tierney, R. J., and J. W. Cunningham. 1984. Research on teaching reading comprehension. In P. D. Pearson (ed.), *Handbook of reading research.* New York: Longman.

CHAPTER
F I V E

BUILDING COMPREHENSION

PROCESSES AND SKILLS

*Reading comprehension must also be regarded as a set of
discrete processes. The simple fact is that you cannot deal
with the universe of comprehension tasks at once. . . . We
recognize that for the sake of instructional convenience
and sanity, you have to start somewhere and move toward
something else.*—Pearson and Johnson, 1978, p. 227

In this chapter, you will learn

1. what modeling is and how it fits into the directed reading lesson,
2. how metacognition relates to modeling,
3. strategies for teaching and modeling comprehension skills and processes,
4. how to model comprehension skills and processes within guided silent reading,
5. a strategy for teaching students to monitor their own comprehension,
6. questions to ask to help you analyze a reader's comprehension problems,
7. types of computer software that can be used for helping students practice comprehension skills.

One of the components of the instructional program in reading comprehension is building the processes and skills of comprehension (see Chapter 2). The need for direct instruction in this activity has been clearly documented (Durkin, 1978, 1981; Duffy, Roehler and Mason, 1984). The processes and skills component is the part of comprehension instruction that involves the most direct teaching and the heaviest use of modeling, for it is here that the teacher clearly shows students how to use the skills and processes of comprehension. This component, however, must not be emphasized to the exclusion of the other two components of the instructional program—developing background and vocabulary and correlating writing.

The building processes and skills component of comprehension involves teaching students to use specific strategies to determine clues from the text and specific processes to relate the text to their prior experiences. It also involves helping readers comprehend different text structures. This chapter develops the concept of building comprehension processes and skills, especially focusing on the use of modeling. Chapter 6 focuses more specifically on the process of teaching and modeling text structure.

MODELING DEFINED

Modeling was defined earlier in this text as the act of showing or demonstrating for students how to use and think through a given skill or process. Various dictionaries define modeling as the act of showing or presenting a model to be imitated. Modeling is used frequently to describe what teachers should do to help students learn to comprehend and write. In all instances, modeling means essentially the same thing—showing or demonstrating how to use and think through a particular skill, process, or strategy.

Modeling has often been called a "think aloud" strategy (Clark, 1984); in comprehension-modeling, the teacher shows students how to think through the use of comprehension skills and processes. However, in the literature on reading comprehension, the term modeling has been used loosely and the act of modeling has been elusively defined, mainly because comprehension has not been understood well enough for researchers to be able to provide clear definitions and guidelines for instruction. Recent research, however, has improved our understanding of comprehension; with knowledge gained from this research, teachers should be able to improve their strategies for modeling. Suggestions for doing so are presented in this chapter.

Throughout this text, the importance of incorporating direct instruction into the framework of the directed reading lesson has been stressed. Direct instruction involves three specific parts: teaching, practicing, and applying. Modeling is a component of the teaching part of direct instruction. Frequently, modeling is used synonymously with teaching, but teaching is more inclusive than modeling. Within the framework of direct instruction, teaching includes four distinct but related parts:

1. letting students know what is to be learned and helping them relate it to prior experience,
2. modeling the skill, process, or strategy and verbalizing the thinking that takes place,
3. providing guided practice in the use of the skill, process, or strategy,
4. summarizing what was learned and verbalizing how and when to use it.

The act of teaching, as it is used in this text, involves showing students how to use a skill, process, or strategy and guiding them to internalize it.

When modeling a comprehension skill or process for students, the teacher should not only show the students how to use and think through the process, but should also help them begin to verbalize when to use the process. This latter aspect of modeling helps students develop the metacognitive processes that appear to be very important to the effective comprehender (Baker and Brown, 1984a, 1984b).

For the teaching portion of direct instruction to be effective, it must be followed by opportunities for the reader to practice the skill or process that was modeled and to apply it in the reading of real text. The most significant part of direct instruction may well be application; if students are unable to use whatever they have learned in actual reading situations, the teaching will have been worthless. Therefore, application in real text must come as quickly as possible after the teaching and practicing portions of direct instruction and must be carried out in a way that will allow students to see the connection between what they have learned and what they should apply.

THE DIRECTED READING LESSON AND MODELING

The directed reading lesson (DRL) format was suggested in Chapter 2 as a way to organize and approach reading instruction that would account for the three components of the instructional program in reading comprehension. The modeling of comprehension skills and processes is most likely to take place in the skill building and the guided silent reading and discussion sections of the DRL.

During skill building, teachers have normally carried out whatever activities they consider to be the teaching of skills. It is at this point in the DRL that the teaching (and modeling) of most comprehension skills and processes occurs. However, for the teaching to be effective, it must be followed by practice and application activities that provide students with the experiences they need to develop the skill or process to the point that makes it theirs. If modeling is not followed by practice and application activities, it will not help students learn to use and apply the skills and processes being taught.

Before having students apply a skill or process to longer text, the teacher may want to model the skill again; guided silent reading would be the best place to do this. Most of the comprehension skills and processes can be modeled in this part of the lesson, and sometimes it really is necessary to model a given process in both skill building and guided silent reading. A discussion of modeling in guided silent reading is presented later in this chapter. The teacher must clearly understand that guided silent reading and discussion has two purposes—guided application and modeling. The format and structure of the guided reading will vary depending on the purpose for its use.

METACOGNITION AND MODELING

The term metacognition has been used by researchers and educational writers rather prolifically during the past decade. Because of its widespread use with lack of clarity, many educators have made fun of the term and all the other "meta" words that have seemed to become the by-words of the 1980s. However, the research of the metacognitive psychologists is important and must not be dismissed as a passing fad. The information researchers are learning about metacognition and the role it should play in reading comprehension is providing new insights into what should be done in teaching comprehension.

Metacognition refers to the knowledge and control which students have over their own thinking and learning activities (Brown, 1980). It appears to involve two basic components (Baker and Brown, 1984b):

1. awareness of the processes and skills needed to complete a task successfully,
2. the ability to tell whether one is performing a task correctly and to make corrections during the task if needed; this process is termed cognitive monitoring.

Both aspects of metacognition play an important role in reading comprehension. Although the research does not indicate absolutely that teaching readers metacognitive processes will make them better comprehenders, there is sufficient evidence to lead one to believe that teachers should begin to incorporate these aspects into their modeling strategies (Mier, 1984).

Teachers have often taught students a particular skill or process without helping them develop an awareness of when and how the skill or process would be useful in reading. During modeling, it is important for the teacher to have students verbalize how they used the skill or process they have just learned and when it might be useful. Assume that a teacher has just modeled for students how to note the sequence of events in a selection; as a part of modeling, the teacher showed students how to use clue words, dates, and numbering devices to detect the sequence. Modeling should not end there. As a concluding part of modeling, the teacher should ask students to verbalize how they used the process of noting sequence and to tell when they would expect to use this process in their reading. The dialogue between the teacher and students might sound like the dialogue in Example 5.1.

EXAMPLE 5.1   MODELING DIALOGUE FOR SEQUENCE
OF EVENTS

Teacher: Now that you have learned how to detect the sequence of events in a story, who can describe for me the process that you used?

Student: As we read, we looked for words that told us the order in which things happened.

Teacher: Who can give examples of the types of words you looked for?

Student: First, next, last, then, after.

Teacher: Did you just look for words?

Student: No, we looked for numbers—1, 2, 3, and so on—and for dates, like 1941, 1968, 1982.

Teacher: But how did all of these things help you note the author's sequence of ideas?

Student: As we read, we paid attention to the numbers, words, and dates so we could tell the important things that happened first, second, and third.
Teacher: Who can tell me when you might use this skill in reading?
Student: All the time.
Teacher: Yes, but what types of things do you read where it is important for you to note sequence?
Student: Directions for putting things together.
Teacher: What else? What about your other subjects in school?
Student: (No response.)
Teacher: How about history? Does it require sequence?
Student: Yes.
Teacher: Why?
Student: Because it tells things the way they happened and it gives dates.
Teacher: What other subjects require the use of sequence?

(The dialogue continues until the teacher feels comfortable that students understand where the use of sequencing would be important.)

The purpose of this type of discussion between the teacher and students is to help students bring to a level of consciousness the process they have learned and when they might use it in their reading. The dialogue is part of the summarizing that occurs at the end of the teaching step. The same kind of summary should also occur after students have had opportunities to apply the skill in the reading of natural text. Each time students are taught a new comprehension skill or process, the verbalization of how it works and when it might be used should be repeated. As much as possible, it should be the students who verbalize what they have learned and when they might use it, but the teacher may have to prompt the students by asking the right questions.

Metacognitive development must continue during the guided silent reading and discussion part of the directed reading lesson. Each time students read a selection, they should be aware of the comprehension skills and processes they will need to apply in their reading. Teachers should call the students' attention to these skills and processes before the silent reading begins. For example, the teacher could say:

You have been learning how to determine the main ideas of paragraphs. In the selection you are about to read, think about using this skill to help you understand what the author is telling you about life in space.

This type of reminder helps students make the connection between what they were taught and what they should apply.

In actual reading, students use many skills and processes of comprehension at once. However, in guided application, the teacher is usually concerned about only one skill at a time. Once students have learned to use several comprehension skills, the teacher should provide some lessons that require students to apply several skills at one time; such applications are called cumulative applications. As discussed earlier in this text, teachers can ask questions that will help them determine whether the students are applying the skills they have been taught.

Teachers must exercise caution in developing this aspect of the metacognitive processes in comprehension. Students should not be asked to memorize and recite rules or names of skills. As teachers and students, we can recall times when we were required to memorize phonic rules only to discover later that they were not applied in actual reading. Further, in some instances, good students can recite the rules, but they cannot use them. When teaching metacognition in relation to reading comprehension, the teacher's objective is to help students become aware of the skills and processes of comprehension that they need in order to read and understand a specific text selection. This aspect of metacognitive development should be built into all teaching/modeling strategies for comprehension. Example 5.2 presents a skill reminder for a comprehension skill that is to be applied in a basal reading selection.

Teachers must not simply teach a skill or process; they must also guide students to see how the skill or process works and when it might be needed in reading. On the other hand, teachers must not get so caught up with having students identify processes that they fail to see whether students can comprehend. It is possible for a student to be able to comprehend effectively without being able to tell what skills and processes are being used. The teacher must remember that it is comprehension that is most important, and not the recital of skills.

The second part of metacognitive development that should be built into instruction is cognitive monitoring (Palincsar and Brown, 1984b). In terms of reading, this is referred to as comprehension monitoring (Baker and Brown, 1984b). Comprehension monitoring means that readers are constantly checking themselves as they read to make certain they understand what they have read; if they do not understand, they stop, go back, and reread to try to correct their lack of understanding. This process of monitoring must be modeled for students in the same manner that the other skills and processes of comprehension are modeled. The modeling can take place during the guided reading portion of the DRL. This type of activity brings to a level of consciousness for students the need to constantly check on their own comprehension as they are reading. A strategy for modeling comprehension monitoring is presented on page 259.

In summary, metacognitive development should be built into the direct instructional strategies for reading comprehension. Metacognition involves two components: (1) knowing the skills and processes needed to effectively comprehend a selection; (2) being able to monitor one's own comprehension during reading. Awareness of the skills and processes needed to perform a comprehension task can be developed as part of the skill building portion of the DRL (when the teacher models skills and processes), but it must be further developed in guided silent reading (when the teacher points out to students which comprehension skills and processes to apply in reading a given selection). The second aspect of metacognition, comprehension monitoring, should be modeled through direct instruction and can occur during guided silent reading.

EXAMPLE 5.2 BASAL SERIES METACOGNITIVE SKILL REMINDER —

Farolas are shaped like regular hanging lanterns, but in parades, they are often carried on long poles. In the evening, the light inside the farola adds color and light to the busy festivities of the parade.

Tell children that the story they will read today is about a parade where farolas are used. At this particular parade, people come dressed in many costumes and the costumes tell something about where they work.

- Print *Dora Rivera* on the board. **This is the name of the girl in the story. Her first name is Dora (Door** *eh***). Her family name is Rivera (***Riv ear eh***). Say her name with me. Dora Rivera.**
Print *Ramón* on the board. **This is the first name of Dora's brother. His name is Ramón (Rah** **móan).**
Print *Rosa* on the board. **This is the first name of Dora's sister. Rosa (Rose** *eh***).**

Skill Application **Now let's see how many syllables you hear in each of these names. When I point to a name, say the name softly to yourself. Then hold up one, two, or three fingers to tell how many syllables you hear in that name. Point to the names Dora, Rivera, Ramón, and Rosa.**

Skill Reminder

Comprehension: Drawing Conclusions (C2 · G1b)
Explain to children that sometimes when they are reading, they will find that the author tells them some things they need to know but lets them figure out other things for themselves. Remind children that as they read, they should use what the author tells them along with what they already know from their own experience to figure out some things for themselves.

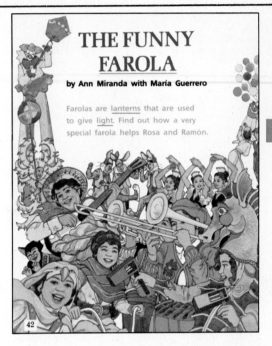

THE FUNNY FAROLA

by Ann Miranda with María Guerrero

Farolas are <u>lanterns</u> that are used to give <u>light</u>. Find out how a very special farola helps Rosa and Ramón.

1

42

Reading

Page 42: Purpose Setting for *The Funny Farola*

Ask children to open to **Reader** page 42, and look at the picture on this page. Ask children how they think the people in the picture might be feeling and why they think that.

After children have had a chance to read the page silently, call on volunteer to read the page aloud. Point out that this story was written by Ann Miranda with help from María Guerrero.

Tell children when they read the story they'll find out how a farola helps Rosa and Ramón.

STRATEGY FOR TEACHING AND MODELING
COMPREHENSION SKILLS AND PROCESSES

The Preparation Step

The strategies used for teaching and modeling comprehension skills and processes must not only show and demonstrate how to use the skills and processes but must also help students understand when to use them. Before beginning to teach any comprehension skill or process, the teacher must

1. consider the backgrounds of the students in relation to the material to be used,
2. consider the reading levels of the students,
3. determine the objective for teaching.

Considering Students' Backgrounds

The students' backgrounds and schema are vitally important for their comprehension of any text; thus, these factors must be considered in selecting the material to be used in teaching. Because the concern in teaching is to teach students a given skill or process, and not to develop the background and/or schema needed for a particular topic, the material used for the teaching should be on topics already within the students' backgrounds of experience. The teaching step should require as little background development and schema-building as possible. This does not mean that teachers should not be interested in broadening the background experiences of students; they certainly should! (See Chapter 3.) However, the focus here should be on helping students learn the process or skill, and the more closely related to the students' existing background the material is, the better it is for teaching.

Considering Students' Reading Levels

The second factor that must be considered in preparing for the teaching of a comprehension skill or process is the difficulty level of the material to be read. The success factor is crucial to learning in the classroom (Squires, Huitt, and Segars, 1983). Therefore, the text used for the initial teaching of any comprehension skill or process should be at a level of difficulty that can be easily handled by students. If the students are having trouble learning, the material used in teaching should be at their independent level (level at which students can read with complete ease). If they are learning at what would be considered a normal pace, the material can be at their instructional level (level at which students miss a few words but still have good comprehension).

By accounting for both the topic of the material in relation to the students' background and schema and the difficulty level of the material in relation to the students' reading abilities, the teacher can create a teaching situation that will focus directly on the skill or process to be taught and modeled. Thus, the teacher's concern will be on teaching, not on overcoming lack of background or trying to guide students through text that is too difficult. These two factors must be considered as part of the preparation for teaching.

Determining Teaching Objective

The third factor the teacher must consider before beginning instruction is the teaching objective. Too often teachers begin a lesson without having clearly in mind what it is they want students to learn and what behavior on the part of students will signify that they have learned it; such circumstances lead to poor teaching or no teaching. The teaching objective has been referred to as both a behavioral and a performance objective; however, it does not really matter what term is used. What does matter is that the teacher clearly state the teaching objective before beginning to teach. By clearly defining an objective, the teacher will know exactly what he or she wants students to learn and will be able to determine whether they have learned it.

The following are examples of possible objectives for comprehension lessons:

1. Given paragraphs of narrative text, students will demonstrate their ability to pick out relevant details by answering specific fact questions correctly.
2. Given text with information that leads to inference of additional information, students will be able to explain how they used the stated information to infer as they read.

Notice that the second objective is oriented toward having students explain the process they used in inferencing. The first objective is directed toward students' actual performance of the comprehension ability. Both objectives let the teacher know what it is he or she wants students to learn and the performance that will indicate that it has been learned. The teacher can make the objectives more precise by including the level of performance expected (e.g., by stating, "by answering eighty percent of the specific fact questions..."); however, such precision is really needed only when the objective relates to a test to check for mastery. Once the objective is identified, the teacher is ready to begin teaching.

The Teaching Step

Letting Students Know What Is to Be Learned

In the first part of teaching, the teacher uses a simple dialogue to let the students know what they are going to learn and to relate it to their prior knowledge. In determining the objective, the teacher decided what he or she wanted students to learn. Now, the teacher is informing students of the objective. For example, when teaching students the skill of inferencing, the teacher might say:

Do authors give you facts or details in their writing? (Students respond, yes.) Do they always tell you all the exact information they want you to know about a topic? (Students respond, no.) You have learned to identify the important facts or details as you read. Today, you are going to learn how to use those facts and details to figure out information the author doesn't tell you specifically.

The teacher could, but does not have to, use the term inferencing.

Modeling

Modeling, the second component of teaching, is the one that is the most involved and takes the most time. In modeling, the teacher shows students how to think through the use of the comprehension skills and processes. There are three steps to the modeling of any comprehension skill or process (Cooper et al., 1979):

1. Develop the *concept* of the skill or process.
2. Check to see if students can use the skill or process at the *listening* level; develop its use at the listening level, if necessary.
3. Demonstrate the use of the skill or process at the *reading* level and verbalize the thinking required to use the skill.

Developing the Concept of the Skill: The first step in modeling involves making certain that students understand the concept underlying the skill or process being modeled. When teaching inferencing, for example, the teacher can start the modeling with an activity that requires students to look at some concrete material, such as a picture, and make an inference from it. One possible activity is shown in Example 5.3.

At the beginning reading levels, it will be necessary for the teacher to do most of the verbalizing of how a skill or process was used; as students mature in their reading, the teacher should prompt them with questions to help them do the verbalizing. Through verbalization, the students will become more aware of how they are using the skill or process being taught; this is a part of the metacognitive development needed for effective comprehension.

At the beginning reading levels, the teacher will need to emphasize *developing* the concept of the skill or process; at the more advanced levels, this aspect of modeling will become more of a checking activity to be certain that students understand the concept.

In concept development and checking activities, the teacher should use concrete materials as much as possible. At the more advanced levels, the checking activities may be carried out verbally, but even when they are, the questions used should always draw on the most concrete examples possible. For example, to check whether sixth graders understand how to predict outcomes, the teacher might say:

If you were asked to make a prediction about which team was going to win a basketball game, how would you go about doing it?

EXAMPLE 5.3   MODELING INFERENCE: DEVELOPING THE CONCEPT

Pass around copies of this picture or post it on a bulletin board.

Ask students to look at the picture and describe the weather as they see it. Then ask them to tell what they see in the sky (dark clouds and the sun) and what the person is carrying (an umbrella). Next, ask students to tell what the weather may be like later in the day in this scene. Accept reasonable answers (such as, It might be raining). Have students tell how they used the existing facts to help them reach their answers. Discuss all answers the students give, but accept only those that are verifiable. If students are unable to figure out what the weather may be like, answer the question for them and explain how you were able to determine your answer. Then, point out to students that they should use the existing facts in the picture to help them formulate their answers.

This is a verbal concept checking activity. Student responses would let the teacher know whether the students understand the concept. Note that even though the concept is being checked verbally, the question used for checking understanding of the concept draws on a concrete example. Verbal checking should not replace concrete materials when the concrete materials, such as pictures, would indeed be a better way to develop a process or skill concept.

Developing the Skill at the Listening Level: The second step in modeling is checking or developing the skill or process at the listening level. The purpose of this step, which is a transition between oral language and reading, is to make certain that students are able to use the skill in their listening. The teacher should begin by telling the students that they are going to listen to a sentence or short passage in order to find the answer to some specific question or other purpose for reading. The teacher should then give the purpose, read the material, and have the students respond. Not only should students answer the question posed as the purpose for listening, but the teacher and students together should verbalize how the answer was reached. Example 5.4 shows how this can be done when teaching inferencing.

EXAMPLE 5.4   MODELING INFERENCING: LISTENING ─────────

Ask students to listen to a paragraph you are going to read and tell you what happened about Mr. Lind's appointment:

Mr. Lind only had fifteen minutes to make his appointment. He hurried from his office and pushed the elevator button, but the elevator didn't come. Finally, after some nervous moments of waiting, it arrived. Down the forty-two floors and out into the parking garage he ran. As he got into his car, he noticed it was leaning to the right. He got out and went to the other side to find a flat tire. Mr. Lind looked at his watch and saw that he had five minutes and eight miles to go.

In some instances, especially at the beginning stages of instruction, you may find it necessary to give students choices of what might happen. For example:

1. Mr. Lind made his appointment.
2. Mr. Lind got stuck in the elevator.
3. Mr. Lind was late for his appointment.

When choices are given they should be written on the chalkboard before the students are directed to listen to the passage.

After students have listened to the passage, discuss their answers. Point out that although the paragraph does not tell what happened about Mr. Lind's appointment, it does give clues that can lead them to formulate an answer. Ask students to verbalize how they used the existing facts within the text to reach their answers. Explain to students that although there may be several possible answers, you can only accept those that can be verified. Again, this type of verbalization is a part of the metacognitive development that is essential to effective comprehension.

─────────────

For some students, it will be necessary to do more work at the listening level before moving on to the reading level. Because of the close connection between listening comprehension and reading comprehension (Sticht and James, 1984), it is important that the skill or process be carefully checked and developed, if necessary, at the listening level before it is taught at the reading level.

Modeling at the Reading Level: The final step of the modeling process is demonstrating how to think through the use of the skill or process at the reading level—that is, showing students how to use the skill or process when they read. This part of the modeling should begin with the teacher presenting students with a portion of text and giving them a purpose for reading that requires the use of the skill or process. After students have read the text, the teacher should give the answer required by the purpose and go back through the passage to show and explain how the answer was reached. The teacher should then repeat the procedure with a second portion of text, but this time should have the students do the answering and verbalizing; the teacher should prompt and direct the students with questions as needed. The actual name of the skill or process—for example, inferencing—can be used in the discussion, but teachers should be cautious about burdening students with unnecessary information, particularly at the beginning reading levels.

The teaching of inferencing has been used as an example throughout this section to illustrate the steps of modeling. First, the concept of the skill was developed; then the skill was checked at the listening level. In the final part of modeling, the skill must be demonstrated at the reading level. One way of doing this is shown in Example 5.5.

EXAMPLE 5.5   MODELING INFERENCING: READING ─────────

Distribute a copy of the following paragraph to students and ask them to read it silently to tell what happened to Larry and Ted. (Also put a copy of the paragraph on the chalkboard, a chart, or a transparency.)

Larry and his friend Ted were getting ready to play their last baseball game of the season. Ted was the team's most valuable player, and they needed him to pull off this victory. For the first time, Ted was going to get to play in the championship; something had always kept him out of the last game of the season. All that Larry and Ted could think about was winning as they leaped and jumped over the benches in the locker room on their way to the field. Neither of them saw the hole the plumbers had left uncovered in the floor as they jumped the last bench and turned the corner to the hall. Neither of them knew what trouble was to follow during the rest of the afternoon.

After the students have completed the reading, write the most likely answers on the board. For example:

1. Larry and Ted got hurt and couldn't play.
2. Ted got hurt and couldn't play.
3. Larry got hurt and couldn't play.

Then explain the thinking that led you to each answer. By doing this, you are showing students how to think through the process of inferencing.
Say: As I began to read the paragraph, I could tell that Ted was an important player for the team. (Underline the relevant part of Sentence 2.) As I read on, I could tell that this was the first time he was going to get to play in the champion-

ship because something had always caused him trouble before. (Underline Sentence 3.)

As I read further, I could tell that both boys were excited about the game. I could tell this from Sentence 4, but the author doesn't say so exactly. (Underline the relevant part of Sentence 4.)

The beginning of Sentence 5 tells me that neither boy saw the hole left in the floor by the plumber. (Underline it.) Finally, from Sentence 6 I can tell that neither boy knows what trouble is about to follow. (Underline the relevant parts of Sentence 6.)

The author doesn't tell me what happened to Larry and Ted, but the author gives clues telling me that Ted is important to the team, that he has run into trouble in past years and hasn't yet played in the championship game, and that this year there will be trouble in the afternoon. From my experience, I know that these kinds of circumstances are likely to lead to trouble. Therefore, all three of my answers are possible. I really think the best answer is number two, Ted got hurt and couldn't play, but I can't really tell until I read further.

Here is how the paragraph used in modeling would look after the process was complete. The comments at the left explain how each underlined passage relates to the dialogue above.

Sets the scene about how important Ted was to the game.

Larry and his friend Ted were getting ready to play their last baseball game of the season. Ted was the team's most valuable player, and they needed him to pull off this victory. For the first time, Ted was going to get to play in the championship; something had always kept him out of the last game of the season. All that Larry and Ted could think about was winning as they leaped and jumped over the benches in the locker room on their way to the field. Neither of them saw the hole the plumbers had left uncovered in the floor as they jumped the last bench and turned the corner to the hall. Neither of them knew what trouble was to follow during the rest of the afternoon.

Lets you know Ted hasn't played in the final game before.

Shows that the boys were excited and not thinking about much besides the game and winning.

These last two sentences give clues that *neither* boy knows what is about to happen.

You would then have students model the skill as you have just done, using another paragraph. For the paragraph that follows, have students read to tell what was so unusual about Captain Sanders. Tell them to be ready to explain how they reached their answer(s), just as you did.

The giant jumbo jet rolled slowly onto the taxiway. For Ron Vickers, the copilot, this was a new experience. All of the other pilots he had worked under had been great guys, but never before had he had a boss who had received so much publicity just before boarding the plane. The press, the lights, the questions, and all the passengers watching the new 747 pilot for International Air made Ron a little nervous. But Captain Sanders wasn't affected by all of the attention. International Air was proud to be first in its new hiring policies.

As the captain and the copilots went through their last minute routines, Ron couldn't help but be a bit excited himself as he looked over at the captain. This was indeed a first being shared by the passengers, including the captain's son, daughter, and husband.

After students have read the paragraph, have one student give the answer or answers and model as you did with the first paragraph. Have the student underline sentences or parts of sentences that support his or her ideas. Ask directive questions and provide prompts as needed to coach students through the modeling.

Conclude the modeling by pointing out to students that they used clues in the text plus their own background to formulate ideas the author did not state directly. Indicate that as one reads, it is always necessary to use ideas in the text plus one's own experiences to determine information the author does not state.

The three parts of the modeling process, concept, listening, and reading development, are summarized in Table 5.1. All three parts should be included in the modeling of all comprehension skills and processes. Teachers of primary-level students will probably need to spend more time on concept development than will teachers of intermediate-level students. The intermediate-level teacher will probably put the bulk of emphasis on reading development, carrying out concept and listening development primarily as checking activities. Often there is a temptation on the part of intermediate-level teachers to omit the first two parts of modeling because they assume that older, more mature readers have already developed the concept and listening aspects related to the skills and processes being taught. However, such assumptions should not be made.

Table 5.1 Steps for Modeling Comprehension Skills and Processes

Step	Purpose	Comments
Concept development	Develop the underlying concept of the skill or process.	Use concrete materials and/or examples.
Listening development	Check to see if students can use the skill at the listening level; if not, develop the skill.	This step bridges the gap between a student's oral language and reading.
Reading development	Model the use of the skill or process and verbalize how it is used.	The verbalization of the process is an explanation of the thinking one goes through when using it.

Guided Practice

The next part of the teaching step is guided practice, which is where students complete a directed-choice activity under the teacher's direction. In directed-choice activities (fill-in-the-blank, multiple choice, and so on), the student's attention is drawn directly to the skill or process being taught, and the teacher is given an opportunity to tell whether students have learned what was expected. It is at this point in direct instruction that the teacher can check to see if students have accomplished the objective that was identified as a part of the teaching. The teacher should go through the guided-practice activity item by item, having students complete each exercise and explain how they reached their answer(s). The teacher should prompt, question, and reteach during the guided practice as needed. If students are unable to complete the exercises in the guided practice, a complete reteaching should be done before independent practice and application are carried out. Example 5.6 illustrates a guided-practice exercise for inferencing.

EXAMPLE 5.6 GUIDED-PRACTICE ACTIVITY FOR INFERENCING ——

Directions to Teacher: Have students read each of the following paragraphs silently, one at a time, and answer the question given at the beginning. Go over each exercise as it is completed, and have students prove their answers by reading aloud parts of the paragraph that are supportive. If students have difficulty completing the inferencing activity, go over each exercise and model how you, the teacher, would have reached your answer.

1. What happened to the July 4 relay race?
    a. It was canceled because of rain.
    b. It was run on time.
    c. It was run after the rain.

    The July 4 relay race was about to begin just as it started to rain. The runners ran from the track to the cover of the stands. Everyone waited, hoping the rain would stop. In about an hour the sky cleared and the runners returned to the track.

2. What did Mark discuss with his teacher after school?
    a. the cheating on the test
    b. his low test score
    c. the assignment for the next day

    Mark always believed in being fair. One day his class was taking a science test that he and most of the other students had studied very hard for. During the test, he saw Sarah copying answers from her book. When the test papers were returned the next day, Mark had a good score. However, Mark stayed after school to talk to his science teacher.

3. What was the surprise when Ted came home from school?
   a. The plumbers were digging holes to repair broken pipes.
   b. Dad was having a swimming pool put in.
   c. Dad was having another room put on the house.

   Ted came home from school and saw several trucks in front of his house. A large bulldozer was digging a huge hole in his backyard. His dad came out of the house. "Surprise!" he said. "It won't be long until you can have a swimming party at home."

Summarizing

The final part of the teaching step is the summary. Here, the teacher asks students to tell what they have learned in a given lesson and how and when it might be useful to them in their reading. It is easy to fall into the trap of telling students what they have learned, but by doing so, the teacher does not accomplish the purpose of this part of teaching, which is to get students to think about what they have just learned and begin to internalize it into their thinking and reading. This is a part of the readers' metacognitive development. Therefore, the students must be the ones doing the summarizing, although the teacher can prompt and guide students by asking questions. The dialogue in Example 5.7 illustrates the summarizing step for inferencing.

EXAMPLE 5.7 SUMMARIZING DIALOGUE FOR INFERENCING ───

Teacher: Who can tell me what you have learned about determining information when the author does not state the information directly (inferencing)?
Student: You look at the facts the author gives and figure out your ideas based on those.
Teacher: What do you use to figure out your ideas?
Student: You use the clues from your reading.
Teacher: What else do you use?
Student: What you already know.
Teacher: Yes, you use the clues in the text plus the ideas you have in your head to form these new ideas. Do you always come up with one absolute idea?
Student: No, sometimes there are several possible ideas.
Teacher: But how do you know which one or ones to accept?
Student: You think about the ones that have the most support in the author's writing. You can accept more than one possible idea.
Teacher: When are you likely to use this comprehension skill?
Student: When you read mysteries and the author gives you clues to who committed the murder.
Teacher: Yes, that's right, but are there other times?
Student: Anytime you read material where the author does not tell you everything and you sort of have to read between the lines.

This type of dialogue between the teacher and students brings out the points that have been taught, gives the students an opportunity to put the ideas into their own words, and helps students think more about how and when they would use what has been taught.

The teaching/modeling strategy that has been presented here is one that can be used in the skill-building portion of the DRL or at any other time that a specific comprehension skill or process is to be taught. The teaching/modeling activity should always be followed by independent practice and application.

The Practice Step

The teaching step for a particular comprehension skill or process should be immediately followed by an independent-practice activity. This activity should be very similar to or match exactly the type of activity used for the guided practice. The major difference between the guided practice and the independent practice is that the latter is done by the students independent of the teacher. The independent-practice activity should be a directed-choice exercise and should be discussed with students after completion.

The purpose of independent practice is to focus the students' attention on the skill or process being taught and provide them with opportunities to internalize it. The independent practice for the inferencing example that has run through this chapter would follow the same format as the guided-practice activity (page 212). If students successfully complete the independent-practice activity, they are ready to move on to application. It is not necessary for students to complete three or four workbook pages practicing a skill after they have demonstrated their ability to perform it.

The Application Step

Following independent practice, students must be given many opportunities to apply the comprehension skill or process they have learned to the reading of connected or natural text. Short paragraphs or sentences should not be used for the application; rather, real text in a basal selection, trade book, content book, or other source should be used. The power of direct instruction resides in application. It has been shown that teaching and practicing without the appropriate application do not have the desired impact on a student's reading (Baumann, 1984).

Within the framework of the directed reading lesson, application takes place during guided silent reading. However, the background and vocabulary for the selection to be read must be developed prior to the reading. (See Chapters 3 and 4.) After the background and vocabulary have been developed, the following steps should occur:

1. *Remind the students of what comprehension skill or process they are to apply in the selection.*

    This is done to help students develop their metacognitive processes and to direct their thinking toward using the skill or process that was taught. Although students will use many comprehension skills and processes simultaneously as they read, the skill reminder should alert the students to the one skill that they should focus on as they are reading. Therefore, in direct instruction the teacher should focus on one skill at a time even though students will be using several at once.

2. *Have students read the text to determine the intent of the selection.*

Students should be given an appropriate purpose to guide their reading. The purpose can relate to the skill or process being applied, but it will not always do that. It should be stated so that it requires the students to focus on the entire selection and not on one isolated detail. The purpose should also help students relate their prior knowledge to their reading. (See Chapter 3.)

3. *Discuss the text.*

The reading of the text is followed by discussion during which the purpose is checked and the story line or main ideas are brought out; this is followed by questions meant to extend the reader's thinking. (See Chapter 2 for a detailed discussion.) The teacher can also ask questions to check the students' application of the skill or process that was taught.

4. *Summarize what was learned and how it was used in reading.*

At the conclusion of the teaching step of direct instruction, the teacher had students summarize what they had learned up to that point about the skill being taught. Now that the students have applied the skill or process in reading natural text, they should be asked to summarize again what they have learned and to talk about how they were able to use the skill or process in their reading. This is done to further develop the students' metacognitive awareness.

Students need many more opportunities to apply comprehension skills and processes than they do to practice them. Therefore, students should be given many opportunities to read selections and discuss them with the teacher (guided application) and to read selections on their own and share what they have read with others (independent application).

Example 5.8 illustrates guided application for the skill of inferencing, using the background and readiness and guided silent reading and discussion portions of the DRL. The selection "Ernie and the Mile-Long Muffler" is used for the application.

SAMPLE LESSONS FOR TEACHING AND MODELING

This section presents sample lessons for teaching and modeling selected comprehension skills and processes. Each sample follows the basic guidelines presented for the teaching phase of direct instruction and may be used by teachers as given or may serve as models for developing other lessons. The modeling part of each sample uses the three components for modeling a comprehension skill or process presented in this chapter—concept, listening, and reading development.

(text continues on page 232)

Ernie and the Mile-Long Muffler

by Marjorie Lewis

When Ernie was sick, his uncle showed him a good way to pass the time. Little did Ernie dream what would happen because of his hobby.

290

One October afternoon Ernie was home from school waiting for the scabs from his chicken pox spots to fall off. Even though nobody could catch the chicken pox from him anymore, he looked pretty awful. Now that he didn't itch and feel terrible, he was bored. Ernie was so bored he couldn't wait to get back to school. He wondered what exciting things his friends in the fourth grade and Mrs. Crownfeld, his teacher, were doing while he spent his time waiting for scabs to fall off. When the doorbell suddenly rang, Ernie was glad. Even answering the door was something to do.

When Ernie looked through the peephole in the door to find out who was there before opening it, he saw it was his Uncle Simon, his mother's brother, who was a sailor. Ernie and his mother hadn't seen Uncle Simon in two years because he had been away at sea. Ernie had thought of Uncle Simon often during those two years and had imagined Uncle Simon climbing the rigging, doing things with the mizzenmast, swabbing the deck, and standing watch with a spy glass — all the things that sailors did in the stories Ernie read.

Ernie and Uncle Simon sat and talked with each other while Ernie's mother made dinner. Uncle Simon showed Ernie pictures of the places he had been and of the ship he'd sailed on.

Then Uncle Simon asked Ernie what he liked best to eat. Ernie told him his best thing was a hamburger with red onion circles, lots of ketchup on the top part, lots of

mayonnaise on the bottom part, and a roll with seeds to hold it all together. Ernie told Uncle Simon his worst thing to eat was anything that shook. Uncle Simon said he didn't like shaky things either, especially tapioca pudding because the tapioca beads looked like fish eyes. Uncle Simon told Ernie all about the strange foods he had eaten all over the world: rattlesnake, turtle soup, candied grasshoppers, rabbit stew, cows' eyes, calves' brains, and chocolate-covered ants. Ernie began to feel sick.

Uncle Simon changed the subject and asked Ernie what kinds of things he liked to do. Ernie told him about reading comics and cereal boxes, trading baseball cards, making cookies, and shooting baskets.

Uncle Simon told Ernie he liked most to read mystery stories; next, to bake bread; and third, to knit. He told Ernie that on his ship, when he wasn't working, he had lots of time to do all three. Ernie said that he didn't know that men knitted. Uncle Simon said that men have knitted for hundreds of years, especially men in armies and navies who spent a lot of time waiting for things to happen. Uncle Simon opened his seabag and took out a sweater that looked like a rainbow and let Ernie try it on. Ernie thought it was the most terrific sweater he had ever seen. Then Uncle Simon took some knitting needles out of his bag and a big ball of yellow yarn. By the time Ernie's mother called them for dinner, Uncle Simon had taught Ernie to knit.

The next few days, while Ernie waited for the scabs to fall off and his spots to fade, he knitted a sweater for his dog Buster, socks for his father's golf clubs, a Christmas stocking for his canary, and a muffler for his mother for her birthday. The muffler was so beautiful and fit his

mother's neck so well that Ernie decided to make one for everyone he knew. Then he had a better idea. The idea came to him one morning while he was eating breakfast and reading his world-record book for the millionth time. Ernie decided that he would knit the world's longest muffler. He would make it a mile long! Ernie wrote a letter to Uncle Simon, who was back at sea, and told him about his plan.

He asked his mother to get all the record books she could find in the library. Ernie looked through all of them and found that none of them had a record for muffler-knitting. Ernie pictured himself holding the victorious knitting needles crossed in front of him, with foot after foot of muffler looping around the throne he would be sitting on when they took his picture for the record book.

Ernie told his mother about his idea. She told him that there were 5,280 feet in a mile. Then Ernie and his mother figured out that there were 63,360 inches in a

mile. Ernie's mother said that it would surely be a lot of muffler to knit!

Ernie asked his mother to ask her friends to give him all the extra yarn they had. By the time Ernie was well enough to go back to school, he had finished about two feet of muffler. Ernie thought that the two feet had been done so quickly that it wouldn't be hard at all to do a mile of knitting.

His first day back at school, Ernie packed his gym bag with his gym shorts, his T-shirt, and his knitting. He kept his knitting with him all morning. When he was sitting and waiting for late-comers to be present for morning attendance, or for the assembly program to begin, or for the fire drill to be over, Ernie knitted. Mrs. Crownfeld said she thought it was wonderful to be able to knit and asked Ernie if, after recess, he would show the class how to knit. Ernie said he would.

At recess, the class went outside. Ernie sat down on the bench to wait for his turn to shoot baskets. He took out his knitting.

"I can't believe you're doing that," said Frankie.

"I mean my *mother* does that!" said Alfred.

"So what," said Ernie. "Your mother bakes cookies, Alfred, and so do you. So do I."

"It's different," Alfred said. "Knitting is different."

Alfred watched while Ernie's fingers made the needles form stitches. When Edward came over, Frankie and Alfred moved away. Edward leaned over and watched Ernie.

"No boy I ever saw did that," Edward said. "Boys don't do that." Edward reached out and grabbed the ball of yarn, tearing it off from the knitting. Ernie watched

silently while Edward, Frankie, and Alfred played basketball with the yarn ball. Then they dropped it into a puddle. They fished it out and tossed it to Ernie.

Ernie looked at the ball of yarn with glops of mud and leaves tangled in it. Then he put his needles and the two feet of muffler on the bench and threw the ball of yarn away into the bushes.

The three boys, Frankie, Alfred, and Edward, formed a circle around Ernie. They began to run around madly with their thumbs in their ears and their fingers flapping, yelling, "Nyah, nyah, Ernie knits!" Over and over again. Then the three boys called Ernie a nitwit (or was it a *knitwit?* thought Ernie miserably). The other children in the class came over to watch. Some of them joined the group around Ernie.

"Hey, Ernie," called Richard. Raising his voice to a screech that sounded like a girl's voice, Richard said, "Oh, Ernie. Would you make me a pink sweater?"

By the time the bell rang for the end of recess, Ernie felt terrible. When Mrs. Crownfeld asked him to show the class how to knit, everyone began to giggle. Ernie walked up to the front of the classroom. In his hands, he held the needles and the two-foot piece of the record-making mile-long muffler. He took a deep breath and waited until the class quieted down.

He told them all about his Uncle Simon's being a sailor. He told them about the strange things Uncle Simon had eaten and the places Uncle Simon had been. He told them about Uncle Simon's terrific sweater. He told them that Uncle Simon liked best to read mysteries; next, to bake bread; and third, to knit. He told them what Uncle Simon had said about people in armies and navies having lots of time while they waited for things to happen, so soldiers and sailors for hundreds of years knitted to keep from being bored.

Finally, Ernie told the class that he was going to knit the longest muffler in the world, a mile long, and get his name and his picture in the record books. The class was absolutely quiet.

Mrs. Crownfeld said that she would be very proud to have one of her fourth-grade students be a record maker. Then Mrs. Crownfeld asked Ernie to demonstrate how to knit. Ernie said that he couldn't because he had lost his ball of yarn during recess. Ernie promised to show Mrs. Crownfeld and the class how to knit the next day.

At the end of the day, Ernie was walking home by himself with his knitting in his gym bag.

"Ernie, Ernie," called Frankie. "Wait up!"

Frankie walked along with Ernie. "Thanks for not telling the teacher what happened to your yarn," he said. "I think it's neat how you're going to win the muffler-knitting record."

Ernie and Frankie went to Ernie's house and ate some cookies that Ernie had baked when he was sick. Ernie showed Frankie all the stuff he had knitted when he had been home with the chicken pox. Frankie admired the dog's sweater most of all. Ernie next showed Frankie the bags of different-colored yarns that his mother's friends had given him for his muffler project.

"Say, Ernie," said Frankie. "I'll bet my mother's got some yarn left over from the sweater she knitted for my sister. I'll ask her if I can give it to you."

"That would be great, Frankie," said Ernie. "I'm going to need all the yarn I can get!"

The next day in school, Ernie showed the class how one needle went in front of the stitch to make a knit stitch and how it went in back to make a purl stitch. He showed them how the two kinds of stitches together made the bumpy ridges that kept the sleeves tight at the wrists. He showed the class how to make the pieces get bigger and smaller to fit next to each other, so that they could be sewn together to make a swell outfit. He offered to teach anyone in class who wanted to learn. Mrs. Crownfeld was the first to ask Ernie for lessons.

After a while, everyone in the fourth grade learned to knit. Mrs. Crownfeld made a deal with them: The class could knit during homeroom, fire drills (while they were outside waiting to go back in), or rainy-day recess, plus a special knitting time right after lunch each day when the class could knit while Mrs. Crownfeld put her knitting aside and read them a story from the library.

In return for all the knitting lessons from Ernie, the class brought in all the yarn they could get from anyone who would give it to them. Ernie kept the yarn in a big plastic garbage bag in the corner of the classroom. Each day, a knitting monitor measured Ernie's muffler and wrote the length in a notebook Mrs. Crownfeld had given the class as a present.

By Thanksgiving, Ernie's muffler was sixteen feet long, and Ernie was looking pale. He never went outside to play. He didn't do anything at all but go to school, do his homework, eat his meals, and knit. Cynthia, who was very good in math, subtracted the sixteen feet Ernie had finished from the 5,280 feet in a mile. That left 5,264 feet to go before the end of school. Since school would be over and summer vacation begin in twenty-eight weeks, Ernie would have to knit over 188 feet of muffler *every week,* or about twenty-seven feet *every day* (including

Saturday and Sunday) to finish the muffler by the end of fourth grade.

Ernie listened to Cynthia very carefully. He remembered the picture he had dreamed of: sitting on a throne, his knitting needles crossed in front of him, foot after foot of muffler looping around him. His name and photograph would be in the record books. Pride would be in the faces of his parents and his teacher. He would have the admiration of all his friends. Then Ernie thought of how long it had been since he played with his friends or baked cookies or read a book — or even a cereal box.

Ernie decided to take it easy. It wasn't important when the muffler got finished. He could finish it someday. So maybe it wouldn't be the longest muffler in the world. Mrs. Crownfeld would be disappointed not to have a fourth-grade record-breaker, but Ernie figured if he ever did finish it — in fifth grade maybe, or sixth — he would publicly thank her for her encouragement when he became famous.

Ernie told his mother, Mrs. Crownfeld, and his friends what he had decided. Now he could go out and shoot baskets during recess. He began to read his cereal boxes again. Sometimes, while he was watching television or waiting for the dentist to see him, or riding in the car for a long time, he would knit. He even had time to write to Uncle Simon and tell him everything that had happened since he learned to knit.

Ernie's class continued to bring in yarn for him. Ernie decided to give the yarn to the class because now that they all could knit, they could have a fair or something to raise money to buy games and books for children in the town hospital.

All the things sold at the fair were knitted by the fourth grade. Frankie was good at mittens and so was Edward. Frankie knitted all the right-hand ones and Edward all the left-hand ones. Between them, they made five pairs of mittens for the fair. Alfred made bean bags. Cynthia made pot holders. Other people made mufflers (the regular length). Mrs. Crownfeld made cat and dog sweaters. Someone else made pincushions. Everyone in the fourth grade made something. The fair was a huge success. They sold $173.42 worth of stuff, including six

pairs of slipper socks in bright colors that Ernie made and
cookies that Frankie, Alfred, and Ernie baked and sold.

By the time spring came, the fourth grade was famous. Everyone in town knew about their knitting and
Ernie's muffler, which was getting very long even if it
wasn't anywhere near a mile. When the local paper did a
story about the class and took a picture to go with it, on
the front page right in the middle of the photograph was
Ernie sitting on a chair, holding his knitting needles
crossed in front of him. Ernie's muffler was looped

303

around each member of the class and Mrs. Crownfeld, with several feet left over. It made Ernie as happy as if he had finished his mile of muffler. Suddenly, Ernie decided the time had come. Even though people were always saying you should finish everything you start, Ernie knew better. Three hundred fourteen feet was long enough. Long enough, Ernie thought, is long enough.

He asked Mrs. Crownfeld, who was an expert fringe maker, to put fringe at each end of the muffler. When the muffler was done, it was exhibited all over school — in the fourth-grade room, down the hall, in the principal's office, and in the library. People came to see it and admire the way Ernie made all the colors of fuzzy and thin yarn come together into a multicolored muffler. People who had contributed yarn could recognize their bits and were very pleased to see them used in Ernie's muffler.

When summer vacation came, Ernie's mother took the muffler home. Ernie helped her wrap it and put it away in a box. Then he went out to ride bikes with Frankie, Alfred, and Edward.

Author

Marjorie Lewis says, "I believe in stories — in giving children delight. I believe in the power of words to create music, laughter, and tears." Mrs. Lewis, a school librarian, has written several books for young readers. Like Ernie, she enjoys knitting projects that don't take too long to finish.

Source: ERNIE AND THE MILE-LONG MUFFLER by Marjorie Lewis, text © 1982 by Marjorie Lewis. Reprinted by permission of Coward, McCann & Geoghegan. In William K. Durr et al.: *Flights*, pp. 290–304 (Houghton Mifflin Reading), 1986.

Sample Lesson

Background and Readiness

To prepare students to read this selection, you must first develop the background and vocabulary they will need to be able to read it with understanding.

Background
1. Students need to know about knitting and to realize that most people think that only women knit.
2. Students need to know that people often set very high goals or expectations for themselves.

Vocabulary
   The following key-concept words should be pretaught: knit, muffler, purl stitch. (*Purl stitch* is not crucial to understanding the selection, but it does relate to the topic. The specific words to be pretaught will depend on the students' backgrounds.)

Procedures
   Direct students in a background-generating activity and a discussion of the two background concepts listed above. (See Chapter 3.) Throughout the discussion, integrate the teaching of vocabulary using the context procedure. (See Chapter 4.) Provide students with guided practice with the new words, and summarize the points covered in this section of the lesson.

Guided Silent Reading and Discussion

Remind Students of the Skill to Apply
Say: You have been learning how to use the information an author gives you to determine things the author doesn't actually say. (This is called inferencing.) You must use clues from the text and facts you already know to figure out the points you don't know. As you read "Ernie and the Mile-Long Muffler," think about using this skill.

Provide a Purpose for Reading
Say: Read the selection on pages 290–304 of your reader and be prepared to tell me what Ernie learned as a result of his knitting experience. (This purpose guides students' reading but also serves as a check on their application of inferencing.)

Discuss the Text
After students have finished reading the story, ask them questions that are designed to bring out the story line:

1. Who were the characters in the story?
2. Why was Uncle Simon so important in this story? *(Note: This is checking the application of inferencing.)*

3. Where does this story take place?
4. What was it that Ernie wanted to accomplish?
5. When Ernie first returned to school, what did the other students think of him and his knitting? *(checking the application of inferencing)*
6. After Ernie showed the class about knitting, how did they feel about him? *(checking the application of inferencing)*
7. What did everyone in the class want to learn to do?
8. How did the class offer to pay Ernie for the knitting lessons?
9. By Thanksgiving, what was Ernie beginning to learn about knitting his muffler? *(checking the application of inferencing)*
10. What did Ernie decide to do with some of the yarn he had collected?
11. What did the class do with all the things they had knitted?
12. By the time spring came, what had happened to the fourth-grade class?
13. What did Ernie decide about his muffler by the end of the year?
14. What did Ernie learn as a result of his knitting experience? *(checking purpose for reading; checking the application of inferencing)*

Discussion Extension
Next, ask students questions designed to extend their thinking about the selection:

1. What kind of person do you think Ernie was? Why? *(checking the application of inferencing; checking critical thinking)*
2. If you had been Ernie, how would you have felt when you went back to school? Why? *(relating students' experiences to the selection)*
3. What do you think the class learned as a result of this experience? Why? *(checking the application of inferencing; checking critical thinking)*

Summary About Inferencing
Say: In today's selection, you used your skill of inferencing to help you understand the story. How and when did you use that skill? (Guide students to see that they used inferencing when they figured out things the author did not directly tell them. Also, help them see that they got clues from the text, but much of the inferencing came from their own heads and the information they already knew. Refer to the story to show specific examples—pages 295, 296, 297.)
Say: When will you make use of this skill? (Guide students to see that they will use inferencing over and over again as they read; specific places might be in mysteries, social studies, and so on.)

The approximate level of difficulty is indicated for each sample, but the teacher should keep in mind that the basic strategy for teaching the comprehension skills and processes is independent of the difficulty level. Therefore, the teacher should not ignore a particular sample because its difficulty level does not match that of his or her students; the teacher may be able to utilize the basic strategy while altering the lesson to fit the appropriate level of teaching.

When developing teaching and modeling strategies for comprehension, or when adjusting the lessons presented here to fit the difficulty level of his or her students, the teacher will find it necessary to draw paragraphs and sample text from a variety of sources, including, of course, basal readers. There is one important criterion for the text the teacher selects: it must clearly illustrate the skill or process that is being taught.

Because of space limitations, the independent practice and application steps are not presented for all of the lessons that follow. However, Example 5.8, on the application of inferencing, and other examples presented earlier in this text can serve as models for developing the independent practice and application steps for these lessons.

Noting Details

Students must be taught the skill of noting relevant details in narrative and expository text. Strategies for teaching students how to read and comprehend these two different types of text are presented in Chapter 6. The following lessons (Examples 5.9 and 5.10) illustrate strategies for teaching students the process of noting relevant details.

EXAMPLE 5.9   SAMPLE LESSON ON NOTING RELEVANT DETAILS IN NARRATIVE TEXT

Level: Primary

Objective

Students will be able to answer questions that will show that they can identify details relevant to their purpose for reading narrative text.

Letting Students Know What Is to Be Learned

Say: In this lesson you will learn how to read a story and figure out some of the important things the author is saying. When I read you stories, we talk about such things as who the important characters are. Those are important details. So, you see you have already learned to note important details in your listening.

Modeling

Developing the Concept
Have students tell you important details that would describe their classroom. To guide students, ask such questions as:

1. What color are the walls?
2. Where is the teacher's desk?
3. What other things do you see that describe the room?

As students answer the questions, ask them how they were able to figure out their answers. (They could see the things in the room; the answers were clearly observable.) Point out that students are telling important details that describe the room. Continue this procedure with other examples until you are sure the students understand the concept of what it means to note relevant details. Then, explain to students that authors also tell important details; they tell them in the stories they write. Just as the students noted relevant details in their classroom, they can note relevant details in the stories they read.

Developing the Skill at the Listening Level
Tell students that you want them to listen to a short story to tell who went to the zoo. Read the following story to them:

It was a warm summer day. Phil and Ruth went to the zoo with their mother. They had lots of fun.

Have students answer the question. (Phil, Ruth, and Mother)
Say: As you were listening, you were looking for who went to the zoo; that was your purpose for listening. Therefore, you identified the people who went by the purpose I gave you. Can you remember any other things that the story told? (warm summer day; they had lots of fun)
Say: This information is important, but you weren't listening for that purpose. When you listen for a purpose, you know what is important. (Ask students how they were able to figure out the answer to the question, Who went to the zoo? They should tell you that the information was given in the story, or that the author told it.)

Developing the Skill at the Reading Level
Present students with a copy of the following story:

The kids went to the park. They ate lunch and played games. They all had fun. The park was filled with people.

Ask students to read the story silently and then tell you what the kids did at the park.
After students have read the story, give answers to the question, and explain your thinking. *(Note: This is the teacher modeling part of direct instruction.)*

> They ate lunch.
> They played games.
> They had fun.

Say: As I read the story, I knew I was looking for things the kids did in the park. The first sentence told me where they went. The next sentence told me they ate lunch and played games. (Underline the relevant parts of the sentence.) These are things they did in the park. The next sentence said they had fun. (Underline "had fun.") This is also something they did in the park. The last sentence tells that the park is full of people. That does not tell me what the kids did. Therefore, I know that the kids ate lunch, played games, and had fun. (Point to the underlined words as you mention them. Then, present students with a copy of a second story.)

Say: Read this story silently and then tell me what the fox and the rabbit did in the woods. After you finish reading, I want someone to explain how they figured out the answer as I did with the first paragraph. *(Note: This is the student modeling part of direct instruction.)*

The fox and the rabbit lived in the woods. They played games together. They had fun. There were also birds and squirrels in the woods.

(After students have read the story, have them answer the question—they lived in the woods, played games, had fun. Next, ask one student or several students working together to explain how they figured out the answer by going through each sentence and underlining the relevant words as you did. It may be necessary for you to prompt the students with questions, especially at levels where these types of lessons are new to students. If students need more practice, repeat the teacher modeling/student modeling process with other paragraphs.)

Guided Practice

Say: Now I want you to try out what you have just learned. (Give students a copy of the following story. Have them read the question and possible answers aloud; then, have them read the story to find the answer.)

Who was swimming in the pool?
  a. Jill
  b. Jill and Janet
  c. Larry

Jill and Janet were having fun. They were swimming in the pool. Larry came to play, but he did not go swimming.

(After students have read the story, have them answer the question and then explain, as they did in the modeling step, how they figured out the answer. If students do not understand, model the process for them. [*Note: Here the teacher is providing corrective feedback and additional modeling as needed.*] Have students repeat the procedure with another story.)

What did Tom do on the plane?
  a. talked to people
  b. ate lunch
  c. read a book

Tom and his mother were flying on a plane. It was Tom's first trip. Tom talked to the people around him. His mother ate her lunch and read a book.

(Have students answer the question and explain how they got their answer as they did with the first example. Continue to prompt as needed. If students are still unsure of how to complete this process, provide more practice with additional examples.)

Summary

Say: In this lesson you have learned to look for the important information that a story tells you. How do you do that? (Encourage students to tell in their own words:

1. You must know the question you want to answer as you read [your purpose for reading].
2. You must look for sentences or parts of sentences in your reading that answer that question.)

Say: Where would you use this skill in your reading? (Encourage students to tell, in their own words, places they would use this skill:

> In school when reading assignments
> At home when reading books

Accept all reasonable answers; prompt students with questions as needed.)

EXAMPLE 5.10   SAMPLE LESSON ON NOTING RELEVANT DETAILS IN EXPOSITORY TEXT

Level: Intermediate–Junior High

Objective

Given passages of expository text, students will be able to identify relevant details according to their purpose for reading.

Letting Students Know What Is to Be Learned

Say: When you read science or other content materials, you need to be aware of the details that an author tells you. In this lesson you will learn how to read and identify the details that are important to your purpose for reading.

Modeling

Developing the Concept
Say: Suppose that an artist is working on a painting and says that he must finish the details of the faces. What does he mean by the details of the faces?

(Students should respond: eyes, nose, expression, mouth, and so on. Have students discuss what it means to focus on the details. Provide additional examples until you are sure the students understand the concept.)
Say: It is also important to focus on details when you read. The author gives you the details you need.

Developing the Skill at the Listening Level
Tell students to listen to the paragraph you are going to read to tell what kind of bird the gray owl is. Read them the following paragraph:

The great gray owl is a "squatter" bird and a bird of prey. It lives in the northern pine forests of the United States. It is called a squatter because it moves into the nests of others to live and to hatch its young. It uses its claws to catch food. As the owl sees its prey moving along the ground, it swoops down and picks it away with its strong claws.

Discuss students' responses to the purpose question, pointing out that the author has given many details about the gray owl in one paragraph. The details that are most important really depend on what the listener wants to know. As they listened to the selection, the students paid most attention to the details about the kind of bird the gray owl is because that was their purpose for listening.

Developing the Skill at the Reading Level
Present students with a copy of the following paragraph and tell them to read silently to find at least two important details that researchers have recently learned about the "killer whale." Remind students that you will be reading silently while they are reading.

Killer Whales?
The seas are filled with many creatures but none so mysterious and feared for years as the *orcinus orca* or killer whale. This great black and white twenty-five foot long creature weighs as much as six tons and has been known as the ruler of the sea. Only in recent years have researchers discovered that the so-called killer whale has never been known to kill a human being. They have also found the great giant, who uses the thrust of its tail to leap from the water, to be social, intelligent, and even gentle.

After students have read the passage, list on the chalkboard some of the details that researchers have learned about killer whales:

> never killed a human
> gentle
> social

Say: As I read this paragraph, I knew I wanted to identify important details that researchers have recently learned about killer whales. The first two sentences give details about killer whales, but they don't relate to my purpose for reading. The third sentence tells me something researchers have recently learned: that no killer whale has ever killed a human. (Underline the relevant words.) In the next sentence, the author tells more about the killer whale, but only the last three points tell what has been learned recently. (Underline social, intelligent, and gentle.) Therefore, I can identify the details that are relevant to my purpose for reading: *(Note: This is the teacher modeling part of direct instruction.)*

Now, I want you to read a second paragraph on the killer whale and tell me two important details about how killer whales live. (Have students read the paragraph silently. Tell them that you are going to ask them to explain how they reached their answers in the same way that you explained your answers in the first example.) *(Note: This is the student modeling part of direct instruction.)*

Each summer a census, or count, of the killer whale is made off the shore of Vancouver Island. It is from this census and other activities that scientists have learned so much about how killer whales live. The scientists can recognize each whale by the distinct shape of its dorsal fin. It is estimated that males live as long as fifty years and that females, or cows, live a century. Killer whales live together in groups called pods; it appears that each whale must be born into its pod and stays with it until death. Each pod has its own language or set of sounds that is different from the other pods.

After the students have finished reading, have them give the important details about how the killer whale lives and explain how they determined their answers as you did in the first paragraph.

Guided Practice

Say: Now, I want you to read a paragraph with me and use what you have learned about identifying relevant details in expository (or content) materials. First, read the question and possible answers to yourselves. (Have someone read the question and answer choices aloud.) Now, read the paragraph to find the correct answer and be ready to explain how you determined your answer as we have been doing in this lesson.

What evidence from ancient times do scientists have that animals can predict weather?
a. Scientists continue to study the phenomena all over the world.
b. Scientists say animals are close to nature and can read the signs of nature to predict storms.
c. Ancient Romans saw changes in the behavior of birds, cows, mice, and other animals before weather changes.

Some scientists think animals can predict events such as earthquakes and rain storms. This is not a new idea to man. Ancient Romans thought that swallows flying too near the ground or cows looking up at the sky meant that it was going to rain. They also noted that mice, moles, and weasels swarmed out of the ground before a 373 B.C. earthquake. Zoologists have tried to explain how animals could predict earthquakes and violent storms by showing that animals could read signs in their own environments. They point out that animals are so close to nature that they can predict what is going to happen. Scientists continue to study this phenomenon all over the world.

(After students have read the paragraph, have them give their answer and explain how they determined it. Prompt students with questions as needed. Provide reteaching by modeling the process with other passages if needed.)

Summary

Ask students to tell what they learned in this lesson about how to note important details in reading content material. Encourage them to tell in their own words:

1. You must first know what your purpose for reading is.
2. You read for those details that relate to your purpose; you pay most attention to them.

Next, ask students when this skill might be useful to them in reading. Guide them to note such times as when they are doing an assignment in science or social studies, or when they are reading a newspaper to find information on their favorite teams.

Both of these strategies for teaching readers the process of noting relevant details should be followed by opportunities for independent practice and application in natural text.

Main Idea

Teaching readers to identify the main idea of passages has traditionally been carried out in a very rigid, stilted manner. Many times main idea has been taught using narrative materials when, in fact, main idea is more appropriately taught using expository text. Also, students have been led to believe that main idea is usually stated, when most of the time it must be inferred. With the following process, students can determine the main idea whether it is stated or implied, and whether the text is expository or narrative. This process should guide students in seeing how the relevant details of both types of material are related to the main idea.

Step 1: Read the material to determine the general topic. Do this by noting which of the ideas are related to one another. Together, they form the general topic. *(This is identifying relevant, related details of the text.)*

Step 2: Look for a sentence that seems to summarize the related details of the text. This sentence may appear at any point in the text. If such a sentence exists in the text, it is likely to be the main idea.

Step 3: If there is not one sentence that summarizes the related, relevant details of the text, look to see what ideas are irrelevant to all the others. These should be ignored.

Step 4: Use the related, relevant details to formulate the main idea in your own words.

Teaching readers to use this process will require a series of carefully sequenced lessons, each one building upon the lessons before. The lessons can begin as soon as students know how to determine relevant details. The teacher should provide lessons on each of the four steps in close sequential order, and conclude with lessons on the entire process. The following examples (5.11 and 5.12) illustrate two of these lessons:

1. Identifying the topic by noting related, relevant details
2. Using the complete process

EXAMPLE 5.11 SAMPLE LESSON ON IDENTIFYING THE TOPIC OF A PARAGRAPH

Level: Intermediate–Junior High

Objective

Given paragraphs, students will be able to identify the topic by noting related, relevant details.

Letting Students Know What Is to Be Learned

Say: When you read, it is often necessary to think about what the most important idea or ideas are in the text you are reading. You have learned how to identify the relevant details in text. In this lesson, you will learn how to identify the topic of passages by noting how the relevant details are related.

Modeling

Developing the Concept
Begin by listing the names of some of the students in the class on the chalkboard. In one column, list both boys' and girls' names; in a second, list girls' names only; and in the third, list boys' names only.
Say: If you had to give one or two words as a heading or label for each of these columns, what would they be? (Accept all reasonable answers, such as:

> Column 1—Students in our Class
> Column 2—Girls
> Column 3—Boys

Point out that each column has a label that best describes what the whole column is about. Ask students to tell why you couldn't use a name listed in one of the columns as the column's heading. Be sure students understand that such a label does not represent what the whole column is about. Explain that when you read paragraphs, you have to think in the same way and look to see what most of the paragraph is about. Use additional examples to develop this concept if needed.)

Developing the Skill at the Listening Level
Tell students to listen to the paragraph you are going to read them and tell you the topic of the paragraph. Tell them that they can do this by noting how most of the sentences in the paragraph are related:

SAMPLE LESSONS FOR TEACHING AND MODELING

Birdfeeders are helpful to both birds and people. Because birdfeeders are available during during the winter, many birds are saved from starvation. The seed, bread crumbs, and suet that people put in feeders help give the birds the food they need. Birdfeeders also help people by providing them with much entertainment during the cold winter months. It is fun to feed the birds and watch them flutter for their food.

After students have listened to the paragraph, ask them to identify the main topic.

Say: In this paragraph, all sentences were about birdfeeders. Although each sentence told something different about birdfeeders, each is related to birdfeeders—the overall topic. (Continue the activity with other paragraphs if more practice is needed.)

Developing the Skill at the Reading Level
Present students with a copy of the following paragraph.
Say: Now, I will show you how to identify the topic of a paragraph when you read. Read this paragraph to yourself and see if you can identify the topic by noting how all the sentences are related:

Sawbuck, a slang term for a ten-dollar bill, comes from a comparison with a sawhorse. A sawhorse is a rack used to support a piece of wood being cut. Many sawhorses have *X*-shaped legs, and the letter *X* is the Roman numeral for ten. Thus, saw, or ten, was combined with buck, meaning "dollar."[1]

Say: I can determine the topic of this paragraph by noting that each sentence is related to the others. All the sentences tell me something about the overall topic. The first sentence presents the topic, sawbuck. Each sentence that follows is related to this topic and tells me something about it. (As you explain your thinking, underline the appropriate parts of the sentences to show how they are related.) *(Note: This is the teacher modeling part of direct instruction.)*
Say: Now I want you to read a second paragraph to yourselves and identify the topic. Be ready to explain how the sentences are related. (Distribute copies of the paragraph.)

Nellie Bly was the pen name for newspaper reporter Elizabeth Cochran, who was born in Pennsylvania in the mid-1880s. By putting herself into unusual situations, she was able to get information and write stories that no other reporter could. For example, she pretended to be a thief so she could be arrested and learn how women were treated in jail. Such unusual and daring acts made Nellie Bly one of the most famous newspaper reporters.[2]

(Have students identify the topic, explain how the sentences are related, and explain how they reached their answer. *[Note: This is the student modeling step of direct instruction.]* If students give incorrect answers, guide them with questions to the correct answer.)

[1]Paragraph from William K. Durr et al.: *Banners, Teacher's Guide,* p. 198 (Houghton Mifflin Reading Program). Boston: Houghton Mifflin Company, 1983.
[2]Paragraph from William K. Durr et al.: *Banners, Teacher's Guide,* p. 198 (Houghton Mifflin Reading Program). Boston: Houghton Mifflin Company, 1983.

Guided Practice

Say: We are now going to read some paragraphs together to identify the topic and tell how the sentences are related. (Have students read each of the following exercises one at a time. Have them select the main topic from the list of choices and explain their answers. If students make errors, provide corrective feedback and reteach as needed.)

Sample One
The topic of this paragraph is
  a. things in the air
  b. dust in the air
  c. airplanes

    Look up in the air. What do you see? Sometimes there are insects flying around. Airplanes and birds can be seen in the sky. There are even little pieces of dust that the eye can't see. There are many different things in the air: some of them you can see, and some of them you can't.

Sample Two
The topic of this paragraph is
  a. farmers
  b. people who go to work early
  c. life in the city

    The bus driver works long hours on the job. Early in the morning, the farmer is out in the fields. Many days he works until dark. Some people in cities go to the factories very early and stay late. There are many occupations that require people to go to work early.

Summary

Ask students to tell in their own words how to identify the topic of a paragraph. If they are unable to explain what they have learned, ask questions that will lead to the following:

1. Most paragraphs have a single topic.
2. You determine the topic by reading the whole paragraph and deciding how the sentences are related.

    The lesson in Example 5.11 should be followed by the appropriate independent practice. However, because this lesson is part of the overall process of learning to select the main idea, the application can be delayed until the complete process is taught.

EXAMPLE 5.12   COMPLETE-PROCESS LESSON ON MAIN IDEA ———

Level: Intermediate–Junior High

Objective

Students will formulate the main idea of an expository paragraph when it is not stated, by using a four-step process.

Letting Students Know What Is to Be Learned

Say: You have learned some important things about how to determine the main idea as you read. In this lesson, you will learn how to put what you have already learned to use in a four-step process on determining the main idea.

Modeling

By this point in the teaching process, students will already have developed the concept of main idea and should be able to use it in their listening. Therefore, the first two parts of the modeling process—developing the concept and developing the skill at the listening level—can be skipped.

Developing the Skill at the Reading Level
Say: Today, you are going to learn to use four steps for determining the main ideas of paragraphs. (Write the steps on the chalkboard or overhead projector, or photocopy them and distribute them to students:

1. Read the paragraph to determine the topic.
2. Look for a sentence that summarizes the related details of the paragraph. This is the main idea.
3. If there is not a sentence giving the main idea, decide if any of the details are not important to the topic. Ignore them.
4. Use the related, important details to form your own main-idea statement.)

Say: Now, we are going to read a paragraph together to see how to use this process. Read the following paragraph to yourself while I read it silently.

> Sometimes you can see blue-green lights in seawater at night. These lights may be jelly fish. Tiny living things called plankton sometimes glow in the dark, too. There are also some deep-water fish that glow. On warm summer nights, fireflies and glowworms light up the air. It is fun to catch fireflies at night.[3]

Say: Here is how I used the four steps to help me determine the main idea. *(Note: This is the teacher modeling part of direct instruction.)*

[3]Adapted from Ira E. Aaron et al.: *Golden Secrets, Teacher's Edition,* p. 78. Glenview, IL: Scott, Foresman and Company, 1983.

1. I could tell that all the sentences in the paragraph are about living things that glow in the dark. (Underline parts of sentences that show this.) Therefore, the topic is living things that glow in the dark.
2. As I looked at all the sentences, I could not find one sentence that summarized all the related details.
3. Next, I looked to see if all the sentences related to the topic about things glowing in the dark. The last sentence is not related to the others. Therefore, I didn't pay any attention to that sentence in trying to come up with my main idea.
4. I used all sentences except the last one to form my main idea, which is "There are many living things that glow in the dark."

Say: Now, I want you to read a paragraph and show me how you can use these four steps to determine the main idea. (Have students read the following paragraph and give their main idea. Have them go through the four steps and explain the process they used.) *(Note: This is the student modeling part of direct instruction.)* (Students may need prompts to guide them as they explain the process they used.)

Nature has offered us many tall tales over the years. Some people think that bats, for example, are dangerous mammals that willingly tangle in your hair and carry bedbugs. There is a belief that birds return to the same nest each year. Tall tales such as those are often believed, but without scientific proof. Oh, let's not forget the notion that porcupines throw quills; this, too, is untrue.[4]

Guided Practice

Say: Now, I want you to determine the main idea of another paragraph, again using the four-step process. (Distribute copies of the following paragraphs.) Read this paragraph and select the statement at the end that you think is the main idea; use the four-step process to decide, and be ready to explain how you used the process.

A form of comedy involving wild chases, crashes, and practical jokes is called slapstick. This noisy and active type of comedy still exists. Slapsticks, however, are no longer used. Slapsticks were two sticks tied together at one end. The sticks would slap together loudly when used by one performer to hit another.[5]

The main idea of this paragraph is:
a. Slapstick is a form of comedy.
b. Slapstick gets its name from two sticks that were slapped together.
c. Slapstick is still in existence.

[4]Paragraph from William K. Durr et al.: *Banners, Teacher's Guide,* p. 198 (Houghton Mifflin Reading Program). Boston: Houghton Mifflin Company, 1983.
[5]Paragraph from William K. Durr et al.: *Banners, Teacher's Guide,* p. 198 (Houghton Mifflin Reading Program). Boston: Houghton Mifflin Company, 1983.

Summary

Say: What have you learned about determining the main idea of paragraphs? (Have students summarize the four steps of the process in their own words.)

Say: When will you be able to use this in your reading? (Guide students through discussion to show them that they can use this process when they are reading any material in which they need to determine the main idea.)

Lessons on teaching the four-step process for determining main idea should be followed by the appropriate independent practice and many opportunities for students apply the process in reading real text. It may be necessary to teach this process several times before students become comfortable with its use.

Critical Reading

When students read critically, they take clues and ideas from the text and relate them to information they have in their prior experiences in order to evaluate and judge what they are reading. Students must learn certain skills to become critical readers, but they must also learn to use a process that will allow them to put these skills together to achieve understanding (see Chapter 1). Example 5.13 illustrates the teaching of a specific critical reading skill—fact versus opinion. Example 5.14 illustrates the teaching of a four-step process that students can use to help them become more effective critical readers. The steps include:

Step 1: As you read, try to get a general idea of what the author is saying and what the author is trying to persuade you to think.

Step 2: Look for writing techniques the author has used that might lead you to question what the author has said (for example, bias, assumptions, propaganda, mixing facts and opinions).

Step 3: Compare the information you are reading with what you already know, or, if necessary, check the information in another source.

Step 4: Evaluate what you read.

Is it of value to you?
Can you accept what the author has told you?
Should you wait to make a judgment until you have more information?
Should you reject what you have read based on your critical thinking?

EXAMPLE 5.13   SAMPLE LESSON ON CRITICAL READING—
FACT/OPINION

Level: Primary

Objective

Given statements, students will be able to identify the facts and the opinions.

Letting Students Know What Is to Be Learned

Say: Good readers always question what they read as they read. In this lesson, you will learn to do this by recognizing facts and opinions.

Modeling

Developing the Concept
Have a student count the number of boys in the class.
Say: There are _____ boys in our class. (Ask students if this is true. They should answer yes.)
Say: A statement that is true and can be proven is called a fact. Is the statement "I like spinach" a fact?
(Discuss with students that because not everyone likes spinach, the statement is not a fact. It is an opinion. Explain that a statement of opinion tells how someone feels or believes about something. Then, give other statements of fact and opinion and have students do the same until you are sure the group clearly understands the concept.)

Developing the Skill at the Listening Level
Tell students to listen to pairs of sentences you are going to read them and tell you which is the fact and which is the opinion. Read the following sentences:

> Dogs have four legs. (*fact*)
> Dogs make good pets. (*opinion*)
>
> Warm weather is better for your health. (*opinion*)
> Snow falls in cold weather. (*fact*)

After presenting each pair, discuss why the statements are facts or opinions. Use other examples if needed.

Developing the Skill at the Reading Level
Present students with copies of the following pair of sentences. Tell them to read the sentences silently while you do the same to tell which is a fact and which is an opinion.

1. Boys and girls have eyes and ears.
2. All boys can run faster than girls.

Tell students that Statement 1 is a fact and Statement 2 is an opinion.
Say: Statement 1 can be proven. You can see that boys and girls have eyes and ears. Therefore, it is a fact.
   Statement 2 is not necessarily true. It is only true for some boys. Therefore, it is an opinion. It tells how the person making the statement feels. *(Note: This is the teacher modeling part of direct instruction.)*
Say: Now I want you to read another two statements silently and then tell me which is the fact and which is the opinion. (Distribute the sentences. Have the stu-

dents tell how they identified the statements as fact or opinion. Use other statements if needed.) *(Note: This is the student modeling part of direct instruction.)*

1. Trees make the yard look pretty.
2. Trees have leaves in summer.

Guided Practice

Say: Now, I want you to read some more sentences and decide, like we did before, which are facts and which are opinions. After you read each pair of sentences, I want you to explain how you knew which was a fact and which was an
opinion. (Complete the pairs one at a time.)

Set One
1. Snow melts when it gets warm.
2. Snow is nice to have on the ground.

Set Two
1. It is fun to fly in an airplane.
2. Airplanes carry people and other things.

Summary

Say: In this lesson you learned to recognize facts and opinions. Tell me how you
do that. (Encourage students to summarize in their own words.)
Say: What are facts? (statements that are true or can be proven)
Say: What are opinions? (statements of belief or statements that cannot be
proven)
Say: Why should you know the difference between facts and opinions? (so that
you will be able to determine whether statements you are reading in textbooks or
newspapers are true)

Example 5.14 illustrates a sample lesson on the teaching of the four-step process for critical reading suggested at the beginning of this section. As you study
this lesson, notice how the lesson reviews the techniques of critical reading and
then teaches the four-step process. Included in the lesson are the modeling,
guided practice, and the summary.

MODELING IN GUIDED SILENT READING

Earlier in this text (see Chapter 2), it was suggested that guided silent reading and
discussion could be used for two purposes: (1) to check the application of comprehension skills and processes and (2) to model certain comprehension skills and
processes. In the previous sections of this chapter, strategies were presented for
developing comprehension skills and processes in the skill building part of the

BUILDING COMPREHENSION PROCESSES AND SKILLS

EXAMPLE 5.14   CRITICAL READING SELECTION FROM A BASAL READING SERIES

Thinking and Reading Critically

Suppose that, in looking through a magazine, you come across several articles with the following titles: "Government Favors Big Business," "Orange Juice Cures Common Cold," "New Discovery Helps You Lose Weight," "Studies Show Link Between House Plants and Happiness." Would you stop to read any of these articles? Do you believe the claims in the titles to be true? Because of what you already know, which of the articles would you doubt to be correct?

The questions above require you to think critically about the articles. Critical reading and thinking are very important skills. They give you the ability to evaluate information for yourself.

Much material is written by individuals who hope to persuade you to accept their point of view. They may want you to buy a certain product, to support or oppose a certain candidate or political issue, to accept or reject a certain idea. Rather than simply going along with an author, you need to judge what he or she tells you. You need to think and read critically to make your own evaluations.

This lesson will help you to be a better critical thinker and reader in three ways. First, it will review the techniques that authors use to influence readers' thinking. You have already learned to recognize these techniques — the use of bias, assumptions, propaganda, and the mixing of fact and opinion. Second, the lesson will give you a plan to follow that will help you read and think critically. Third, it will give you some practice in applying that plan to what you read.

Techniques That Influence

The following techniques are used to influence readers' thinking.

Bias

Someone who is biased (or who has a bias) favors or is opposed to a subject. When that person writes about the subject, often he or she doesn't try to present a fair view of it. Rather, the author tries to convince you, the reader, that you should feel about the subject as the author feels. This is biased writing, writing that shows the writer's feelings either for or against the subject.

You can recognize biased writing in several ways. First, biased writing takes a stand for or against something, although the author may not come right out and state what he or she is for or against. You can figure out how the author feels by the kind of information the author gives you. Biased writing often uses emotion-laden words to arouse feelings of support or opposition in the reader. Rather than simply giving the facts, it uses a careful selection of facts to influence the reader to share the writer's views. While some facts may be introduced that do not support the point of view of the author, these facts are made to seem less important than the ones favoring the author's point of view.

Read the following statements to see if you can tell which of them show bias:

Author 1 — The new pollution laws are sure to make for a cleaner, more attractive community.

Author 2 — New pollution laws will go into effect next month. Government leaders are watching to see the impact of the new laws.

Author 3 — The new pollution laws are going to be an expensive burden to many small businesses in our community.

Can you tell which of the statements are biased? Those of Authors 1 and 3 are both biased. Author 1 is for the new laws, and Author 3 is against them. Author 2 takes no position; this author's statement simply offers information about the laws.

Overall, biased writing creates the impression of support for or opposition to a particular subject. If you recognize the bias in an article, you can seek information on the other side of the story before accepting what the author tells you.

Assumptions

An assumption is a statement that is accepted as true without being proven to be true. For example, look at this sentence: "The new ambulance, too expensive for a town of ten thousand, has been a source of argument in the town council." Can you identify the assumption in this sentence? That members of the town council have argued about the new ambulance can be proven to be true. That part of the sentence is *not* an assumption. However, whether or not the ambulance actually is too expensive for a town of ten thousand has, in this sentence, been accepted as true without having been proven. That the ambulance is too expensive is an assumption. To determine whether or not this assumption actually is true, the reader would need to find out more information about the ambulance and the town's need for it. For example, how much would another type of ambulance cost? Is there any way to provide emergency medical services for the town's citizens without the ambulance? For how many years will it be in operation? Can it be shared with a neighboring town? Perhaps, when all of these factors are considered, it can be demonstrated that the ambulance is *not* too expensive for the town.

This example shows you how assumptions frequently persuade readers to agree with something without carefully examining it. If you are able to recognize assumptions in your reading, you will not automatically accept them but will ask questions that can help you to decide for yourself about the information presented.

Propaganda

Propaganda is the spreading of information or ideas to persuade people to be for or against something. You come across a great deal of propaganda every day — in radio and television advertisements, posters, billboards, and newspaper and magazine articles. Some propaganda is easy to recognize while other propaganda is less obvious. There are eight commonly used types. You have probably already studied the first five:

Bandwagon — Writers use this technique to encourage people "to get on the bandwagon" and do something because everyone is doing it.

Testimonial — In this type of propaganda, the writer has a famous individual recommend something or someone in the hope that people who admire the famous individual will be influenced to support whatever he or she recommends.

Transfer — In this technique, a writer associates an idea or product with something or someone the reader already feels positive toward, hoping that the reader will transfer these positive feelings to the new product or idea.

Repetition — The writer repeats names, words, or phrases to emphasize them and make the reader remember and think about them.

Emotional Words — The writer chooses words that arouse, rather than inform, hoping that readers will be persuaded to be for or against something on the basis of their emotional response.

The other three types of propaganda include:

Name Calling — With this technique, a writer uses belittling names instead of facts to make an individual or group look bad. *Example* — "The candidate, wearing a striped bow tie and looking like a clown, is dangerously incompetent."

Faulty Cause-Effect — The writer says or implies that one thing causes another when there is actually no logical relationship between the two. *Example* — "If you want a wonderful vacation, wear Sun Fashions."

Compare and Contrast — In this approach, the writer compares similar products or ideas to convince the reader that one is better than the other. However, the claims for the supposedly better product are difficult to prove. *Example* — "Soap powders were good, liquid detergents were better, but new Wonder White Crystals are best for cleaning your clothes."

When you encounter propaganda, you should ask yourself two questions: (1) What am I being persuaded to think? (2) How is this persuasion being done? As a critical reader and thinker, you can learn to recognize propaganda and make your own judgments about it.

Combining Fact and Opinion

A statement of fact is given as true and can be checked. An opinion is a statement of what an individual or group thinks, feels, or believes. On any subject there can be more than one opinion because groups and individuals do not all think alike. Read the following three sentences.

A. Chicago's O'Hare International is one of the busiest airports in the world.

B. O'Hare International is the best airport in the world.

C. O'Hare International, one of the world's busiest airports, is the best in the world.

Statement A can be checked — the number of planes and people using O'Hare International Airport can be compared with the number using other airports to show that O'Hare is one of the busiest airports in the world. Statement A is a fact.

Statement B, however, expresses how someone feels about O'Hare International Airport. Someone else may think that another airport is the best. Therefore Statement B is an opinion.

To get you to accept their opinions, writers may combine them with facts in their writing, sometimes even in the same sentence, as in Statement C. Therefore, as a critical reader and thinker, you should always check to see if authors are mixing facts and opinions. While you cannot disagree with facts, you can decide for yourself whether you think that an author's opinion is valid or whether you have another opinion.

A Plan for Critical Thinking and Reading

As you can tell, it is important to question and evaluate what you read. The following four steps will help you to be a more effective critical reader and thinker:

Step 1 — As you read, try to get a general idea of what the author is saying and what the author is trying to persuade you to think.

Step 2 — Look for techniques that might lead you to question what the author has said:

Does the author show bias?

Are the author's ideas based on assumptions?

Does the author use any of the techniques of propaganda?

Does the author mix facts and opinions?

Step 3 — Compare the information you are reading with what you already know or, if you think it is nec-

essary, look for more information in another source.

Step 4 — Evaluate what you read. First decide whether the information is useful or important to you. It may not be, in which case you can simply store it in your mind, remembering that you have neither accepted nor rejected it. If it is information that matters to you, you need to evaluate it in terms of what you learned about it in Steps 1 through 3 and decide on one of the following reactions:

Accept what the author has told you.

Consider what you have read but wait to make a judgment until you have more information.

Reject what you have read because your critical thinking has convinced you that the article is not fair or correct.

Following the Plan for Thinking and Reading Critically

Use these four steps as you read the following letter. Suppose that you are a resident of the city of Oakton and you have received this letter in the mail:

Dear Citizen:

Our community needs a clean-up! Radio Station KMIL and Ann Whitmore, the Citizens' Party candidate for mayor, are sponsoring a Community Cleanup on Saturday, August 15.

There hasn't been a single community cleanup since our humdrum mayor was put in office three years ago. Oakton has had second-rate leaders far too long. Ann Whitmore will change that. You can join her and the celebrities from KMIL in helping to make Oakton the scenic, beautiful town we all want it to be. After Saturday, there will be no more litter-covered sidewalks, trash-filled alleys, or filthy roadside gutters. Together we will show the current mayor what a clean, well-run community looks like.

Join all of your friends and neighbors on Saturday. Throw out trash, rake up leaves, and clean up your neighborhood. KMIL and prospective mayor Ann Whitmore have arranged to have the Booster Club pick up and haul away any trash that you have deposited on the sidewalks by 11:00 A.M.

Then join Ann Whitmore and disc jockey "Mean Joe" Ferroni at 11:30 in cleaning up the Oakton Community Park. Bring community spirit back to Oakton by cleaning up our city and supporting Ann Whitmore for mayor.

Sincerely,

Robert Capener
Manager, KMIL

Read this letter again, and then read the following model that shows how you should use the four-step plan for effective critical reading and thinking:

Step 1 — What is the general idea the author is telling you? What is he trying to persuade you to think? Mr. Capener clearly wants you to participate in the cleanup drive on August 15, but did you notice the other message you are being persuaded to believe? Mr. Capener is also trying to convince you that the present mayor is not very good and that Ann Whitmore will be a better mayor.

Step 2 — Does the author use any techniques that might give you any reason to question what he says? For example:

Does the letter show bias? Mr. Capener is obviously biased against the present mayor and for Ann Whitmore, the new candidate. How do you know that?

Is any part of the letter based on assumptions? There is an assumption that the community needs a cleanup. Perhaps the city's regular cleaning workers keep it free of litter. There is also an assumption that because there hasn't been a cleanup for three years, Oakton's city leaders are second-rate. To judge the current mayor fairly, one would need to look at the rest of her record.

Does the author use any of the techniques of propaganda? The letter is obviously filled with propaganda.

There are examples of each of the following propaganda techniques: bandwagon, transfer, repetition, emotional words, name calling, and faulty cause-effect. Can you find them?

Does the author mix facts and opinions? The statement that Oakton hasn't had a community cleanup for three years is given as a fact, but it is an opinion that the leaders are second-rate. It is also an opinion that Ann Whitmore will be a better mayor than the current one. Can you find other opinions in the letter?

Step 3 — Compare the information in the letter with what you already know. Because Oakton is an imaginary city, you don't have more information about it. But suppose that, as a citizen of Oakton, you know that one of the first priorities of the current mayor, when she was put in office, was to improve the city's sanitation department, to increase garbage collection to twice a week, and to have every street cleaned at least once a month, and that all of her goals have been achieved. How would that information affect your response to the letter from KMIL?

Step 4 — Evaluate what you read. There are several ways in which you may choose to respond to this letter. You may choose to participate in the cleanup and support Ann Whitmore for mayor. You may choose to ignore the cleanup and support the current mayor. (You may also want to write a letter to the station manager at KMIL protesting the letter's unfair treatment of the current mayor.) Or you may choose to attend the cleanup and withhold your decision about which candidate will be the better mayor until you get more information. Which of these responses would you choose? Why? Be ready to explain how your judgment of what to do is based on your critical reading of the letter.

As you read this letter using the plan for critical reading and thinking, you learned that the KMIL station manager was trying to influence you not only to join in the community cleanup but also to support Ann Whitmore for mayor. If you had not been reading critically, you might have simply accepted what you read. As a critical reader and thinker, however, you are alert to the persuasive techniques the author uses.

Thinking and Reading Critically

Keep in mind the four steps designed to help you be a more effective critical reader and thinker as you read through the following "Letter to the Editor." Make notes so that afterwards you will be prepared to discuss in class how the steps can be specifically applied to this example.

To the Editor:

I am fed up with the inconsiderate, thoughtless clowns who allow their dogs to run loose! I know I speak not only for myself but for all the other law-abiding citizens living in Wellsville. We are tired of our lawns being dug up, our trash cans overturned, and our children threatened. These vicious dogs roam free, causing nothing but trouble. It is about time for a leash law, and it should be enforced without exception. This situation, very simply, can no longer be tolerated.

Daniel Lawson
Wellsville

Skill Summary

The techniques that authors use to influence their readers' thinking include:

Bias — Writing that shows the author's feelings for or against the subject and uses emotion-laden words and a careful selection of facts to influence the reader to share the writer's view.

Assumptions — Statements that are presented as true without being proven to be true.

Propaganda — Information developed to persuade people to be in favor of or opposed to something, including the following techniques: bandwagon, testimonial, transfer, repetition, emotional words, name calling, faulty cause-effect, and compare and contrast.

Combining facts and opinions — Mixing statements that can be objectively confirmed (facts) with statements of how a group or individual feels (opinions) to get the reader to accept the opinions.

To read and think critically, you should:

1. Form a general idea of what the author is saying and what the author is trying to persuade you to think or do.
2. Look for evidence that the author is trying to influence you.
3. Compare the information you are reading with what you already know, or look up more information in another source.
4. Evaluate what you read by deciding to accept it, reject it, or wait until you have more information to make a judgment on it.

Critical reading and thinking are skills that will help you throughout your life. You will be better informed and more independent if you read and think critically about the hidden tactics and messages that authors use to persuade you in newspapers, magazines, and books.

257

Source: William K. Durr et al.: *Triumphs*, pp. 250–257 (Houghton Mifflin Reading). Boston: Houghton Mifflin Company, 1986. Used by permission.

DRL with the applications taking place in the guided silent reading. In this section, a strategy for modeling skills and processes in guided silent reading and discussion is presented.

There are two reasons why modeling comprehension skills and processes in guided silent reading is appropriate:

1. By modeling comprehension in guided silent reading, the modeling is imbedded in actual reading and is therefore closer (than when modeling is done in skill building) to the type of activity students will ultimately be required to do.
2. Even when comprehension skills and processes are taught in skill building, there is often a need to show students how to use the skills in the reading of longer text.

One of the major problems in skill teaching is that if it is handled without systematic provision of the teach, practice, and apply activities needed, it is too far removed from the actual reading act, and there is little or no transfer from the skill teaching to reading. This may be a greater problem with comprehension than it is with decoding. Even when teaching and practice are closely tied together, there is a need to show many students how to apply or use a skill or process in their reading. The skill reminder that is given before students apply a comprehension skill helps to accomplish this. However, it is often not enough.

Modeling in the guided silent reading portion of the DRL helps to accomplish this purpose. When the modeling of comprehension is done in guided silent reading, the teacher is showing students how to apply the skills and processes. In most instances, the strongest instruction occurs when the teacher models the skills or processes first in skill building and then models them a second time in guided silent reading. When that is done, all three steps suggested in the previous section for modeling comprehension skills (concept, listening, and reading development) are conducted in skill building and only the reading step is repeated in guided silent reading.

After a skill or process has been taught in skill building and students have practiced it sufficiently for the teacher to feel that the students know how to use it, then the skill or process can be modeled in guided silent reading. Prior to beginning the modeling, the teacher should remind students about the skill or process that they are going to use. The dialogue in Example 5.15 illustrates how a teacher could model the skill of identifying the main idea of an article in guided silent reading. The article the teacher is using in the lesson is entitled "Insect Zoo" and is presented before the dialogue.

EXAMPLE 5.15   SELECTION AND MAIN IDEA DIALOGUE ────────

Selection: "Insect Zoo"

1. Years ago during a World's Fair in Chicago, Brayton Eddy got the idea of building an insect zoo. For some time everybody thought that his idea was crazy. Who would want to look at bugs?

2. But Eddy would not give up his idea. At last a few people helped him to get an empty house in a public park. This house he could use for his insect zoo. Then he and his wife got busy. In their hunt for bugs, they turned over logs, climbed trees, and walked through swamps.

3. What strange ways they thought up to catch bugs! They put an open umbrella upside down under a bush and shook the bush. Out fell a fine lot of crawling things. They caught many bugs just by painting rings around tree trunks. The rings were made from sticky molasses mixed with beer!

4. On the day the zoo opened, Eddy had 165 different kinds of insects to show. The zoo was a hit. People who visited it learned a lot about insects. Eddy, in turn, learned a lot about people! He found that they liked to stand and watch the insects.

5. "An insect zoo should be a place where things are always happening," Eddy said. He told about a woman who shouted to him one day and pointed to a chrysalis. A beautiful Monarch butterfly was coming out of it. Said the woman, "I have been all over the world. But I have never seen anything like this!"

6. Such moments were very pleasing to Eddy. He was a born showman.

7. Eddy found out how to make his insects show off for visitors. He knew that beetles love dampness, so he put them in a dry cage with a damp log. Of course, the beetles stood on the log, in plain sight.

8. The tumblebug always tried to hide a little ball in the sand. Eddy did not give him enough sand. The tumblebug worked very hard trying to get his ball out of sight. Then he moved on to another spot to try again.

Source: T. E. Murphy, "Insect Zoo." In *Reader's Digest Reading Skill Building,* Level 4, Part 2, pp. 92–95. Pleasantville, NY: Reader's Digest Services, Inc., Educational Division, 1960.

Main Idea Dialogue

Teacher: You have learned how to identify the main idea of paragraphs. Today, we are going to read an article in order to learn how to identify the main ideas of paragraphs in a longer selection. Who can tell me what is meant by a main idea? (Students respond.)

Teacher: The article we are going to read is entitled "Insect Zoo." What do you think an insect zoo would be? (Students respond. Encourage discussion that will bring out the background students have on the topic. Develop the discussion to the point that students have an understanding of what an insect zoo would be and some of the problems that might be associated with creating an insect zoo —getting a place, convincing people the idea is a good one, and so on. During the discussion present key vocabulary in written context as needed.)

Teacher: Remember that when authors write, they have a main idea for each of their paragraphs. Sometimes they state the main idea in a sentence, and other times the reader has to pull together the main idea from all the information in the paragraph. Let's read the first paragraph to figure out what its main idea is. Remember to use the four-step process you have learned for determining main idea.

Teacher: This paragraph does not have a main idea sentence. There is no sentence that tells what the whole paragraph is about. But, the paragraph does have a *main idea*—Brayton Eddy wanted to build an insect zoo, but some people thought it was foolish. You have to look at all the sentences to figure out the main idea.

The next paragraph is different. It has a main idea sentence. Read to tell what it is. (Students read.)

Teacher: Who can tell me what the main idea of this paragraph is?

Student: Brayton Eddy got an idea to build an insect zoo. (If students had responded incorrectly, the teacher would have pointed out the main idea in Sentence 1 and then would have proceeded.)

Teacher: The first sentence tells the main idea. All of the other sentences tell something about how Brayton Eddy didn't give up—people helped him find a house; he and his wife hunted for bugs. In this paragraph where was the main idea stated?

Student: The first sentence.

Teacher: The main idea, when it is given in a sentence, is not always the first sentence. It can come any place in the paragraph. Now, it's your turn. Figure out the main idea of the next paragraph and explain how you did it. Read silently to do that. (Students read.)

Teacher: What is the main idea of the paragraph?

Student: The first sentence.

Teacher: Read it aloud. (Student responds.)

Teacher: Explain how you figured out the main idea.

Student: The other sentences tell about different ways they caught bugs. (If students are unable to explain how they figured out the main idea, the teacher should prompt them with questions such as: What is the second sentence about? Is the whole paragraph about using an umbrella to catch bugs?)

Teacher: Now, let's read the next paragraph to find the main idea. It is stated in one of the sentences, but it is not the first one. (Students read.)

Teacher: What is the main idea of this paragraph?

Student: The zoo was a hit.

Teacher: Where was the sentence in the paragraph?

Student: In the middle.

(At this point, the teacher can continue the guided reading by alternately modeling and having students model how to find the main idea or can assign students the remainder of the article to read on their own to identify the main ideas of the rest of the paragraphs.)

The guided reading portion of the DRL can also be used as a place for modeling comprehension monitoring. Such modeling takes the form of reciprocal teaching—first the teacher models and then the students model. Reciprocal teaching is described in the next section. It has many values for teaching students both how to comprehend and how to think (Palincsar and Brown, 1984a).

A TEACHING STRATEGY FOR COMPREHENSION MONITORING

The effective comprehender keeps track of his or her comprehension during reading, constantly checking to see whether what is being read makes sense. If the material doesn't make sense, the effective comprehender takes action immediately, while reading, and tries to clarify what is not clear in order to achieve some understanding. In other words, the effective comprehender knows whether he or she is understanding what is being read while the reading is taking place, and if there is a lack of understanding, does something immediately to correct the situation. This is the aspect of metacognition known as comprehension monitoring. The monitoring part of metacognition is closely interwoven with the other component, that of knowing which skills and processes are needed to successfully complete a task.

A student's ability to monitor comprehension appears to be a developmental task. Beginning readers seem to be less aware of a lack of understanding when reading and less able to explain why this lack of understanding occurs than are more mature readers (Myers and Paris, 1978). At the same time, however, the ability to monitor comprehension appears to be something that can be taught (Palincsar and Brown, 1984b).

Much of the emphasis in helping students comprehend has been focused on what to do before reading and after reading, such as using study techniques similar to SQ3R (see Chapter 8) (Robinson, 1962). Such strategies are helpful, but they do not account for the actual reading time, during which the bulk of a reader's comprehension activity takes place. The teacher cannot assume that comprehension takes place automatically during reading. He or she must teach students how to monitor their own comprehension.

As was noted earlier in this chapter, the teaching of comprehension skills and processes in isolation from the context of reading is of little or no value to students; the skills and processes must be systematically taught and tied together in reading with the appropriate type of application. For some skills and processes, however, the modeling is more effectively done during reading. Comprehension monitoring is one of those skills (Palincsar and Brown, 1984b).

The following teaching strategy is suggested for helping students learn to monitor their own comprehension. It is basically the strategy developed and tested by Palincsar and Brown (1984a, 1984b; Baker and Brown, 1984a). The strategy consists of four basic steps[1] for the reader to engage in during silent reading:

1. Summarize
2. Clarify
3. Question
4. Predict

Summarizing is simply stopping at a given point in text and telling what has been read. *Clarifying* is asking yourself, "Is this clear to me?" If it is not, then you try to clarify what is not clear by carefully rereading or by discussing as a group.

[1]These four steps are sometimes listed as Summarize, Question, Clarify, Predict.

Table 5.2 Strategy for Comprehension Monitoring

Step	Questions the Reader Asks While Reading
Summarize	What did I read? (Tell it.)
Clarify	Was it clear to me? (Reread or discuss parts that are unclear.)
Question	What question could a teacher ask in a test or discussion about this material? (Pose the question.)
Predict	What is likely to happen next (or later) in this text? (Make predictions.)

Questioning is asking yourself questions a teacher might ask in a discussion or a test. *Predicting* is trying to tell what will come next in the text or in later sections of the text. The basic strategy is summarized in Table 5.2.

The teacher and students work through the steps of this strategy together, taking turns being the leader. First, the teacher takes the lead and directs the discussion, and then one of the students serves as the leader. The teacher and students silently read a given portion of text—a paragraph or more (in the beginning of the exercise, no more than a paragraph should be read at a time). After the silent reading is completed, the teacher directs the group through the four steps, modeling the strategy for the students. First, the teacher summarizes orally what was read and asks students if they would add anything. Second, the teacher notes any points that were not completely clear and asks students to do the same. The teacher and students then reread parts of the text to clarify the points raised; portions can even be read aloud for clarification. Third, the teacher suggests a question that might be asked in a discussion or on a test. (Sometimes the material may not lend itself to questions; the leader should indicate if that is the case.) And, fourth, the teacher predicts what is likely to come next or later in the text.

The teacher and students then silently read the next portion of the text. At the conclusion of the reading, the teacher calls on one of the students to serve as the leader, and the student leader carries on the discussion as the teacher did with the previous portion of text. The teacher assumes the role of student and responds as a student would respond. At first, it is likely that students will have difficulty assuming the role of leader, and it may be necessary for the teacher to prompt the leader with questions. After the leader has completed the four steps involved in the monitoring process, the group reads the next portion silently, and the teacher reassumes the leadership role. This process continues with teacher and students alternating as leader until the selection is completely read. This process is known as reciprocal teaching.

Prior to the beginning of this reciprocal teaching/modeling activity, the teacher should present the four steps involved in the process, explain and model each for the students, and tell how this procedure is to be used. Students should be told that the purpose of this activity is to help them

1. use all the comprehension skills and processes they have been taught,
2. learn to think more about what they are reading,
3. remember what they have read.

It must be kept in mind at all times that this is a modeling strategy to help students learn to monitor their own comprehension. Students will begin to internalize the monitoring process into their reading and to think more about what they are reading as they read by observing the teacher as model and other students as models. Therefore, the teacher must work to always demonstrate the monitoring process as clearly as possible, by summarizing clearly, asking good questions, and making realistic predictions. This strategy should be built into a natural dialogue between the teacher and students that draws the steps of the strategy into the discussion without making them appear to be artificial or discrete.

Teaching students to monitor their own comprehension should begin as soon as students have the basics of reading under control and can silently read several sentences or a short paragraph. At the beginning reading levels, the strategy should be simplified and turned into a "reading game" for students, having students take turns being teacher, which they always enjoy doing. The monitoring activity should not replace the other components of reading instruction, such as the effective modeling of other skills and processes followed by guided silent reading to check application. Although research has been conducted on this and other reciprocal teaching strategies designed to help students monitor comprehension, much of the research has been done with older students, many of whom were having reading problems (Palincsar and Brown, 1984b; Manzo, 1968). However, this strategy is not unlike what many good primary teachers have always done with students—encourage them to think about what they are reading and reread parts if they are not clear.

The monitoring strategy suggested here should not be confused with the traditional guided silent reading and discussion that has typically been used as a part of reading instruction. The purpose of the monitoring strategy is to make students assume the responsibility for thinking about their reading and for automatically trying to clear up any problems that arise with understanding during reading.

In helping students develop the process of monitoring, the teacher should use the suggested strategy on a systematic basis. At the primary levels, the strategy should be used at least one time every other week, and at the intermediate levels, at least once a week until students are proficient at using the strategy on their own. The research that has been conducted on this strategy found thirty-minute sessions on approximately fifteen to twenty consecutive days to be effective (Palincsar and Brown, 1984a). Teachers at the intermediate and junior-high levels may want to experiment with different patterns of days and different blocks of time to determine which are most effective with their own students; for example, the teacher might compare the effectiveness of two days a week for ten weeks to that of the twenty consecutive days.

Every time students are assigned independent reading, they should be reminded to follow this thinking/monitoring strategy. Further, each time the monitoring strategy is taught, the appropriate preparatory activities for background and vocabulary should be completed before the teacher and students carry out the reciprocal teaching.

The dialogue in Example 5.16 illustrates how a teacher and students can carry out reciprocal teaching by imbedding the steps of the strategy in a natural discussion. The text used as the reading sample is presented prior to the dialogue.

EXAMPLE 5.16   SELECTION AND RECIPROCAL TEACHING DIALOGUE

Selection: "Lightning—Its Wonder and Danger"

When you see lightning, it has already missed you. When you hear thunder, don't worry! The show is over.

Lightning moves about 30,000 times as fast as a bullet. If a big stroke were to hit you, you'd never know it. Sound travels much slower than light. By the time you hear thunder, the lightning that caused it is over.

Lightning is helpful as well as harmful. It is true that it kills about 400 people and injures 1,000 in the United States every year. Also, more than 7,000 forest fires are started by lightning each year. But without lightning we could not have any plant life.

Source: Ira Wolfert, "Lightning—Its Wonder and Danger." In *Reader's Digest Reading Skill Building*, Level 4, Part 3, p. 31. Pleasantville, NY: Reader's Digest Services, Inc., Educational Division, 1960.

Reciprocal Teaching Dialogue for Comprehension Monitoring

Teacher: Today, we are going to read an article together and take turns being the discussion leader. I will go first, and then one of you will take a turn. The article we are going to read is called "Lightning—Its Wonder and Danger." What do you know about lightning? (The teacher leads students in a discussion about their knowledge of lightning and presents any background information that might be missing. The teacher presents any needed key vocabulary in written context.)

Teacher: After we read each paragraph, we are going to talk about it and think about it together. We're going to do four things. First, we'll summarize what we have read. We'll ask ourselves, "What did we read?" In summarizing, we only tell the most important things. Second, we'll ask ourselves if what we read was clear. If it wasn't, we'll reread it and talk about it. Third, we'll think of a question a teacher might ask about the paragraph. And, fourth, we'll make a prediction about what is likely to come next or later in the article. (It is a good idea for the teacher to have these four points on a chart in front of the students so that the students and teacher can refer to them as the activity is conducted. The teacher should not be concerned if the discussion is a bit awkward in the beginning. It will flow more smoothly with practice.)

Teacher: Now, let's read the first paragraph silently. While you are reading, I will also be reading. (Students and teacher read the paragraph.)

A TEACHING STRATEGY

Teacher: Let's talk about this paragraph. It states that when we see lightning, we should know it has missed us, and that the thunder tells us the show is over. *(Note: This is the summarizing step.)* I have noticed that lots of times during storms. Have you?

Student: Yes. (One or two students relate experiences.)

Teacher: The one sentence in the paragraph that wasn't really clear to me was the second one: "When you hear thunder, don't worry!" I had to reread it after I finished the paragraph because I needed to know what the last sentence said before I could really understand the third sentence. Are there any points in the paragraph that aren't clear to you? *(Note: This is the clarification step.)* (The teacher allows students to respond and clears up any problems by rereading and discussing.)

Teacher: If I were going to ask you a question about the paragraph, I might ask, "In storms, how can you tell that you are safe from the lightning and thunder?" How could you tell? (The students respond.) *(Note: This is the questioning step.)*

Teacher: I think the next paragraph will probably tell us more about lightning. *(Note: This is the prediction step.)* Let's read it to ourselves to see if I'm correct. (All read silently. Then, the teacher calls on a student.)

Teacher: _____, I want you to talk about the paragraph we just read, like I did. It's your turn to be teacher. (The teacher prompts with questions as needed.)

Teacher: Look at the four steps on our chart. The first step is to tell about the paragraph.

Student 1: Lightning moves faster than a bullet. (Student 1 pauses.)

Teacher: What else did the paragraph tell? Tell us more about it.

Student 1: Sound moves slower than light, and when you hear the thunder, the lightning is over.

Student 2: Lightning moves so fast, you would never know it hit you.

Teacher: Was everything in this paragraph clear to you?

Student 2: What does it mean that sound travels slower than light?

Student 1: The light is fast. You see the lightning first, but the thunder from the lightning doesn't get to your ears as fast as the flash of lightning gets to your eyes.

Teacher: That's right. What question could I ask you about this?

Student 1: How much faster than a bullet does lightning travel? (The teacher accepts any question given; the quality of the questions will improve with practice.)

Teacher: What do you think the next paragraph will be about?

Student 1: It's probably going to tell more things about lightning.

Teacher: Let's read it to find out if that's right. As you read, think about using the four steps on our chart—summarize, clarify, question, and predict. (The students and teacher now read the next paragraph silently, and the teacher takes the turn as leader. The teacher should try to keep the process in a natural dialogue. The teacher and students continue to take turns as leader until the selection has been completed. At the conclusion of each reciprocal teaching session, the teacher should remind students to think about the four steps and use them while they are reading at other times.)

COMPREHENSION PROBLEMS

Typically, teachers have examined readers' comprehension problems by determining whether they could use a particular skill or process (Ekwall and Shanker, 1983). A teacher would give a student a test designed to measure the use of the skill in question or would give an Informal Reading Inventory (an informal test to determine reading levels) and analyze the questions missed in terms of the different types of comprehension required (that is, details, inferences, main idea, and so on.) Although this type of analysis has merit, recent research and theory points to the need to examine some of the underlying factors, such as background, vocabulary, and ability to monitor, which are directly related to effective comprehension (Palincsar and Brown, 1984b; Markman, 1981). A teacher can do this by asking a series of questions about the comprehension of those students who are having difficulty.

1. *Does the reader have the background (schema) for the text being read?* Because a reader's background for the topic being read is so important to successful comprehension, background should be a prime consideration in determining a comprehension problem (see Chapter 3). The teacher should ask students to tell what they know about the topic. Responses will indicate whether students know enough to read and understand the topic.
2. *Is the text clearly written?* Sometimes readers have the needed background to read a text, but the text may not be clearly written or the author may not have given enough information or background to get the ideas across. Therefore, the text must be carefully examined to see if it is a part of the cause of the reader's difficulty. A reader may have difficulty comprehending a particular author's writing style or a particular type of text.
3. *Does the reader know the key vocabulary needed to comprehend the text?* Because vocabulary is a significant component of reading comprehension (Davis, 1968; Rosenshine, 1980), it is important to determine whether the reader knows the meanings of key-concept words in the text being read (see Chapter 4). Too often, teachers are concerned about *all* the words a student doesn't know in a text when the real concern should be those key words that are most related to the main points. If there are an excessive number of words a student doesn't know in a text, the text is probably too difficult.
4. *Can the reader monitor his or her comprehension?* One way to tell whether readers are able to monitor their own comprehension is to have them read and answer questions about the text and then ask them to tell whether they think their answers are correct. Good comprehension monitors know when their answers are correct but may think some of their answers are wrong when they are actually correct. Poor comprehension monitors will think that their answers are right when they are really wrong (Palincsar and Brown, 1984b).

Analyzing a reader's comprehension problems is not an easy task, but teachers can be more effective in seeking the possible causes than they have been in the past. By asking these four questions in addition to looking at how readers perform on tasks requiring them to use the various skills and processes of comprehension, teachers will be able to do a more viable job of determining why students do not comprehend given text and determining how to go about correcting the problems. The teacher should always remember, however, that a student's ability to comprehend will vary according to the type, topic, and difficulty level of the text. Therefore, global generalizations about a reader's overall ability to comprehend should not be made.

COMPUTER SOFTWARE FOR COMPREHENSION INSTRUCTION

As noted in Chapter 4, there is a lot of computer software available for use in instructional programs in reading. However, most of the software is designed for drill and practice rather than teaching. Thus, it should only be used after the appropriate teaching has been provided. Following is a list of some of this software.

Title   Cloze Plus
Source   Milliken Publishing Company
Grade   3–8

This program contains tutorial lessons that develop comprehension and vocabulary skills through context-analysis activities.

Title   Fact or Opinion
Source   Learning Well
Grade   2 and above

This program presents reading selections based on advertising slogans and techniques. Students must decide if the advertisements are based on fact or opinion. Material is presented in a game format. Other programs produced by Learning Well of a similar nature are

> Context Clues
> Cause/Effect
> Drawing Conclusions
> Following Directions
> Getting the Main Idea
> Inference

Title   Missing Links
Source   Sunburst Communications, Inc.
Grade   3 and above

This program uses the cloze technique to allow students to make educated guesses based on their knowledge of word structure, meaning in context, spelling, and grammar. Three different programs are available:

Young People's Literature
Classics, Old and New
Micro-Encyclopedia

These programs have features that allow the teachers to add materials of their own.

Title   Newbery Winners
Source   Sunburst Communications, Inc.
Grade   3–8

These software–book packages include an instructional manual and teacher's guide. Four drills and games are keyed to each of fifteen Newbery Awards.

Title   Snooper Troops II
Source   Spinnaker Software Corporation
Grade   5 and above

In this adventure game, students assume the role of a detective and try to solve a mystery. Problem solving and critical reading/thinking skills are emphasized.

Title   Extra, Extra
Source   Media Materials
Grade   3 and above

This program allows students to read clues, track down the facts, and submit their stories to the press. The program works on who, what, where, when, and how. The game format program allows for three levels of difficulty.

SUMMARY

The instructional program in reading comprehension must include activities to build the processes and skills of comprehension; this involves the important step of *modeling*—that is, of showing or demonstrating for students how to use the skills and processes and helping them verbalize how and when to use them. Modeling can be done as a part of the DRL during skill building and also in the guided silent reading portion of the lesson.

Metacognition, an important aspect of reading comprehension, involves (1) knowing what skills and processes are required to successfully complete a task and (2) being able to tell whether one is performing a task correctly and to make corrections during the task if needed. This later component is known as cognitive monitoring or comprehension monitoring. These metacognitive aspects of learning must be integrated into the modeling strategies for comprehension.

The modeling of a comprehension skill or process includes three parts:

1. developing or checking the concept of the skill or process,
2. developing or checking the skill at the listening level,

3. demonstrating the use of the skill or process in reading, and verbalizing how and when to use it.

These three steps should be used to model comprehension skills and processes in both skill building and guided silent reading. If modeling is done in guided silent reading, it should be preceded by an initial full teaching of the given skill or process—including modeling—in skill building.

Students should also be taught to monitor their own comprehension while they are reading. A basic strategy for doing this includes teaching students to summarize, clarify, question, and predict during their reading. A reciprocal modeling strategy can be used to do this where the teacher and students alternate taking the lead in using these four steps while reading text. In this strategy, the teacher models for students how they should monitor as they read.

Determining a reader's comprehension problems is more involved than just looking at whether he or she can use a particular skill or process. To determine the cause of a comprehension difficulty, the teacher should look at the reader's background, vocabulary, and ability to monitor comprehension as well as at the clarity of the text.

REFERENCES

Baker, L., and A. L. Brown. 1984a. Metacognitive skills and reading. In P. D. Pearson (ed.), *Handbook of reading research*, pp. 353–394. New York: Longman.

Baker, L., and A. L. Brown. 1984b. Cognitive monitoring in reading. In J. Flood (ed.), *Understanding reading comprehension*, pp. 21–44. Newark, DE: International Reading Association.

Baumann, J. F. 1984. The effectiveness of a direct instruction paradigm for teaching main idea comprehension. *Reading Research Quarterly*, 20, 93–115.

Brown, A. L. 1980. Metacognitive development and reading. In R. J. Spiro, B. C. Bruce, and W. F. Brewer (eds.), *Theoretical issues in reading comprehension*, pp. 453–481. Hillsdale, NJ: Lawrence Erlbaum Associates.

Clark, C. M. 1984. Teacher planning and reading comprehension. In G. G. Duffy, L. K. Roehler, and J. Mason (eds.), *Comprehension instruction: Perspectives and suggestions*, pp. 58–70. New York: Longman.

Cooper, J. D., et al. 1979. *The what and how of reading instruction*. Columbus, OH: Charles E. Merrill Publishing Company.

Davis, F. B. 1968. Research in comprehension in reading. *Reading Research Quarterly*, 3, 499–545.

Duffy, G. G., L. R. Roehler, and J. Mason (eds.). 1984. *Comprehension instruction: Perspectives and suggestions*. New York: Longman.

Durkin, D. 1978. What classroom observations reveal about reading comprehension instruction. *Reading Research Quarterly*, 14, 481–533.

Durkin, D. 1981. Reading comprehension instruction in five basal reader series. *Reading Research Quarterly*, 16, 515–544.

Ekwall, E. E., and J. L. Shanker. 1983. *Diagnosis and remediation of the disabled reader*, 2nd ed. Boston: Allyn and Bacon.

Manzo, A. V. 1968. *Improving reading comprehension through reciprocal questioning*. Ph.D. dissertation, Syracuse University.

Markman, E. M. 1981. Comprehension monitoring. In W. P. Dickson (ed.), *Children's oral communication skills*. New York: Academic Press.

Mier, M. 1984. Comprehension monitoring in the elementary classroom. *The Reading Teacher, 37*, 770–774.

Myers, M., and S. G. Paris. 1978. Children's metacognitive knowledge about reading. *Journal of Educational Psychology, 70*, 680–690.

Palincsar, A. S., and A. L. Brown. 1984a. A means to a meaningful end: Recommendations for the instruction of poor comprehenders. Urbana, IL: University of Illinois, Center for the Study of Reading. (reprint)

Palincsar, A. S., and A. L. Brown. 1984b. Reciprocal teaching of comprehension-fostering and comprehension-monitoring activities. In *Cognition and instruction*. Hillsdale, NJ: Lawrence Erlbaum Associates.

Pearson, P. D., and D. D. Johnson. 1978. *Teaching reading comprehension*. New York: Holt, Rinehart and Winston.

Robinson, F. P. 1962. *Effective study*. New York: Harper & Row, Publishers.

Rosenshine, B. V. 1980. Skill hierarchies in reading comprehension. In R. J. Spiro, B. C. Bruce, and W. F. Brewer (eds.), *Theoretical issues in reading comprehension*. Hillsdale, NJ: Lawrence Erlbaum Associates.

Squires, D. A., W. G. Huitt, and J. K. Segars. 1983. *Effective schools and classrooms: A research-based perspective*. Alexandria, VA: Association for Supervision and Curriculum Development.

Sticht, T. G., and J. H. James. 1984. Listening and reading. In P. D. Pearson (ed.), *Handbook of reading research*, pp. 293–317. New York: Longman.

CHAPTER
S   I   X

TEXT STRUCTURE

*The importance of text structure theory for educators is
that students need to learn different reading strategies for
different text types.*—Beach and Appleman, 1984, p. 116

In this chapter you will learn

1. what is meant by text structure and what is included in teaching it,
2. how to teach students to recognize narrative text structure and use clues from
   it to aid comprehension,
3. how to teach students to recognize different expository text structures and use
   clues from them to aid comprehension.

A basic premise throughout this book has been that readers construct meaning
by relating the ideas in text to their own schema. They do this by learning to use
different strategies that ultimately help them identify what is relevant information in text and by separating that information from irrelevant information. A
part of this process includes being able to recognize how an author has organized,
or structured, the ideas presented in text and learning to use the structure to anticipate or predict what information is to follow. All texts are different; the style
and structural characteristics depend on the author. However, there are com-
monalities among text types that can be utilized in teaching readers to comprehend more effectively.

Research on the value of teaching readers to be aware of an author's organizational structure to improve comprehension has produced conflicting results.
Some researchers have found that teaching students to focus on structure does
lead to improved comprehension (Bartlett, 1978; Taylor and Samuels, 1983;
Taylor and Beach, 1984). Others, however, have noted the contrary (Dreher and
Singer, 1980; Mathews, 1982). A part of the problem resides in how students are
taught to use text structure. Just teaching students to recognize and categorize

different text types without focusing on how to use the clues within the texts to construct meaning is not likely to improve the students' comprehension. However, if instruction is directed toward showing students how to use the structure of text to identify the relevant information to construct meaning, the instruction will be effective in helping readers improve their comprehension; this is particularly true when the content of text is unfamiliar to the reader.

A major component of the instructional program in reading comprehension is the building of processes and skills. This includes teaching—and modeling for students—how to use different organizational structures of texts to construct meaning. Chapter 5 focused in detail on how to use direct instruction, including modeling, to teach the processes and skills of comprehension. This chapter extends that concept by illustrating how to use direct instruction to teach students the processes they need to understand different text structures.

UNDERSTANDING TEXT STRUCTURE

Text structure refers to the way in which an author organizes his or her ideas. There are two basic types of text: narrative and expository. Narrative texts tell a story and are organized into a general pattern of characters, setting, problems, action, resolution of the problems, and theme. Narrative texts may present true or fictional accounts. Expository texts present facts and information organized into patterns that show relationships among the ideas presented. The pattern of text and type of writing an author uses depend on his or her purpose for writing. Both narrative and expository texts communicate ideas and information, but they do it in different styles and formats.

The first thing readers must learn about text structure is that authors use different types of text in their writing and each type of text is organized differently. Readers must then be taught that when they are reading they can use their knowledge about text structure and clues within the structure to help them formulate understanding.

Narrative Texts

Narrative texts are organized into a sequential pattern that includes a beginning, a middle, and an end. Within this pattern, any given narrative may be composed of several different episodes, each consisting of characters, a setting, a problem, action, and resolution of the problem. By identifying these elements the reader identifies the story's grammar or basic plan. Example 6.1 illustrates in diagram form how the elements of a story's grammar fit together, with episode *N* representing any number of episodes that might be included in the story. The graphic representation of a story's grammar is called a story map. There are many different forms of story maps (Freedle, 1979), some of which will be shown in this chapter. The exact map for a story depends on the structure of the story.

The *theme* of a story is the basic idea about which the whole story is written; the theme can be stated or unstated. The *plot* is the way in which the story is organized; it is made up of episodes. The *setting* is the place and time at which the

EXAMPLE 6.1   A STORY GRAMMAR

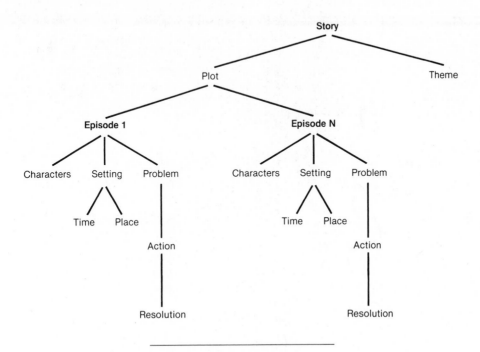

story occurs. The *characters* are the people or animals who carry out the action in a story. The *problem* is the situation or situations around which an episode or the whole story is organized. The *action* is what happens as a result of the problem; it is made up of events that lead to the solution of the problem, which is called the *resolution*.

Understanding the technical elements of narrative structure is more important for teachers than it is for students. The teacher should organize the elements into a map of the story and use the map to develop the questions he or she will ask in guided silent reading and discussion (see Chapter 2). Such questions will cause students to focus on the relevant elements in the story—those elements that they will need to understand the story. As research has shown, asking questions that focus on the story line leads to improved student comprehension of the story (Beck, 1984). Students, however, only need to know enough about the structural elements to anticipate the type of information that will appear in the text. This knowledge will help them distinguish the information that is relevant to their understanding of a story and will make it possible for them to separate that information from the irrelevant information.

Let's consider a story that you are likely to know—"The Three Pigs"—to illustrate the elements of narrative text and see how knowing those elements would help the reader improve his or her comprehension of the story. A story map of "The Three Pigs" is shown in Example 6.2.

EXAMPLE 6.2   STORY MAP OF "THE THREE PIGS"

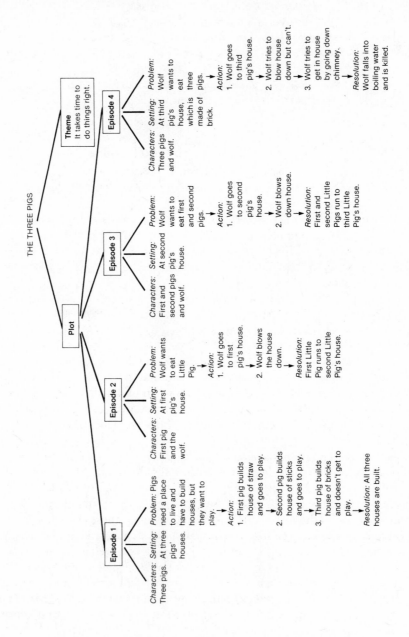

As you can see by studying this story map, you need only the essential elements to understand the story. Each episode leads to the next, which culminates by leading the reader to the overall understanding, or the theme, of the story. Notice that three of the episodes have essentially the same problem, but the third ends with a different resolution. By thinking about stories in this way, the reader focuses only on the essential elements, which leads to better comprehension. Also, by knowing the elements of a narrative, the reader can anticipate the information that will be included in the story, and that will also aid comprehension of the text.

Expository Texts

Expository texts present information and are the types of materials commonly found in textbooks, newspapers, and magazines. Students generally have more difficulty reading expository texts than narrative texts because they have had less experience with them and because expository texts do not follow a set pattern like narrative texts do. There is not one basic pattern that the reader can expect to find in expository texts; how the information is organized really depends on the type and purpose of the information. There are five patterns of expository writing that are frequently used by authors (Meyer, 1975; Meyer and Freedle, 1984): description, collection, causation or cause-effect, response or problem-solution, question-answer or remark-reply, and comparison. Not all of these types are used with the same frequency in all textbooks at all levels, but these are the types that are most frequently used overall.

The reader must learn two basic things about expository structures:

1. The only purpose for the particular structure is to present the content or information in a clear manner.
2. By knowing different structures, the reader can begin to anticipate the type of information that will be presented or that should follow, based on the structure itself.

In the next paragraphs, these points will be illustrated for each type of expository text structure.

Descriptive expository text presents information about a particular topic or gives characteristics of the topic or the setting. The following passage is an example of this type of expository text structure:

The tiger is the master of the Indian jungle. It stalks its prey in deadly silence. For half an hour or more, it carefully watches and then slowly, placing one foot softly in front of the other, closes in.

Unlike the other types of expository text structure, descriptive passages do not provide readers with clue words to aid in comprehension; readers must use the basic strategies they have learned for noting details and selecting the important information from the passage. However, the structure of descriptive passages can help the reader anticipate the type of content that is likely to follow. For the passage about the tiger, the content can be graphically represented as:

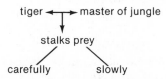

If the reader is taught that descriptive passages present important details relevant to a particular topic, then the reader can anticipate the content of the passage. The first sentence of the tiger paragraph lets the reader know that the passage is going to be about the tiger, which is the master of the jungle. The second sentence lets the reader know that the passage is going to be about how the tiger stalks prey, which should lead the reader to expect ideas that describe how the tiger stalks.

Collection is the type of expository text structure in which the author presents a number of ideas or descriptions in a related group. This structure is often called a listing. It is frequently used in magazine or newspaper articles where the writer is presenting lists of related points, but it is also used in many textbooks. The following passage is an example of this type of expository text structure:

> As master of the Indian jungle, the male tiger plays many roles. First, he is the hunter of prey who stalks in deadly silence. He is the beauty of the jungle who is an expert at doing nothing in order to rest to be ready for his hunt. Finally, the lord of the jungle is the active seeker of mates who begins his mating with a nuzzle but ends with a roar.

In the collection type of passage, the author frequently uses clue words such as first, second, next, and finally to denote the related points. When reading a collection type of passage, the reader must be able to infer the relationship between the listed points and the overall topic. It is important for the reader to note details and to identify the sequence of ideas in the passage.

In this type of structure, the reader must be taught to recognize the clue words given by the author and to use them to anticipate the content of the passage. In the paragraph presented above, the author immediately lets the reader know that there are many roles played by the tiger. The author then lists the roles, using the words "first" and "finally" to clue the reader into the beginning and end of the list. The content of this passage can be graphically depicted as follows:

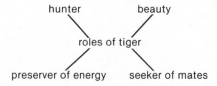

The *causation*, or cause-effect, type of expository structure presents ideas grouped in a sequence so that a causal relationship is either stated or implied.

This type of structure is frequently used in science, social studies, and mathematics textbooks; it is also found in newspaper and magazine articles—for example, those that discuss the relationship between environmental factors and health. Following is an example of this type of expository text structure:

> We observed the tiger from our vehicle as it stalked the herd of deer. As a result of the slight noise from our running camera, the tiger turned and knew we were there. This didn't stop it from returning to its intended prey. Slowly and carefully it moved forward, not making a sound. The deer were initially unaware of its presence but because of the shifting winds, they caught the tiger's scent. This was enough to scare them away.

In the causation type of passage, the author often uses such clue words as "therefore," "consequently," "because," "as a result of," "since," or "the reasons for." When reading text with this type of structure, the reader must be able to identify the elements that are being related and either recognize or infer the cause-effect relationships. In the paragraph presented above, the reader can use the clue words "as a result of" and "because" to identify the cause-effect relationships. The content of the passage could be graphically represented as follows:

$$\text{noise of camera} \xrightarrow{\text{cause}} \text{tiger turned to observers}$$

$$\text{winds shift} \xrightarrow{\text{cause}} \text{deer smell tiger} \xrightarrow{\text{cause}} \text{deer run away}$$

In the *response* type of expository structure, the author presents a problem, question, or remark followed by a solution, answer, or reply. This type of structure is often used in mathematics, science, and social studies. Sometimes (in mathematics, for example) the author presents the problem but the reader is expected to provide the solution. Following is an example of this type of structure:

> One problem to be resolved in tiger watching is transportation. How is it possible for observers to get close enough to a tiger without scaring it away or being attacked? Nature has helped solve this problem by making the tiger and the elephant friends. It is possible for an elephant carrying several people to get very near a tiger without even being noticed. If it weren't for this natural friendship, tiger watching would be virtually impossible.

In the response type of text structure, the author may use clue words such as "the problem is," "the question is," "one reason for the problem," "a solution," or "one answer is," but the author does not always use such words. When an author does not clearly identify the problem, the reader must look for clues to help clarify it. Upon identifying a problem, the reader should anticipate that a solution to the problem will follow.

In the first sentence of the paragraph on tiger watching, the author lets the reader know that there is a problem to be resolved in tiger watching. The reader should then anticipate finding a solution and note only those points that are relevant to the problem. The content of the tiger-watching passage can be graphically depicted as follows:

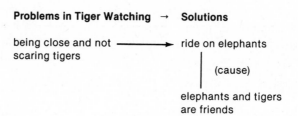

Note that the elephant and tiger's friendship makes it possible for the elephant to be the solution to the problem.

The *comparison* type of expository structure requires the reader to note the likenesses and differences between two or more objects or ideas. This type of structure is frequently found in social studies and science texts. Following is an example of the comparison type of expository text structure:

The power of the great tiger is like that of no other animal in the jungle. With one steady lunge, it can destroy its prey, seemingly without any effort at all. Unlike other predators, the tiger basks in the sun after an attack in order to prepare for its next kill. The actions of the tiger resemble those of no other animal in the Indian jungle.

In the comparison type of passage, the author uses clue words such as "like," "unlike," "resemble," "different from," "same as," "alike," or "similar to" to make comparisons. When reading comparison structures, the reader must be able to recognize the objects or ideas being compared and the points of similarity or difference between and among them. Often the comparisons will not be directly stated.

In the paragraph about the power of the tiger, the author lets the reader know in the first sentence that the tiger is being compared to the other animals in the jungle. From this sentence and the clue words "like," "unlike," and "resemble," the reader can anticipate the information relevant to the comparison. The author does not directly state the information about the other animals of the jungle; the reader must infer that information. The content of this passage can be graphically depicted as follows:

	Tigers	*Other Animals*
Power	kill prey with one lunge	*kill with more than one lunge
After kill	bask in sun to rest for next kill	*do not bask in sun and rest

*This information must be inferred. It is not directly stated.

Look back over each of the five types of expository structure presented. Notice that each is organized differently to present a different type of content clearly. That each presents a different type of content can be seen by comparing the main ideas of the example passages:

Passage	*Main Idea*
Description	Tigers are master hunters.
Collection	Tigers play many roles.
Causation	Tigers encounter problems when hunting.
Response	How to watch tigers safely.
Comparison	Tigers are like no other animal in the jungle.

The *description* passage describes the tiger as a master hunter. The *collection* passage lists the roles the tiger plays. The *causation* passage shows some of the problems the tiger encounters in hunting and identifies the resulting effects. The *response* passage poses a problem and then provides a solution. The *comparison* passage compares the tiger to other animals.

In summary, a part of helping readers become effective comprehenders is teaching them to recognize and interpret different text structures. Teaching text structure involves teaching readers

1. to recognize that different texts have different types of structures and that the structure of the text can help them anticipate information,
2. to read narrative texts and know how to anticipate the information in them,
3. to read and interpret the five basic patterns of expository text structure and know how to use clues in the text to anticipate and understand the ideas presented.

USING DIRECT INSTRUCTION TO TEACH TEXT STRUCTURE

In Chapter 2, a model for direct instruction was presented. In Chapter 5, the model was used in teaching strategies for building the processes and skills of comprehension. The same model can be used to teach students how to comprehend different text structures. The elements of the model for direct instruction include:

Teaching
1. Let students know what is to be learned.
2. Model for the student the skill, process, or strategy. (Comprehension skills and processes can be modeled by developing the concept, checking the skill at the listening level, and demonstrating the use of the skill at the reading level.)
3. Provide guided practice.
4. Have students summarize in their own words what has been learned and verbalize how and when they can use what they have learned in reading.

Practice
Provide students with an independent, directed-choice activity that requires them to focus their attention on what was taught.

Application
Have students use what they have been taught in reading text. Within the framework of the directed reading lesson, this takes place during guided silent reading.

The elements of direct instruction will be used throughout the remainder of this chapter to illustrate how to teach text structure.

TEACHING STUDENTS THE CONCEPT OF TEXT STRUCTURE

As soon as students are able to read independently and perform some of the basic processes of comprehension, they are ready to begin to learn the concept of text structure. The students would have already developed some concept of narrative structure from their experiences of listening to stories. In lessons on the concept of text structure, the teacher's emphasis should be on teaching students to recognize that different authors organize their ideas differently. It is not necessary to burden the students with the terms *text structure*, *narrative*, or *expository*. The terms can be used, but the mastery of the terms themselves should not become the goal of the lessons. The exact number of lessons that will be required to teach this concept will depend on the students.

Students need to have the concept of text structure well developed before they are given specific lessons on reading narrative and expository material. Further, it is always wise for the teacher to review the concepts of text structure with students before teaching lessons on any aspect of text structure.

Example 6.3 presents a sample lesson in which direct instruction is used in teaching the concept of text structure. The passages used in the lesson are approximately third to fourth grade level but passages from lower or higher levels could be used with the same format. Before students begin this lesson, they must have developed the concepts of "story" and "information."

EXAMPLE 6.3   SAMPLE LESSON ON THE CONCEPT OF TEXT STRUCTURE ━━━━━━━━━━━━━

Purpose of the Lesson

To teach students to recognize that authors use different types of writing in their selections.

Materials Needed

Two drawings of houses: one showing a one-story house made of wood; the other showing a two-story house made of wood.
An overhead projector and screen or a chalkboard.
Copies of the passages used in this lesson to distribute to students.

Teaching

Letting Students Know What Is to Be Learned

Say: Do all cars look alike? (Students respond. Have a brief discussion about the fact that cars are built differently.)

Say: The selections you read are also not alike. Different authors write differently and use different types of writing. In this lesson you will learn to recognize two different types of writing by the way the text is organized.

Modeling: Developing the Concept

Show students the drawings of the houses.

Say: How are these two houses different? How are they the same? (Students respond. Guide them to see that one house has one floor and the other has two, but both houses are built with wood.

Say: Could people live in each of these houses? (Students respond.) Did the builders of these houses use the same materials and structures? (Students respond. Guide students to see that the two houses have different structures even though they are made of the same material.)

Say: Both of these pictures are of houses, but the houses are different in how they have been built or structured. Both are made of wood, but they have different windows, a different number of levels, and so on. *(Note: Concrete materials such as building blocks can also be used to develop the concept of structure.)* In the same manner, the paragraphs and stories that you read are also structured differently. Authors structure what they have to say in different ways.

Modeling: Developing the Concept at the Listening Level

Say: As I read you the following two paragraphs, listen to what each paragraph is about. (After reading each paragraph, have students summarize the information presented. List the points they tell you on the chalkboard or overhead projector.)

Paragraph 1

Sara had gone to Mark's house. "Hello, Mark!" said Sara. "I'm here to go with you to the movies." "Great, Sara," Mark replied. "I didn't want to go by myself. It will be fun for us to go together."

Paragraph 2

Indiana is a beautiful state in the spring. The trees and grass begin to turn green, and the flowers add splashes of color everywhere. Jonquils, tulips, and hyacinths add color to this beautiful season.

Say:　The two paragraphs are different because they present different types of information. They are also different because of the way they are written. The first paragraph is telling a story. Listen as I reread this paragraph and then tell me who the characters are. (Reread the paragraph. Have students respond.)

Say:　We can tell that this paragraph is a part of a story because it has characters and there is some action taking place. Now, listen as I read the other paragraph again and tell me what facts are being told about Indiana. (Reread the paragraph. Have students respond.)

Say:　This paragraph is not a story. There are no characters or action. The purpose of the paragraph is to present facts and information about Indiana. These two paragraphs present different types of information, and they are written differently to do that.

Modeling: Developing the Skill at the Reading Level

Say:　Now we are going to see how to recognize different types of writing when we are reading. (Distribute the two paragraphs that follow.) Read these paragraphs to yourselves to see if you can determine whether the author is telling a story or giving facts. Think about which paragraph you would find in a science book and which you would find in a story book. *(Note: These paragraphs should be reproduced on a transparency as well as on sheets for the students to use.)*

Paragraph 1

Scientists study whales by watching them where they live. Two whales that scientists are just beginning to learn more about are the sperm whale and the blue whale. These whales have both been seen in the Indian Ocean and have been studied there. Blue whales are the largest creatures to inhabit the earth. Sperm whales are not as large as blue whales; under the water, sperm whales are graceful and flexible.

Paragraph 2

Suddenly, the wind began to blow. The warm breezes turned to strong gusts that seemed to come from dark clouds. Larry yelled for Eddie to hurry. He knew they would never make it to cover before the storm if they didn't hurry. All at once there was a loud crack. Larry saw the huge tree falling in their direction. He grabbed Eddie just in time to get him out from under the tree's path. There was no chance to reach cover before the storm broke.

Say:　In which paragraph is the author telling a story? (Students respond. Explain to students why this (Paragraph 2) is a story. If students are unable to determine which paragraph is a story, tell them which one it is and underline the sentences and parts of sentences in the paragraph that show that it is a story.)

Say: This type of writing is called narrative text. When an author is telling a story, he or she is writing a narrative. (Put the words *narrative text* on the chalkboard for students to read. If the terms are too difficult for students to understand at this point, delete this portion of the lesson.)

Say: In Paragraph 1, the author is telling us facts about whales. Who can underline these facts? (Have students take turns underlining the words that show that the author is giving information. If students are unable to do this, do it for them and verbalize your reasoning.)

Say: This type of writing is called expository writing. When an author is telling facts or information, he or she is using expository text. (Put the words *expository writing* and *expository text* on the chalkboard. Again, if the terms are too difficult for students to understand, delete this portion of the lesson.)

Providing Guided Practice
Say: Now, we are going to see if you are able to identify when an author is using narrative writing—telling a story—and when an author is using expository writing—giving facts—in two related articles. (Distribute sheets with the following two articles.)

Article One

Yellowstone National Park is a great place to go for a vacation. There is much to do. The bears and the geyser, "Old Faithful," are two of the things that everyone wants to see on their trip.

The bears are beautiful but can be dangerous. When they are low on food, they come into the campsites to find what they need.

Article Two

Last summer our family went to Yellowstone on vacation. I remember the night we were asleep in the camp. There was a loud sound outside our tent. My brother Artie and I both heard it. I wanted us to go out to see what it was. Artie wouldn't go.

As I looked out the tent, I saw two bears at the picnic table eating away. I called Artie to come see. We didn't make a sound and watched the bears finish their meal.

Say: Read these selections to yourselves and then tell me how the articles are different in the way their information is presented. Be ready to support your answers. (After students have read the articles, have them tell how the two articles differ. Be sure they see that the basic topic is the same in both articles. Have students justify their answers by pointing out words and elements that show the different writing styles. If students are unable to do this, do it for them and give your reasoning. If students still seem uncertain about the differences between narrative and expository text and cannot recognize when the structure of passages is the same and when it is different, reteach the lesson using different passages.)

Summarizing

Say: What have we learned in this lesson about how authors write differently? (Encourage students to give the following points in their own words:

1. Authors write differently in different texts.
2. Narrative writing tells a story.
3. Expository writing tells information.)

Practice

Give students the following exercise and have them complete it by themselves. *(Note: This is independent practice.)* When students complete the exercise, go over it with them, having them justify their answers.

**Independent Practice for Recognizing
Different Types of Text Structures**

Name _____ Date _____

Directions: Read each of the following groups of passages and decide whether they are the same type of writing or different. Place a checkmark next to the correct answers. Be ready to explain your reasoning. *(Note: The correct answers have been marked for the teacher.)*

1. a. The praying mantis is a very interesting insect. It catches its food with the sharp spines on its front legs and eats its food alive. It always catches its food while it is at rest on leaves or flowers.
   b. The Congo River is a dark and mysterious river in Africa. The banks of the river are covered with many thick, green plants that help to give the river a dark, mysterious look. All living things around the river must depend on the river for life.
      __X__ same types of writing
      _____ different types of writing

2. a. The old man could hardly walk down the path. He had been sitting so much during the winter that his legs had grown stiff. Now he needed to be able to move quickly to escape from his attackers. The hungry wolves were much too swift for him.
   b. Termites are insects that can cause much damage to wooden structures. These tiny creatures live underground and find their way to the wood in old trees and houses. Once these insects swarm to start new colonies, the workers begin to eat away at the wood. Sometimes these tiny creatures go unnoticed until their damage is done.
      _____ same types of writing
      __X__ different types of writing

Application

Students could apply the skill taught in this lesson by comparing the passages they read in natural text to tell whether they are written the same. However, such an activity is really not pertinent at this time because the focus of this lesson was simply to help the students *develop the concept* that different authors structure text differently. It is best to hold off on application until students have been taught to read and interpret different text structures.

TEACHING STUDENTS TO READ NARRATIVE TEXT

Teaching students to read narrative text involves helping them learn to recognize the elements of narrative text and to use those elements to improve their comprehension of selections. Three effective ways to help students learn to read narrative text are described in the following sections: (1) teaching the elements of narrative, so that students can anticipate the type of information they should be looking for as they read; (2) teaching students to construct a story map; and (3) using guided reading questions, which help students develop an understanding of the story's structure.

Teaching the Elements of Narrative

Students can learn the elements of narrative text even before they begin to read. When reading stories to students, the teacher can conduct a discussion focusing on the setting, characters, problem, action, resolution, and theme without using the technical terms. After the story has been completely read, the teacher can ask questions that bring out the elements of narrative. The questions can be similar to the following, although all of the questions listed will not be relevant to all stories.

Setting	Where did this story take place? When did this story occur?
Characters	Who was the story about? Who were the characters in the story? Who was the most important character in the story or the star of the story?
Problem	Did the characters (people/animals) in the story have a problem? What was the big problem that the whole story was about? As you listened to this story, what did you think the characters were trying to do?
Action	What were the important things that happened in the story?
Resolution	How did the story end? How did the characters in this story finally solve their problem?

Theme   What was this story really trying to tell us?
What lesson could be learned from this story?

If these types of discussions are carried out routinely, students will develop a good concept of narrative structure. Such discussions should be held whenever stories are read to students, even after students begin to read; this practice will continue to reinforce the narrative structure concept.

As students begin to develop a good understanding of narrative structure, the terms *setting, characters, problem, action, resolution,* and *theme* should be gradually introduced. The teacher should write the terms *setting* and *characters* on the chalkboard as soon as the students seem to understand these elements and should relate the terms to a story that has been read to the students. After reading another story to the class, the teacher should begin the discussion by asking students to identify the story's setting and characters. This pattern should continue until all the terms of narrative are introduced. If the students seem unable to handle the terms, the teacher should postpone their introduction until later.

As soon as students have developed the concept of text structure and realize that different authors use different types of writing, lessons on the elements of narrative text, such as that in Example 6.4, should be incorporated into the reading program. The sample lesson in Example 6.4 uses passages that are approximately second to third grade level. The lesson teaches all elements of narrative structure; it is possible and in some cases necessary to teach one or two elements at a time and then focus on all elements in a single lesson.

EXAMPLE 6.4 SAMPLE LESSON ON RECOGNIZING THE ELEMENTS OF NARRATIVE TEXT ───────────

Purpose of the Lesson

To teach students to recognize the information needed to comprehend narrative text.

Prerequisites

Students should be familiar with narrative structure and should know that narratives have characters, setting, problem, action, resolution, and theme. It is not necessary that students have mastered these terms.

Materials Needed

An overhead projector or chalkboard.
Copies of the stories used in this lesson to distribute to students.

Teaching

Letting Students Know What Is to Be Learned
Say: You have listened to stories that I have read to you, and you have read stories on your own in your reader and in other books. You have learned that stories have different parts. What are they? (Students respond. If they cannot recall all the parts immediately, tell them—characters, setting, problem, action, resolution, and theme.) In today's lesson, you are going to learn how to identify which information in stories is important to remember.

Modeling
By this time students will have developed a concept of narrative structure through listening to and reading stories. Therefore, it should not be necessary to include the concept and listening parts of modeling in this lesson.

Modeling: Developing the Skill at the Reading Level
Say: You have learned enough about stories to know that as you read them you can expect to find certain things in them, such as characters. Today, I'm going to show you how to determine which information in stories is most important for helping you understand the stories. *(Note: This is the teacher modeling part of direct instruction.)* I want you to read this story to yourselves to get a general idea of what it is about. (Distribute copies of the following story. Have a copy on a transparency or on the chalkboard.)

Huggie and the Big Top

It was a warm spring day in Loganville. Beth was so excited she couldn't eat her breakfast of bacon and eggs. Today, Beth and her friend Lisa were going to the circus.

"Huggie, you must eat," said Beth's mother. Her mother and friends always called her Huggie because she liked to hug people. "I just can't eat," said Beth. "I'm too excited." Beth knew that what she was really going to do was try to get a job at the circus. She had always wanted to be a clown.

Lisa arrived at 9:30. Beth and Lisa left for the circus right away. Beth told Lisa about wanting to work in the circus.

"What in the world would you do?" asked Lisa. "Be a clown," Beth answered. "I just have to find the right person to talk to."

When Beth and Lisa arrived on the circus grounds, they walked around. They saw elephants, people dressed in work clothes, and some dressed in costumes. As they went by one tent, they heard someone crying. Beth peeped inside. She saw an old clown sitting in a chair crying. He saw Beth.

"Come in," he said. Beth and Lisa stepped into the tent. "Why are you crying?" asked Lisa.

"I had someone to help me with my new act, but she quit this morning. I don't know what I'm going to do! She was supposed to be a funny little girl. Now I have no one. I'll get fired."

"Maybe I can help you," said Beth. "I would be a great little girl clown, and I'm the right age."

"I couldn't let you do that," said the clown.

"Sure you could!" yelled Lisa. "We'll make her look just right."

It didn't take much to change the clown's mind. He had no choice.

The band began to play. It was time for the clowns. Out they came!

The last clown into the ring got a special drum roll. In marched this big old clown carrying a sign that said "HAPPY AND HUGGIE." At last Beth had her dream come true. She ran around the ring hugging everyone. She was a hit.

Say: As you read "Huggie and the Big Top," you knew that this was a story. How could you tell? (Students respond. If they are unable to answer, help them see that it has characters, a setting, a problem, action, a resolution, and a theme. Remember, it is not necessary for students to give the terms so long as they give the general ideas. List the terms on the chalkboard as students describe them.)

Say: The names of these parts are unimportant, but it is important to know that when you are reading stories you can expect to find this information in them. As I read "Huggie and the Big Top," I looked for information to help me understand the story. As I read the first paragraph, I asked myself the question, Do I need this information to understand the story? (Read the first paragraph aloud or have a student read it aloud.)

Say: The first sentence tells me when and where this story takes place. (Write "Loganville" and "warm spring day" in a box on the chalkboard.) The last sentence of the paragraph tells me that this story is going to happen at the circus. (Add "at the circus" to the box.)

```
┌─────────────────────────────┐
│                             │
│                             │
│   Loganville                │
│                             │
│   warm spring day at        │
│   the circus                │
│                             │
│                             │
└─────────────────────────────┘
```

Say: I know that this information is important and that I will need to know it to understand the story. There are also some other things in this paragraph that are going to be important to understand the story. For example, there are two characters mentioned—Beth and Lisa. The story wouldn't make sense if I didn't know who the characters were. (Write "Beth" and "Lisa" in a box on the chalkboard, or have students go to the board and do this. Leave room for additions to the box. Place this box right under the first box.)

```
┌─────────────────────────────┐
│                             │
│                             │
│   Loganville                │
│                             │
│   warm spring day at        │
│   the circus                │
│                             │
│                             │
│                             │
└─────────────────────────────┘


┌─────────────────────────────┐
│                             │
│                             │
│                             │
│   Beth                      │
│   Lisa                      │
│                             │
│                             │
│                             │
│                             │
└─────────────────────────────┘
```

Say: Now, let's look back at the paragraph. I can see that there is some informa-tion that doesn't seem too important right now. The paragraph says that Beth was excited and that she had bacon and eggs. These pieces of information don't seem to be important to the story. If I find out that they are important, I can come back to them later. As I read this first paragraph, I knew I was reading a story so I looked for things that made up a story. I kept asking myself the question, Would this story make sense without this information?

Say: Now, I want you to reread the next paragraph and tell me what information in that paragraph is really important to understanding the story. Ask yourselves the question, Would this story make sense without this information? I want you to explain your thinking as I did. *(Note: This is the student modeling part of direct in-struction.)* (After students have reread the paragraph, have one or more give their answers and explain their thinking. If students are unable to answer and explain on their own, guide them with such questions as:

1. What other character was introduced?
2. What does this paragraph tell you Beth wants to do at the circus?
3. Is the information about Beth eating and being called Huggie really that impor-tant to helping you make sense of the story?

Conclude the discussion by writing on the board that Beth wanted to get a job as a circus clown. Place this information in a box under the other two boxes. Add "Mother" to the box with "Lisa" and "Beth.")

```
Loganville


warm spring day at
the circus
```

```
Beth
Lisa
Mother
```

```
Beth wanted to get job
as a circus clown.
```

Say: Now, let's reread the next five paragraphs to ourselves to see what other information is given that is important to our story. (After students have reread the paragraphs, continue by explaining your thinking.) *(Note: This is teacher modeling.)*

Say: The first of these paragraphs told me that Beth and Lisa went to the circus. I know that's important to the story. In the next paragraph, Beth and Lisa are talking about Beth's wanting a job at the circus; that paragraph doesn't tell me anything new. The next paragraph just tells me what Beth and Lisa saw as they walked around. But the last part of that paragraph and the paragraph that follows tell me that Beth and Lisa met a clown who was crying because the girl who was supposed to help him quit. The story wouldn't make sense if Lisa and Beth had not gone to the circus and if they had not met the clown with the problem. The clown is another character in our story. (Write the two events in boxes on the board beneath the other boxes and add "clown" to the box with the other characters.)

Loganville

warm spring day at
the circus

Beth   clown
Lisa
Mother

Beth wanted to get job
as a circus clown.

Beth and Lisa went to
the circus.

Beth and Lisa met a
clown who had lost his
little girl partner.

Say: Now, I want you to reread the remainder of the story to tell what other information is given that is needed to make sense out of the story. Be ready to explain your thinking. *(Note: This is student modeling.)* (After students have completed their reading, call on one or two students to answer. If they have difficulty or are unable to answer, guide them with the following questions:

1. What did Beth and Lisa do?
2. How did the story end?

Conclude the discussion by adding the students' answers to the boxes on the board and connecting the boxes as shown. Don't add the labels "setting," "characters," and so on at this time; they can be added later, during further discussion.)

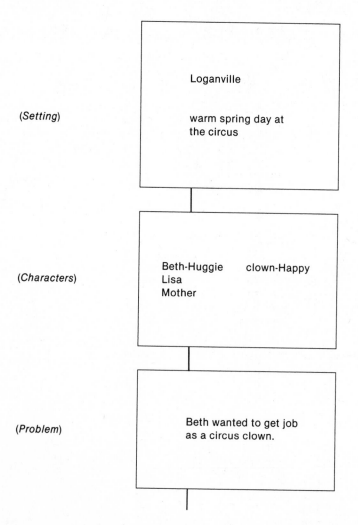

(Setting)

Loganville

warm spring day at the circus

(Characters)

Beth-Huggie   clown-Happy
Lisa
Mother

(Problem)

Beth wanted to get job as a circus clown.

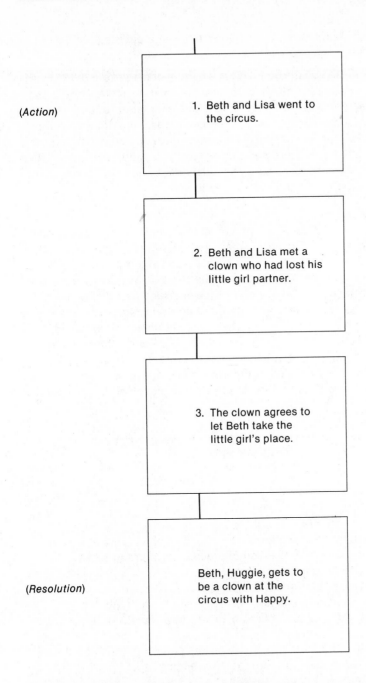

(*Action*)

1. Beth and Lisa went to the circus.

2. Beth and Lisa met a clown who had lost his little girl partner.

3. The clown agrees to let Beth take the little girl's place.

(*Resolution*)

Beth, Huggie, gets to be a clown at the circus with Happy.

Say: As you read these paragraphs, you looked for only that information that was needed for the story to make sense. Look at what I have written on the board. If I left out any part of this information, would the story make sense? *(Note: This is teacher modeling.)* (Students respond. Be certain that students see that if any part was left out, the story wouldn't make sense.)

Say: What I have written on the board gives a picture or map of our story. This is called a story map; it shows all those parts that are needed for the story to make sense. (At this point, you can add the terms setting, characters, and so on to the map, but they really are unimportant to what the students are doing. The labels should only be added for discussion purposes.) As we have been reading this story together, we have been learning how to identify the important information that is needed for a story to make sense. The other information that is given by the author is not important to understanding the story.

Providing Guided Practice

Say: Now, we are going to read a story together to identify which information we will need to know for the story to make sense to us. (Distribute copies of the story "A Different Day," which is reprinted on pages 293–295 of this book. Also distribute copies of the exercise sheet, printed on pages 292–293.) We will read the story in parts. As we read each part, I want you to put a checkmark next to the information on your sheet that you really need to know for the story to make sense. As you complete each part, be ready to tell why you selected the information you did. (Have students read the first section of text—pages 1–2—and complete the exercise sheet for that section. Discuss their answers and provide corrective feedback and reteaching as needed. Follow the same procedure for the other sections indicated on the exercise sheet. A map of the story is presented on page 295 for the teacher's use.)

Exercise Sheet

Pages 1–2

_____ The story takes place at the zoo.

_____ It was Edgar the Elephant's birthday.

_____ Edgar was twenty-five years old.

_____ Mr. Carr was the head zoo keeper.

_____ Mr. and Mrs. Cortina were asked to prepare food for the party.

_____ Ruby and Ricardo are the children.

_____ Ruby and Ricardo ate breakfast.

_____ Mr. Cortina was on the phone.

_____ Mr. and Mrs. Cortina don't have anyone to help them with the big party.

Pages 3–4

_____ Ruby and Ricardo help prepare food for the party.

_____ They prepare three hundred tamales.

_____ The tamales were cooked in a big pot.

_____ Ruby and Ricardo had to help with the party and weren't going to get to see the animals.

_____ Mom and Dad put the food in big boxes.

_____ When they got to the zoo, Ruby, Ricardo, Mom, and Dad got things ready for the party.

_____ The tent was red and white.

Pages 5–6

_____ The zoo workers came to the party.

_____ The people danced at the party.

_____ Mr. Carr took the party to Edgar; he went by the other animals and Ruby and Ricardo got to see them.

Pages 7–8

_____ The TV News people came to take pictures of Edgar's party.

_____ The TV people came to the zoo in a truck.

_____ The Cortina family saw themselves on the TV news and knew that it had been a different day.

Selection: "A Different Day"

Today is a very special day at the zoo. It's Edgar the Elephant's birthday. Edgar was born at the zoo twenty-five years ago.

Mr. Carr, the head of the zoo, decided it would be fun to have a birthday party and invite everyone who worked at the zoo.

Mr. Carr asked Mr. and Mrs. Cortina to prepare the food for the party. They own Cortina's Kitchen, and everyone says Cortina's Kitchen makes the best Mexican food in town.

Mr. and Mrs. Cortina got up early to start preparing the food while their children, Ruby and Ricardo, ate breakfast. Ruby wished she could go to the zoo with her parents, but she and Ricardo were going bowling, just as they did every Saturday.   1

As Ruby was getting her bowling ball, she heard the phone ring. Mr. Cortina answered it.

"Hello, Cortina's Kitchen," Mr. Cortina said. Mr. Cortina was on the phone for only a minute, but he had a troubled look on his face.

"Carmen has a cold, and she can't help us cook today," he said.

"Oh, no!" said Mrs. Cortina. "Ann and Carlos are on vacation, and we can't fix all the food for such a big party without help!"

"We can help," said Ruby.

"Right," said Ricardo. "I don't care if I miss bowling just once. I think we really can help."

"That's great!" said Mom and Dad, almost at the same time.

"Where do we start?" asked Ruby.

"We'll have to make the tamales first," said Mom. "We're going to make three hundred of them!"   2

"Three hundred!" said Ricardo.

Marginal numbers indicate pages in original story.

"Yes," said Mom. "That's why we really do need help. We'll have to prepare the meat filling for the tamales. And we'll need to make the corn dough for them."

Ruby and Ricardo worked all morning helping Mom and Dad fix the tamales. After lunch they put the tamales into big pots to cook.

"We have enough tamales to feed an elephant!" said Ricardo. Everyone laughed.

3

"I can't wait to get to the zoo," said Ruby. "I want to see the lions, tigers, kangaroos, and Edgar the Elephant."

"I'm afraid you won't be able to see the animals today," said Mom. "We need you to help with the food and to help clean up."

"Oh," said Ruby, "I forgot." Ruby looked sad. She really did want to see the animals. Ricardo looked a little sad, too.

"Someday we'll all see the zoo," said Mom.

Mom and Dad put all the food in big boxes, and Ruby and Ricardo helped put the boxes into the truck.

When the Cortinas arrived at the zoo they found the big, red and white tent that had been put up for the party. Tables and chairs had been set up inside.

Ruby and Ricardo helped place all the food on a long table in the tent. Mom put flowers and paper hats on all the small tables where people would eat.

4

"Everything looks beautiful!" said Ruby.

The zoo workers started coming into the tent, and the party began. They laughed and sang and danced—and ate tamales. It wasn't long before all three hundred tamales had been eaten.

Mr. Carr came over to talk to Mr. and Mrs. Cortina. "Thank you. Just as everyone says, Cortina's Kitchen makes the best Mexican food in town."

5

"We couldn't have done it without our children," said Dad. "They helped cook."

Mom smiled and hugged Ruby and Ricardo. Ricardo looked up at his mom and said, "It's too bad Edgar can't be here at his own party."

Just then Mr. Carr stood up and made an announcement. He said, "Because Edgar can't come to his birthday party, we're going to take the party to him! Come on everybody, follow me." He led the party past the lions, tigers, bears, and kangaroos.

6

"We are getting to see all the animals after all," Ruby said to Ricardo.

As the crowd reached Edgar, a TV truck with the letters WHTZ pulled up. Out jumped a man with a microphone and a woman with a TV camera on her shoulder. The man went to Mr. Carr and shook his hand.

"This is Paul Zepp from the TV news," Mr. Carr announced. "Now let's all sing 'Happy Birthday' to Edgar! Ruby and Ricardo Cortina, from Cortina's Kitchen, will lead us!"

7

That night, a tired Ruby and Ricardo watched the TV news. They jumped up and hugged each other when they heard Paul Zepp say, "Now a special story from the zoo. Edgar the Elephant has turned twenty-five!"

Right there on TV, leading the others at the party in singing "Happy Birthday" to Edgar, were Ruby and Ricardo.

Ruby laughed and said, "This has been quite a day. I did get to see the animals."

"Yes," said Mr. Cortina, "I found out my children are great helpers and good cooks."

"We were on TV!" added Ricardo.

Mrs. Cortina said, "This really has been a different day!"   8

Source: Ann Miranda with María Guerrero, "A Different Day." In William K. Durr et al.: *Discoveries*, pp. 58–67 (Houghton Mifflin Reading Program). Boston: Houghton Mifflin Company, 1986. Used by permission.

Story Map Based on "A Different Day" (For Teacher Use Only)

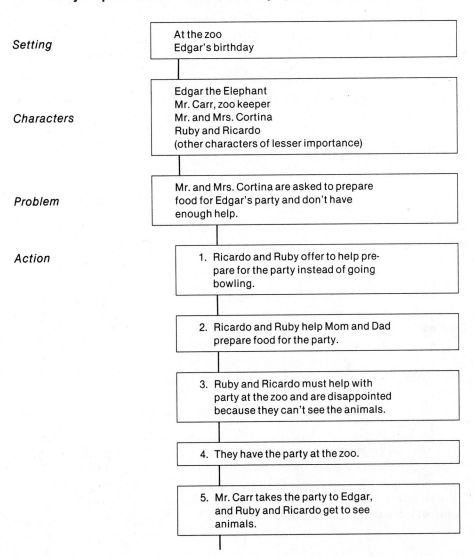

Setting	At the zoo Edgar's birthday
Characters	Edgar the Elephant Mr. Carr, zoo keeper Mr. and Mrs. Cortina Ruby and Ricardo (other characters of lesser importance)
Problem	Mr. and Mrs. Cortina are asked to prepare food for Edgar's party and don't have enough help.
Action	1. Ricardo and Ruby offer to help prepare for the party instead of going bowling.
	2. Ricardo and Ruby help Mom and Dad prepare food for the party.
	3. Ruby and Ricardo must help with party at the zoo and are disappointed because they can't see the animals.
	4. They have the party at the zoo.
	5. Mr. Carr takes the party to Edgar, and Ruby and Ricardo get to see animals.

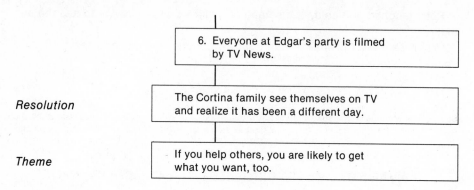

6. Everyone at Edgar's party is filmed by TV News.

Resolution

The Cortina family see themselves on TV and realize it has been a different day.

Theme

If you help others, you are likely to get what you want, too.

Summarizing

After students have completed the guided practice, continue as follows.

Say: You have learned how to read a story and tell what information is important. How did you do that? (Guide students to conclude:

1. I knew that characters, setting, problem, action, and resolution are found in stories.
2. As I read, I asked myself the question, Would the story make sense without this information?
3. I can use this procedure everytime I read a story.)

Practice

The independent practice for this lesson should follow the same format as the guided practice.

Application

For application of this lesson, select a narrative for students to read on their own. Develop the needed background and vocabulary. Remind students that they have learned how to identify which information they will need to understand a story. Have students read the selection. Tell them that you are going to ask them to tell the story in their own words after they have read it. Notice whether students are able to present the story line.

Comments About the Lesson

The focus of this lesson has been to teach students how to recognize the important elements in narrative text so that they understand the story. The emphasis was not on teaching students to label different parts of a narrative. It cannot be overemphasized that students do not need to learn the labels for parts of narrative structure. What they need is to learn to recognize the information that is important for understanding the story.

Using Story Maps

Earlier in this chapter, the concept of a story map was presented. The story map is another means of helping students learn the elements of narrative text and become aware of narrative structure (Reutzel, 1985). After students know the elements of narrative text and have been taught how to read narrative as they were taught in the last lesson, the story map can be used to graphically reinforce the concepts and help students visualize how the elements of narrative text are related. Lessons similar to that in Example 6.4 can be used to teach students to construct a story map. The same basic procedures would be followed, but the emphasis would be on constructing the map.

After students have read a selection under the teacher's direction, they can construct a map of the story. This will help them clarify each of the elements of narrative text. After students become proficient in constructing story maps, they can be given assignments to construct their own maps as a follow-up to their reading. Students who have read the same story can compare their maps to note variations. By comparing maps, students will develop an appreciation for the various ways different individuals interpret the same story.

Using Guided Reading Questions

As noted in Chapter 2, researchers have found that students comprehend narrative text better if the questions used for guided silent reading help them develop the flow of the story (Beck, 1984). Therefore, questions that focus on the elements of narrative structure should help students develop a better overall understanding of what they are reading. (See Chapter 2 for further discussion about guided reading questions.)

In situations in which the teacher carries out page-by-page guided reading with students, the questions used should come in the order necessary to help bring out the elements and flow of the story. The follow-up discussion should help synthesize the story and give students an overall understanding of the selection.

In situations in which students are given an entire selection to read for a single purpose, the questions in the initial follow-up discussion should bring out the elements of the narrative. The remainder of the discussion should help students draw the story together.

Guided reading questions will not directly teach students the elements of narrative. They will, however, help students develop a better understanding of narrative text if they focus on the narrative elements and are asked in an order that helps students understand the selection.

TEACHING STUDENTS TO READ EXPOSITORY TEXT

As students learn to read expository text, they should be taught to recognize the basic patterns of expository writing and to interpret those patterns as they read. As with narrative text, the teaching should incorporate direct instruction with systematic teaching and practicing followed by many opportunities to apply the patterns in natural reading situations. Researchers have concluded that students can improve their comprehension of expository text by learning to recognize and interpret the common patterns found in such materials (McGee and Richgels, 1985).

Another sound way to help students become more aware of an author's organization of ideas in expository writing is to teach them to outline as they read (Taylor and Beach, 1984; Slater, Graves, and Piché, 1985). Students are frequently taught to outline from notes to organize information before they write, but the concept of teaching outlining as an aid to comprehension during reading is often overlooked or assumed to be transferred by students once they have learned to outline for writing. Such an assumption should not be made.

When using direct instruction to teach students to read expository writing, the teacher must consider all the principles and guidelines that have been discussed earlier in this text. The sample lesson in Example 6.5 illustrates one way to use direct instruction to teach students to read and interpret the comparison type of expository text structure. The same strategy can be used to teach the description, collection, causation, and response structures. The emphasis should be on teaching the students to see how the structure of an expository passage helps them understand the information, not on identifying the type of structure. The following lesson is approximately fourth to fifth grade level. Other passages can be used to make the lesson more simple or more sophisticated.

EXAMPLE 6.5   SAMPLE LESSON FOR TEACHING THE COMPARISON TEXT STRUCTURE

Purpose of the Lesson

To teach students to use clues from the comparison expository text structure to anticipate information that is to follow in the text.

Materials Needed

Photograph or drawing of two airplanes parked at an airport—one a jet and the other a small propellor-driven private plane.
Copies of the paragraphs used in this lesson to distribute to students.
An overhead projector and screen.

Teaching

Letting Students Know What Is to Be Learned
Say: You have learned that when authors write to tell you facts and information they are using expository writing. In this lesson you will learn how to recog-

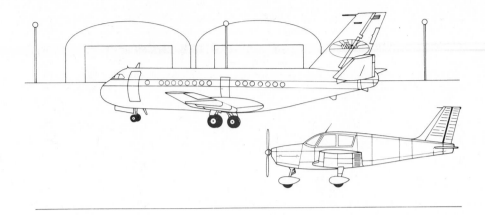

nize and interpret one type of expository writing, called comparison. (Distribute copies of the airplane picture to students, or show the picture on the overhead projector.)

Modeling: Developing the Concept
Say: Look at this picture and tell me what you see. (Students respond. If necessary, provide guidance in describing the picture.) How are the planes in the picture alike? (Students respond. Guide them to see that:

  Both planes have wings and a tail.
  The planes are alike because they both have engines.
  The jet plane and smaller plane are similar because they can both fly.)

Say: How are the two planes different? (Students respond. Guide them to see that:

The two planes are different because the jet plane is larger than the one with propellers.
The engines on the jet plane are different from those on the smaller plane.
The two planes are different because one has a propeller and the other doesn't.)

Say: As you look at the picture of these two planes, you can compare the planes and tell how they are alike and how they are different. Authors often use comparisons in their writing. To help you understand comparisons when you are reading, you must be able to recognize what the author is comparing and know which words help you anticipate and interpret the comparison.

Modeling: Developing the Skill at the Listening Level
Say: Listen to the paragraph I am going to read you and tell me what two things are being compared. As you listen, note the words that the author uses to make the comparisons.

Radios and televisions are used by people throughout the world. Both are forms of entertainment as well as means of passing along news and information. The radio is similar to the television because it carries the voices of individuals talking or singing. The television is different from the radio in that it also provides a picture for the user to watch. Years ago, televisions were much larger than radios. But today, the television and radio can be similar in size; some televisions, just like radios, are small enough to carry anywhere one wants to go.

Say: What two things are being compared in this paragraph? (Students respond.) What are some of the statements in the paragraph that compare the radio and the television? (Reread the paragraph to students if needed. List the statements on the board as students respond.)

Say: What words or phrases did the author use to help you recognize the comparisons that were being made? (Students respond. List the words on the chalkboard; the list should include the words both, similar to, different from, similar, and just like.)

Say: These are some of the words that authors use to help you recognize and interpret comparisons.

Modeling: Developing the Skill at the Reading Level
Say: Now we are going to see how to use the author's comparisons in a paragraph to tell what information is important. (Distribute copies of the paragraph that follows.) Read this paragraph to yourselves and then tell me what you learned about the things being compared.

People who travel in outer space today and the pioneers who traveled west in our country years ago have much in common. Both the pioneers and the space travelers were charting new territory; they were venturing into places where people had not gone before. The space travelers, like the pioneers, face many unknown dangers. The methods of travel used by the pioneers were very different from those used by today's space explorers. The crude wagons drawn by horses or oxen moved the pioneers much slower than the mighty rockets of today's space travel. But even some parts of the travel were similar: Life in a space capsule and life in a covered wagon both have their rough moments and hardships.

Say: What things were compared in this paragraph? What did you learn about them? (Students respond.) Now, I want to show you how I used the structure of this paragraph to help me understand the author's ideas and relate them to what I already knew. (*Note: This is teacher modeling.* As this dialogue is carried out, underline the appropriate parts of the paragraph and circle the clue words. A copy of the marked paragraph is presented at the end of this dialogue.)

Say: The first sentence let me know right away that the author is comparing people who travel in outer space to pioneers; I knew they were being compared because of the phrase "have much in common." The next clue word I saw was "both"; from it I knew that the author was going to tell me how the two things are alike. *Both* were charting new territory and venturing into unknown places. The word "like" in the next sentence alerted me to look for another similarity. However, in the following sentence the author told me to look for differences with the phrase "were very different." The horses and oxen were much slower than the rockets. Finally, in the next sentence the author directed my attention to again think about how the pioneers and space travelers are alike by the word "similar." Therefore, as I read this passage I began to expect what type of information would follow because of the important clue words.

Sample Marked-up Passage

People who travel in outer space today and the pioneers who traveled west in our country have much in common. Both the pioneers and the space travelers were charting new territory; they were venturing into places where people had not gone before. The space travelers, like the pioneers, face many unknown dangers. The methods of travel used by the pioneers were very different from those used by today's space explorers. The crude wagons drawn by horses or oxen moved the pioneers much slower than the mighty rockets of today's space travel. But even some parts of the travel were similar: Life in a space capsule and life in a covered wagon both have their rough moments and hardships.

Say: I can diagram the information in the paragraph so I can see at a glance the things that are alike and the things that are different. (Draw the following diagram on the board and explain.)

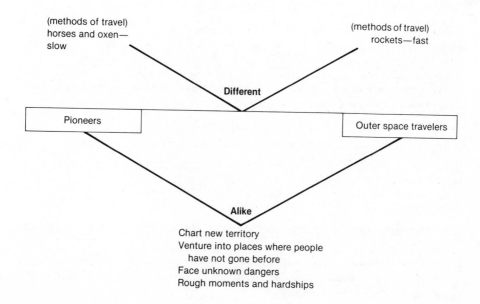

(methods of travel)
horses and oxen—
slow

(methods of travel)
rockets—fast

Different

Pioneers

Outer space travelers

Alike

Chart new territory
Venture into places where people
    have not gone before
Face unknown dangers
Rough moments and hardships

Say: As you read expository passages, you can recognize the comparison structure by the clue words "alike," "both," "similar," "different," "different from," and so on. These words should help you know what is being compared and should help you anticipate the type of information you will find as you read.

Providing Guided Practice
Say: Now, we are going to look at a paragraph together. I want you to read the paragraph to identify the comparisons and the clue words that help you interpret them. I'm going to ask you to explain your thinking as I did in the first example. *(Note: This is student modeling.)* First, read the paragraph to yourself to see what things are being compared. (Allow students time to read the following paragraph.)

Water skiing and snow skiing are great sports. Both require careful preparation and training on the part of the participant. The skis used for water skiing are similar to those used for snow skiing, but they are not exactly alike. Snow skis are narrower and longer than water skis and are usually made of different materials. Snow skiing is very different from water skiing in that the skier's weight is kept forward on snow skis and backward on water skis. Also, snow skiing is different from water skiing because water skiing requires more than one person; snow skiing can be done alone.

Say: What was being compared in this paragraph? (Students respond. Have a student read aloud the sentences and parts of sentences in which comparisons are being made. Have the student underline these sentences and circle the clue words that helped him or her identify and interpret the comparisons. Have the student explain how he or she used the information in each sentence to gain understanding of the comparisons in the paragraph. If the student misses comparisons, guide him or her with questions. If the student still fails to see the comparisons, point them out. The completed paragraph should look like the following:

Water skiing and snow skiing are great sports. (Both) require careful preparation and training on the part of the participant. The skis used for water skiing are (similar) to those used for snow skiing, but they are (not exactly alike). Snow skis are narrower and longer (than) water skis and are usually made of different materials. Snow skiing is very (different from) water skiing in that the skier's weight is kept forward on snow skis and backward on water skis. Also, snow skiing is (different from) water skiing because water skiing requires more than one person; snow skiing can be done alone.)

Summarizing
Say: What have you learned in this lesson about reading one type of expository text? (Guide students with questions to conclude the following points in their own words:

1. In comparison type of text, the author looks at how things are alike and different.
2. An author usually uses clue words such as "different," "different from," "both," "like," "alike," "similar," "similar to," "than," and "but" to help the reader identify comparisons.)

Practice

Have students complete the following exercise by themselves. When they have finished, go over their work with them. *(Note: This is independent practice.)*

**Independent Practice for Recognizing
and Interpreting Comparison Text Structure**

Name _____ Date _____

Directions: Read each of the following sentences and paragraphs to yourself. Below each exercise, check the answer showing what is being compared. Circle the clue words in the sentence or paragraph that helped you identify and interpret the comparison. The first exercise has been done for you. In some cases, you may check more than one answer.

1. Cats and dogs are(both)common pets with wild ancestors.
    __×__ Tells how cats and dogs are alike.
    _____ Tells how cats and dogs are different.
2. Oak is considered a hard wood but pine is a soft wood.
    _____ Tells how oak and pine are alike.
    _____ Tells how oak and pine are different.
3. Making pottery is becoming a popular craft again. Stoneware cups, mugs, bowls, and dishes are being made by many potters today. Porcelain, another kind of pottery, is also very popular. Porcelain and stoneware are alike because they are both types of clay.
    _____ Tells how potters are different today.
    _____ Tells how porcelain and stoneware are alike.
    _____ Tells how different things are made of porcelain.
4. Wool, cotton, and silk are three very popular cloths. Unlike nylon, wool, cotton, and silk are natural fibers. Wool, cotton, and silk are each different because they come from different living things.
    _____ Tells that nylon is different from wool, cotton, and silk.
    _____ Tells that wool, cotton, and silk are different from each other.
    _____ Tells that wool and cotton are similar to nylon.

Application

For application, use a selection from a basal reader, textbook, or trade book that uses comparisons. Before having students read the selection, develop the background and vocabulary with students and help them set an appropriate purpose for reading. After the students have finished reading, discuss the selection, asking questions that require students to interpret the comparisons. Do not ask students to identify the comparisons or clue words unless they are unable to answer the questions. (If you have students identify the comparisons or clue words, the activity becomes practice and not application.)

Comments About the Lesson

This lesson has focused on teaching students to think through the process of using the comparison structure to anticipate information and construct meaning. The emphasis has not been on having students identify the comparisons, but on modeling the thinking process involved. Each of the other types of expository structure should be taught in the same manner, with emphasis being placed on the process and not on identification of the structure.

Outlining as an Aid to Understanding Expository Text Structure

As was noted earlier, students' understanding of expository text structures can be improved by teaching them outlining. Many teachers emphasize outlining only as an aid for organizing notes before writing papers. Although outlining is certainly helpful to students in this situation, it is also a valuable skill for students to use as they read and study expository text.

If students read expository text with the idea in mind that they are going to outline the text, they will focus on the overall structure of the writing. In the beginning stages of outline instruction, teachers should have students develop written outlines as they read; as students progress in the use of this skill, teachers should encourage them to develop mental outlines. One of the advantages of teaching students outlining to help them understand expository text structures is that it requires them to focus on the interpretation of the text and prevents them from focusing on the identification of the different types of structures. Too often students simply learn to identify the type of structure without really learning to read and interpret the structure.

Learning to use outlining will help students begin to predict or anticipate the information that is likely to be in the text. By outlining, students can construct the meaning of text more readily—through an outline they can see how the author has organized his or her ideas and they can relate those ideas to their own existing schema. Learning to outline in written or mental form during reading helps the reader develop a strategy that he or she can use when reading any type of expository text.

Outlining should be taught very systematically, using the steps of direct instruction that have been presented throughout this text. Once students have learned to identify main ideas and note important details (see Chapter 5), they can be taught to outline with a focus on text structure. Outline instruction should proceed through sequential steps and phases such as those suggested below. (Only one form of outlining is presented here.)

Step 1: Teach the concept of outlining. Here, the teacher should introduce students to the concept of an outline by telling them that an outline is a written framework of the author's most important ideas. The teacher should show students a simple outline form, such as:

I. _____
   A. _____
   B. _____
II. _____
   A. _____
   B. _____
   C. _____

The teacher should then explain that the Roman numerals represent the main ideas of paragraphs and that the capital letters represent the supporting details. After students have learned to use this simple form, they can be introduced to a more complex form showing specific subpoints of supporting details.

I. _____
   A. _____
   B. _____
      1. _____
      2. _____
      3. _____
II. _____
   A. _____
      1. _____
      2. _____
   B. _____
      1. _____
      2. _____
   C. _____
      1. _____
      2. _____
      3. _____

Outline form and the concept of outlining should not be taught as things that are rigid. Students should be made to feel that they can adapt the outline to help them develop a good picture of an author's ideas and how they are structured.

To illustrate the concept of outlining, the teacher should select three or four paragraphs from one of the students' content textbooks, develop a simple outline, and have students read it to tell what they think is going to be covered in the text. The teacher should then have them read the paragraphs in the text to see if their predictions were correct. In this way, students will learn that an outline can give them a picture of what is covered in the text.

Step 2: Teach students to listen to passages and select the main points that represent each paragraph. For this step of instruction, the teacher should select two or three paragraphs of expository text, make a list of statements representing the main ideas of the paragraphs, and write the list in scrambled order on the board. The teacher should then tell students to listen as he or she reads the paragraphs and note on their paper the number of the statement that gives the main idea for each paragraph. The teacher should point out that the students are developing an outline for the paragraphs. The teacher can make this activity more difficult by including statements that are distractors in the list.

Step 3:   Teach students to listen to paragraphs and generate their own main-idea statements. After students have become proficient at selecting the main-idea statements that represent paragraphs, the teacher should have them listen to other paragraphs and formulate their own main-idea statements. This step requires considerable teacher modeling, which can be done using two or three sample paragraphs from content texts.

When teaching students to generate their own main-idea statements, the teacher should continuously require the students to put their ideas in outline form. The teacher should point out that the students can use the skill of outlining while they are listening to others talk as well as when they are reading. This skill is especially useful in classes in which teachers lecture.

Step 4:   Teach students to listen to paragraphs and select the supporting details. Here, the teacher should select three or four paragraphs to read to the students and should list the main headings in outline form on the board. The same paragraphs used in earlier steps can be used here. The teacher should then list in scrambled order, the details found in the paragraphs. The teacher should include in the outline the number of supporting details there are for each heading. (see Example 6.6). The students should listen to the paragraphs and complete the outline under the teacher's direction. After students have developed the ability to perform this task, the teacher should have them listen to other passages and generate their own supporting details.

Step 5:   Teach students to read paragraphs and identify the main ideas from a given list. In this step, the teacher should select three or four paragraphs of connected expository text, determine the main idea for each paragraph, and list them for students in scrambled order. The teacher should then model for students how to determine the main idea for the first paragraph and should instruct students to follow the same procedure for the other paragraphs. This type of activity should continue until students are proficient at identifying the main points for paragraphs. The written portion of the activity should always be in outline form.

Step 6:   Teach students to read paragraphs and generate their own main-idea statements. Using several paragraphs of connected text, the teacher should model for the students how to generate their own main ideas. As students become more proficient, they can do this on their own. The teacher should use sections of text with subheadings and should show students how to use the subheadings to anticipate the main idea of a paragraph or section. This instruction should be combined with the teaching of SQ3R (see Chapter 8).

EXAMPLE 6.6   SAMPLE EXERCISE FOR OUTLINING WITH MAIN IDEAS LISTED ──────────────

I. The main uses of hardwood trees
   A. _____
   B. _____
II. How man has destroyed hardwood trees
   A. _____
   B. _____
III. Problems in raising hardwood trees
   A. _____
   B. _____
   C. _____

Choices

1. Through forest fires
2. To make lumber for furniture
3. Takes years to grow
4. Cut too many trees at once
5. Having the proper soil conditions
6. Scraps used as mulch in landscaping
7. Having money to start a tree farm

─────────────────────

Step 7: *Teach students to read connected text to pick out supporting details for the main ideas.* The teacher should select several paragraphs of connected expository text and list for students the main-idea statements for each paragraph. The teacher should then give students a list of the supporting details in scrambled order and model for students how to pick out the details that support the main idea. Finally, the teacher should instruct students to generate their own details without a list of scrambled choices.

Step 8: *Have students outline text without any choices.* This is the final step in teaching outlining. By this time students should be familiar with outlining and outline form. If each of the previous steps was carefully modeled for students, the teacher should need to do only minimal modeling now.

Throughout the teaching of outlining, the teacher must model the processes involved (see Chapter 5). Modeling should be done systematically, with passages from the students' textbooks used as examples. The teaching of outlining should be followed by many opportunities to practice and apply the skill in reading different types of texts.

SUMMARY

An important part of helping students comprehend is teaching them to read and interpret different text structures. There are two basic types of text, narrative and expository. Narrative text tells a story. Expository text presents facts and information. There are five basic patterns of expository writing that authors use frequently—description; collection; causation or cause-effect; response or problem-solution, questions-answer or remark-reply; and comparison.

Students can be taught to comprehend different text structures through the use of direct instruction. In teaching students to understand narrative text, story maps and guided-reading questions that bring out the elements of the narrative are helpful. Expository structures can be taught through the use of specific lessons that conclude with application in real text. Outlining is also an excellent way to focus the reader's attention on an author's structure.

REFERENCES

Bartlett, B. J. 1978. Top level structure as an organizational strategy for recall of classroom text. Ph.D. dissertation. Arizona State University, Tempe.

Beach, R., and D. Appleman. 1984. Reading strategies for expository and literary text types. In A. C. Purves and O. S. Niles (eds.), *Becoming readers in a complex society*. Eighty-third yearbook of the National Society of Education, pp. 115–143. Chicago: University of Chicago Press.

Beck, I. L. 1984. Developing comprehension: The impact of the directed reading lesson. In R. C. Anderson, J. Osborn, and R. J. Tierney (eds). *Learning to read in American schools: Basal readers and content texts*, pp. 3–20. Hillsdale, NJ: Lawrence Erlbaum Associates.

Dreher, M. J., and H. Singer. 1980. Story grammar instruction unnecessary for intermediate grade students. *Reading Teacher, 34*, 261–272.

Freedle, R. O. 1979. *New directions in discourse processing*. Hillsdale, NJ: Lawrence Erlbaum Associates.

Mathews, S. R. 1982. The impact of prior knowledge on accessibility and availability of information prose. In A. Flammer and W. Kintch (eds.), *Discourse processing*. Amsterdam: North Holland Press.

McGee, L. M., and D. J. Richgels. 1985. Teaching expository text structure to elementary students. *The Reading Teacher, 38*, 739–748.

Meyer, B. J. F. 1975. *The organization of prose and its effects on memory*. Amsterdam: The Hague North-Holland Press.

Meyer, B. J. F., and R. O. Freedle. 1984. Effects of discourse type on recall. *American Educational Research Journal, 21*, 121–143.

Reutzel, D. R. 1985. Story maps improve comprehension. *The Reading Teacher, 38*, 400–404.

Slater, W. H., M. F. Graves, and G. L. Piché. 1985. Effects of structural organizers on ninth-grade students' comprehension and recall of four patterns of expository text. *Reading Research Quarterly, 20*, 189–202.

REFERENCES

Taylor, B. M., and R. W. Beach. 1984. The effects of text structure instruction on middle-grade students' comprehension and production of expository text. *Reading Research Quarterly, 19,* 134–146.

Taylor, B. M., and S. J. Samuels. 1983. Children's use of text structure in the recall of expository material. *American Educational Research Journal, 20,* 517–528.

CHAPTER
S E V E N

CORRELATING COMPREHENSION

AND WRITING

The more I delve into children's writing, the more I want
to study the connections between reading and writing.
—Calkins, 1983, p. 160

In this chapter you will learn

1. what the relationships are between reading and writing,
2. how to integrate reading and writing,
3. how to teach the writing process,
4. how to use student-written materials in the reading program,
5. activities that correlate and integrate reading and writing.

For many years researchers have contended that the four language arts—read-ing, writing, speaking, and listening—were closely related and should be taught in a more correlated manner (Loban, 1963), and recently researchers have em-phasized the importance of correlating reading and writing instruction (Tierney and Leys, 1984). Yet classroom teachers have not been given clear direction on how to correlate these activities. In a discussion with a group of teachers in a re-cent workshop, some teachers related that they correlated reading and writing by simply having students read selections in their basal reader and write answers to the accompanying questions in sentence form. This is certainly not what is meant by correlating reading and writing.

This chapter focuses on developing an understanding of the relationship be-tween reading comprehension and writing and shows how the two processes can be correlated in instruction. Strategies and activities that can be used in the class-room are presented.

RELATIONSHIPS BETWEEN READING AND WRITING

One of the relationships between reading and writing that has been examined by many researchers is that of reading and writing achievement. Most of the studies have shown a moderate relationship between these activities that fluctuates with the age of the students (Tierney and Leys, 1984; Shanahan, 1980). The relationship is not causal; the teaching of writing does not necessarily improve reading nor does the teaching of reading necessarily improve writing. However, some research indicates that selected reading activities influence writing performance and selected writing activities influence reading performance (Tierney and Leys, 1984; Graves and Hansen, 1983; Birnbaum, 1982).

The relationships that exist between reading and writing that are important to instruction can be seen by noting the similarities between the two processes. Reading and writing are both language processes that depend heavily on the students' oral language and background experiences. That reading and writing involve similar processes is obvious from Pearson and Tierney's (1984) description of the reader as a composer. They describe the thoughtful reader as one who plans his or her reading around a given purpose for reading; with this purpose in mind, the reader thinks about the reading and begins to activate his or her background relative to the topic. The writer goes through a very similar process. The writer has some purpose for writing and begins to think about what he or she knows or needs to know about the topic before beginning to write.

Next the reader begins to read and construct or compose meaning in light of his or her purposes and background. The cues in the text help the reader compose these meanings. The writer begins to write and construct meaning; the writer's task is to compose meaning so it can be conveyed to a reader. As the writer writes about the topic, he or she thinks about the topic and develops it; the writer may have a general idea when he or she starts to write, but the idea really develops as the writer thinks more about the topic.

As the reader continues to compose meanings, he or she thinks about what is being read and rereads and changes meaning as necessary. The writer goes through the phase of revision to clarify meanings. He or she thinks about what has been written, rereads it, and rewrites it to make it clearer.

Finally, the reader reaches a point where he or she thinks about what has been read and finalizes the meaning composed as being the best possibility for this given point in time. The writer performs this task in developing his or her final copy. Pearson and Tierney refer to each of these four phases of the reader as planner, composer, editor, and monitor. The similarities between the reader and writer as composers of meaning are summarized in Table 7.1. As readers and writers go through these steps, they do not proceed through them one after another. They go back and forth between them as they perform the overall process (Pearson and Tierney, 1984; Murray, 1985; Graves, 1984).

As proficient readers and writers work, they tend to use the two processes simultaneously. Think about your own experiences in writing. As you write your ideas, you reread them to see if they make sense. Often you turn to books or other

Table 7.1   Readers and Writers as Composers of Meaning

	Reader	Writer
Planner	Have purpose for reading	Have purpose for writing
	Generate background	Generate background
Composer	Read and compose meaning	Write and compose meaning
Editor	Reread, reflect, revise meaning	Revise
Monitor	Finalize meaning	Finalize copy

sources to get more information to include in your writing. The processes of proficient reading and writing not only have many similarities in how they function, but they also tend to be processes that are used together.

Teaching students to write helps their reading comprehension by making them more aware of how authors organize their ideas. As students learn to write and organize their own ideas, they will have a greater appreciation and understanding of how other authors have organized their thoughts.

INTEGRATING READING AND WRITING

Integrating reading and writing means teaching reading and writing in a closely connected manner and helping students see how they are related. Whenever possible, reading and writing activities should be tied together and not taught as separate subjects. The teaching of reading and writing together involves

1. teaching students the writing process,
2. pointing out the relationships that exist between reading and writing,
3. using writing activities as a part of the reading lesson and using reading materials as a stimulus for writing.

The teacher should not assume that the teaching of writing automatically improves comprehension or vice versa. Students must be taught how to write just as they must be taught how to comprehend. However, if the two processes are systematically taught and related to each other, they will reinforce each other.

Students often think that what they learn in reading has no relationship to what they do in writing or in the other language areas. It is the responsibility of the teacher to point out these relationships and help students make the connections. Reading, for example, provides students good models to use in their writing. If the author of a selection makes excellent use of descriptive language and uses many figures of speech, the teacher should follow-up the reading by discussing the author's use of descriptive language and having students locate in the selection examples of such language. In subsequent writing assignments, the students should be encouraged to make use of descriptive language. The same strategy can be carried out with all writing techniques that students encounter in their reading. However, students should not be expected to copy or model any author exactly.

TEACHING WRITING

Teachers have often been afraid to teach writing because they haven't known how to teach it. Many times it has been assumed that children learn to write simply by being told to write. That is not so. An important element in integrating reading and writing is teaching students how to write.

In the 1970s and 1980s, there has been considerable research devoted to writing and learning how to teach it (Calkins, 1983; Graves, 1983). From this research we have learned that writing is a process that must be taught. Writing, just like reading comprehension, is influenced by the individual's background and language abilities. Students who lack sufficient background on a topic and do not have the ability to relate to the topic in their oral language are not likely to be able to write about it.

The process of teaching writing involves five basic steps (Graves, 1983):

1. Organizing the classroom
2. Selecting topics
3. Modeling writing
4. Revising
5. Publishing

Each of these steps must be included in an ongoing program for teaching students how to write.

Organizing the Classroom

Organizing the classroom is the first step in the successful writing program. The classroom must become a laboratory of excitement, enthusiasm, and motivation that makes children want to write and at the same time makes it possible for them to write. By organizing the classroom for writing the teacher is also making the classroom conducive to reading.

Make the Classroom Motivating

The classroom should be alive with good books, art, and displays that give students things to experience and discuss. A table with unusual rock formations or a bulletin board with photographs of tropical birds might be just the things that provide students the interest and background they need to start writing. Things that are brought into the classroom should be discussed with students; the thoughts and ideas expressed during these discussions will help the students build the background needed for good writing. Students should be encouraged to use the topics brought up in the discussions in their writing, but they should not be required to use them. Bulletin boards and classroom exhibits should be changed frequently to keep interests high.

Good books for students to read and have read to them should be available in the classroom. Even though the school might have a central library, a collection of good books should be in the classroom for students to use. Having a featured book of the week or month is an excellent way to motivate students to read a particular book. The teacher should have the book on display and read portions of it to students, taking time to let students react to the story and talk about it. The teacher should encourage the students to read the book on their own. By reading good literature, students expand their backgrounds and develop a foundation for good writing.

Develop a Writing Attitude

Creating a writing attitude is a part of organizing the classroom and making it conducive to writing. This attitude begins with the teacher who is willing to accept the ideas of students in their writing and who shows sincere pleasure and satisfaction in what students have accomplished in writing no matter how small the amount or insignificant the topic. Too often, students are made to feel that their ideas just aren't good enough. Even if a child writes only a single sentence, it is a beginning, and the effort should be supported.

Another way the teacher can enhance a writing attitude is by writing and sharing his or her writing with students. Letters, notes, poems, stories—anything the teacher has written—can be shared with the class. The teacher should let students know his or her thoughts and see how he or she writes them. If students think their teacher values writing, they will value writing, too.

Have Places for Students to Keep Their Writing

It is important for students to have a place to keep their writing as they are working on it because writing is an ongoing process. A writing folder works well. The folders should be kept where students can easily get to them if they have time to work on some writing or have ideas that they want to jot down for future writing. The writing folder should contain only the work that is the current interest of the student and lists and ideas for future topics. Completed writing samples should be kept in a second folder. That folder provides the teacher and student with a record of the progress the student is making in writing.

Identify a Time for Writing

Finally, organizing the classroom for writing involves having an identified time for writing. Some writing researchers feel that students should write every day (Graves, 1983). Whatever the writing time, it must be clearly specified, and students should know that it is appropriate to write at other times as well—for example, when they have completed their other work. The students should not feel that they must finish their writing in one writing period. Writing is not something that can be rushed. Some writers write for long periods of time at once while others write in short spurts.

One way to accommodate the different writing speeds of students is to work writing in with the instructional needs of the rest of the language arts program. For example, all of the language arts can be taught in the same block of time so that rigid time lines do not need to be drawn between each of those activities. In many classrooms, writing is something that gets worked in when there is extra time. The teacher should make up his or her mind that there *will be time for writing* and then work the other things that need to be taught in with it.

Organizing the classroom so that it becomes a place that promotes and encourages students to write is the first step to helping students learn to write, no matter what the level or age of the students. A checklist for organizing the classroom for writing and reading is presented in Example 7.1.

EXAMPLE 7.1 CHECKLIST FOR ORGANIZING THE CLASSROOM FOR WRITING

Questions to Ask	Yes	No
1. Are there exciting displays and bulletin boards in the classroom?		
2. Are there good books and magazines available for students to read or have read to them?		
3. Is there a place for students to keep their writing, such as folders or compartments?		
4. Do you share your own writing with students?		
5. Is there an identified time for students to write daily?		

Selecting Topics

As students learn the process of writing, they should begin to select their own topics. The teacher's role in this process is that of guide and facilitator. Selecting a writing topic can be a painful process for students who have gotten used to writing on assigned topics or using story starters or opening sentences provided by the teacher. However, selecting a topic is an important part of writing, and it should be given considerable time and attention, especially in the beginning stages of teaching writing. As students become accustomed to selecting their own topics, they will do so almost automatically, although, periodically, even the best writers hit snags in selecting their topics and need some guidance from the teacher.

From the start of instruction in selecting topics, students must get the idea that they really can select their own topics. Time should be taken to give students the needed encouragement to think of ideas on their own. The following steps can be used:

Step 1:   Give each student a blank sheet of paper and ask the students to make a list of anything that they might like to write about. While students are making their lists, do the same, and tell students that is what you are doing. After finishing your list, move around the room trying to spot those who are having trouble. Stop and ask these students such questions as:

"What have you read that you would like to write about?"
"What topics are you thinking of?"
"What do you like to do at home?"
"Have you been any place that you really enjoyed?"
"Would you tell me some topics you would like to write about, and let me write them on your paper?"

Such questions may be the encouragement that some students need. Be careful not to sound critical or insulting to the students. The object is to get students to begin to think for themselves and to generate their own ideas.

After about five minutes, stop the group and share with students the list of topics you have made, commenting on the topics you selected. Be certain that your list is not too long or overwhelming. Next, ask for volunteers in the group who are willing to share their lists. (Students should not be required to read their lists aloud if they don't want to do so.) As students read their lists, encourage them to comment on any of the topics they selected. Comment about their topics with such remarks as:

"Those are all exciting topics."
"It sounds like you have good ideas."
"You have so many topics you are going to have to really think about which one you want to write on."

Be certain that your comments are supportive and encouraging for all students; they should not be reserved for students with lengthy lists.

After several students have shared their lists, help students to see that it doesn't matter that some have long lists and others have short lists—all you need is one idea to begin writing. Don't be disappointed or discouraged if very few students want to share their ideas. You will find that in some classrooms all students will be eager to share; in others very few want to do so. Accept the class for what it is and go on from there.

Step 2:   Have students look over their lists to see if they want to add any topics. You can model the process with your own list. You might add a topic similar to one a student selected. By doing so, you will let students see that it is all right for them to get ideas from other students.

Step 3: Following this activity, have students look over their lists to select the topic they would most like to use for their first piece of writing. Suggest that they consider the following points as they make their decisions:

1. Which topic is the most interesting to you?
2. Which topic do you feel that you know the most about?
3. Which topic do you think others might enjoy reading the most?

Have students circle their choices. Follow this by sharing your choice with the group and having volunteers, other than those who volunteered earlier in the lesson, do the same.

By following these steps, the teacher can guide students to the selection of their first topic for writing. It doesn't really matter what the topics are; the choices are the students', and the students want to write about them. The topics and choices of two students from a fourth-grade class are shown in Example 7.2. Note the differences in their lists.

EXAMPLE 7.2 SAMPLE LISTS OF WRITING TOPICS ———————

> Student A
>
> playing in the park
> ~~fishing~~ (circled)
>
> Student B
>
> My dog
> My brother
> Going to the circus
> Building a race car
> (The ball team) (circled)
> Cutting

This procedure for helping students select topics is similar to the procedure suggested by Graves (1983). It works! It can be used at all levels, even the first grade. The teacher may find that some adaptation is required for first graders and students who have limited writing abilities or poor writing attitudes. For them, the teacher may find it helpful to move around the room and record the ideas for students on the students' own papers or to record the ideas in a master list on the board, writing each student's name beside his or her topic.

The procedure suggested here for helping students select topics is a part of the modeling process that should be employed in the teaching of writing. Just as comprehension processes must be modeled, so must the writing process. As the teacher goes through the process of selecting a topic with students, he or she demonstrates to students how this is done. This is the teacher modeling step in direct instruction.

Students should keep their lists of topics in their writing folders and should be encouraged to add to their lists when they think of new ideas. Students should not be made to feel that they will have to write on every topic on their lists. Their ideas change; therefore the lists can be changed.

There are many other ways to have students select topics for writing. These should also be tried from time-to-time throughout the year:

Partners: Many times students get good ideas for writing from one another. Have each student work with a partner to develop lists of possible topics. This is a good strategy to use for the student who appears to have few ideas or for the student who doesn't want to write.

Look for Ideas Away From School: Encourage students to look for writing ideas on the way home from school, at home, or in places that they visit. Have them jot down their ideas on 3×5 cards and bring them back to class.

Camera Ideas: Provide students with instant-developing cameras. Let them use the cameras to take pictures of things they might like to write about. If the cameras can be taken out of the school, have students take pictures away from school as well. If cameras are not available, encourage students to bring to class photographs from home that show things they would like to use as topics for their writing.

TV Topics: Encourage students to look for interesting topics as they watch their favorite TV shows.

Selecting topics for writing is not always easy for students. Some of the problems students encounter (and suggestions for the teacher for overcoming these problems) include:

No Ideas: Some students will say that they have no ideas to use for writing. One way to help these students is to talk with them and get them to tell the things that they do at home or in some other place. As they tell their ideas, the teacher can suggest that each of these can be a topic for writing. Another tactic is to ask the students if they have ever dreamed about going somewhere or doing something special and pointing out that these can also be ideas for writing. The teacher in this situation might even serve as the student's secretary and jot down the ideas.

Too Many Ideas: Some students will have so many ideas that they won't know which one to select for writing. Teachers can help students by discussing the ideas with them. Through discussion, a student may get excited about a particular topic. If discussion doesn't work, the teacher can select one of the topics for the student. One teacher, who had tried other strategies to no avail, finally said to a student, "Close your eyes and point to a topic. Since you like them all, write about the one you point to." That was enough encouragement to get the child started.

Don't Like to Write: This problem is tougher to deal with, and there are really no easy solutions. Some students simply don't like to write and don't want to write for a number of reasons. (Likewise, some teachers don't like to write and don't want to teach writing.) These students need to be encouraged to write and to see some of the fun of writing. The teacher can begin by serving as the student's secretary and recording not only the topics but the first draft of the writing. Another tactic is to have the student dictate his or her list of topics onto a tape recorder and then have the student write the first draft on a word processor. In schools where computers are available, the computer and word processor can be used in this way to encourage writing.

Selecting the topic for writing is an important part of the writing process, and students need to see that they can use their own ideas. Although there are times in classes and subjects when students must write on assigned topics, students must be allowed to choose their topics when they are learning "how" to write. Even in classes such as social studies in which students are required to write reports, teachers are likely to get better products if they let students have some choice of the topic.

As the writing program gets underway, students will always be at varying stages. The teacher must be the guide and facilitator throughout the process. The teacher must help to create the atmosphere that makes students feel they can write, but at the same time the teacher must show students how to write. From time to time, the teacher will find it necessary to talk about topics with an individual student or the group, always keeping in mind that students should have the right to select their own topics for writing. As students develop in their use of the writing process, they will be looking for topics in a great many places. The more comfortable the students and teacher become with writing, the more students are likely to be ready with a new topic for their next writing assignment.

Modeling Writing

Once students have selected their topics they are ready to begin to write. The teacher and students have already modeled the process of selecting topics; now, the teacher must show students how to write. Writing includes three stages: planning, writing, and composing. All three stages should be modeled for students.

Planning

Good writers think about what they are going to write and organize their ideas. Students need to be shown how to do this. The teacher can model the process using his or her topic and the following steps:

Step 1: Tell the class a little about your topic and what you want to write about. Have them ask any questions they want. Next, on the chalkboard, overhead projector, or large sheets of paper, jot down some of the ideas you have about the topic. Group ideas that go together but don't be concerned about getting all of the ideas organized at this point. Tell students that you now have a general plan of what you want to include in your writing and you know how you want to begin. Example 7.3 shows the notes one teacher made while planning to write about her family's camping trip.

EXAMPLE 7.3 TEACHER'S NOTES FOR PLANNING WRITING ──────

where we camp
>
> in the mountains
> at the campgrounds
> in national parks

what we take
>
> sleeping bags
> tents
> stove
> plastic jugs
> lanterns
> matches

what we do
>
> walk trails
> sing around fire
> go on nature hikes
> fish

Step 2: Have students work in pairs, telling each other about their topics. Afterwards, have each student jot down some ideas or words about his or her topic on a sheet of paper. Have some volunteers share their ideas with the class and talk about what they want to include in their writing. Help students understand that this is a beginning plan for their writing and that it might change as they do their writing.

As students mature in their writing abilities, outlining can be introduced and how to use outlining can be included in modeling. Students will find outlining a useful planning tool for such activities as report writing. Outlining as it is taught in reading can be directly related to writing.

The more students mature in their writing, the less necessary it will be to go through the planning phase as a group. However, students should be provided enough teacher modeling to see how planning is done and how it can help them in their own writing. The more students write, the more automatically they will carry out the process of writing.

Writing

The next phase in the writing process is the actual writing. Students should be told to write their first draft on lined paper using every other line. This practice helps them develop a positive attitude toward revision; it lets them know that changes can and will be made and that it is all right to make mistakes and/or changes in one's writing.

The teacher must model this activity as well. It is important that the students see the teacher write. Although the teacher and students can write independently and share their results later, this type of modeling works best with older, more mature writers. It is not satisfactory for younger, beginning writers. It does not really let students see all of the process of writing being modeled. For most students, the following procedure will be most effective:

Step 1: Using the chalkboard, overhead projector, or large sheets of paper, begin to develop the topic you selected, pointing out what you are doing along the way. Note the mechanics of starting a sentence and paragraph and show students how to organize ideas into sentences and paragraphs. Ask students to suggest words or make changes in your writing. Don't be afraid to tell students that you don't know what to say next, and you need some help. Example 7.4 shows a sample of the teacher's draft for modeling the family camping trip story.

Step 2: After the initial teacher modeling, have students start their own writing. Encourage them to use the notes they made as a part of their planning. While students are writing, move about the room offering guidance, assistance, and encouragement to those who need it. If there are students who are not writing, offer to be the student's secretary to encourage the beginning few sentences of their draft.

If the writing is going smoothly, continue to move about the room offering assistance and support. A few minutes of talking about the topic or a few questions

EXAMPLE 7.4 TEACHER'S DRAFT FOR MODELING WRITING

> Our family likes to go camping. We usually go to a
> campground
> nearby ~~camp~~, but sometimes we go to the mountains or a national park.
>
> Getting ready to go camping is a big job. We have to take our tents, sleeping bags, and things needed for cooking. Plastic jugs are always needed to store water.

from the teacher are often enough to keep students writing. Give students as much time to write as the schedule will allow and as much time as they can use productively. If you see that the writing time is producing little or nothing, it is probably best to resume modeling or to stop the writing at this time.

Step 3: If you find it necessary to resume modeling, return to your story and continue to write, explaining as you go. Continue to encourage students to offer assistance. As you model your writing, you can note different elements of good writing, but do not overemphasize the teaching of isolated mechanics. The needs of the students will determine what you should stress during the modeling; areas stressed might include writing complete sentences, using more descriptive language, paragraphing, or using conversation in writing. If many students are weak in a particular writing convention, you may want to stress only that convention in the modeling. Keep in mind that the modeling of writing must include modeling of how the content is created and organized. Do not dwell on writing mechanics at the expense of the content and flow of ideas.

In modeling, the teacher should focus on one or two elements of writing mechanics at a time. If students are having particular difficulties in certain areas, these should be worked into the modeling. The teacher can consult the English textbook or curriculum guide for help in deciding which other areas of mechanics should be included in modeling. The modeling of writing not only teaches students how to write, but it also provides an opportunity to teach the mechanics of grammar and usage in a natural setting.

Composing

Composing is the phase of writing in which students develop their topic. Usually, they will have been given enough direction up to this point that they can proceed with their own writing without additional instruction. During this part of the writing program, students should be given uninterrupted writing time to develop their topic. Modeling occurs as the teacher moves about the room offering assistance as needed.

In this phase of writing, the object is for students to express their ideas freely and creatively; students should not be hampered by worrying about spelling. The best way to deal with the spelling issue is to encourage students to spell words the way they think they sound (invented spellings). This will allow students to be free to write, realizing that they can take care of any spelling problems during their revision. For those students who are so concerned about having words spelled correctly or are unable to use invented spelling, the teacher can provide the correct spellings by writing the words in question on a sheet of paper or the chalkboard. Other techniques such as having one student serve as a spelling helper or having a list of troublesome words on the board or a chart can also be used, but nothing works as well as having students try to spell words the way they think they sound and then making corrections during revision.

The amount of time allowed for the composing phase of modeling depends on the students, their writing abilities, and the length of time allocated to writing in the classroom. Usually the composing phase will extend over several days or writing periods. Students can place their writing in their writing folders and return to it at the next writing period or when they have some extra time during the day. The writing, especially in the beginning stages, should be done at school.

Throughout the composing phase, the teacher should continue to be available to help students with their writing. If a student gets stuck, he or she should be encouraged to ask the teacher for suggestions. For example, if a student can't think of a good word to describe his old dog, the teacher might give several suggestions and let the student select the one he or she wants to use. Asking questions and offering suggestions as the students are writing is an extension of modeling.

Revising

Revision or editing is the step in the writing process in which the students begin to look at their work to examine two broad areas:

1. Content—ideas, choice of words, and so forth
2. Writing mechanics—such as spelling and punctuation

Revision involves modeling by the teacher, conferences between student and teacher, and individual student work on the writing. During the revision stage, students should develop an appreciation for improving both the content and the mechanics of their writing. Revision involves two steps—checking content and proofreading—which will be described in the following sections. Revision is not a natural step for students to employ (Graves, 1984). Therefore, teachers must help students learn to revise by systematically working through this stage with them.

Checking Content

The teacher can extend the modeling process into revision by using his or her writing as an example of what should happen during this phase of the writing process. The teacher and students should first discuss what to look for when revising the content of writing. During discussion, the following points should be raised:

1. Have I expressed my ideas clearly?
2. Are there other ideas that I should add to my writing?
3. Are there other words that I could use to make my writing more exciting and interesting?
4. Are there better ways that I can express my ideas?

The items considered in content revision will vary according to the level of the students and their sophistication in writing.

After the teacher and students have developed their guidelines for content revision, the teacher should show the students how to go about revising their writing. The teacher should check each of the points listed in his or her writing and discuss problem areas with students. Changes should be made with the students' help. Better ways of expressing the ideas should be tried. Throughout the revision step, the teacher should stress to students how important it is to express oneself clearly and correctly because the writing is going to be read by someone else. Example 7.5 shows a copy of the teacher's story about the family camping trip after the teacher and students revised the content.

EXAMPLE 7.5   TEACHER'S STORY USED FOR MODELING CONTENT REVISION ——————————

Our family likes to go camping.
They all have fun.
∧ We usually go to a nearby campground, but sometimes we go to the mountains or a
    The campground is my favorite
national park. ∧   spot.

    Getting ready to go camping
is a big job. We have to take
our tents, sleeping bags and
~~equipment~~
~~things~~ needed for cooking.
Plastic jugs are always
needed to store water.

Students are now ready to begin to work on their own revisions. At this point the teacher should begin to have revision conferences with students to talk about their writing and help students look for places where content changes might be made. The teacher takes on the role of an editor who asks questions and points out places where students need to make changes. Many students will already know where some of the problem areas are. The teacher should not become the "fixer" of the student's writing; rather, the teacher should mark the places that need work, discuss them with the student, and have the student try to make the necessary corrections or changes. The teacher should not cover the student's paper with red ink. It is more effective to use a pen or pencil the same color as the student's; in this way there is less feeling of being graded, and the student begins to feel that he or she is working together with the teacher.

Proofreading

The second aspect of revision is proofreading, which should take place after students have made all the content changes they feel are necessary. In proofreading, students get their writing in order for final copy, checking spelling, writing mechanics, and sentence structure. The teacher and students should work together to develop a list of things to look for in proofreading, and the list should be posted in the room so that students can refer to it as they work on their revisions. In addition to spelling, the list should reflect the writing mechanics that were modeled throughout the writing. For example, it can include such points as

1. Sentences and questions begin with capital letters.
2. Sentences end with a period (.) or an exclamation point (!).
3. Questions end with a question mark (?).
4. Each new paragraph is indented.

The items will vary according to the level and sophistication of the students. The teacher can check proofreading in individual conferences or small-group conferences.

Holding Revision Conferences

Finding time for conferences with students during revision is usually a big concern for teachers. However, after the writing program gets underway the problem usually takes care of itself because all students are not finished with their writing and ready for revision at the same time.

The teacher should set aside blocks of time during the writing program or other periods of the day for writing conferences. The conferences should take place at two different times: before the student begins his or her revisions and after the student has worked with a partner, checking each other's revisions. The conferences need not be lengthy. Many times a few minutes of discussion will get many students on their way to making the (additional) revisions needed.

Before students come to the first revision conference, they should prepare by reading their writing and noting places that they think need attention. Simple guidelines like the following can be taught to students to help them look at their writing and prepare for the conference with the teacher:

1. Draw one line under places where you think the sentence could be better.
2. Circle places where you think another word might be used.

3. Draw two lines under words that you think are misspelled.
4. Draw a box around places where you think there is a need to correct the grammar.

After the conference, students should work on their revisions. When they have finished, they should be encouraged to work with a revision partner. The revision partner looks at the writing, asks questions, and notes places where corrections or clarifications still need to be made. In one school, the revision partner was designated the editor and wore a hat that said "Editor." The editor and student read through the writing and checked the points noted on the list developed by the class. Every student had a chance to be an editor; some were better than others. Through this activity, the students learned to think about their writing, and by the end of the year revision took place almost automatically.

The students should then go to the teacher for another revision conference. During this conference, the teacher and students look again at the student's writing as a final check for clarity of ideas and for writing mechanics. The teacher might read places from the writing aloud and ask the student to listen to see if the idea is clear or if there is anything wrong with the writing.

Conferences are modeling sessions, too. The teacher is not only trying to get the student to think about and question his or her writing but is also trying to show students different ways to write and express themselves. The teacher must be careful to not try to do too many things at once. Many times it is better to have several conferences to get the writing in shape than to overwhelm students with too many things in a single conference. In the school mentioned earlier with the student editors, the teachers usually looked at content and correctness of writing in different conferences. Students were encouraged to see their partner editors between conferences to get more input.

The teacher must remember that the students are just learning to write; therefore, they are expected to have errors in their writings. The purpose of the revision phase is to help them begin to look at their writing and see ways to improve it. The number of times a piece of writing should be revised depends on what is to be done with the writing and the level of sophistication of the students. If the teacher has taken the student as far as is possible in a single revision, then the revising should stop.

The teacher can schedule either individual conferences or, to save time, group conferences. In the latter, the teacher and three or four students should gather around a table; while the teacher is looking at the work of one student, the others can be looking at each others' work, making suggestions for revisions.

Publishing

The final stage of the writing process is publishing, which has two parts:

1. Making a final copy of the writing.
2. Putting the writing in a published form to be shared with others.

All students should make a final copy of their writing. They should do so after completing their revisions. However, not all writing should be put in published form. The decision to actually publish the student's writing should be made by the teacher and student together. Both the quality of the writing and how the student feels about it should be taken into account. In a conference, the teacher should ask the student such questions as

How do you think others will feel about this piece of writing?
Do you think it is a good idea to publish this one?

The teacher's questions should help guide the student in making the decision about publication. Sometimes it is appropriate for the teacher to say, "This is not one of your best pieces of writing. Maybe you should just make your final copy for me and your file and start work on something new." If a student feels strongly about the piece being published, it is probably best to proceed. However, the teacher must always weigh the consequences of having a student publish a piece that is really not ready.

Publishing is important for all students, not just a special few. This phase of the writing creates a sense of reason for writing and gives students pride and enjoyment in their own work. The more students publish their writing, the more they will grow in the writing process. One precaution: A few students will not want to create final copies or publish. The teacher must direct these students and not let this happen.

When the decision is to make final copy only, the copy should be put in the student's writing folder so it can be used to determine his or her growth in writing. Even papers that are not published should be saved for this purpose.

Producing Final Copy

After students have completed their revision and hold their initial publishing conference with the teacher, they are ready to make a final copy of their writing. In making their final copy, students should be encouraged to be as neat and accurate as possible. The appropriate writing tools for the age and level of the students should be used.

The teacher and students should work together to develop a list of guidelines for students to follow in making final copies. The list should be kept in a place where students can refer to it. Points such as those given below can be included on the list, but each list must reflect the needs, abilities, and level of the students:

Final Copy Guidelines
Be neat.
Indent each new paragraph.
Keep margins at the top, bottom, and sides of the paper straight.
Check punctuation.
Check spelling.
Reread your final copy to be sure it is correct.

The manner in which the final copy is prepared will depend on whether it is to be published. If the copy is not going to be published, it should be placed in the student's permanent writing folder for review by the teacher.

Ideas for Publishing

Publishing is a very important part of the writing process (Graves, 1983). Students need this aspect of the writing to help them develop a sense of importance for their writing and a sense of understanding as to why one must learn to write.

The most common way for students to publish their writing is in book form. Individual students can produce their own book or several students can work together on one. The excitement and pleasure on the face of a student after producing his or her first book is almost indescribable. Publishing brings closure to the student's writing.

Books can be produced in many forms, the simplest being colored paper covers stapled over a few pages of tablet paper to look like hard-cover books. It is best for students to first make more simple types of books; they can move on to more complex procedures as they become more accustomed to producing books. Following are examples of types of books students can make:

Construction Paper Books: Use two pieces of construction paper for the book cover and the student's writing paper for the pages. Staple the cover and pages together. The students can letter and decorate the cover in any manner desired.

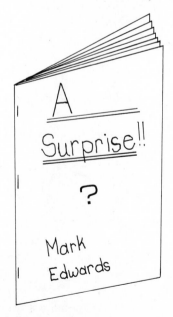

Folder Books: Manila folders can be used to create bookcovers. Cut the tab from the folder and place the student's writing inside. Staple together. Have students decorate the cover to reflect the contents of the writing.

Shape Books: Before students write their final copy, cut the pages in a shape that relates to the topic. Cut construction paper covers in the same shape, but a bit larger than the pages inside. Staple the cover and pages together or tie them with yarn. Students really like these books because the shape gives clues to the contents. When several students have written on the same topic, their papers may be combined into a class book.

Sewn Bookcovers: These book covers are more sturdy and have a more professional look. These types of books should be undertaken after students have tried some of the others suggested above. The procedure for constructing a sewn bookcover is shown in Example 7.6.

EXAMPLE 7.6   PROCEDURE FOR CONSTRUCTION OF SEWN BOOK COVERS ━━━━━━━━━━━━

Materials Needed

Cardboard or heavy tagboard, approximately 9½" × 6½"
Ditto or mimeograph paper, white, 8½" × 11"
White glue or rubber cement
Cloth tape
Colored construction paper, old wallpaper, fabric scraps, or other materials to
  use in covering the book
Needles and button thread, yarn, or dental floss
Scissors, ruler, and a device to punch holes

Steps

1. Cut two pieces of cardboard or tagboard to 9½" × 6½" or whatever size is
   approximately one inch larger than the final book pages. (Note: pages are
   going to be folded in half so if 8½" × 11" paper is to be used, the final book
   pages will be 8½" × 5½". All measurements in this example will be for that
   size book; they will have to be adjusted for other sizes.)

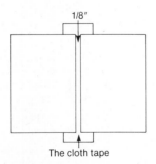

1/8"

The cloth tape

2. Cut a piece of cloth tape approximately 11½" × 3". Attach the tape to the two
   pieces of cardboard, leaving 1/8" between them. Fold the ends of the tape up
   over the top and bottom of the cardboard.

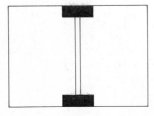

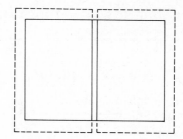

3. Cut two pieces of construction paper, or whatever material you are using for the cover, to approximately 7″ × 11″ (about two inches larger than cardboard). Place the cardboard pieces face down so that the nonsticky side of the tape is up. Glue the outside covering material to the cardboard. Be sure the material is even with inside edge of cardboard.

4. Turn the cover over so that the cardboard is face-up. Fold in the corners of the covering in material and glue them down. Then fold in the sides and bottoms and glue.

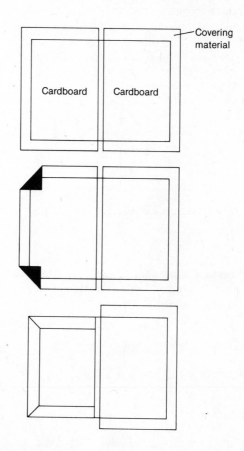

5. Fold a sheet of 8½" × 11" ditto or mimeograph paper in half so that it becomes 8½" × 5½". Do the same for three other sheets, folding them one sheet at a time.
6. Fold an 8½" × 11" piece of construction paper in half to be 8½" × 5½".
7. Put all of the folded sheets of writing paper together, inside the sheet of folded construction paper.
8. Open the pages and colored construction paper so that they are laying flat. Make approximately five marks in the center of the pages and punch holes.

9. Thread a needle and sew from the back of the construction paper through the center hole leaving two inches hanging to tie. Sew through all the other holes so that you end up back on the outside of the center hole with two more inches to tie.

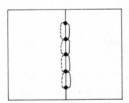

10. Tie the thread on the construction paper side of the pages.
11. Open your cover and lay the pages inside. Glue the construction paper to the inside cover. The book is complete.

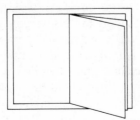

12. Letter the cover.

USING STUDENT WRITTEN MATERIALS FOR READING

One way to correlate reading and writing is to have students use the materials they have written for reading. As students begin to construct books, they can read each others books; they enjoy seeing what their peers have written.

Student-written books should be displayed in both the classroom and school libraries and should be used as a part of the reading material for the reading program. In many schools where this is done, it is reported that student-written books are among the books most frequently selected and checked out.

Developing a collection of student-written books is a simple procedure.

The teacher should begin the school year by telling students that there will be a special section in the school library for books or magazines they have written. (This gives purpose to the writing program and a means for correlating reading and writing.) Students should also be told that there will be a classroom library of their books and that throughout the year selected books will be placed in the school library.

The teacher should have students begin to write and work on their books.

The teacher and students should develop criteria for selecting books to be placed in the school library. These criteria should cover such points as

1. best written,
2. favorite topic or story,
3. topic others would most likely enjoy,
4. book student would like others to read.

The student-written book collection for the library should become a school project with all classes participating. At the conclusion of each school year, students should be asked to donate a certain number of their books to the library for its permanent collection. When this is done, photocopies or handwritten copies should be made so that students can keep a copy of the books they have given to the school.

As student-written books are added to the school library, special announcements should be made for all in the school to see. This can be done through the use of a school newspaper or a bulletin-board display similar to that in Example 7.7.

A special time should be designated in the reading program for students to read the books that have been written by their peers. For example, teachers can designate an hour every other week for this purpose and can increase the time to an hour or longer each week as more student-written books are available. Students should use the time to read the student-written books and talk about them with their classmates. Discussions can be handled in small groups or as class discussions; they should focus on telling about the books, not evaluating them.

Having a time in the reading program for students to read books written by their peers gives a special importance to both reading and writing. It helps to show students that reading and writing are related and also provides the motivation and incentive for reading and writing.

EXAMPLE 7.7   BULLETIN BOARD FOR PUBLICIZING STUDENT BOOKS IN THE SCHOOL LIBRARY ———————————

USING PREDICTABLE BOOKS TO CORRELATE READING AND WRITING

Predictable books are books written with a repeated pattern; they are often rhythmic. The text of these books usually matches the illustrations closely. One very popular predictable book is *Brown Bear, Brown Bear* by Bill Martin, Jr. This and other predictable books are listed in a bibliography at the end of this chapter.

   Predictable books can be the basis of activities correlating reading and writing. Teachers often read predictable books to the class (or students can read them on their own) and then have students use the text as the basis for their own writing. For example, consider the following portion of text from *Brown Bear, Brown Bear:*

Brown Bear, Brown Bear
What do you see?
I see a red bird looking at me.
Red Bird, Red Bird
What do you see?

Part of this pattern can be left out and students can create their own stories.

Brown Bear, Brown Bear
What do you see?

I see a _____ _____
           (color)   (animal)
looking at me.

_____ _____ , _____ _____
   (color)   (animal)   (color)   (animal)
What do you see?

I see a _____ _____
          (color)   (animal)
looking at me.

The stories can be published and read by other members of the class.

In another activity, students can use the patterns from predictable books to write new outcomes for stories. They can rewrite the pattern and create their own ending.

Using predictable books is a good way to get reluctant readers or writers moving. The rhythmic patterns and simple story lines are enjoyed by students and are often enough to motivate them to read and write on their own.

ACTIVITIES THAT REINFORCE READING AND WRITING

Current research indicates that correlating selected reading and writing activities has an impact on student performance in both areas (Tierney and Leys, 1984). The research, however, does not provide a definite listing of all possible types of activities that can be used in this way. Some of the activities for correlating reading and writing that are supported by current research are described in the following sections. These activities can be incorporated into the guided silent reading and extension sections of the directed reading lesson (see Chapter 2).

Story Summaries

One way to correlate reading and writing is to have students write a summary of a story or part of a story they have just read. In the primary grades, students can write single sentence summaries. As they progress in their reading abilities, they can expand their summaries to a paragraph or more.

Students must be taught how to compose a summary. Research by Brown and Day (1983) offers guidelines for teaching the process of summarizing paragraphs to students. The following steps are based on their findings:

1. Determine the topic of the paragraph; identify unnecessary information or trivia. Delete this information; it should not be included in the summary.
2. Look for information that is repeated. Such information should only be included in the summary once.

3. Note places where ideas or terms can be grouped together. For example, if the paragraph being summarized discusses travel by plane, ship, train, and car, all of these can be referred to as transportation.
4. Identify a topic sentence for the paragraph.
5. If no topic sentence exists, try to form a topic sentence of your own.

The process of writing a summary should be modeled for students using procedures similar to those suggested for teaching the writing process.

Writing summaries after reading can be handled in many creative ways. For example, teachers can give students such writing assignments as:

Pretend to be newspaper reporters or TV newscasters who must present a summary of what they have read. The students should first write the summary and then distribute it to other students in newspaper form or give the summary as a part of a TV news report.

Maintain a log, journal, or diary that reports a summary of your readings. Write the log entries after reading your favorite selections. Students can also be instructed to write log entries for particular selections assigned by the teacher.

Story Frames

Story frames are another way to correlate comprehension and writing (Fowler, 1982). A story frame is a basic outline for a story that is designed to help the reader organize his or her ideas about what has been read. The story frame consists of a series of spaces hooked together by transition words; each story frame usually follows a single line of thought or aspect of a selection. Example 7.8 presents a story frame that focuses on a particular character from a selection.

EXAMPLE 7.8 SAMPLE STORY FRAME FOCUSING ON A CHARACTER

This story is about _____ .

_____ is an important character.

_____ tried to _____

_____

The story ends when _____

_____ .

_____

After students read a selection, the teacher can use the story frame as an oral discussion starter. Students should be encouraged to fill in the slots in the frame basing their responses on their reading; however, they should also be encouraged to express the ideas creatively in their own words. When students have become familiar with the concept of using story frames, the teacher can use story frames in written activities following reading.

Story frames can be written for specific selections. However, some of the basic patterns can be used repeatedly. Example 7.9 presents three additional story frames, focusing on setting, plot, and character comparison.

A variation to the story frame activity just described is having students write their own frames. These can be given to other students who have read the same

EXAMPLE 7.9 SAMPLE STORY FRAMES ――――――――――

Setting Frame

This story takes place _____

_____ . I can tell this because the author uses such words as _____

_____ to tell where this story happens.

Plot Frame

This story begins when _____ .

Next _____ .

Then _____

_____ . The story ends when _____

_____

_____ .

Character Comparison Frame

_____ and _____ are two characters

in our story. _____ is _____

while _____ is _____ .

For instance, _____ tries to _____

and _____ learns a lesson when _____

_____ .

_____

selection. After the frames are filled in, the students can get together and discuss their completed products. This variation of the activity puts more of the responsibility for learning on the students.

Creative Writing Activities

A third way to correlate reading and writing is through creative writing activities. After students have completed the reading of a selection, the teacher can have them use the topic, structure, or some other aspect of their reading as a basis for their own writing. Such activities could include:

1. Writing a paragraph on a topic of the students' own choice in which they try to use descriptive language as the author of the selection did. This type of activity would be used as a follow-up to reading a selection in which an author did an outstanding job of using descriptive language. After writing their paragraphs, students should compare their writing to that of the author and discuss the comparisons.
2. Writing an expository paragraph or article similar to the one just read. Students should begin by noting how the author presented his or her information. They should be encouraged to use similar techniques in their own writing but should not be limited to using only those techniques.
3. Writing a story or article that utilizes a particular type of passage that an author has used. The teacher should first discuss the type of passage (for example, cause-effect or sequence) and have students identify examples of passages using these techniques in the selection. Students should then be instructed to write a paragraph or story on their own topic, making use of similar paragraphs.

Many good activities for correlating reading and writing are suggested in more recent basal readers. Example 7.10 shows a page from the Riverside Reading Program on which correlating reading and writing activities are described.

SUMMARY

This chapter has focused on the importance of correlating reading and writing. Although the relationships between reading and writing are not completely understood, it is becoming increasingly evident that the relationships that do exist between the two processes should be accounted for in instruction. Correlating reading and writing involves

1. teaching students the writing process,
2. helping students see the relationships between reading and writing,
3. using writing activities as a follow-up to reading.

Instruction in reading and writing should be correlated as much as possible.

EXAMPLE 7.10 WRITING ACTIVITIES SUGGESTED IN A BASAL READING SERIES

Extending Language Skills

Writing: Stories

As you found out in reading "The Whopper Club," sometimes the truth sounds like a whopper. Let's see if we are any better at judging the truth than Joy, Muriel, Beverly, and April were. I want you to write a story about something you did. It can be either the truth or a whopper. After you've finished, the class can decide whether you belong in The Whopper Club. If necessary, help individual children write their stories. Then have each child read his or her story and let the class vote on whether it's true. Ask volunteers to explain their reasons for believing or not believing a story.

For more practice with writing stories, use Practice Master 54.

Speaking: Interviews

In the story "The Whopper Club," why did TV and newspaper reporters interview Beverly? (Because she captured an escaped baby elephant in her garage.) Pretend you are a reporter sent to interview Beverly about this experience. What are some of the questions you will ask? Encourage discussion and write children's responses on the chalkboard. If you were Beverly, how would you answer these questions? Encourage discussion.

What are some things you might do that would make an interesting news story? Encourage discussion of probable and improbable events and list some responses on the chalkboard. Then have children work in pairs. Pick a topic or make up one of your own. Plan an interview about this event. When pairs have had time to prepare, have them act out the interviews for the whole class or for small groups. Encourage the listeners to comment on both questions and responses.

Enrichment

For Groups

For work with vocabulary, use the Home-Study materials from the Teacher's Resource Book.

■ Read the Aesop fable "The Shepherd Boy and the Wolf" to the class (a good version appears in *Childcraft, The How and Why Library, Vol. 2*) and ask children to compare the situation of the boy in the fable with that of Beverly in the story "The Whopper Club." Ask how the stories are the same and how they are different. Extend discussion to the difference between telling whoppers and lying —that is, between telling tall tales for fun and telling lies that can hurt people. Ask children which story they like better and why.

■ Have children sit in a circle to compose a group whopper. Begin the story with a sentence such as "I'll never forget the day of the big snowstorm." Each child in turn is to add a sentence to the tale to make up a real whopper.

■ Show the filmstrip set *Pinocchio* (Walt Disney Educational Media, 12 min. each) or some similar audiovisual material that has exaggeration as its theme.

For Individuals

■ Have a child look through newspapers or magazines to find a story that is so fantastic it is hard to believe. After a story has been found, ask the child to write it as a whopper. Have the child read the whopper to the class, ask for comments, and then read and display the original article.

■ Tell a child *Pretend one of the whoppers told in "The Whopper Club" really happened. I want you to write a television news story about it, making it sound as real as you can.* Ask the child to "broadcast" the TV news story to the class.

266

Source: Leo Fay et al.: *Blue Ribbon, Teacher's Edition*, p. 266. The Riverside Reading Program, Copyright 1986 by The Riverside Publishing Company, Chicago, IL.

BIBLIOGRAPHY OF PREDICTABLE BOOKS

Adams, Pam. *This Old Man*. New York: Grossett and Dunlap, 1974.

Alain. *One, Two, Three Going to Sea*. New York: Scholastic, 1964.

Aliki. *Go Tell Aunt Rhody*. New York: Macmillan, 1974.

Asch, Frank. *Monkey Face*. New York: Parents' Magazine Press, 1977.

Balian, Lorna. *The Animal*. Nashville: Abingdon Press, 1972.

Balian, Lorna. *Where in the World Is Henry?* Scarsdale, NY: Bradbury Press, 1972.

Barohas, Sarah E. *I Was Walking Down the Road*. New York: Scholastic, 1975.

Becker, John. *Seven Little Rabbits*. New York: Scholastic, 1973.

Beckman, Kaj. *Lisa Cannot Sleep*. New York: Franklin Watts, 1969.

Bellah, Melanie. *A First Book of Sounds*. Racine, WI: Golden Press, 1963.

Brandenberg, Franz. *I Once Knew a Man*. New York: Macmillan, 1970.

Brown, Marcia. *The Three Billy Goat Gruffs*. New York: Harcourt Brace Jovanovich, 1957.

Brown, Margaret Wise. *Goodnight Moon*. New York: Harper and Row, 1947.

Brown, Margaret Wise. *Home for A Bunny*. Racine, WI: Golden Press, 1956.

Brown, Margaret Wise. *The Important Book*. New York: Harper and Row, 1949.

Carle, Eric. *The Grouchy Ladybug*. New York: Thomas Crowell, 1977.

Carle, Eric. *The Mixed Up Chameleon*. New York: Thomas Crowell, 1975.

Carle, Eric. *The Very Hungry Caterpillar*. New York: Philomel Books, 1983.

Charlip, Remy. *Fortunately*. New York: Parents' Magazine Press, 1969.

Charlip, Remy. *What Good Luck! What Bad Luck!* New York: Scholastic, 1969.

Cook, Bernadine. *The Little Fish That Got Away*. Reading, MA: Addison-Wesley, 1976.

Cory's Counting Game. Los Angeles: Intervisual Communications, 1979.

de Regniers, Beatrice Schenk. *Willy O'Dwyer Jumped in the Fire*. New York: Atheneum, 1968.

Domanska, Jania. *If All the Seas Were One Sea*. New York: Macmillan, 1971.

Duff, Maggie. *Rum Pum Pum*. New York: Macmillan, 1978.

Emberley, Barbara. *Simon's Song*. Englewood Cliffs, NJ: Prentice-Hall, 1969.

Emberley, Ed. *Klippity Klop*. Boston: Little, Brown, 1974.

Ets, Marie Hall. *Elephant in a Well*. New York: Viking Press, 1972.

Ets, Marie Hall. *Play With Me*. New York: Viking Press, 1955.

Flack, Marjorie. *Ask Mr. Bear*. New York: Macmillan, 1932.

Galdone, Paul. *The Little Red Hen*. New York: Scholastic, 1973.

Galdone, Paul. *The Teeny-Tiny Woman*. Boston: Houghton Mifflin, 1984.

Galdone, Paul. *The Three Billy Goats Gruff*. New York: Seabury Press, 1973.

Ginsburg, Mirra. *The Chick and the Duckling*. New York: Macmillan, 1972.

Guilfoile, Elizabeth. *Nobody Listens to Andrew*. New York: Scholastic, 1961.

Hawkins, Colin, and Jacqui Hawkins. *Pat the Cat*. New York: Putnam's Sons, 1983.

Hill, Eric. *Where's Spot?* New York: Putnam's Sons, 1980.

Hoffman, Hilde. *The Green Grass Grows All Around.* New York: Macmillan, 1968.

Hutchins, Pat. *Good-night Owl.* New York: Macmillan, 1972.

Hutchins, Pat. *One Hunter.* New York: Greenwillow Books, 1982.

Hutchins, Pat. *Rosie's Walk.* New York: Macmillan, 1968.

Hutchins, Pat. *Titch.* New York: Collier Books, 1971.

Keats, Ezra Jack. *Over in the Meadow.* New York: Scholastic, 1971.

Kent, Jack. *The Fat Cat.* New York: Scholastic, 1971.

Kraus, Robert. *Whose Mouse Are You?* New York: Collier Books, 1970.

Langstaff, John. *Oh, A-Hunting We Will Go.* New York: Atheneum, 1974.

Laurence, Ester. *We're Off to Catch a Dragon.* Nashville: Abingdon Press, 1974.

Lobel, Anita. *King Rooster, Queen Hen.* New York: Greenwillow Books, 1975.

Lobel, Arnold. *A Treeful of Pigs.* New York: Greenwillow Books, 1979.

Mack, Stan. *10 Bears in My Bed.* New York: Pantheon, 1974.

Martin, Bill. *Brown Bear, Brown Bear.* New York: Holt, Rinehart and Winston, 1983.

Matin, Bill. *Fire! Fire! Said Mrs. McGuire.* New York: Holt, Rinehart and Winston, 1970.

Mayer, Mercer. *If I Had. . . .* New York: Dial Press, 1968.

McGovern, Ann. *Too Much Noise.* New York: Scholastic, 1967.

Memling, Carl. *Ten Little Animals.* Racine, WI: Golden Press, 1961.

Moffett, Martha. *A Flower Pot Is Not a Hat.* New York: E. P. Dutton, 1972.

Peppe, Rodney. *The House That Jack Built.* New York: Delacorte, 1970.

Polushkin, Maria. *Mother, Mother, I Want Another.* New York: Crown, 1978.

Quackenbush, Robert. *She'll Be Comin' Round The Mountain.* Philadelphia: J. B. Lippincott, 1973.

Rokoff, Sandra. *Here Is a Cat.* Singapore: Hallmark Children's Editions.

Seuss, Dr. *Dr. Seuss's A B C.* New York: Random House, 1963.

Seuss, Dr.. *There's a Wocket in My Pocket!* New York: Random House, 1974.

Stover, JoAnn. *If Everybody Did.* New York: David McKay, 1960.

Tolstoy, Alexei. *The Great Big Enormous Turnip.* New York: Franklin Watts, 1968.

Welber, Robert. *Goodbye, Hello.* New York: Pantheon, 1974.

Who's Your Furry Friend? Los Angeles: Intervisual Communications, 1981.

Wolkstein, Diane. *The Visit.* New York: Alfred A. Knopf, 1977.

Wondriska, William. *All the Animals Were Angry.* New York: Holt, Rinehart and Winston, 1970.

Zemach, Harve. *The Judge.* New York: Farrar, Straus and Giroux, 1969.

Zemach, Margot. *Hush, Little Baby.* New York: E. P. Dutton, 1976.

Zolotow, Charlotte. *Do You Know What I'll Do?* New York: Harper and Row, 1958.

REFERENCES

Birnbaum, J. C. 1982. The reading and composing behavior of selected fourth- and seventh-grade students. *Research in the Teaching of English, 16,* 241–260.

Brown, A. L., and J. D. Day. 1983. Macrorules for summarizing texts: The development of expertise. *Journal of Verbal Learning and Verbal Behavior, 22,* 1–14.

Calkins, L. M. 1983. *Lessons from a child on the teaching and learning of writing.* Exeter, NH: Heinemann Educational Books.

Fowler, G. L. 1982. Developing comprehension skills in primary grades through the use of story frames. *The Reading Teacher, 36*(2), 176–179.

Graves, D. H. 1983. *Writing: Teachers and children at work.* Exeter, NH: Heinemann Educational Books.

Graves, D. H. 1984. *A researcher learns to write.* Exeter, NH: Heinemann Educational Books.

Graves, D., and J. Hansen. 1983. The author's chair. *Language Arts, 60,* 176–182.

Loban, W. D. 1963. *The language of elementary school children.* Champaign, IL: National Council of Teachers of English.

Murray, D. M. 1985. *A writer teaches writing,* 2nd ed. Boston: Houghton Mifflin Company.

Pearson, P. D., and R. J. Tierney. 1984. On becoming a thoughtful reader: Learning to read like a writer. In A. C. Purves and O. S. Niles (eds.), *Becoming readers in a complex society.* Eighty-third yearbook of the National Society for the Study of Education, pp. 144–173. Chicago: University of Chicago Press.

Shanahan, T. 1980. A canonical correlational analysis of learning to read and learning to write: An exploratory analysis. Ph.D. dissertation, University of Delaware.

Tierney, R. J., and M. Leys. 1984. *What is the value connecting reading and writing?* Reading Education Report No. 55. Urbana, IL: University of Illinois, Center for the Study of Reading.

CHAPTER

E I G H T

CONTENT TEACHING AND

READING COMPREHENSION

*Subject matter texts are instructional tools; students should
not be expected to read them independently.*
—Herber, 1984, p. 227

In this chapter you will learn

1. the role of reading in content classes,
2. a plan to help students improve their comprehension of texts,
3. how to use study guides to improve students' comprehension.

The first seven chapters of this text focused on how to teach students to comprehend. Emphasis was placed on showing teachers how to employ direct instruction to teach students the specific skills, processes, and strategies they would need
to be effective comprehenders. Everything that has been said thus far about the
teaching of comprehension can and should be applied to improving comprehension in the content areas. However, the content areas and content teaching pose
some circumstances that affect the way in which reading instruction can and
should be viewed.

Much of the recent research in comprehension relative to content areas has focused on the organization of textbooks (Anderson and Armbruster, 1984). Although this research is important, it will not be dealt with in this text. Rather this
chapter presents a basic position on the role of reading in content classes and presents a plan that all content teachers can use to help students comprehend their
texts better. The organization of text is important to a reader's comprehension,
but it takes more than improved text organization to help a student comprehend
(Herber, 1984). Teachers cannot change the organization of the texts they use,
but they can do certain things to assist students in comprehending any text, re-

gardless of its organization. No attempt is made in this chapter to present all of the alternatives available to content teachers. The emphasis is placed on one sound alternative that teachers can use at any level and in any class. Throughout the discussion, references are made to earlier chapters.

THE ROLE OF READING IN CONTENT CLASSES

The goal of any content class or content teaching at any level is for students to understand the concepts and ideas presented. Students are expected to gain a significant portion of the information needed for this understanding by reading textbooks. Therefore, a major goal in content teaching is to help students to comprehend the texts they read.

Content area teachers generally expect students to be able to read their textbooks and comprehend them. Even elementary teachers who teach students how to read often approach the teaching of a content area as though all students are able to read the textbook. In the elementary classroom, it is common to see several reading groups in the morning but all of the students placed in a single group with a single text for science or social studies classes in the afternoon. In content classes at other levels, it is common to see instruction based on the assumption that students can read the text. "Read Chapter twelve; tomorrow we will have a quiz" is frequently heard from content teachers. In any classroom where this approach to content teaching is taken, the teacher is assuming, conscientiously or unconscientiously, that the students have the abilities to read and comprehend their texts. When this type of activity occurs, there is no teaching. Although content teachers generally expect students to read to learn, this expectation is not valid—even in content areas students must be taught how to read their specific texts. The reading skills they have learned do not automatically transfer to the various content areas (Herber, 1984; Singer and Donlan, 1980).

Content teachers at all levels usually have a single textbook to use for instruction. The wisdom of this circumstance can be debated at length, but the reality is that most content teachers must teach all students, regardless of reading ability, from a single text. Authorities in teaching reading in content classes often recommend that content teachers rewrite materials for their students (Shepherd, 1982). On a large scale basis, such suggestions just aren't reasonable or realistic. Teachers can't carry out their teaching responsibilities and rewrite their textbooks, too.

Another factor that must be considered in determining the role of reading in content classes is the preparation of the teachers to teach reading. Content teachers at the middle, junior, and senior high levels have little or no preparation in how to teach reading; most of the teachers at these levels have been educated/trained in a discipline. At most, these teachers have had one class related to reading in content areas. Even elementary teachers who have been trained in reading often fail to make use of that training when they are teaching from content texts.

A basic premise of this chapter is that content teachers should not perceive themselves as reading teachers, especially those at the middle, junior, and senior high levels. Rather, they should think of themselves as teachers who can and should be able to help students do a more effective job of comprehending the texts that they read. All teachers can help students comprehend without being reading specialists. If a content teacher has students who have severe problems in learning how to read, the expertise of a reading specialist is needed.

Content teachers in every class can help students improve comprehension of the texts they read by accounting for those elements in the instructional program in reading comprehension that relate most directly to content classes (see Chapter 2). These include developing background and vocabulary, helping students understand how the ideas in their texts are organized, and correlating writing activities to reading.

A PLAN TO HELP STUDENTS IMPROVE THEIR COMPREHENSION OF TEXTS

In Chapter 2, the concept of the directed reading lesson was presented. The teacher can use a modified version of that plan to help students improve their comprehension of connected text in any content area. The modified version, which will be referred to as the content teaching plan, has four steps:

1. Preparation
2. Developing Vocabulary and Background
3. Guided Reading
4. Follow-up

Systematic use of the content teaching plan will not only help teachers guide students to improved comprehension but will also lead students to improved learning of content. Each step of the plan is designed to direct the content teacher in accounting for the factors that research has indicated are important in helping students comprehend text more effectively.

The preparation step of the plan is carried out by the teacher before he or she has students read any text. In this step, the teacher

1. identifies the key concepts, generalizations, ideas, or facts that students should learn as a result of reading the text.
2. identifies the key terminology that relates to what is to be learned.
3. identifies the background that students need to comprehend the text.

In order to guide students to successful comprehension, the teacher must have a clear understanding of what he or she expects students to learn as a result of their reading. Not all information covered in a text is equally important. A part of what is significant is determined by the author in how he or she writes the text, but what the teacher thinks students should learn influences the way in which the teacher will guide students in reading that text. Once the teacher has determined what students should learn from the text, he or she will be able to guide students in determining the relevant information from the irrelevant. This is difficult for students to do, particularly when they do not know what it is they are supposed to learn.

It has already been established that teaching vocabulary is an important part of helping the reader comprehend (see Chapter 4). The words that should be taught before students read text are the terms that relate most directly to what is to be learned. As the content teacher identifies the key ideas to be learned in the text, he or she can also identify the related key terms.

Basic to the reader's ability to comprehend text is his or her background (see Chapter 3). While reviewing the text, the teacher should ask him- or herself the question, "What do my students need to bring to this text in terms of background in order to comprehend it successfully?" The time the teacher spends in preparation is crucial to the success of the plan. All of the remaining steps of the plan are built on the preparation step.

The second step in the plan is developing vocabulary and background. Helping readers learn the key terms and activating or developing the background needed to comprehend text are activities that should be carried out together because they are closely related (see Chapters 3 and 4). In this step of the lesson, the teacher should provide direct instruction for the key terms identified and weave this together with activities that will help the reader activate or develop his or her background relative to the text. Included in this step should be some written practice with the vocabulary if students seem to need it.

The guided reading step of the lesson is where the teacher helps the students comprehend the text and understand how the author has organized his or her ideas. The teacher gives students purpose questions or purpose statements or helps students formulate their own purposes to guide their silent reading. This step concludes with a discussion that helps students draw together the ideas that were presented in the text.

The final step of the lesson is the follow-up, during which the teacher provides activities that will help students further clarify points in the text, extend the text, and relate the knowledge gained to information they already possess; these activities assist the reader in developing his or her meaning of the text. The activities in this part of the lesson can include such things as writing that is related to the text, vocabulary extension, going to other sources for additional information, and using creative activities. The parts of the content teaching plan and the types of activities that should take place in each step are summarized in Table 8.1. Specific instruction in how the content teacher can use this plan to help students improve comprehension is provided in the remainder of this chapter. Examples from a fourth-grade science text and a high-school U.S. history text are used as illustrations.

Preparation

The first step of the content teaching plan, preparation, requires that the teacher read the text with three questions in mind:

Table 8.1 Content Teaching Plan

Step	Activities	Comments
Preparation	The teacher identifies: a. Key concepts, generalizations, ideas, and facts that students should learn. b. Key terms that should be pretaught. c. Background that students will need to comprehend the text.	The teacher carries out this step as preparation to instruction, deciding what should be done to help students comprehend the text. The activities in this step are the basis for the remaining steps in the plan.
Developing Vocabulary and Background	Prior to students reading the text, the teacher: a. Uses direct instruction to teach the key terminology. b. Provides activities that help the student develop or activate the background needed to comprehend the text. c. Weaves vocabulary and background together.	This step of the lesson helps the reader activate his or her schema relative to the topic of the text. The activities in this step help the reader develop a framework for understanding the text.
Guided Reading	The teacher helps the students comprehend the text and understand how the author has organized ideas by: a. Providing the students with purposes to guide their reading of the text. b. Helping the students formulate their own purposes for guiding their reading. c. Conducting a discussion after students have completed their reading to help them pull together the information from the text and clarify points.	Through the activities of this step the teacher helps make the text more readable and guides the students to construct meaning from the text. The teacher guides the students by showing them how to read the text. The discussion at the end of the guided reading helps the reader relate new ideas from the text to what he or she already knows.
Follow-up	The teacher provides activities that: a. Help students clarify points. b. Help students extend ideas developed in the text.	This step helps students achieve closure on the lesson and further develops the concepts or ideas presented. The activities utilized can also include writing.

1. *What do I want students to learn as a result of reading this text?*

   The answer to this question should reflect the main points brought out in the text as well as the emphasis of the teacher. What is determined as the answer to this question sets how the teacher should guide the students in comprehending the text.

2. *What terminology is likely to cause students difficulty in reading this text?*

   As the teacher reads the text, he or she should decide which words are likely to cause students difficulty, paying special attention to those words that relate most directly to the key ideas to be learned. The teacher should think about

the words that typically cause students difficulty as well as the reading needs of students in the class. A list of the terms that students may find difficult should be made.
3. *What background will students need in order to comprehend the text?*
      When thinking about the first two questions, the teacher should also consider the type of background students will need to comprehend the text. The specific backgrounds of students in the class must be considered.

The selection "Minerals," presented in Example 8.1, will be used to illustrate the teacher preparation step for a content text selection. Following the selection is a discussion of each of the above questions as they relate to that text.

Developing Vocabulary and Background

Chapters 3 and 4 of this text focused on the significance of teaching vocabulary and developing background to help students improve their comprehension. The importance of relating vocabulary teaching to background development was stressed. The activities that take place in the developing vocabulary and background portion of the lesson help students develop their schema or frame of reference for constructing their understanding of the text. The more closely connected vocabulary teaching and background development are in the lesson, the more effective they are likely to be.

Selecting Words to Teach

It is not possible or necessary to teach students all the vocabulary in a text. The emphasis should be placed on teaching those words that relate most directly to the key ideas and those that are not fully taught in the text itself. To make this determination, the teacher should examine each of the words that he or she identified in the preparation step in light of the following questions:

1. Is this word directly related to the key concepts or ideas covered in the text? If not, it should be deleted from the list.
2. Can this word be learned from the text either by definition, through context, or by the structural elements such as prefixes, suffixes, base words, or root words? If so, it does not need to be taught to students before they read the text. It can be used in follow-up activities to extend vocabulary after the chapter has been read.

The words that remain on the list after these questions have been asked are the ones that should be pretaught. If the number of words to be pretaught exceeds six to eight, the teacher should develop the words over several days before students read the selection.
      Now, let's apply these questions to the list of words determined during preparation as being the words that are likely to cause students difficulty in reading this

EXAMPLE 8.1 SCIENCE TEXT SELECTION AND TEACHER PREPARATION

Chapter One
Minerals

What are minerals? How are they formed? Where are they found? How are they alike? How are they different? How are they used?

Some substances found in the Earth's crust are not formed from plants or animals. They are not alive. They are made of one or more chemicals. These substances always have the same properties. What are these substances called?

Minerals and Their Uses

The substances you have been reading about are called minerals. **Minerals** are solid chemical substances formed in the Earth's crust. They are not alive. They do not come from living things. They are natural solids formed from Earth's chemicals. They are found in the Earth's crust.

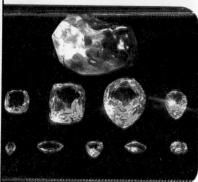

Some minerals are used in industry. One, called hematite, is used in making steel. Hematite is a source of iron. Iron is used to make steel.

Diamonds are minerals. Some diamonds are used in industry. They are very hard. They are used on the cutting edges of some saws. Some drill bits have diamond tips. Diamonds cut through most kinds of matter.

Some diamonds are more valuable for their beauty. Some very large diamonds are kept on display. Others are cut and polished for jewelry. How might the diamonds in the picture be used?

Physical Properties

The boy and girl are looking at physical properties of some minerals. A **physical property** is a characteristic that can be observed.

A **geologist** (jee AHL uh just) is a scientist who studies the Earth. One way to learn about the Earth is from minerals. Some have special physical properties. These can be used to identify a mineral.

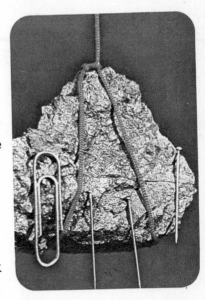

Magnetite has a special physical property. It acts like a magnet. Look at the picture. See how the pins and clip are stuck to the magnetite. How might this property help you identify magnetite?

Another property that can be used is appearance. This is not the only way to identify minerals. Some minerals may look the same.

Look at the minerals in the picture. Only one is real gold. The other is not real gold. It is a mineral called "fool's gold." Which do you think is real gold? How could you be sure? Why should you use more than one physical property to identify a mineral? Why should appearance not be the only property used?

Activity

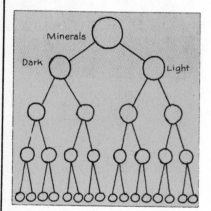

How Can You Make a Mineral Property Chart?

What to use:

poster paper   16 mineral samples
color marker   pencil and paper

What to do:

1. Place all samples in one pile at the top of the paper. Draw a circle around the pile.

2. Move all the dark samples to a separate pile. Make a separate pile of light samples. Draw a circle around each pile.

3. Observe the dark samples. Choose a physical property that will allow you to divide the samples into 2 piles. Draw a circle around each pile. Write the property you used by each circle.

4. Repeat step 3 using the light samples.

5. Keep dividing the piles using physical properties. Do this until each mineral is by itself.

What did you learn?

1. What properties did you use to divide the light samples?

2. What properties did you use to divide the dark samples?

Using what you learned:

1. How might a mineral property chart be used?
2. Make another chart. Do not tell or write what properties you used. Find out whether a classmate can guess the properties.

Hardness

Hardness is a physical property of a mineral. It is used to identify a mineral. **Hardness** is the measure of how easily a mineral can be scratched. Hardness is tested by scratching a mineral with an object. It is measured on a scale from 1 to 10. Soft minerals are given low numbers. They are more easily scratched. Hard minerals are given high numbers.

Streak

A streak test is a color test. Soft minerals leave a powder trail. A mineral is scratched across a tile. The powder trail left by the mineral is called a **streak.** The color of a mineral may change. Contact with air and soil can cause a color change. The streak test shows the true color of a mineral. Why would the streak test not work well with hard minerals? Here are some minerals and their streak colors.

Mineral	Streak Color
Magnetite	Black
Galena	Gray
Hematite	Reddish-brown
Pyrite	Greenish-black

Luster

Luster is the kind of shine a mineral has when light strikes it. Minerals with metal look shiny. They have metallic luster. Minerals without metal look dull. They have nonmetallic luster. Which of these minerals show metallic luster? Which show nonmetallic luster?

120

Crystals

Tiny particles, or atoms, that make up minerals are arranged in patterns. The pattern may be repeated. When the pattern is repeated enough, it makes a shape. The shapes have smooth, flat surfaces. They also have corners and sharp edges. The visible shape of a mineral's atom pattern is called a **crystal.** Many minerals have a special crystal shape. Crystals grow by adding on to their atom pattern.

Mineral crystals grow in special places. Matter that forms crystals must be a liquid or gas. Crystals form when the matter becomes a solid. There must be enough space for crystals to grow. Crystals must not be disturbed while they are growing. Crystals that grow slowly and have plenty of room grow to be large.

The crystals of a certain mineral always have the same shape no matter where they grow. How do you think crystal shapes are used to identify minerals?

People and Science

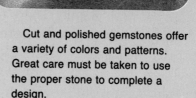

Geology Useful to Jewelry Designer

Some of the minerals that come from the Earth are used by people who make objects of beauty such as jewelry. Several kinds of precious and semiprecious metals are taken from the Earth in ore.

Refining processes are used to separate the metal from the ore. Gold, silver, copper, tin, zinc, aluminum, and nickel are some of the metals used to make jewelry. These metals are usually mixed together, or alloyed, to produce harder, longer lasting materials such as sterling silver, bronze, brass, pewter, karat gold, and nickel silver. Different colors can be made by alloying different metals.

Metals can be shaped into almost any design by bending, pounding, cutting, melting, or casting.

Cut and polished gemstones offer a variety of colors and patterns. Great care must be taken to use the proper stone to complete a design.

During the day, Professor William Shearman teaches art to college students. The rest of his time is given to designing and making jewelry and other art objects. He has learned many things about precious metals and gemstones. Professor Shearman uses this knowledge to create beautiful pieces of art.

What field of science should a person, such as Professor Shearman, study to help with artistic work?

Chapter Review

Summary

- Minerals are solids found in nature.
- Minerals are not formed from living things.
- Minerals can be identified by their physical properties.
- Color, hardness, streak, luster, and crystal form are physical properties of minerals.
- A crystal is the visible shape of a mineral's atom pattern.
- Mineral crystals grow in the Earth's crust in special places.

Science Words

minerals	**hardness**	**luster**
physical property	**streak**	**crystal**
geologist		

Questions

1. Where are minerals formed?
2. How are some minerals used?
3. How are minerals identified?
4. List three physical properties of minerals.
5. What is mineral hardness?
6. What kind of test is a streak test?
7. Which physical property is determined by reflected light?
8. What things affect mineral crystal growth?

Source: Robert B. Sund, Donald K. Adams, Jay K. Hackett, and Richard H. Moyer: *Accent on Science*, pp. 114–123. Columbus, OH: Charles E. Merrill Publishing Company. 1985. Used by permission.

Teacher Preparation

1. *What do I want students to learn as a result of reading this text?*

    Each teacher will answer this question somewhat differently depending on his or her focus—teachers with a more factual orientation will be concerned about specific facts, and those with a more concept orientation will focus on the main ideas. The main-idea focus is more appropriate for the fourth-grade level. The main ideas for this chapter are given in part in the chapter summary on page 123. A complete listing of the main points to be learned in this chapter would include:

    Minerals are solids found in nature.
    Minerals are not formed from living things.
    Minerals are used in industry.
    Minerals can be identified by their physical properties.
    Color, hardness, streak, luster, and crystal form are physical properties of minerals.
    A crystal is a visible shape of a mineral's atom pattern.
    Mineral crystals grow in the Earth's crust in special places.

    These are the points that students should understand as a result of reading this chapter. If the teacher has a more factual orientation, concern might be directed toward the names and qualities of the specific minerals mentioned, but that is not really the focus of this chapter.

2. *What terminology is likely to cause students difficulty in reading this text?*

    There are numerous words in this text that are likely to cause students difficulty. Some of them are listed at the end of the chapter in the section entitled "Science Words." However, some additional words must be considered. These words include:

minerals, p. 114–115	hardness, p. 119	crystal(s), p. 121
hematite, p. 116	streak, p. 120	atom(s), p. 121
physical property, p. 116	luster, p. 120	precious, p. 122
geologist, p. 117	metallic, p. 120	semiprecious, p. 122
appearance, p. 117	nonmetallic, p. 120	gemstones, p. 122

    All of these words will not need to be taught before students read the text. You will learn how to limit this list in the developing background and vocabulary section of the lesson.

3. *What background will students need in order to comprehend the text?*

    As you examine the chapter, you will find that students need to know something about nature, plants, animals, and scientists prior to reading the text. Students must certainly understand the concept that nature is composed of many types of things. You do not have to activate background about minerals because that is what the text is developing.

    Having determined the answers to these three questions, you are ready to proceed to the next step of the content teaching plan.

science text. There are fifteen words on the list (see page 360). All of the words relate directly to the key ideas that students are expected to learn in reading the
chapter. The last three words in the list—precious, semiprecious, and gemstones—are found in the extension reading, "People and Science." These do not
have to be pretaught as a part of the words for the body of the chapter; they can
be taught just prior to the reading of the extension article after the main text has
been read. Of these twelve remaining words, eight are defined in the text by definition or through context:

> minerals
> hematite
> physical property
> geologist
> hardness
> streak
> luster
> crystal(s)

Most students reading at the fourth-grade level should be able to figure out the
pronunciations and meanings of these words using the reading skills they have
developed up to this point. If students lack the skills to decode these words, the
words will need to be pretaught.

One of the words, metallic, is defined in the text but is not defined as
thoroughly as it needs to be. Three of the words are definitely not defined in the
text—appearance, nonmetallic, and atom(s). Therefore, using the questions just
cited for deciding which words to teach before students read the text, we have determined that four words must be taught prior to reading—metallic, appearance, nonmetallic, and atom(s). Precious, semiprecious, and gemstones will be
taught just before students read the article "People and Science." If students have
learned the prefix non, it might not be necessary to teach nonmetallic; however,
it will be included in the sample vocabulary teaching provided in Example 8.6.

Some teachers will feel it necessary to teach words that are defined in the text
even though students should be able to get the meanings on their own as they
read. Teachers should, however, look realistically at the amount of time this will
take. Although it is important to spend enough time to do a good job teaching vocabulary, time would be better spent doing something other than developing
word meanings if students can obtain the meanings from the text as they read.
The teacher should begin by not teaching words defined in the text. If the students encounter difficulty with the words, then the teacher can take that as a clue
that the words must be pretaught.

Teaching Vocabulary Prior to Reading

The purpose for teaching vocabulary before students read a text is to ensure that
students know the meanings of key words that they will encounter in their reading. These are the words that carry the major meanings of the text. In Chapter 4,

a detailed discussion on the preteaching of vocabulary was presented (see pages 134–166). All the strategies that were presented there are appropriate for use in content areas. However, many content teachers lack strong backgrounds in teaching reading and thus may not feel comfortable in using all of the strategies. The three strategies repeated in Examples 8.2, 8.3, and 8.4 include some variations that should make it possible for any content teacher to feel comfortable using them. First, the strategies are discussed; then, sample practice activities are provided in Example 8.5. Then, a sample lesson utilizing the strategies in the teaching of vocabulary and the development of background is presented (Example 8.6).

EXAMPLE 8.2   STRATEGY FOR USING CONTEXT CLUES ──────────

Purpose

To have students use context clues to decode words and learn their meanings.

When to Use

Use this strategy to teach *any* words prior to having students read text.

Materials

Chalkboard or overhead projector.

Procedures

Step 1:   Tell students that they are going to use the familiar words in a sentence to help them figure out the pronunciation and meaning of a word they may not know.

Step 2:   Give students a sentence using the vocabulary word. Underline the word.

The new government was voted out by the people.

Ask for a student to read the sentence. (If students can read the sentence, pronouncing the word correctly, proceed to Step 4.)

Step 3:   If students were unable to complete Step 2, read the sentence aloud for them pointing to the underlined word. Then have a student read the sentence aloud.

Step 4:   Discuss the meaning of the word. Ask students to tell what they think the word means. If students are unable to give a meaning for the word, tell them what it means. Use additional materials, such as pictures or other concrete materials, to develop the meaning of the word as needed.

Step 5: Have students give other sentences using the word. Their ability to use the word in a sentence will show that they really understand the meaning of the word and are not just parroting the original sentence used.

Step 6: Write at least one of the sentences given by the students on the chalkboard and have someone read it aloud.

Comments

This strategy can be used to teach any words from a content text. The sentences used for introducing the words should provide the strongest context clues possible to help students determine the meanings. The sentences should use the words in the same way they were used in the selection.

EXAMPLE 8.3 STRATEGY FOR USING STRUCTURAL ELEMENTS ——

Purpose

To have students use the structural elements of a word to figure out its pronunciation and meaning.

When to Use

Use this strategy to teach any word that has a prefix, suffix, base, or root that students know.

Materials

Chalkboard or overhead projector.

Procedures

Step 1: Tell students that they are to use what they know about the structure of words—prefixes, suffixes, base words, and roots—to try to figure out the pronunciations and meanings of words.

Step 2: Write the vocabulary word on the chalkboard.

scientific

Ask students if they can pronounce the word. If they pronounce it correctly, proceed to Step 4.

Step 3: If students are unable to pronounce the word, ask them to identify the prefix, suffix, base, or root (whichever is appropriate for the word). Have them discuss the word's parts and then try again to pronounce the word. (If students are still unable to pronounce the word, pronounce it for them.)

Step 4: Have students give the word in a sentence or give them a sentence using the word.

The <u>scientific</u> study of living things is called biology.

Have a student read the sentence aloud or read it aloud to the group.

Step 5: Discuss the meaning of the word, pointing out the relationships of the appropriate parts.

Step 6: Have students give other sentences using the word. Write one of these sentences on the chalkboard and have a student other than the one who gave the sentence read it aloud.

Comments

This strategy is often useful for teaching words in mathematics and science, but it can also be used in other content areas for any words that contain structural elements.

EXAMPLE 8.4 STRATEGY FOR USING WEBBING

Purpose

To teach students the meanings of a group of words from text by focusing on how they are related.

When to Use

This strategy can be used when a chapter has a group of words that are clearly related to one another.

Materials

Chalkboard or overhead projector.

Procedures

Step 1: Print the list of words to be taught on the chalkboard. Have a student read the list aloud or read the list to the group.

test tube
flask
Bunsen burner
centrifuge

Step 2: Select one word to begin the discussion. Print it on the board.

flask

Ask students to tell what this word means. If they don't know, tell them the meaning and use the word in an oral sentence.

Step 3: Select another word and print it on the chalkboard near the first word. Have students discuss the meaning of the new word. Then ask students how or if this word can be related to the first word. Draw a line to show the relationship.

flask
|
Bunsen burner

Step 4: Continue adding words in this manner until all words have been discussed. Draw lines to show relationships that students identify.

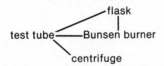

Step 5: Have students give sentences using each word. Write the sentences on the chalkboard and have other students read them aloud.

The <u>flask</u> held a mixture that separated after a few minutes.

Comments

This strategy is excellent for building background and teaching the meanings of words. It is also useful as a follow-up activity to extend and enrich vocabulary because it helps students see how words are related. It helps them internalize the words into their existing schemata.

Several strategies can be combined for more effective lessons. Vocabulary preteaching should be thorough, fast paced, and interesting. After word meanings have been taught, many students may need written practice using the new words; this is especially true when a day or more has elapsed between the teaching of the vocabulary and the reading of the text. The exercises in Example 8.5 illustrate some activities that can be used for this purpose. These exercises require minimal teacher preparation time, are not complicated for students to complete, and provide good practice for students.

EXAMPLE 8.5 MATCHING, CONTEXT COMPLETION, AND SYNONYM EXERCISES

Matching

Directions: This exercise will help you become more familiar with the terms you have learned to help you read patterns. Match each word listed in column 1 with the appropriate symbol in column 2.

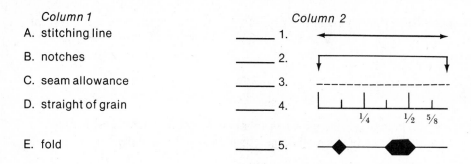

Column 1

A. stitching line

B. notches

C. seam allowance

D. straight of grain

E. fold

Column 2

_____ 1.

_____ 2.

_____ 3.

_____ 4.

_____ 5.

Comments

This type of exercise can be used with terms and definitions in any content area.

Context Completion

Directions: This exercise will help you learn the words you will need to know as you read the chapter "Oceans and the Life of Man." On your paper write the correct word from the list that would complete each sentence.

waves	surf	tide
tidal waves	crest	currents

1. Huge waves of water that travel at high speeds and are caused by earthquakes are called _____ .
2. The _____ refers to the rise and fall of the ocean's water level.
3. The patterns of powerful movement in the ocean's waters are

   _____ .
4. _____ are the most common form of motion in oceans.
5. The _____ is the white foam that forms when a wave breaks on the shore.
6. The wave's _____ is the high point of the water as the wave is formed.

Comments

Students can also be given a paragraph with blanks to be filled in.

Synonyms

Directions: This exercise will help you learn some words you may not know that are in the next chapter of your English text. Match each word in column 1 with its synonym in column 2.

Column 1	*Column 2*
1. advertise	A. anticipate
2. agree	B. attack
3. contends	C. coincide
4. foresee	D. broadcast
5. assail	E. believes

Comments

Synonym exercises can be used in any content area. They are also useful in helping students expand their vocabulary after reading.

Developing or Activating Background

A major factor in helping a reader comprehend text is making certain that he or she has the background for the text to be read. This was discussed in detail in Chapter 3 (see pages 79–121), and it is true for students in any content areas. To construct meaning for a chapter, the students must have the appropriate background relative to the key concepts or ideas to be learned. Thus, every content teacher should take time prior to having students read a chapter to help them develop or activate this background. Time spent on background development will lead to improved comprehension so long as it relates directly to the key concepts or ideas to be learned.

Vocabulary teaching prior to reading is one aspect of background development. In the preparation step of the lesson for the science chapter, it was determined that the student would need background on

> the concept of nature,
> how plants and animals operate within nature,
> scientists.

This background relates directly to the key points to be learned. Because the chapter focuses on basic information about minerals, the background that students will need will also be basic. The development of background should not be confused with telling students what they will learn from the chapter. Although that information is also important to helping students comprehend, it is not the same thing as background development.

As students approach the reading of any text, they bring with them the accumulation of many experiences. They may not have thought about some of those experiences for a long time. Therefore, the experiences need to be activated or reactivated in students' thinking. If the students totally lack the background, it must be developed.

There are many procedures for activating and/or developing background (see Chapter 3). Several procedures can be combined to ensure that students have the needed background, but the one that is most useful to content teachers is that of directed discussion. Simply taking the time before students read a chapter to discuss the background topics or concepts with students will help activate or build the background needed. Having students tell what they know about a particular topic and discussing this with the group can also be helpful, as can discussing pictures, diagrams, and illustrations from the text that relate to the needed background.

It cannot be stressed enough that content teachers should take the time before having students read chapters to help them develop background relative to the text. This will pay off in improved content learning.

The sample lesson in Example 8.6 illustrates how a teacher preparing students to read the fourth-grade science chapter presented on page 350 could combine vocabulary teaching and background development or activation. Some of the elements of direct instruction are used. The lesson incorporates the points that the teacher determined, during the preparation step, were important for students to learn from the chapter and the related key terms.

The amount of time that any teacher will devote to developing vocabulary and background will always depend on the needs of the students. However, if at all possible, this step should be completed within one class period so that students can get on to the reading of the text.

As you read the lesson, notice how background and vocabulary development are woven together. Pay attention to how the elements of direct instruction are utilized.

EXAMPLE 8.6   SAMPLE LESSON COMBINING VOCABULARY
TEACHING AND BACKGROUND DEVELOPMENT ———

Purpose

To teach students the terms *metallic, appearance, nonmetallic,* and *atom(s).*
To develop background on the concept of nature, how plants and animals operate within nature, and what scientists are.

Materials

Chalkboard or overhead projector.

Teaching Step

Let Students Know What Is to Be Learned

Say: In today's lesson you will learn some new words, and we will talk about some ideas that will help you read the next science chapter on minerals. Has anyone ever heard of minerals? Where would you find minerals? *(Note: This is activating and developing background.)* (Encourage students to tell what they know about minerals and where they're found. Record the major ideas on the chalkboard. Discuss them briefly. If students have no background relative to minerals, continue as follows.)

Say: When I say the word nature what do you think of? (Record student responses on the chalkboard and discuss them. Make certain that students understand that nature is both living and nonliving things and how they work together. If students do not seem to know much about nature, provide some specific information about nature. For example:

> It is made up of plants and animals including humans.
> Things in nature live and die together.
> Nature includes rocks and other things you would find in the soil.)

Say: What would we call a person who studies nature? (Allow students time to respond. If students do not know, tell them that this person would be called a scientist.

Say: What kinds of things do scientists do? (Students respond. Make a list of their responses and add your own suggestions. Discuss them.)

Say: Scientists study nature and look at how different things in nature work together. In the chapter on minerals, you are going to learn about some things in nature.

Model Vocabulary

Say: There are some words in the chapter that you will need to know to understand the chapter. Let's look at them now. (Write the word metallic on the chalkboard.)

Say: Here is a word that has an ending and a base word you should recognize. What is the base word? (Students respond. If they can't identify it, identify it for them.) *(Note: This is modeling vocabulary using the structural-elements strategy presented in Example 8.3.)*

Say: What is metal? (Students respond. Help them see that metal is usually a shiny, hard substance.

Say: If you add the ending *ic* to the word metal, the new word means having the properties or characteristics of metal. Who can say this word? (Point to metallic.)

Say: Give me a sentence using the word metallic. (Students respond. If students are unable to respond, give them a sentence. For example:

The silver paper had a metallic look.)

Say: Now look at this word. (Write the word nonmetallic on the chalkboard.)

Say: This word has a prefix that you know, added to it. What is this word? (Students respond. If they can't read the word, tell them what it is.)

Say: What does *non* mean? (Students respond. If they don't know, tell them it means *not.*)

Say: What does the word nonmetallic mean? (Students respond.)

Say: Nonmetallic is the opposite of metallic. It means that something is not like metal. Give me a sentence using the word nonmetallic. (Students respond. If they need help, give them a sentence.

The wooden box was painted a nonmetallic gray.

Discuss the meaning of the word in the sentence given.)

Say: Let's look at two other words. (Write the following sentence on the chalkboard: The man could tell that the car was new because of its shiny, clean appearance.) *(Note: This is modeling vocabulary using the context-clues strategy presented in Example 8.2.)*

Say: Read this sentence to yourselves to see if you can figure out the meaning and pronunciation of the underlined word. (Students read.) Who can read the sentence for me? (Have a student read the sentence. If no one can read the sentence, read it for them.)

Say: What does appearance mean? (Students respond. Discuss its meaning.)

Say: Give me another sentence using the word appearance. (Students respond.)

Say: How are metallic, nonmetallic, and appearance related to nature? *(Note: This is relating vocabulary to backgrounds.)* (Students respond. Help them see that when you look at things in nature, one way to tell one thing from another is by its appearance. Some things are metallic and some are nonmetallic. Put the following sentence on the chalkboard: Everything in nature is made of small units called atoms.)

Say: Read this sentence to yourselves and see if you can figure out the meaning and pronunciation of the underlined word. (Students read.) What is the word? (Students respond. If they can't read the word, read the sentence aloud.)

A PLAN TO HELP STUDENTS

Say: An atom is the smallest unit things are made of. You can't see a single atom. Give me another sentence using the word atom. (Students respond. Discuss the sentence given. List all words introduced on the chalkboard: metallic, nonmetallic, appearance, and atoms.)

Say: Since we are going to read a chapter about minerals and nature, how do you think each of these words is related to nature? *(Note: This is relating background and vocabulary.)* (Students respond. Discuss briefly how each word might be related to nature.)

Guided Practice
Say: Now I want you to give me a new sentence using each word on our list. (Have students respond. If students don't know the words, go over the meanings again, giving other examples.)

Summary
Say: What have you learned in this lesson that will help you as you read the chapter on minerals? (Students respond. Guide them to conclude in their own words the following points:

1. Nature is the world of living and nonliving things and how they work together.
2. Scientists study nature.
3. The words metallic, nonmetallic, appearance, and atoms all relate to nature and minerals.)

Practice Step

If students seem to need a written practice and/or if there is a day between the reading and this lesson, use the following exercise for independent practice.

Independent Practice for Vocabulary

Name _____ Date _____

Directions: Complete the crossword puzzle by selecting the correct word to match the definitions.

appearance	metallic
atoms	nonmetallic

1. Does not look like metal
2. Looks like metal
3. The smallest unit that things are composed of
4. How something looks

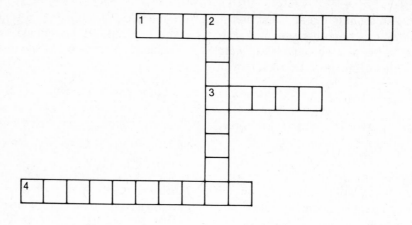

Application Step

The application of what was taught in this lesson will come when students read the chapter on minerals.

Guided Reading

During the guided reading portion of the content teaching plan, the teacher helps the students learn how to read the assigned text and construct meaning by asking them questions, by giving them purpose statements, and by discussion. As students become more proficient readers, they should begin to set their own questions to guide their reading.

Basically, in this step the student is reading the text silently. Teacher-posed or students' self-posed questions help the reader relate prior experiences to the text and focus on specific points to assist in constructing meaning. The more responsibility the students assume for setting their own purposes for reading and posing their own questions, the more effectively they will be able to monitor their comprehension and tell whether what is being read makes sense. It is important for effective comprehenders to monitor their comprehension as they read (Baker and Brown, 1984).

Teacher-Posed Questions and Purposes

Students should be given an overall purpose to guide their reading, and the purpose should be discussed immediately after the reading is completed. The purpose should be broadly based, requiring students to focus their attention on the entire reading. For example, a purpose statement for the chapter on minerals might be, "Read the chapter on minerals to tell the important things that you should know about minerals." Such a purpose statement would be sufficient to guide some readers, but many students would need more teacher guidance to help them comprehend the text. For them, the teacher can guide reading more precisely by asking questions about different parts of the chapter. The questions should follow the order of the chapter and should help students see the main ideas and general flow of ideas in the chapter. Questions should not focus the students' attention on insignificant details and should not be presented in a scrambled order. Teacher-posed questions are meant to help the students get an overall understanding of the chapter. The questions should be directed toward the key ideas that the teacher identified in the preparation step.

Elementary-level teachers will be familiar with using guided reading as a part of reading instruction (See Chapter 2 for a discussion of guided reading.) The teacher has the students read the chapter under his or her direction, posing questions and discussing the questions as portions of the chapter are read. The same procedure can be used at the middle, junior, and senior high school levels. Many teachers feel that this procedure is too immature for their students, but that assumption is false. If the procedure is handled properly by the teacher, the students will respond well. However, there are alternative ways to use teacher-posed questions to guide students' reading that appear more adultlike. For example, the teacher can write the guided reading questions in a list on the chalkboard, overhead projector, or a duplicated sheet. Again, the questions should be listed in the order in which they appear in the chapter. Questions listed in written form are referred to as a study guide. Study guides are excellent ways to incorporate many of the elements of the content teaching plan. They are very useful for helping students comprehend text at all levels, but especially at those levels beyond the elementary school. Study guides are discussed in more detail later in this chapter.

Throughout the guided reading of a chapter, students should be encouraged to ask themselves if what they are reading is making sense. This process is called comprehension monitoring. If students are not understanding what they are reading, they should try to clarify points by rereading or seeking assistance from the teacher. Poor readers have great difficulty monitoring their comprehension. The teacher should be alert to students who have trouble doing this and should help them with strategies such as the one suggested on page 259.

Student-Posed Questions

Another way to approach guided reading is to teach students a system of study where they pose their own questions or set their own purposes for reading. The advantage of such a system is that it puts the responsibility of comprehending more directly on the students and makes the students more aware of monitoring their own comprehension. One system that has been widely recommended and researched is SQ3R (Robinson, 1962). This system is composed of five basic steps:

Survey: The reader makes a quick survey of the text to get a general idea of what it is about. The title, subheadings, introduction, and summary are read. Illustrations, photographs, diagrams, and maps are examined. (The reader now reads the text in sections, carrying out the Question, Read, and Recall steps for each section.)

Question: The reader poses a question that he or she thinks can be answered in reading the first portion of the text. If the section begins with a subheading, it should be turned into the question. For example, in the chapter on minerals, the first subheading is "Minerals and Their Uses." The reader could turn this heading into the question, "What are minerals and how are they used?" As the reader reads through the sections of text, the questions posed focus his or her attention and help improve comprehension of the text. The questions can be written down to guide the reader in taking notes.

Read: The reader reads as much of the text as needed to answer the question. If a subheading was used to generate the question, the reader reads to the end of that section. Throughout the reading, the reader's attention is focused on answering the question.

Recall: After completing the portion of text, the reader looks away from it and answers the question in his or her own words. If the reader cannot answer the question, he or she rereads the text. The reader can write down the answer to the question. The reader continues reading the text and using the Question, Read, and Recall steps until the entire text is read.

Review: When the entire text has been read, the reader reviews what was learned by looking over his or her notes. The reader looks away from the notes and tries to recall the points learned from the reading. The notes are used for study purposes prior to a test.

Direct instruction should be employed when teaching students to use this system of study. The teacher must model the strategy repeatedly using different types of text (see Chapter 5 on modeling). Students need a great deal of teacher modeling in formulating the appropriate questions. By the time many students reach the junior/senior high school levels, they have been taught to use SQ3R. However, because each content area text is constructed differently, each content teacher should model the use of SQ3R to show students how it can be applied to his or her particular text.

Discussion as a Part of Guided Reading

After students have read the text, there must be a discussion that helps them draw together and clarify the main ideas and extend their thinking about the text. The discussion should be viewed in two parts:

1. bringing out the main points of the text,
2. relating the main points to an overall understanding of the text and getting students to think critically about the text.

During the first part of the discussion, the teacher should focus on making certain that students understand the main ideas covered in the text. The first question the teacher asks should always relate to the overall purpose or to specific questions that students were given to guide their reading. The rest of this part of the discussion should consist of questions that will help students recall the main ideas in the order in which they were presented in the text. Many times when guided reading is used, students will read chapters in sections. Therefore, the discussion should be used to help unify the chapter for students by pulling together the key ideas and concepts developed.

In the second part of the discussion, the teacher should direct students to think about and react to the text. The questions should be generated by both the students and the teacher. Emphasis should be on critical thinking and evaluation.

The lesson in Example 8.7 illustrates one way in which guided reading can be carried out to help students more effectively comprehend text. The science chapter presented on page 350 is used in this example as it has been in the examples that illustrated the preparation and developing vocabulary and background steps of the content teaching plan. Before proceeding with the lesson, reread the science text, noting that pages 118, 119, 122, and 123 are special pages that will be completed under the teacher's direction at another time; they will not be a part of the guided reading, but the lesson will illustrate how and when these pages can be used.

As you read the script for the lesson, notice how the teacher relates the guided reading to vocabulary and background development and how the questions used in the guided reading help students develop the main points identified in the preparation.

EXAMPLE 8.7   SAMPLE LESSON ILLUSTRATING GUIDED READING OF A CONTENT TEXT ─────────────────

Lesson Script

Say: Yesterday, we talked about nature and what it was and some of the things that happened in nature. What do you remember about our discussion? (Students respond. Review briefly the background discussed in the previous lesson.)

Say: We also talked about four words that will be in the chapter we are going to read today. Who can tell me what those words are? (Students respond. If they are unable to recall the words, list them on the chalkboard and have students quickly review their meanings.)

Say: Today, we are going to read the chapter on minerals. (Place the following questions on the chalkboard or distribute copies to students to guide their reading:

Questions

1. What is a mineral?
2. How are some minerals used?
3. What is meant by physical properties of minerals?
4. What physical property does magnetite have?
5. How can appearance help you identify minerals?
6. What problems can you have if you use only appearance to identify minerals?
7. What is hardness?
8. How can hardness be used to identify minerals?
9. What is streak?
10. How can a streak test be used to identify minerals?
11. What is luster?
12. How can luster be used to identify minerals?
13. What are crystals?
14. How can crystals be used to identify minerals?

Students should write out their answers. Alternatively, you can ask students the questions one at a time and have them read to locate the answers.)

Say: Open your text to page 114. As you read this chapter remember to use the words and information that we discussed yesterday. Use the questions on the chalkboard to help you understand the main ideas in the chapter. Write your answers on your paper. I want you to read pages 115–117 and from the middle of page 119 to page 121. We will do the activities together later.

Discussion

The discussion that follows the reading of the chapter should first focus on the questions that are meant to guide students' reading. As students answer questions, it is often good to go back and have them prove their answers by reading supporting sentences and phrases in the text.

The second portion of the discussion should focus on such questions as:

1. Why is more than one test used to identify a mineral?
2. Why do scientists study mineral properties?
3. What interesting careers might result from the study of rocks?

The activity pages included in the chapter can be completed after students have read and discussed the text or can be viewed as a part of follow-up of the content teaching plan.

Follow-Up

The final part of the content teaching plan is follow-up. The focus of this part of the lesson is to extend the text that was read and bring closure on the overall concepts developed in the text. The activities used in this part of the lesson will vary. They should include such things as

Activities that further develop the vocabulary of the chapter.

Activities that require students to use the information from the chapter in written form.

Reading other sources or seeing films or filmstrips that further develop the information in the chapter.

Creative activities such as role playing, drawing, and so forth, that would be appropriate to the content area.

Some type of follow-up should be done for the reading of every chapter. It is not necessary to cover all areas of follow-up for each chapter.

In Example 8.8, some follow-up activities that could be used with the chapter on minerals are presented. Of course, only one or two of the activities would be used.

EXAMPLE 8.8   SAMPLE FOLLOW-UP ACTIVITIES ━━━━━━━━

Vocabulary

Science Words: Use each of the words presented on page 123 of your text in a sentence and write the sentences in your notebook of new words. Refer to your text to check the meanings if necessary.

Minerals: Your chapter lists many different minerals. Make a chart listing them and giving some information about each. Refer to an encyclopedia if necessary.

Writing

Summary: You have read and identified the main points in this chapter. Now, write a summary of these ideas in your own words.

Report: Select one of the minerals listed in your chapter. Look it up in the encyclopedia and write a one-paragraph report telling some important facts about it.

────────────────────────

USING STUDY GUIDES TO IMPROVE COMPREHENSION

A study guide is just what its name implies—a guide for studying. It is a set of questions and activities designed to direct students' reading of a text with emphasis on helping them comprehend more effectively. The study guide can include vocabulary and other types of activities as well as questions that the student can use to guide his or her reading. The study guide does not replace the teacher in the content teaching plan. It does, however, give the teacher an organized way to provide vocabulary practice, questions to guide reading, and follow-up activities. If a teacher uses a study guide, it is still necessary to teach vocabulary, build or activate background, and have discussion after reading. The use of a study guide enhances the content teaching plan but does not replace it.

Study guides have a number of different purposes, which will be described in the following paragraphs. It is important that the users, both teacher and students, understand the purposes for the study guide. Also, the purpose for using the guide will influence its construction.

The primary purpose for study guides is to direct the students' reading and help them draw out those points that are important in the text. The activities of the guide direct the students' attention to the points that are most significant to their overall comprehension of the text.

Another purpose for study guides is to stimulate students' thinking. A significant portion of learning and learning to read is thinking. Therefore, the study guide is a useful tool for organizing learning activities that can lead students to develop various types of critical, creative thinking abilities.

A third purpose for study guides is to meet the individual needs of students. Some students need more direction and guidance in their reading than others. Therefore, the study guide can be designed to meet those needs.

Factors to Consider in Designing a Study Guide

For the teacher and students to get the most out of a study guide, it must be carefully designed and constructed. The teacher must remember that the purpose of the guide is to help students improve their comprehension of the text. To do this, a well-designed guide should include

1. questions that guide the students' reading of the text,
2. some vocabulary practice and/or extension activity,
3. activities that require students to think critically.

The guide might also include a variety of follow-up activities appropriate to the content area and the text.

The questions that are included to guide the students' reading should be given in the order in which the answers appear in the text. If they are presented in that order, the questions will serve as a guide for the readers and will lead them to the overall points of the chapter. The question format can be varied to provide more guidance for those who need it by including the page number on which the answer can be found. For example:

p. 21   Who was the first scientist to work in blood research?

The questions in the guide can also be multiple choice, but multiple-choice questions should only be used if students are having great difficulty in comprehending the text and need this type of guidance.

The vocabulary practice and extension activities should include a variety of formats including puzzles, categorizing activities, and matching activities. The traditional sentence-completion activities can also be used but should be varied with other formats to keep interests high.

The activities that require students to do critical thinking should include appropriate questions but should also involve other types of activities. The same formats suggested for vocabulary can be used here.

Constructing study guides is obviously a time-consuming task. As this task is undertaken, the teacher must keep a number of points in mind:

1. There must be a clear purpose for the guide. Teachers should not create a study guide simply because other teachers are doing so.
2. The guide is meant to assist students, not hinder them. The guide should not be so complicated, confusing, or tricky that learning is impaired.
3. The teacher should start small and not try to write a set of guides for an entire book at one time. It is best to begin with a small portion of material and try out the guides as they are written. It is impossible to really know the strengths and weaknesses of study guides until they are used with students.

Example 8.9 shows a portion of a chapter from a U.S. history text and an accompanying study guide.

EXAMPLE 8.9 SELECTION FROM A U.S. HISTORY TEXT AND ACCOMPANYING STUDY GUIDE ────────

CHAPTER 8
Under the First Presidents
1789–1800

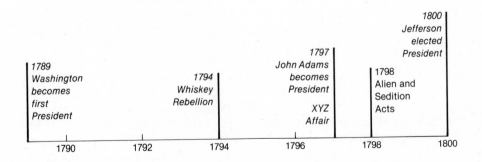

CHAPTER OUTLINE

1. The new government is launched.
2. Hamilton tackles the nation's money problems.
3. Political parties are formed.
4. Federalist power declines.

George Washington was the most trusted man in the United States. Unanimously elected President in April, 1789, he gave the new government respectability even before it was fully organized. Still, the work that lay ahead was a challenge no one had ever faced.

Differences between the northern and southern states had showed themselves at the Philadelphia Convention. Business leaders and farmers were not in agreement on the policies the new nation should pursue. Americans on the frontier were so far from the seat of government that they found it hard to feel involved in the changes taking place.

In spite of such uncertainties, the people's energies were turned to making the Constitution work. The architects of the new government had understood that at the Philadelphia Convention they had written only an outline of the new government. Indeed, people called it "the frame of government." What was now needed was the enthusiasm of men and women who would give it life and direction.

April 30, 1789, the day that the nation began its life under a President, was notable in the history of the world. A country not ruled by a king or queen was so novel that for many years people everywhere would refer to the United States as the "American experiment." No one could know for sure if the experiment would succeed. Few could imagine that its features would become a model for other nations for centuries to come.

The New Government Is Launched

The task of getting the country off on the right foot was taken on by the group that had been enthusiastic for the ratification of the Constitution. The goal of the Federalists was now one of making the new government effective and respected.

George Washington is inaugurated. In the spring of 1789, the President-elect left Mount Vernon for New York City, where he would be inaugurated. The journey took eight days over roads muddy from rain. It was a triumphant procession. In every town and village George Washington passed through, thousands of people greeted him with speeches, banners, and flowers. They treated him like a Roman hero, even building triumphal arches in his honor. Many veterans who had served under his command in the Revolution were on hand to greet him and wish him well. Already the nation was coming together under Washington's leadership.

Washington had not wanted to return to public life. "My movements to the chair of government," he wrote, "will be accompanied by feelings not unlike those of a culprit who is going to the place of his execution." His beloved Martha was also distressed by his re-entry into the limelight. She agreed only reluctantly to uproot herself again from their Virginia home.

Martha Washington missed her husband's triumphant entry into New York City. He crossed the Hudson River aboard a special barge decorated in red, white, and blue with everything in thirteens to symbolize the thirteen states. When Martha Washington traveled north to join her husband a month later, she too was cheered along the way to New York. Then Washington crossed the Hudson from New York to fetch her. When they landed in Manhattan, guns boomed in salute.

On April 30, 1789, Washington took the oath of office on the balcony of Federal Hall. The strain of the occasion showed, for his hands trembled and his voice could hardly be heard. A senator in the audience observed, "This great man was agitated and embarrassed more than ever he was by the leveled cannon or pointed musket." Washington was dressed in a dark brown suit of American manufacture, but he also wore a sword and white stockings, in the fashion of court ceremonies in Europe. When the ceremony was over, the crowd below cheered, shouting "Long live George Washington, President of the United States."

Both Washington and the American people would have to learn how to deal with this new office, the presidency. A heated discussion had already taken place in the Senate as to how a President should be addressed. One participant suggested "His Highness the President of the United States of America and Protector of their Liberties." Another proposed "His Elective Highness." Yet another offered "His Patriotic Majesty." Finally it was agreed that the Chief Executive was to be called simply "President of the United States."

Washington was not eager for a fancy title, but he was not a "man of the people" either. Naturally aloof and reserved, he never shook hands as President. On social occasions, moreover, he always greeted guests while standing on a raised platform.

Happily, the spring and summer brought no crisis and so the new government was launched under favorable conditions. The country was experiencing general prosperity, furthermore, and people were pleased to credit the new government for the good times.

Washington chooses a Cabinet. At the outset the only other member of George Washington's administration was Vice President John Adams of Massachusetts. Adams and the President were not friendly, however, and they could not work closely together. For advice, the President turned to the heads of the executive departments. Those departments, set up by Congress in 1789, included State, Treasury, and War, and the office of the Attorney General. Together, the heads of these departments came to be known as the *Cabinet*. Even though the word *Cabinet* does not appear in the Constitution, Cabinet members have become recognized as a group of official advisers to the President.

Washington chose his Cabinet with great care. To be Secretary of State he selected Thomas Jefferson, a fellow Virginian. At the time, Jefferson was serving as minister to France. He would bring to the new office not only his considerable experience of the world, but a sense of the revolutionary stirrings that were beginning to reshape Europe. The appointment of Jefferson was also aimed at winning the loyalty of those people, like Jefferson himself, who had not thought the United States needed the new Constitution at all.

Washington named Alexander Hamilton to be Secretary of the Treasury. Only in his mid-thirties, Hamilton had already devoted much time to working for a strong national government.

The Secretary of War was General Henry Knox of Massachusetts. Knox had headed the War Department under the Confederation government. Weighing over three hundred pounds, he had been a leading artillery officer during the Revolution. Now he was a symbol of continuity with the previous government.

The post of Attorney General went to Edmund Randolph, another Virginian. Randolph had at first been uncertain about the Constitution, but after deciding to support it he had helped to obtain Virginia's ratification.

Congress establishes courts.   One of the first acts of the new Congress, as required by the Constitution, was to pass a law establishing the Supreme Court and other federal courts. The Judiciary Act of 1789 provided for a Supreme Court made up of a Chief Justice and five associate justices.[1] It also established three circuit courts and thirteen district courts.

In filling the Supreme Court, President Washington had the privilege no other Chief Executive would have—that of naming all the members. He chose three justices from the North and three from the South, all of them staunch defenders of the Constitution. The first Chief Justice was John Jay of New York, one of the authors of *The Federalist* essays.

Rival groups emerge in the administration.   In making decisions, President Washington sought all the facts, relying upon advice offered by his Cabinet and by the Chief Justice. He also turned to help from Congress, where James Madison, a member of the House from Virginia, was one of his most trusted friends and advisers.

Because there were no political parties, Washington depended on people in government who had been active in seeking ratification of the Constitution. He assumed that these people would be united in the common goal of working for harmony in the government. The President's hopes soon vanished, however, as two rival groups developed in the administration. One group found its leader in Jefferson; the other, in Hamilton. Each man became a symbol of ideas that had become current in America in the years since the writing of the Declaration of Independence.

Jefferson and Hamilton hold contrasting views.   Jefferson believed that the ideal American nation should be one consisting of farmers who owned their own land. He thought that farmers were the most noble of all people. Jefferson also believed that people were by nature good. The purpose of government, therefore, should be to provide a free atmosphere in which individuals might pursue their personal goals without interference.

America, Jefferson maintained, should not try to become an industrial nation. Having seen "the mobs of great cities" in Europe, he was eager that his own beloved country avoid them. Instead of building large factories, he thought it possible for Americans to develop household manufacturing. At Monticello, his home in Virginia, he had set up a small nail factory run by slave children.

Despite his views on industrialization, Jefferson believed strongly in the will of the majority. He held that if people wished to live in cities and establish factories,

[1]The number of associate justices is now eight.

their leaders must not stand in the way of those goals. Above all, government must constantly merit the approval of its citizens.

Hamilton, on the other hand, maintained that people needed a strong government. Government, he said, must be energetic and efficient. By this he meant that it must exert its power boldly in order to operate properly. He was convinced that by using without hesitation the powers granted it, the new government would prove vigorous and respected. It would benefit all the people, because they would be able to obtain every advantage they wanted.

The two contrasting viewpoints resulted in clashes over policies within the Washington administration. Jefferson wanted to leave most governing to state and local governments. He had particular confidence in the state legislatures, because they reflected readily the will of the people. Still, he held firmly to the view that "that government is best which governs least." Hamilton, on the other side, wanted a strong government led by a strong President. He also supported policies that would benefit people of wealth. Such policies, he believed, would lead to the prosperity of the rest of the people.

It is wrong to think that Jefferson and Hamilton were personal enemies. Indeed, Jefferson kept a marble bust of Hamilton in the entranceway of his home. Their hostility was over policies, and it grew only slowly. Hamilton took office in September, 1789. Jefferson did not return from Paris to assume his post until the following spring. By then, Jefferson, who hoped to be a good Secretary of State, especially wanted to be on good terms with the Secretary of the Treasury. For his part, Hamilton, who did not meet Jefferson until 1790, greatly respected him for his reputation and accomplishments.

Neither Jefferson nor Hamilton had at first a clear sense of the views of the other. Still, their views soon were the driving forces in a struggle for power within the new government. By 1792 Washington was pleading with each of them to be tolerant of the other, lest their differences "tear the machine asunder" and destroy the new union of states.

SECTION REVIEW

1. Vocabulary: *Cabinet.*
2. Name the four members of Washington's Cabinet, and tell which position each held.
3. (a) What courts were established by the Judiciary Act of 1789? (b) Who was appointed Chief Justice?
4. (a) Compare Jefferson's and Hamilton's views on the role and purpose of government. (b) Why were the differences between Jefferson and Hamilton important during Washington's presidency?

Source: H. F. Graff, "Under the First Presidents," Chap. 8 in *America: The Glorious Republic*, pp. 174–179. Boston: Houghton Mifflin Company, 1985. Used by permission.

Study Guide

Name _____ Date _____

Under the First Presidents
(pages 174–179)

Reading the Chapter

Directions: Read pages 379–383 and answer the questions as you read. The questions come in the order of the chapter; the text subheadings are included in the study guide to help direct your reading.

1. Look at the timeline on page 379. What period of time is covered in this chapter? _____

2. Read the introduction on page 380 and answer the following questions.
   a. What kinds of problems faced George Washington as he became the first president of the United States?

      _____
      _____

   b. In spite of the problems, how were people thinking toward the new government? _____

      _____
      _____

THE NEW GOVERNMENT IS LAUNCHED
3. Who were the people who had been enthusiastic about the Constitution? ___

   _____

George Washington is Inaugurated
4. How was George Washington received by the people of the United States? __

   _____

5. What kind of person was George Washington? _____

   _____

Washington Chooses a Cabinet
6. Why did George Washington create a group of people to give him advice? ___

   _____

7. Who are the people who make up the president's Cabinet?

   _____
   _____

8. What kind of men did George Washington appoint to his Cabinet? _____

   _____
   _____
   _____

Congress Establishes Courts

9. What did the Judiciary Act of 1789 provide? _____

_____

10. What made George Washington's first Supreme Court appointments different from those of all other presidents? _____

_____

11. Who was the first Chief Justice of the Supreme Court?

_____

Rival Groups Emerge in the Administration

12. What happened very early in Washington's administration?

_____

_____

Jefferson and Hamilton Hold Contrasting Views

13. What did Jefferson believe about America? _____

_____

_____

_____

14. What did Hamilton believe about America? _____

_____

_____

_____

15. What did the contrasting views of Jefferson and Hamilton do to the government? _____

_____

_____

_____

Using Vocabulary

Directions: In the first section of this chapter, some terms were introduced that you need to know to understand the section. Match the words in column 1 with the definitions in column 2.

Column 1

1. inaugurate
2. Cabinet
3. Judiciary

Column 2

_____ A. Established the Supreme Court, circuit courts, and district courts.

_____ B. To install a high official, such as a president, into office.

_____ C. The advisers to the president.

Thinking About Your Reading

Directions: Think about the following question and answer it in the space provided. Be ready to discuss your answer.

Why were the opposing views of Jefferson and Hamilton so important during Washington's administration?

_____

_____

_____

_____

_____

_____

_____

_____

_____

Varying Study Guide Activities

Questions are an important part of study guides, but other activities should also be included so that the guides won't become dull and boring. Any type of activity can be used as long as it actually guides students' reading. Usually it is best to use the question format for initial guided reading and some other type of activity for follow-up. For example, a follow-up activity for the section of the U.S. history text presented in Example 8.9 might be to complete a chart showing the members of Washington's cabinet, the positions they held, and a possible reason for their appointment. Another type of activity might involve comparing the views of Jefferson and Hamilton in chart form. Both types of charts are illustrated in Example 8.10.

Using Study Guides in Classes

The true test of a study guide's value comes when it is put into the hands of students. Using study guides in content classes provides no panacea. It is simply a way to begin to account for different reading needs and at the same time improve the teaching of content.

The teacher and students must discuss the purpose of the guides before beginning to use them. If study guides become useless busy work or another paper to be graded, their value is diminished or completely lost. The teacher and students must remember that the study guide is a tool to help improve the student's comprehension by guiding the reading of the content text. A discussion with the group about the purpose and uses of study guides will prevent many problems before they occur.

As mentioned earlier in this chapter, after students have completed their study guides there must be a discussion in which the teacher reviews the activities in the guide and helps students pull the ideas from the text together. Emphasis should be placed on clarifying ideas, synthesizing information, and relating it to what students already know.

EXAMPLE 8.10 SAMPLE CHARTS

George Washington's First Cabinet

Position	Person Appointed	Possible Reason
1. 2. 3. 4.		

Comparing the Views of Jefferson and Hamilton

Points to Compare	Jefferson	Hamilton
Purpose of Government		
Type of Nation U.S. Should Be		
The Role of State Governments		
Their Friendship		

Should study guides be graded? This question is frequently asked by teachers. This author's answer is simply, no. The guides are teaching tools. They are not tests. Therefore, grading takes away some of their teaching value and adds an unrealistic burden for a teacher with five or six class preparations. Teachers have many other opportunities to evaluate students' work.

SUMMARY

Every content teacher at every level must help students learn how to read and understand their texts. Although there are many ways to do this, the content teaching plan is one that can be used by all content teachers to improve students' comprehension of text. This plan consists of four steps:

1. preparation,
2. developing vocabulary and background,
3. guided reading,
4. follow-up.

This plan can be enhanced by the use of study guides.

REFERENCES

Anderson, T. H., and B. B. Armbruster. 1984. Content area textbooks. In R. C. Anderson, J. Osborn, and R. J. Tierney (eds.), *Learning to read in American schools: Basal readers and content texts*, pp. 193–226. Hillsdale, NJ: Lawrence Erlbaum Associates.

Baker, L., and A. L. Brown. 1984. Metacognitive skills and reading. In P. D. Pearson (ed.), *Handbook of reading research*, pp. 353–394. New York: Longman.

Herber, H. L. 1984. Subject matter texts—Reading to learn: Response to a paper by Thomas H. Anderson and Bonnie B. Armbruster. In R. C. Anderson, J. Osborn, and R. J. Tierney (eds.), *Learning to read in American schools: Basal readers and content texts*, pp. 227–234. Hillsdale, NJ: Lawrence Erlbaum Associates.

Robinson, F. P. 1962. *Effective study*. New York: Harper & Row, Publishers.

Shepherd, D. L. 1982. *Comprehensive high school reading methods*, 3rd ed. Columbus, OH: Charles E. Merrill Publishing Company.

Singer, H., and D. Donlan. 1980. *Reading and learning from text*. Boston: Little, Brown and Company.

INDEX

Activity. *See also* Directed-choice activity
  generating background, 87–90
  purpose setting, 91–92
Advance organizers, 95
Analogies, 189–190
Anticipating information, 304
Antonyms, 167, 179, 184, 191–192
Application
  of skills, 200–202
  types of, 47–49
Applying step of direct instruction, 47–49
  sample lesson, 49–53
Appositive, 167
  context clue, 168, 169
Attitudes and values, 15
Author's organizational structure, 347. *See
  also* Text structure

Background, definition of, 80
Background development, 22–24, 79–120,
  367–372
  deciding what background, 82–84
  definition of, 80
  preteaching, 104
  sample lessons, 105–119
  selecting strategies, 102–104
  strategies, 84–102
    activities, 80–84, 87–90
    advance organizers, 95
    background-generating activity,
    87–90
    concrete materials, 100–102
    discussion, 85–87
    field trips, 100–102

    objectives, 92
    pictures, 99–100
    prequestions, 90–91
    prior reading, 102
    purpose-setting activities, 91–92
    role playing, 100–102
    semantice mapping, 98–99
    story previews, 95
    webbing, 96–98
Background information, 5–6
Background of readers, 3–5, 8, 12–14,
  16–17, 80, 135–136, 150, 204, 264,
  347
Background and readiness portion of a
  DRL, 56
  sample lesson, 56–57
Background and vocabulary, 56, 360–372
  sample lesson, 56–57
Barrett Taxonomy of Reading
  Comprehension, 3
Base words, 170, 172–173
Bulletin-board activities, 131, 132

Causation type of expository text, 274–275
Cause-effect expository. *See* Causation
  type of expository text
Checking content in writing, 324–326
Clarifying, definition of, 259
Classroom organization, 313–315
Clue words, 200
Clues to understanding text, 8, 10–12. *See
  also* Context clues
Cognitive monitoring, 200, 202
Collection type of expository text, 274

AN INVITATION TO RESPOND

Often changes in future editions of textbooks are based on feedback and evaluations of the earlier editions. Please help us respond to the interests and needs of future readers of *Improving Reading Comprehension* by completing the questionnaire below and returning it to: College Marketing, Houghton Mifflin Company, One Beacon Street, Boston, MA 02108.

1. Please tell us your overall impressions of the text.

	Excellent	Good	Adequate	Poor
a. Was it written in a clear and understandable style?	____	____	____	____
b. Were difficult concepts well explained?	____	____	____	____
c. How would you rate the frequent use of illustrative Examples, including model lessons and reprinted basal selections?	____	____	____	____
d. How comprehensive was the coverage of major issues and topics?	____	____	____	____
e. How does this book compare to other texts you have used?	____	____	____	____
f. How would you rate the text's potential on-the-job usefulness?	____	____	____	____
g. Was its physical appearance appealing?	____	____	____	____

2. Please comment on or cite examples that illustrate any of your above ratings.

_____

_____

_____

3. Which chapters or features did you particularly like?

_____

_____

_____

4. Which chapters or features did you particularly dislike? _____

_____

_____

5. What changes would you like to see in the next edition of this book? _____

_____

_____

6. What was the title of the course in which you used this book? _____

_____

7. Have you taken any other courses in reading education? If so, which courses? _____

_____

_____

8. Was this book used as a supplement to another text? _____ If so, what was the name of that text and by whom was it written and published?

_____

_____

9. Is this a book you would like to keep for your classroom teaching experience? _____ Why or why not? _____

_____

_____

10. Please tell us something about your background. Are you studying to be a classroom teacher or a reading specialist? Are you inservice or preservice? Are you an undergraduate or graduate student? _____

_____

_____